THE POLITICS AND LAW OF DEMOCRATIC TRANSITION

Peaceful legal and political 'changing of the guards' is taken for granted in developed democracies, but is not evident everywhere. As a relatively new democracy, marred by long periods of military rule, Bangladesh has been encountering serious problems because of a prevailing culture of mistrust, weak governance institutions, constant election manipulation and a peculiar socio-political history, which between 1990 and 2011 led to a unique form of transitional remedy in the form of an unelected neutral 'caretaker government' (CTG) during electoral transitions.

This book provides a contextual analysis of the CTG mechanism including its inception, operation, manipulation by the government of the day and abrupt demise. It queries whether this constitutional provision, even if presently abolished after overseeing four acceptable general elections, actually remains a crucial tool for safeguarding free and fair elections in Bangladesh. Given the backdrop of the culture of mistrust, the author examines whether holding national elections without a CTG, or an umpire of some kind, can settle the issue of credibility of a given government.

The book portrays that even the management of elections is a matter of applying pluralist approaches. Considering the historical legacy and contemporary political trajectory of Bangladesh, the cause of deep-rooted mistrust is examined to better understand the rationale for the requirement, emergence and workings of the CTG structure.

The book unveils that it is not only the lack of nation-building measures and governments' wish to remain in power at any cost which lies behind the problems that Bangladesh faces today. Part of the problem is also the flawed logic of nation-building on the foundation of Western democratic norms which may be unsuitable in a South Asian cultural environment. Although democratic transitions, on the crutch of the CTG, have been useful in moments of crisis, its abolition creates the need for a new or revised transitional modality – perhaps akin to the CTG ethos – to oversee electoral governance, which will have to be renegotiated by the polity based on the people's will.

This book provides a valuable resource for researchers and academics working in the area of constitutional law, democratic transition, legal pluralism and election law.

Sonia Zaman Khan, a PhD from the University of London, SOAS, is a Solicitor of the Supreme Court of England and Wales and an Advocate of the Supreme Court of Bangladesh. She has been a legal and social development consultant in London and Dhaka for many years. Her research interest lies particularly in governance.

'*The Politics and Law of Democratic Transition: Caretaker Government in Bangladesh* offers a theoretically grounded, empirically rich, incisive discussion about a unique system of government in Bangladesh, and helps us to understand the challenges of governance and electoral systems in fragile democracies around the world. A must read for those interested in governance and democratization.'

Ali Riaz, Professor, Politics and Government,
Illinois State University, USA

'This incisive work lays bare the obstacles to "substantive" democracy gaining a foothold in Bangladesh. It is an essential read on the pitfalls of endemic friction between political hubris and popular will and opinion. The book's prescription is for complacency to give way to foresight and innovation for a systemic leap forward.'

Justice Dr. Syed Refaat Ahmed, High Court Division,
Supreme Court of Bangladesh

'Sonia Zaman Khan brings into detailed focus a subject that has been pivotal in Bangladesh's transition to democracy but has not been deliberated on to public satisfaction. This work happily fills that gap, for it explains the rationale behind the caretaker political system as a measure toward ensuring fair and free elections in Bangladesh. It enlightens readers.'

Syed Badrul Ahsan, Bangladeshi journalist and author of
From Rebel to Founding Father: Sheikh Mujibur Rahman

'This is an insightful study of the transitional mechanism of caretaker government. It provides relevant facts regarding the liberation movement and its history. Current political realities are presented in the context of which conditions for free and fair elections are to be devised.'

Dr. Kamal Hossain, Jurist, Politician and
Chairman of the Bangladesh First Constitution
Drafting Committee, 1972

THE POLITICS AND LAW OF DEMOCRATIC TRANSITION

Caretaker Government in Bangladesh

Sonia Zaman Khan

Routledge
Taylor & Francis Group
LONDON AND NEW YORK

First published 2018
by Routledge

2 Park Square, Milton Park, Abingdon, Oxfordshire OX14 4RN
52 Vanderbilt Avenue, New York, NY 10017

Routledge is an imprint of the Taylor & Francis Group, an informa business

First issued in paperback 2019

British Library Cataloguing-in-Publication Data
A catalogue record for this book is available from the British Library

Library of Congress Cataloging-in-Publication Data
Names: Khan, Sonia Zaman, author.
Title: The politics and law of democratic transition: caretaker government in Bangladesh / Sonia Zaman Khan.
Description: Abingdon, Oxon; New York, NY: Routledge, 2018. | Includes bibliographical references and index. | Based on author's thesis (doctoral - University of London, School of Oriental and African Studies, School of Law, 2014) issued under title: Democratic transition and the caretaker government in Bangladesh in a culture of mistrust, 2015.
Identifiers: LCCN 2017022362 | ISBN 9780415312301 (hardback) | ISBN 9781351860253 (adobe reader) | ISBN 9781351860246 (epub) | ISBN 9781351860239 (mobipocket)
Subjects: LCSH: Cabinet system–Bangladesh. | Interim governments–Bangladesh. | Bangladesh–Politics and government–1971
Classification: LCC KNG2260 .K48 2018 | DDC 342.5492/04–dc23
LC record available at https://lccn.loc.gov/2017022362

ISBN: 978-0-415-31230-1 (hbk)
ISBN: 978-0-367-88648-6 (pbk)

Typeset in Gaillard
by Deanta Global Publishing Services, Chennai, India

Dedicated to my loving father
Mr. Badiuzzaman Khan

The survival of our democracy and the unity and integrity of the nation depends upon the realisation that constitutional morality is no less essential than constitutional legality. Dharma (righteousness; sense of public duty or virtue) lives in the hearts of public men; when it dies there, no Constitution, no law, no amendment, can save it.

Nani Palkhivala, *Privy Purse Case*
(*Madhav Rao Jivaji Rao Scindia v Union of India*)
[(1971) 1 SCC 85]

CONTENTS

FOREWORD

Democratic systems of governance with periodic elections are the dominant global norm in today's world. Yet even in leading Western jurisdictions, as recent outcomes in the United States, the British Brexit referendum and subsequent fresh elections indicate, manipulations of voting decisions and their consequences are not unknown. While such processes need to be constantly monitored, and no particular electoral system seems inherently perfect, politics remains everywhere a volatile, competitive balancing act, climaxing in periodic elections. Everywhere, often radically disparate aims and perspectives, with many agendas that may not be disclosed, vie for votes. While good election management would appear to involve constructive public engagement, akin to Habermasian conversations within the public sphere, these are manifestly far too romantic expectations. In many countries, not only in Asia and Africa, those in positions of power, or hoping to gain power, will be tempted to play games with people's ballots.

In normal democratic scenarios, voters periodically decide the fate of political parties and leader figures. Yet what if an electorate is manipulated or misguided so severely that a whole country and its political system is thrown into severe and prolonged turmoil? Few people may know that Bangladesh, one of the largest countries in the world in terms of population, has unfortunately suffered this kind of experience, facing what this important study calls 'an arrested democracy'. I am not suggesting here, nor does this book, that Bangladesh is the worst case imaginable of managing democratic elections freely, fairly and peacefully. However, deeply troublesome and serious deficiencies surround the ways in which Bangladesh has, since its blood-stained independence from Pakistan in 1971, dealt with its electoral processes. These troubles have motivated me, as a long-term student of Bangladeshi legal developments, and subsequently supervising the author of this study, as a more directly involved stakeholder, to engage in wide-ranging explorations of why and how the lofty visions of a bright future for a 'Golden Bangladesh' are constantly threatened by various manifestations of wanton violence. While such troubles can be related to the politics and law of democratic transitions, the core question remains of why this turbulence is so prolonged, so persistently brutal and so apparently unresolved. Worse still, dark storm clouds are on the horizon, as the next national elections are due in 2019. Presently, the Bangladesh Nationalist Party (BNP), as the main opposition, does not have a single member in parliament, since they decided to boycott the elections of 2014. This explosive scenario indicates that grave issues of self-righteous reasoning and petty petulance over claims to power cannot be defined away, but where are the solutions? A dysfunctional two-party system is only part of the trouble, while the lack of reliable election management structures and the deep-running culture of mistrust are pertinent, too.

Apart from prolonged periods of military rule, even when democratic elections were held at regular intervals, Bangladesh experienced much more than democratic teething problems. Bangladeshis are acutely political people and their country, the former East Pakistan, was created in a euphoric moment with high expectations of freedom and development, reacting against suppression by the postcolonial Pakistani regime. The shock of discovering very soon that not all Bangladeshis were the same, or shared the same vision, forms one major reason for the continuing electoral struggles in Bangladesh. None of the four major elements of the country's founding vision, nationalism, democracy, socialism and secularism are completely endorsed by all key stakeholders. As this book clearly shows, even the sophisticated Caretaker Government arrangements of Bangladesh, which worked quite well for about two decades, were more recently ruthlessly abused and manipulated, and then suddenly abolished in 2011. Presently, the country seems thrown back into serious turmoil, a troubling fact that news blackouts, restraints on open debate and desperate efforts to control law and order can barely cover up.

This book tells a realistic story, with some important lessons on the need to manage diversity and difference more skilfully, especially if one wants this populous Muslim majority state to avoid the troubles experienced by Afghanistan and Pakistan. What goes on in Bangladesh today is not widely enough known, but urgently needs to be known better, for this experience contains important lessons about how plural societies, in which Muslims are a demographic majority, may manage differences in a sustainable form. Such lessons would apply to Turkey and Indonesia, too, for example. Key questions go much further than asking which Muslims are the 'right' Muslims, as there will always be 'others'. The tragedy of Bangladesh is partly that the deeply politicised conflicts between Muslim secularists and non-secularists play out in a global scenario of ongoing confusion over what Islam actually is, as a religion and a way of life, and what it means, in specific conditions of time and space, to be Islamic. While that is not a topic to which this book aims to make a major contribution, such issues form a major element of the ongoing struggle of Bangladesh to manage difference and diversity through democratic processes. I have theorised this in terms of the somewhat romantic *iccher ghuri*, the wish-kite of Bangladesh, whose four key visionary elements of nationalism, democracy, socialism and secularism match the four corners of the theoretical model of the global kite of law. The dynamic kite image, with (1) natural laws, (2) socio-legal normativities, (3) state-centric laws and (4) international law and human rights principles, rather than depicting leakages in structures of good governance, simply illustrates that any attempt to cut out any of those four corners would lead to a crash scenario for the whole structure. Sadly, as political developments in Bangladesh abundantly confirm, good governance itself becomes a casualty if leader figures cannot even agree on the basics of governance, specifically in terms of whether being an elected ruler is a form of public service, an onerous duty or rather a passport to Austinian rights of domination and abuses of power, only thinly veiled by electoral endorsement.

Even today, the identity of Bangladesh as a separate nation remains challenged by those who push for some kind of imagined uniform Islamic structure and proclaim detestation of the multiple pluralities that underpin this nation. A uniformising vision, based on faulty understandings of law and Islamic jurisprudence, as well as all of history, society and politics, seems to clash over a deeply questionable vision of what it means to be Islamic in today's global, plural world. If Bangladesh, as a Muslim-dominated Asian country, wants to fly its own wish kite towards a golden future, how can some of its leaders behave as though this was an Islamic republic modelled on the very system from which it sought liberation in 1971? The country's vision of a golden future involves a certain kind of path, a form of *shari'a* – and I use that Islamic term deliberately here – that cannot avoid the challenging task of diversity management. All major stakeholders, including the political parties and their prominent leaders, actually know that Islam has a foundational pluralist principle of *ikhtilaf*, the tolerated diversity of human opinion. Islam's pluralist recognition of a diversity of approaches and opinions, also in relation to religion, should thus form the founding element of secularism in the *iccher ghuri* of Bangladesh for all stakeholders. It is clear to all that this means the acceptance of cultural and religious diversity within the context of an Islamic majority. In addition, as Bangladesh knows well, socialism does not feed people, and religion does not feed people either.

This spirited study, which involved much field research, too, is not focused on the impact of political Islam on the election troubles in Bangladesh. It shows, however, that the political struggles over the electoral arrangements in this country reflect a somewhat petty and deeply distrustful fundamental unwillingness to agree on anything, even on a common core of founding principles for this nation. As a result, the common people of Bangladesh are made to suffer and lose out, but the people remain also surprisingly confused, and thus carry a share of the blame for this arrested democracy. Since roughly half of the electorate seems somehow to favour either the BNP or the Awami League, all kinds of dramatic and devious interferences and interventions can easily swing electoral balances in a dangerously simple first-past-the-post system.

The richly documented analysis of this book generates some hope, though, that the people of Bangladesh themselves will learn to realise over time, and with more clarity, that the ballot box can give a sustainable answer for the better management of the country's internal diversity. Even if, as one currently observes, the minority populations are drastically decreased because of violence against non-Muslims and anyone who is perceived as 'other', the problem will never go away. A more mature democracy, freed from the dark powers that currently arrest it, and based on more respect for diversity among the citizens and voters of Bangladesh, is manifestly the only sustainable way forward. Maybe economic progress, which is clearly strongly in evidence in Bangladesh, will carry its own lessons about what kind of governance is better for the country as a whole. For achieving that realisation, the people of Bangladesh may not need a new caretaker arrangement, as the Election Commission is in place and there is no sensible reason why it should not perform its assigned duty, if allowed to work autonomously by the executive. But the people, as well as their rather too self-centred leaders, also need to cultivate a spirit of humanity that respects the deeper implications of democracy and of existing internal pluralities of the politics and law of democratic transition in Bangladesh. Fiddling with some institutions here and there, in light of the still present memory of the Caretaker Government scheme, may be only some drop of medicine that tackles certain peripheral aspects of the deep-rooted cancer of the selfish forms of extremist self-harm in Bangladesh. Only when the people of Bangladesh learn to use their voting powers more wisely will the country as a whole, and its glorious wish kite, be able to experience a real sense of freedom. This is not freedom from 'religion' and 'culture', as so much of Eurocentric argumentation still seeks to posit, but a conscious embracement of the various local manifestations of people's connectedness with their religions and cultures, in a spirit of respect for a higher public interest and global peace, rather than terrorist self-righteousness running amok. That basic message, by the way, is also not irrelevant, as noted earlier, when so-called developed countries are engaged in democratic elections. A defective democracy may arise when leader figures are defective, lack a sense of public accountability or feign aims and ambitions that are clearly not in the public interest. It is an increasingly visible challenge, anywhere in the world, for the common voting public to look through such argumentative scheming and to cast their votes wisely.

Werner Menski
Emeritus Professor of South Asian Laws
SOAS, University of London

PREFACE

What prompted the undertaking of this work was to bring forth the inherent politico-legal difficulties Bangladesh had in managing its national elections. However, delving into the intertwining issues revealed complexities which are far more entrenched into the socio-cultural-religious milieu of the country than meets the eye. The book attempts to identify and disentangle these conflicting factors which weaken democracy – in whatever condition and if at all – it exists in Bangladesh today. Having said that, the initial journey of democracy in any nation is bound to have challenges and, to that extent, Bangladesh is no exception. If the concerned stakeholders are able to sift from this book the intricate issues which continue to remain as stumbling blocks to genuine electoral governance, my humble effort would be worthwhile.

The challenges faced in completing this project have been countless, including my stunted knowledge about the nation's political history and inherent societal dynamics; limited available academic resources on the transition of government in the context of South Asia, the Caretaker Government (CTG) in particular; and the abrupt demise of the CTG structure itself – all compounded with equally complex personal circumstances. Fortunately, I had the support of individuals whose graciousness in imparting their knowledge and experience saw me through this phase.

Although the book and its faults are mine, I know that its perspectives have been sharpened by able scholars, particularly Dr. Werner Menski, Emeritus Professor of South Asian Laws at SOAS, to whom I shall remain enormously indebted. The understanding of the subject has benefitted from constructive insights cordially offered by luminaries, such as the likes of former caretaker chief advisors and advisors, judges of the Supreme Court of Bangladesh, jurists, academics, lawyers, civil and military bureaucrats, civil society members and professionals, to whom I owe immense gratitude and who are Mr. Justice Habibur Rahman CJ, Mr. Justice Mostafa Kamal CJ, Mr. Justice Latifur Rahman CJ, Mr. Justice ABM Khairul Haque CJ, Mr. Justice Shamsuddin Chowdhury, Dr. Kamal Hossain, Barrister Amir-Ul Islam, Dr. Akbar Ali Khan, Dr. Wahiduddin Mahmud, Mr. Hafizuddin Khan, Mr. Abdul Muyeed Chowdhury, General Golam Quader (retired), Dr. Hossain Zillur Rahman, Mr. Azizul Haque, Mr. Asafuddowlah, Mr. Muhammad Nurul Huda, Dr. M Zahir, Dr. Mizanur Rahman, Professor Shah Alam, Mr. Mahbube Alam, Mr. M I Farooqui, Barrister Manzoor Hasan OBE, Dr. Iftekharuzzaman, Dr. Sumaiya Khair, Major General (retired) Syed Muhammad Ibrahim *Bir Proteek*, Major General (retired) Muniruzzaman, Lieutenant General Masud Uddin Chowdhury, Brigadier (retired) Sakhawat Hossain, Professor Khalilur Rahman, Dr Shah M Ali, and Dr Ahsanul Habib. The time they provided was invaluable, both in terms of the quality of information shared altruistically and in fortifying my knowledge and perception about the multiple tensions which play out between ideologies, power-politics, official and unofficial laws, abuses of systems, corruptions and socio-political mindsets.

I also wish to acknowledge with gratitude the kind assistance of Mr. Syed Badrul Ahsan, whose invaluable suggestions with regard to the historical narration of the region alleviated the gaps in the book. I would like to pay tribute to the calm professionalism of the entire team at Routledge, particularly the senior commissioning editor of Taylor & Francis Ms. Alison Kirk, the production editor of Taylor & Francis Mr. Adam Guppy, and the Deanta Project Manager Ms. Anna Snyder, who meticulously ensured that the book met the style and standard of the press. I thank my research assistant Mr. Musavee Reza and remain profoundly indebted to all the educational institutions I was ever part of.

A constant source of strength and encouragement are my parents, Mr. Badiuzzaman Khan and Dr. Dalia Nilufar, whose unconditional love, consistent support and unswerving prayers across the miles and at every step of my life are pure blessings. This project is as much a dream of theirs as of mine. I would also like to mention Mrs. Nora Shariff, my godmother who watches out for me from a different realm. My brother Shafquat Zaman Khan kept my spirits high from afar while my only child, Abrar Ahmed, despite his complex medical needs, endured my relentless preoccupations and erratic dispositions during this journey with such calm and poise, which often made me wonder as to who the real parent is. Last, but not the least, my heartfelt gratitude goes to my spouse, Barrister Muhammad Nawshad Zamir, for his abiding support in sustaining my intellectual pursuits.

Sonia Zaman Khan

ABBREVIATIONS

ACC	Anti-Corruption Commission
AD	Appellate Division
ADC	Appellate Division Cases
AI	Amnesty International
AL	Awami League
APSU	All Party Students Unity
ASK	Ain O Shalish Kendro
BCS	Bangladesh Civil Service
BDR	Bangladesh Rifles
BLAST	Bangladesh Legal Aid and Services Trust
BLD	Bangladesh Law Decisions
BLT	Bangladesh Law Times
BMA	Bangladesh Medical Association
BNP	Bangladesh Nationalist Party
BRAC	Bangladesh Rural Advancement Committee (Formerly)
C&AG	Comptroller & Auditor General
CA	Chief Advisor
CEC	Chief Election Commissioner
CEO	Chief Executive Officer
CJ	Chief Justice
CPD	Centre for Policy Dialogue
CSP	Civil Service of Pakistan
CTG	Caretaker Government
DGFI	Directorate General of Forces Intelligence
DLR	Dhaka Law Report
EC	Election Commission
EPO	Emergency Powers Ordinance
EPR	Emergency Power Rules
EU	European Union
FBCCI	Federation of Bangladesh Chambers of Commerce and Industry
FDD	Foundation for Defense of Democracies

HC	High Court
HCD	High Court Division (of the Supreme Court of Bangladesh)
HRW	Human Rights Watch
HUJIB	Harkat-ul-Jihad al-Islami Bangladesh
ICT	International Crimes Tribunal Bangladesh
IDA	Islamic Democratic Alliance
IGS	Institute of Governance Studies
INC	Indian National Congress
ISIS	Islamic State of Iraq and Syria
JIB	Jamaat-e-Islami Bangladesh
JMB	Jama'atul Mujahideen Bangladesh
JP	Jatio Party
JSD	Jatio Shomajtantrik Dal
LDP	Liberal Democratic Party (Bangladesh)
MOU	Memorandum of Understanding
MP	Member of Parliament
NBR	National Board of Revenue
NDI	National Democratic Institute
NGO	Non-Governmental Organisation
PLD	Pakistan Legal Decisions
PM	Prime Minister
PO	President's Order
PPP	Pakistan People's Party
PPRC	Power and Participation Research Centre
PSC	Public Service Commission
RAB	Rapid Action Battalion
RPO	Representation of People Order
SAARC	South Asian Association for Regional Cooperation
SC	Supreme Court
SHUJAN	'*shushashoner jonno nagorik*' (Citizens for Good Governance)
TAC	Truth and Accountability Commission
TIB	Transparency International Bangladesh
UK	United Kingdom
UN	United Nations
USA	United States of America
USAID	United States Agency for International Development

1

INTRODUCTION

The focus

Across the world, during election periods in general and government transitions in particular, tension, anxiety and fierce competition over the electorate's attention are commonplace and have become a well-known part of the struggles in managing the democratic process. Usually in democracies, a State's electoral system functions smoothly and along democratically acceptable ways to guide and monitor the processes of bringing about the next government. Unfortunately, this has not been the case in many nations, and particularly in Bangladesh, this has remained deeply problematic, even 45 years after independence from Pakistan in 1971. Despite its legacy in terms of inheriting presumably helpful institutions from the British Raj, the nation's historical development of arrested democracy has shaped its political landscape and its legal vicissitudes. In fact, these continuing troubles have not only influenced how Bangladeshi legal and political institutions have developed over the past few decades, but have also from time to time seriously endangered the future of the country as a whole. Even at the time of completing this book, holding acceptable free, fair and participatory elections in Bangladesh remains a burning issue, making this subject even more pertinent than it appeared at the beginning.

Amid this rather troublesome history of perennial failure to address existing problems of electoral governance in Bangladesh, a mechanism called 'caretaker government' (CTG) was devised, from 1990 onwards, to manage general elections and peaceful transitions of power. Since 1990, after ousting the prolonged military regimes, Bangladesh had entered a new phase of democracy in which the 'two' autocratically inclined battling 'Begums', as referred to in popular parlance, have given Bangladeshis no alternative but to choose between the two of them. And Bangladeshis had been content in exercising that choice in an atmosphere of free, fair and inclusive elections conducted through the CTG structure from 1990 to 2008. Given that political deadlock and violent conflict at the country's expense, between the two major political parties, the Awami League (AL) and the Bangladesh Nationalist Party (BNP), have characterised national elections since this new phase of democracy emerged, and given that the nation's democratic institutions have not been strengthened over the years, neither of these two parties believe that it would have a fair chance of winning an election organised by its rival because of the risks of relentless manipulation. This is why the unofficial CTG structure of 1990 formally emerged through a constitutional amendment in 1996. This rather unusual legal structure, created as a remedy by the political élite with the (assumed) will of the people (no referendum was conducted when the CTG emerged, nor when it was subsequently abolished), indicates a certain type of malfunctioning of the State machinery in a developing South Asian country at the critical point of elections. Neighbouring countries, while certainly not trouble-free, have not experienced the kind of intense problems to the extent witnessed in Bangladesh, which indicates that there must be specific factors that play out in creating these kinds of difficulties. Despite delivering four free, fair and participatory national elections over a period of 20 years, this constitutional innovation of the CTG is marred with controversy as to its benefit and effectiveness in assisting democratic transition, thereby fostering democracy in Bangladesh. Its abrupt abolishment in 2011 raised important new issues about the utility and efficacy of this mechanism. Clearly, the general elections of 5 January 2014 were conducted without any CTG, and promptly raised questions over democratic credibility, but to date, Bangladesh has a functioning government that, while of course not unchallenged, has managed to rule it, and rule it in a manner of nonchalance. Although 'on the world stage, Prime Minister Sheikh Hasina has joined a list of leaders who have been elected technically but without an electoral mandate' (Joehnk 2014), the AL government cannot be termed an illegal government, but one lacking serious democratic credibility since Khaleda Zia and her party, BNP, unwisely decided to boycott the poll on the grounds of the absence of a CTG to oversee a free, fair and inclusive election. This decision of non-participation, based on the belief that free and fair elections are not possible without CTG supervision, cost BNP their seats and their standing as an opposition voice in parliament – which is the democratic platform or centre stage. The ensuing violence which followed during the January 2014 election, together with the low turn-out of voters, leaving 154 uncontested seats in the hands of the ruling party, indicates that there is a difference between choosing two candidates rather than just one.

Against this backdrop of election-time tug of war and transition, which cripples the nation prior to general elections every time, the main question posed in this book is: To what extent is there any legal basis of, and justification for, the CTG as a supportive and effective vehicle for democratic transition in Bangladesh? Additionally, to what extent has the CTG mechanism been useful for Bangladesh, and what lessons have been learnt from its operation? To answer these main questions, the book explains and analyses in depth how the CTG machinery of Bangladesh arose and operated, how and why it was abolished and how it has been evaluated by various stakeholders, including the electorate. To capture public perceptions about the CTG and its functioning, a survey of a fairly large sample of people and interviews with stakeholders in Bangladesh regarding the CTG's utility and impact during government transition (if at all) was undertaken. The evidence yielded is integrated throughout the book, particularly in Chapters 4 and 5. While examining the extent to which the CTG is a workable instrument during the transition of power, given that its main role is to ensure that free, fair and participatory elections are regularly held, the book posits that perhaps this temporary institution itself may be a useful and constructive tool in terms of paving the way for good electoral governance in Bangladesh. The reactions to the abolition of the CTG in 2011 suggest that although such an institution may not be ideal in democracies, in the context of Bangladesh, it may still have some utility.

Nagging interrelated questions arise as to why Bangladeshi State election structures have been failing in this particular way, and what the reasons are for the failure of Bangladesh to adequately govern itself. In the troubled conditions of an emerging democracy like Bangladesh, where democratic institutions are not yet fully built, where the pendulum of power has swung between prolonged military rule and unstable civilian order, where there is clear evidence of deep mutual mistrust among most stakeholders and where there is a dysfunctional two-party system as far as holding free and fair elections are concerned, there appear to be many risks for operating an interim structure like the CTG. Despite these clear risks, including the risk of 'politicisation of the judiciary' (as involving the former chief justice as the head of the CTG ran the risk of blurring 'the separation between the judiciary and the executive') (Riaz 2013a: 3), there has nevertheless been a 20-year history of the CTG in Bangladesh. Thus, the book also questions whether the emergence of this structure itself constitutes evidence that the country's democratic system is not yet fully mature enough to handle the challenges of electoral transitions without the crutches of a neutral interim government of some kind.

Given the unscrupulous manipulation of the CTG mechanism from 2006 to 2008, a few subsidiary questions also arise as to whether and to what extent abuses of the system actually continue to pose risks to the country's progression to a satisfactory functioning of electoral governance. Looking at it from a completely different perspective, the book also attempts to examine how a jurisdiction like Bangladesh, in all its cultural specificity and variety, is able to absorb the ethos of a democratic culture when the notion of democracy actually emanates from a Western context and, to that effect, to what extent direct transplants of democratic models from the West actually function satisfactorily in the context of South Asia, specifically in Bangladesh.

The country's electoral history, post 1990, portrays a constant struggle between two deeply opposed political camps, AL and BNP, which have alternated in leading the country when elections were conducted by the CTG mechanism. It would be too simple to explain the electoral and governance troubles of Bangladesh as merely a consequence of this adversarial, vengeful and unremitting battle of AL and BNP, hence the other related questions arise which refuse to fade away: Is it a deeper systemic problem, and to some extent a question of culture, or is it really, as has been suggested, just a personal matter related to the so-called 'battle of the Begums' and thus some form of dynastic warfare? These important questions, elaborating also the wider political context, all relate closely to the main challenge of assessing the operation of the CTG as a legal tool of good governance in Bangladesh.

As the nation witnessed a controversial election, without the crutches of a CTG, in January 2014, in the process it once again succumbed to a series of deadlocks. The lack of desperately needed discourses between the government and the opposition regarding election modalities, the failed attempts of civil society members and the international community to bring AL and BNP members to a dialogue regarding election-time modalities, the boycott of election by the opposition, the ensuing anarchical street violence and crippling *hartals* (labour strikes) by the opposition, the phenomenal number of casualties resulting from the *hartals* and blockades, the ruthless crackdown on the opposition, the poor voter turn-out on election day, the government's winning of large numbers of uncontested seats – all of these tell us about the effects of the manipulation of the law as a tool of governance in a South Asian country like Bangladesh. This results in a series of electoral governance malfunctions, which the populace is compelled to bear year in and year out.

Although the myriad complexities of transitional polities are a work in progress for any nation transiting to democracy, from a vantage point in early 2017, one of the lessons learnt from the CTG experience is, perhaps, that even a CTG can be abused and manipulated. But despite the pitfalls, over a period of 20 years, the fact of the matter remains that the CTGs have delivered free, fair and inclusive elections to Bangladesh over and over again, making the transition from one government to another as trouble-free and non-controversial as possible. Perhaps lessons have been learnt through the CTG experience, but evidently not enough, and it seems that throwing away these crutches of election management completely without creating a reliable alternative may have been a too rushed and somewhat reckless decision.

The context

Bangladesh started out in 1971 as a democracy, based on the legacies of its historical connection with India and Pakistan, but soon saw a regression into an autocratic form of governance. The ruling party, in its attempt to consolidate power, faced with infrastructural challenges, devastating famine, extreme economic hardship, severe deterioration in law and order, rampant corruption and, as a result, decreased popular appeal in the aftermath of a violent war of independence with the Pakistani army, which killed at least three million people 'and sent ten million refugees fleeing to India' (Bass 2014), decided to revert to a one-party system, following the communist parties of China and Russia. This socialist experiment was short-lived and was stopped in its tracks, as a military regime usurped power within a few months of these developments becoming evident, brutally assassinating the founding father of the nation, Sheikh Mujibur Rahman (revered as *Bangabandhu* – 'friend of Bengal') and most of his family members in 1975. Thereafter, the process of going back to a multiparty democratic system started anew, only to be halted again a few years later by fresh military interventions. These military interventions brought religion to the political forefront in a calculative manner, altering the political landscape of Bangladesh by redefining State principles from secularism to Islam and identification of citizens from Bengalis to Bangladeshis. Professor Ali Riaz (2010: 49) identifies the impact of these military interventions in the following words:

> These military regimes succeeded in bringing Islam into the political discourse and facilitated the gaining of legitimacy for the Islamists – both constitutionally and politically. The lasting legacy of this era is the change it has brought to the entire discourse of Bangladeshi politics and the serious blow it delivered to the secular ideal.

This process of Bangladesh's faltering democratisation, coupled with worldwide economic pressures resulting from the oil price hike in the mid-seventies, had a significant impact on the quality of democracy achieved in the country.

Although Bangladesh has had no tutelary period of transition from élite parliamentary politics to parliamentary democracy, the latter is regarded as *the* legitimate form of government by virtually all politically aware and participant groups of the population except for the Islamists (Stern 2001: 17). The deficiency in democratic consolidation was initially due to a lack of democratic experience, a perspective summarised by Hossain (2000: 525) in the following words:

> Political instability should be viewed as a reflection of feudal character of a traditional society in which most people are uneducated, socially backward, and politically uninformed and hence possess unsophisticated character traits, including feudal or tribal rivalry.

The same commentator further points out that '[t]here exists a patron-client culture in all spheres of life that is behind the personalised, factionalised character of Bangladesh's politics' (Hossain 2000: 525). Consequently, the democratic progress is perceived to be constantly disturbed and infected by undemocratic tendencies, worsening the prevalent climate of mistrust in the country. However, the reality is far more complex.

Although Feng and Zak (1999: 162–163) argued that widely held determinants of democratic transitions like low per capita income, low levels of education and a lack of history of democratic experience and practice are factors weighing down the road to sustainable democracy, there are other significant factors which continue to affect the quality of democracy (Fisher 2013; Vigoda-Gadot and Mizrahi 2014). With regard to Bangladesh, Islam (2005) notes that although the rule of law underlies the entire Constitution, the concept is capable of different interpretations by different people and has, therefore, various shades of meaning. Typically, the Constitution of Bangladesh in the preamble proclaims the 'rule of law' as the prime objective of the Constitution and as a new habitat for substantive provisions aimed at achieving the rule of law. By itself, this is merely decorative and is not reflective of Bangladesh's reality. The representative character of the government in Bangladesh is not confined to the central government but to the sphere of local government and all levels of administration. But this truly representative government is a misnomer unless free, fair and inclusive elections to reflect the wishes of the people can be ensured. One could actually go a little further and add that the expectation is that democracy ought to engage the bulk of the population in participation which is political. Such political participation means behaviour on the part of the mass public directed at influencing, directly or indirectly, the formulation, adoption and implementation of governmental or policy choices (Fishkin 2009: 45), for that is a hallmark of an inclusive and perhaps sophisticated democracy. Voting has become by far the most widely shared form of political participation and, although contributing money, time and effort to political causes; demonstrating; writing letters or emails to government officials; and signing petitions are all activities that involve large numbers of people, this level of advanced democracy has not yet been achieved in countries like Bangladesh. For Bangladesh, one can tick the box that there is a basic electoral governance only when the voting is participatory, and political parties enjoy a level playing field when free, fair and inclusive elections are held at regular intervals. Unfortunately, the culture of mistrust in Bangladesh is closely connected to and develops into what one may call a 'culture of non-participation'. This thought arises in view of frequent parliamentary boycotts, *hartals* and a basic refusal of the opposition to engage in constructive discourse. Such obstructions indicate a serious and at times frustrating deficiency in the political culture, which impacts the overall quality of rudimentary democracy in Bangladesh.

It is indeed mainly the 'free and fair election' element of democracy which has been a prominent point of contention in Bangladesh over many years. Hossain (2000: 509) argues that although the common perception of Bangladesh's political instability is fundamentally a self-inflicted national indulgence of trivial issues, in which all social groups willingly or unwillingly show their proclivities, this in itself does not tell the whole story and seems to be marred by rhetoric. Any attempt to identify other, deeper factors that may have caused political instability would require an investigation of the social, cultural, religious and political traits that create social and political disharmony. In analysing the need for a CTG mechanism in Bangladesh, these elements of social, historical, cultural, religious and political aspects are also discussed in this book, in Chapters 2, 3 and 4. In his article, Hossain (2000: 508–529) not only summarises the historical profile of the political parties that dominate Bangladesh's politics, including thumbnail characteristics of voting behaviour, but also attempts to explain why these parties do not cooperate and follow parliamentary norms and practices to establish a mutually beneficial two-party political system. He points out that confrontational politics, as practised by these parties in Bangladesh, are a manifestation of an inbuilt undemocratic political culture in which each party seeks to monopolise State power as if the other does not even have the right to exist. Hossain (2000: 509) concludes that in an underdeveloped society like Bangladesh, the mere transfer of political power from the military to the politicians or the conduct of ritualistic elections does not necessarily establish a stable democratic political system. In such a society, the existing feudal political culture, often under the rubric of dynastic political leadership, is more likely to promote confrontation than stability and cause deterioration rather than an improvement in the governance of the State.

Other State institutions in Bangladesh, such as the judiciary, have been pliant and subject to political intervention and direction. Political and bureaucratic interference are the most significant impediments to police efficiency and have resulted in the worst forms of abuse including illegal detention, death in custody, torture and pervasive corruption. The result is almost universal public disdain for the police force. Political regimes have used the police, since their inception, to regularly harass political opponents, for example, by using the Special Powers Act of 1974 (Act XIV of 1974), which has provisions for preventative detention (promulgated on 9 February 1974), rather than using them to maintain public order or to give them the opportunity to develop as a neutral institution. In addition, since 2004, the Rapid Action Battalion (RAB), an élite anti-crime and anti-terrorism unit of the police, was created to combat criminal gang activity throughout the country. It has been accused by Amnesty International of a lack of accountability and for being responsible for at least 700 deaths from 2004 to 2011, which have been attributed to crossfire, extra-judicial killings and torture. According to Odhikar (a human rights organisation in Bangladesh), the statistics for extra-judicial killings in Bangladesh in 2012 were 70, rising to a massive 329 in 2013; 172 in 2014; and 185 in 2015. In 2013, according to the report, 'among the 329 extra judicially killed by law enforcement agencies, 174 were extra judicially killed in relation to political violence', mostly before the impending January 2014 national elections.

In addition, governmental accountability remains elusive and this lack of accountability stems from two important sources. On one level, it can be traced to the pre-independence legacy, relating to the bureaucratic-authoritarian political institutions that pervaded what was then East Pakistan, which led to bureaucrats yielding a significant amount of political and coercive power, exercising it with considerable impunity. This matter gives rise to questions about the extent to which unsupervised or unchecked bureaucratic discretion is responsible for abuses of power also causing the gradual infiltration of impunity into the electoral system. At another level, the country's shaky transition to democracy, marred by conflicting decisions on what Bangladesh stands for as a nation and the issue of 'Bangladesh's identity', has not done much to instil an atmosphere of accountability in general, including into the country's bureaucracy.

The predicament over Bangladesh's identity has become more pronounced over time. The birth of what appeared to be a homogenous nation, with its majority Muslim population coexisting with non-Muslim and ethnic minorities, bound by the spirit of ethnicity and culture rather than religion in 1971, has altered over the years and has now deeply polarised the very nation into two broad categories: Muslim secularists and Muslim non-secularists. Let us keep the non-Muslim secularists separate for now because that group is in contention for a different reason, namely the issues that minorities face in a State. There is a serious rift between the less-conservative Muslims, who do not perceive secularism to pose any threat to Islam, and the more conservative (including *Wahabi*-influenced) Islamists, who identify secularism as a major threat to their main objective of establishing *Deen*, or Islamic social order, and who wish to declare Bangladesh as an Islamic Republic on the basis of the Sovereignty of Almighty Allah, whereby the Holy Qur'an and the *Sunnah* will be the only source of all laws in the Republic. The interplay and contestation between these two blocs have had a profound impact on Bangladesh's political landscape. Riaz (2016a: 216) pertinently asks whether this contestation is between a 'secularist' understanding of religion's private role and a 'non-secularist' understanding of the public presence of Islam. This contestation and, indeed, how other multiple contestations have played out, both in the context of a domestic historical narrative on identity construction and the global dimension of the relationship between religion and politics, is further explored in Chapter 3.

As parliament has been functioning in a partisan fashion, little effort has been made to scrutinise the bureaucracy on the issue of accountability. While there is political interference with the bureaucracy, which is manifest in the appointment, promotion and transfer of bureaucrats as well as in the allocation of State funds to particular public projects on an openly partisan basis, there is not much routine scrutiny on the work of bureaucracy. In addition, executive scrutiny is rather absent in parliament. Despite being in session, the parliament is often ineffective due to prolonged absences of the opposition from parliamentary sessions (customarily termed as a 'boycott' by the parties in opposition) or because parliament may have an opposition which is 'handpicked or coerced into that role' (Riaz 2014a: 152), as was evident in the post 2014 election with the Jatio Party (JP) – part of the AL-led grand coalition government during its term of 2008–2013 – which was designated as 'the official parliamentary opposition … essentially turning the 10th Parliament into one without any opposition party' (Riaz 2014a: 152–153). Both major political parties, AL and BNP, have justified their respective boycotts over the years by coming up with a myriad of allegations against the ruling party. This has done little to convince the electorate that such boycotts have in any way strengthened pluralistic governance in the country. This clearly also reflects the prevalent 'political culture of non-participation' over many years.

Even today, the political parties remain miles away from each other. Neither is willing to concede ground on any issue of relevance to Bangladeshis. The two political leaders have a well-known aversion to each other that has prevented them from interacting, even at a social level (Ahsan 2011b). Even when parliament is in session, the Speaker, elected generally from the members of the party in power, seldom acts neutrally in terms of allocating time for debates and in giving rulings on issues on procedure. In assessing the parliament's performance at the first session of the tenth parliament, Transparency International Bangladesh (TIB) has observed in its report that merely 1.8 per cent of the total time of the first session was spent on lawmaking.

Another instrument of accountability in a democracy is a free press and media. Although Bangladesh is gradually developing a press that is frequently critical of the ruling regime, journalists who are critical of a regime's performance risk being subjected to harassment (Bhuian 2012) and killings. Both the AL and BNP regimes have been seen to be very sensitive to criticism, among other things, of their human rights records. BNP has reacted with hostility to criticism of its treatment of minorities and the behaviour of some of its radical Islamist coalition partners. Possible ties of a few Bangladeshi political organisations to Islamic radicals have also clearly emerged (Hashmi 2009).

There are other important and mainly historical factors which have played a significant role in the arrested development of democracy in Bangladesh. Prominent here is a deep-rooted culture of mistrust which began first with mistrust of the British during the colonial era, followed by mistrust of the Pakistanis and their hegemonic efforts to suppress what used to be East Pakistan until 1971. Presently, in post-independence Bangladesh, there is ample evidence of blatant mistrust of major forces engaged in ruling the nation, including the aggressive climate of adversarialism which exists between the government and the opposition. This is because determining factors that create the conditions of trust such as fairness, transparency, accountability, reliability and discourse have been largely absent from the political arena. Such deficiencies are embedded in the mindset of respective opposition parties, and even of the electorate, to the effect that no government in power in Bangladesh is able to give a free, fair and participatory election to the citizens that would result in a representative government, as is evident from the electorate and stakeholders' opinions about elections held under political governments. Given this complex backdrop, elections and election results in Bangladesh have almost always been a foregone conclusion, rendering no positive effects on the political process. The 'winner takes all' rule literally means taking it all in Bangladesh, including the civil service, the Election Commission (EC), the police and, these days, most unfortunately to a certain extent, the judiciary.

It is difficult for democracies to operate effectively without mutual trust between various players and institutions, as this is a major pre-condition for effectively managing political, social and economic affairs (Vigoda-Gadot and Mizrahi 2014; Warren 1999). Increasing trust in democracies is thus imperative for improving the management of the democratic State in the wider context of an examination of the various theoretical inputs into a governance system. In this context, in Bangladesh, the need for a neutral umpire in the electoral playground was deemed necessary to increase and foster trust and be an instrument which is legitimate, pragmatic, effective, efficient and essential. While the starting point for the CTG was a desperate attempt to hold free and fair elections after the demise of long-term military rule, there continued a crucial need for such a system to remain in order to develop a system of regular free, fair and participatory election culture, including its necessary management and a peaceful transition of power from one democratically elected government to another. The nation understood that, without this, the country did not stand even the remotest chance of stepping into a basic functional electoral democracy.

Hence the analytical focus of this book falls on the CTG institution as a critical tool for ultimately securing a system of good electoral governance, suitable for Bangladesh. The CTG has had the opportunity of being a bridge between citizens and the political system for 20 years. The political system had suffered the most from a perennial crisis in trust and almost childishly stubborn non-participation, be it in engaging in discourse, in elections or in parliament. Regrettably, this phenomenon prevails. In this wider context, the unilateral abolition of the CTG itself, whose original mandate was to serve as a bridge between peoples' expectations of safeguarding free and fair elections and the frail political realm, has been neither pragmatically altruistic nor constructive.

2

CARETAKER GOVERNANCE

A new dimension to politico-legal philosophy

The purpose of this chapter is to provide a deeper understanding of the criteria by which the effectiveness and contribution of the caretaker government (CTG) to Bangladesh's own brand of democracy may be tested. In order to do so, the CTG is examined here under political science, culture-specific, legal and socio-legal lenses. While these are all interconnected as part of a complex field of normative plurality, the fact that what we analyse here plays out in Bangladesh makes the discussions even more complex. Donlan and Urscheler (2014: 6) note the sovereignty claims of the modern state and observe in this respect that

> Finally, the modern Western 'state legal systems' of the nineteenth century were able to make such claims comparatively more meaningful while also threading together the diverse legalities into a single national common law, though earlier ideas and institutions might continue to exist within reformed structures and substantive law.

Bangladesh, however, is not in Central Europe, and the time/space/situation context evidently creates very significant differences from well-developed 'Western' patterns of governance and even election management. Indeed, Donlan and Urscheler (2014: 7) reiterate that

> In contrast, many non-Western traditions retain a relatively high degree of normative complexity today. In each, there is a set of rules that is seen as equivalent to 'law', but that often plays a very different social role than the latter does in the West. These non-Western traditions also function differently.

It will therefore be necessary here to bring out the hybridity and complexity of Bangladeshi patterns of governance and election management as a *sui generis* sample of postcolonial efforts to make sense of, and to handle in practice, the many challenges posed to governing a fairly new country that is still struggling with its identity as a State. While Western models and prototypes are probably quite powerful as templates, given the colonial impact and related effects of higher education, it will not be sufficient to rely merely on Western or transplanted concepts and patterns. Regional and local influences will inevitably make themselves felt, but have not sufficiently been analysed so far with regards to governance in Bangladesh. This poses restraints in relation to theoretical discussions here, which are, to say the least, undeveloped as far as South Asian patterns of governance are concerned.

The four different lenses applied here are part of an effort to understand in more depth why Bangladesh has been struggling so severely when it comes to election management and has had to resort to CTG techniques, only to abandon those in the most recent elections in early 2014. The political lens approach critically discusses foundational concepts such as democracy, including the rather Eurocentric political theorising of Habermas. It also examines the notion of transition to democracy, the problems of trust and the management of elections. These concepts are discussed in the light of the CTG's role in contributing to the ongoing difficult process of democratic consolidation in Bangladesh. The CTG has been used as a *prima facie* mechanism to hold elections in a free and fair manner during democratic transitions, where trust between political parties and the government in power had been seriously at stake. However, the CTG's abolition has complicated this analysis, and this now perhaps offers the potential for a fresh take on the processes of managing national elections in Bangladesh and their interpretation.

In the case of Bangladesh, the story is complicated by two events of 'liberation': in 1947 from the British Raj and in 1971 from Pakistan. Examined under the socio-cultural lens, these stressful episodes of nation-building assist in understanding that processes of election management in Bangladesh also involve aspects of various competing socio-cultural patterns which consequently impact on legal cultures. These struggles are closely linked to issues of identity formation – an underlying socio-cultural theme that continues to severely trouble Bangladesh. Since Hindu/Buddhist and Islamic elements are deeply embedded in the religious-ethnic-historical mosaic of the region, the creation of a new Muslim-dominated nation state in 1971 had to lead to fresh agonies over that nation's identity. All efforts, including local efforts to construct a vision of a sustainable hybrid nation based on democratic and secular principles, even though standard models and expectations might not be followed, indicate Bangladesh's wish to adhere to a semblance of democracy despite repeated undemocratic interventions. But it is clearly not so simple to operate a country which has increasingly pervasive religiosity, and particularly if many in that country are not at ease with such a 'secular' vision.

Under the legal lens, it is observed that merely examining the CTG structure through a Hartian positivistic lens is not actually helpful. A more sophisticated socio-legal lens, applied under the rubric of legal pluralism, may be more suitable in order to understand the CTG mechanism and its troubled operation. The discussion hence progresses towards the jurisprudential basis of CTG arrangements, drawing primarily on the work of Chiba (1986 and 1989) and Menski (2006) to bring out the importance of legal dynamism in processes of nation building and identity formation of postcolonial states. This book, in addition, traces the various challenges of legal transplantation and the perennial problems which transplanted laws, in this case colonial models and the notion of democracy, face in a new *pluri-legal* environment.

Peaceful transition of power, ruling by consent, free and fair elections and universal suffrage are the usual tenets of democracy. However, as is evident, every nation is different from the other, and the more we research democracies, the more we realise that it is not only difficult to define democracy, but that it is also naive to think that a precise mode of governance can be prescriptive or superimposed worldwide. Perhaps the reason for this messy situation and elusiveness is not only that there is no globally agreed definition of law (Menski 2006: 34; Tamanaha 2009: 17), but that there is also no such notion as a democracy 'blueprint' which can simply be applied to any society or State. Since the nature of law everywhere is culture-specific and situation-specific (Allott 1980; Donlan and Urscheler 2014), specific solutions, whether temporal or permanent, emerge from specific problems. Rather than being rooted in abstract concepts, it seems that democracy and good governance are based on practical experience and continual human interaction in particular scenarios. In order for sustainable democracy to work in any nation, there will need to be a continual state of pragmatic adaptation. It is this adaptive nature which could be a cause for the celebration of pluralism and dynamism. However, pluralism also contributes to the messiness and the complexities of governance. The CTG innovation in the context of Bangladesh is such a pragmatic example of or solution to addressing issues of election management – elections which are free, fair and inclusive.

Although there is no entry for the term 'caretaker government' in conventional law dictionaries, its recent inclusion in online dictionaries, such as the Glossary for Political Terms, defines it as follows:

> A type of governance where those in power refrain from significant actions such as undertaking major legislative programs or senior judicial or public service appointments, but only maintain necessary normal administrative duties. The reason for this is that power would be in transition due to an election being due or being called suddenly due to the success of a vote of no confidence, or some other situation where legitimate democratic government has to be restored.

The CTG mechanism, a comparatively new entry in the field of public law and political science, is supposed to be a temporary phenomenon, in existence for a short time and installed temporarily, usually for holding elections or in an emergency until a regular government takes over. This type of situation may arise where there is an issue of trust or a need for greater transparency or fair play, or where the power of the outgoing government needs to be curtailed for reasons of equilibrium or fair play.

While debates on naturalist theories, legal positivism, sociological interpretations of law, legal realism, contractarian theory, constitutionalism and legal pluralism are in constant motion, the trust of the people in an 'unelected' government, for a certain limited time, with the specific mandate to 'elect' a legitimate government or people's representatives, perhaps enunciates a new legal phenomenon for the management of government and governed relationships. It is evident that the use of CTG arrangement involves, at the same time, political, legal and socio-cultural aspects that require further analysis, to which we now proceed.

Political science lens

Democracy: The ideal model of responsiveness to people's demands?

The general concept of political democracy has of course been debated very widely, and this book takes from this wider arena only those aspects that are pertinent to election management. Broadly speaking, the idea of democracy involves a sharing of power and processes of participation by many stakeholders. According to John Morison (2008: 303–304), 'everyone affected by a decision has a right to participate in the decision-making process'. Democracy, fundamentally thus a struggle over power, and an agreement to share power by a defined group of people, provides however an entirely different experience for those who are elected into positions of power which they then hold, and for those who do not hold so. This may be perceived at two levels, namely in the power struggles between government and opposition and in the relations between governments and citizens.

Viewed from centres of institutions of power, this appears as a set of structures where, ideally, all competing interests are represented by specific methods of governance and full and fair participation is enabled through institutionalised channels and by means of various kinds of voting systems, most prominently for this book, in national elections. This means, first of all, that government and opposition need to work together in the battle for votes, in the election process itself and in post-election arrangements for governance. However, the case study of Bangladesh shows that this very basic model of democratic interactive functioning may not be a lived reality. Yet it would be too simple to just speak of abuses of power or to treat Bangladesh as a failed or failing democracy. All we can say at this stage is that it clearly does not follow the basic model.

Viewed from another perspective, a different problem arises. The principle of one person/one vote, and the confidentiality of the process, turns all those who have voted against the incoming majority into a more or less silent opposition, for expressing any public resentment or critiquing the elected powers may risk negative consequences. The extent to which individuals are freely able to state their views is not at the core of this book, but forms an important consideration, as time and again there has been evidence in Bangladesh that freedom of the press has been curtailed (Bhuian 2012). Moreover, members of minority communities have been perceived as favouring one of the two major political parties, and are thus presumed to be on a particular side of the political spectrum. If that then leads to violence, as is seen in Bangladesh, where Hindus are used as scapegoats to cause trouble for the government, the entire democratic nature of the process of holding elections and managing a state apparatus is thrown into doubt.

These two levels of interaction are often dangerously interlinked. Whether we think of the political opposition or the average citizen, those who are not in power may perceive democracy as a form of exclusion of the losing side. From this perspective, parliamentary democracy becomes, first of all, a means of challenging the government's management of decision-making and instead demanding that a whole range of power relationships be democratised, so that excluded voices are empowered in wider participatory processes. Participation here is instrumental. However, it needs to be constructive and not adversarial for the sake of argument and opposition. Participation is essential not only for electing a democratic government but also for the subsequent management of democracy. Again, we come to the situation that it is all a matter of trust and a willingness to engage constructively – basic conditions which are largely amiss in Bangladesh's political culture.

The CTG of Bangladesh, despite all the political conundrums, clearly provided a response to the first element of such basic failures of participation by creating a free and fair environment, a level playing field, where the electorate could participate in exercising their basic right to vote during elections. The voter turn-out rate, during such democratic transition, was encouraged by the sheer knowledge of the masses that an election conducted by a caretaker regime was not a sham but a genuine opportunity for participation. It generated considerable trust. We also see that basic failures of democratic institutions are not merely a matter of political theory but can have implications on hardcore legal structures.

Good governance, then, is not about producing or shaping the preferences of one specific stakeholder, but about managing a complex system for aggregating competing perspectives and giving effect not just to the will or agenda of those in power, but instead catering to the wider national and therefore public interest, based on a spirit of democratic negotiation. As subsequent chapters of this book demonstrate, these idealised notions of co-operative effort are not a reality when it comes to parliamentary practice in Bangladesh. According to Riaz (2016a: 232), these elections did not always deliver good governance: the ruling party and its leaders have often failed to differentiate between the 'mandate to govern' and the 'license to rule'.

Yet, one cannot dismiss it and say that this is not a democracy. Even if it is democracy at its basic, raw, liminal level, or in name only, it is nonetheless democracy. That it does not function well is a different debate altogether. The question then turns to what kind of democracy is this, and why does it experience such trouble? The more urgent issue becomes how one can improve the operation of the entire system, learning perhaps from past mistakes and failures.

Looking at this conundrum from a vantage point in early 2017, when the CTG is long gone, and when the 'deeply flawed election' of 5 January 2014 was held without any CTG involvement and was clearly not fully democratic, there is, however, no evidently simple answer.

Where do such observations leave political theory and the ubiquitous discussions about democracy? While it may be correct to place the emphasis on voice, it appears that the quality of that voice is what matters. It may help to identify an integrative, constructive approach as opposed to an aggregative, potentially non-participatory, non-inclusive approach. This, then, moves beyond simply counting votes. Instead, it reinforces the idea of the political community as an internally plural collectivity where people nevertheless need to decide issues together. Ideally, a particular value of empowerment which results from such participation is collective decision-making about the actual substance of public action. However, this is not the political reality in Bangladesh.

Examining more closely the relationship between governments and the governed, it is critical to scrutinise the top-down orientation of formal democracy in its manifestations in Bangladesh. In a direct democracy, the decisions of the majority are binding on everyone, including any minority that finds them against their own opinions or interests (Przeworski, Stokes and Manin 1999: 1). This may be tough, but this is the basic principle of democracy. In a representative democracy, decisions are made by elected representatives and implemented by appointed officials to whom the representatives delegate some of the tasks of governing. This obviously illustrates the difference between parliament and executive. The elected representatives, as future law makers, decide what all citizens must and cannot do (Przeworski, Stokes and Manin 1999). This may concern all kinds of matters regarding education, tax, foreign policy, agreements between private parties or the right to information. The people's representatives enforce their rules at times against the wishes of those citizens. While parliamentarians formally represent all persons in their respective constituency, there is of course no complete match between the views and perceptions of the elected representatives and members of the electorate.

In offering one of the most comprehensive discussions on the concept of political representation, Pitkin (1967: 4) reiterates that Hobbes and other theorists have suggested that the representatives are free to do whatever they please but must do what is best and what they think is best using their own wisdom and judgment, since they are chosen to make decisions for their constituency. A minority of the theorists, Pitkin continues, maintains that the representative's duty is to reflect accurately the wishes and opinions of all those s/he represents. Anything else, these theorists consider, is a mockery of true representation. However, this notion may be practically impossible to realise. Pitkin (1967: 4) thus rightly observes that the truth may lie somewhere in between these lines of thinking. Although this analysis is rather broad and general, it raises an essential question: why would rulers, equipped with such powers, act in the best interest of all 'their' people? The ground reality reveals that rulers tend to overstep their limits and prioritise their own perspectives and discretionary decisions. In doing so, they risk forgetting that they, too, are first of all public servants.

Dovi (2014) notes that Pitkin's conclusions about the paradoxical nature of political representation support the tendency among contemporary theorists and political scientists to focus on formal procedures of authorisation and accountability. One hides, it appears, quite conveniently behind notions of 'rule of law' and 'due process', which are ubiquitous, but can and do mean so many different things in different scenarios. There has been considerable theoretical attention paid to the proper design of representative institutions, which is understandable, as one way of resolving disputes about what representatives should be doing is to let people decide through elections in which the entire electorate has a voice, rather than just the representatives. Normally, establishing fair procedures for reconciling conflicts provides democratic citizens one way to settle conflicts regarding the proper behaviour of representatives. In this way, Dovi (2014) notes that theoretical discussions of political representation tend to depict it as primarily a principal-agent relationship. The emphasis on election explains why discussion about the concept of political representation frequently collapses into discourse about democracy. Political representation is understood, firstly, as a way of establishing legitimacy of democratic institutions, and secondly, as creating institutional incentives for governments to be responsive to its people. In both cases, theory and practice should ideally go hand in hand, yet often they do not.

While there has been a broad and stable consensus on conventions of representative institutions of government, people have constantly argued over what is supposed to go on during the processes of representation. In practice, however, as this book confirms, aberrations may and do happen, and certainly not only in Bangladesh. The key example for the book is the abolition of the CTG in Bangladesh in 2011, despite the reality that most people in the country wished the mechanism to remain. Before the January 2014 elections, a May 2013 opinion poll by the newspaper *Prothom Alo* found that 90 per cent of the people surveyed wanted a CTG (Harrison 2013: 120). Riaz (2016a: 96, 265–266) echoes, in a similar vein, that the demand for the CTG had overwhelming public support.

In this current human rights age, there has been an upsurge in the popularity of democracy as the most critical vehicle to fulfil individual aspirations, articulate interests and nurture a civil society. Inoguchi, Newman and Keane (1998: 6) draw a distinction between institutions and procedures of democracy – such as elections, freedom of speech, the rule of law – and the content and substance of democracy. Their emphasis is not only on the institutional criteria of democracy but also on the results. The question is also whether it fulfils the aspirations of citizenship – whatever these are defined as – and whether it serves peace, respect for human rights and development. From a political and legal theoretical perspective, this indicates continued focus on positivist methodology in political as well as legal management. Political systems and cultures, which are also based on State-centricity, today adhere increasingly to the fundamental values of respect for human dignity, justice, equity, participation and accountability that underpin human rights, democracy and good governance (Cheema 2005: 2). Even as democracy proliferates, its nature and models thus diversify. This is particularly true in developing and newly democratic countries in which variables, such as cultural and political differences, economic and social development, the history of democratic governance and globalisation, impact on the way in which and the pace at which democracy evolves (Cheema 2005: 2–3). Moreover, concerns about basic human rights have not been a central consideration in processes of governance in Bangladesh.

Concerning the relationship of government and the governed, according to Dahl (1971: 1), 'a key characteristic of democracy is the continued responsiveness of the government to the preferences of its citizens'. Riker (1965: 31) asserts that 'democracy is a form of government in which the rulers are fully responsible to rule'. Schmitter and Karl (1991: 76) are of the opinion that 'modern political democracy is a system of governance in which rulers are held accountable for their actions in the public realm by citizens'. The question posed thus becomes whether the fact that rulers are 'elected' is sufficient to cause a government to act in a 'representative' manner. Przeworski, Stokes and Manin (1999: 29) assert that 'if elections are contested, if electoral participation is widespread, if citizens enjoy political liberties, then governments are indeed representative'. According to this formula, the national election of January 2014, conducted without the CTG in Bangladesh, makes us question whether the election was truly contested, whether electoral participation was widespread and, as a result, whether the government is indeed representative. While the general health of the institution of democracy in Bangladesh is nowhere and at no time at its fittest, the abolition of the CTG further throws a long shadow of gnawing doubt over the democratic credibility of elections without CTGs.

Despite these doubts, the testing of representativeness and accountability only occurs at specific times, usually five years apart, during the national elections of Bangladesh. Given the specific day-to-day governance problems experienced in Bangladesh, it appears that the present book needs to go beyond this rather formal line of thinking about democracy and cannot just examine the processes of managing elections. Quite apart from the surveillance of governance through parliamentary and other participatory procedures, the topic of this book highlights the need for a fair, transparent and accountable transition before elections, during elections and after elections, and not merely on the day of elections. This is important, because even if elections are contested, even if electoral participation is widespread, even if citizens are able to exercise their political liberty on the election day, this does not mean that the government is representative or the manner in which the government has assumed power is fair and transparent. There may be election engineering years before the actual day of election, as witnessed in Bangladesh before the advent of the CTG system.

With established democracies, institutions or procedures of democracy such as an autonomous Election Commission (EC), a more or less accurate and up-to-date electoral register, reliable ballot boxes, integrity among returning officers in counting votes or lack of an effort to purchase votes or vote rigging, and that there is no election-related violence or deaths, or that returning officers – due to their political allegiance – are not strategically transferred in polling stations, are factors which are so basic that such questions about them usually do not arise. The general nature of European discourse on democracy is therefore usually based on presumptions of equal playing fields and images such as the 'public space', as theorised by Jürgen Habermas, a German sociologist and philosopher, in which such interactions are played out. However, grave doubts are in order about whether such Eurocentric models are in operation throughout the world, particularly in Bangladesh.

To that effect, in the more recent European context, Mark E. Warren (1993: 209–234) argues that Habermas does not equate democracy with any particular set of institutional mechanisms such as voting, separation of powers or representation. Rather, he understands democracy as any institutional order whose legitimacy depends on collective will-formation through discourse. Habermas (1979: 186) emphasises that

> Democracy is a question of finding arrangements which can ground the basic presupposition that the basic institutions of the society and the basic political decisions would meet with the unforced agreement of all those involved, if they could participate, as free and equal, in discursive will–formation. Democracy is the kind of politics that favours discursively mediated consensus over other ways of making collective decisions, namely by means of coercive authority, the authority of traditional or other non–discursively created identities or the authority of the markets.

Habermas here theorises the ideal of democratic functioning, and acknowledges that there may be many other forms which are less democratic. According to Warren (1993: 212), the key institutional embodiment of discourse is what Habermas (1989: 231–232) calls a public sphere, which is an arena where individuals participate in discussions about matters of common concern, in an atmosphere free of coercion or dependencies that would incline individuals towards acquiescence or silence. Following the liberal tradition, Habermas (rather idealistically, as it turns out) views public spheres, not as institutions of political power and action, but as arenas of judgment and decision – arenas that are institutionally separated from collective powers of action, while also serving as their source of direction and legitimacy (Habermas 1989: 231–232). In liberal constitutions, for example, this separation of judgment and power is expressed in the institutional separation of the legislative and executive branches of government (Habermas 1962: 104). He is not suggesting that democratic institutions should conduct all their affairs through discourse; rather they should be structured so that discourse can emerge when ruptures of shared understanding require some kind of resolution. Indeed, this is acknowledged as a work in progress. According to Olson (2007: 129):

> Habermas (1996, 223, 384, 444–445, 454–455, 488–489) sees constitutions as 'unfinished projects' that are constantly amended and revised. They are part of a self-correcting constant learning process in which a society further develops commitments made by earlier generations. In Habermas's case, these commitments are implicit within a discursive conception of democratic lawmaking. They are guarantees of autonomy for all citizens, both in the public, political realm and private, personal one (Habermas 1996: 104–131). This unfolding of basic commitments takes the form of an increasingly sophisticated system of constitutional rights.

Habermas (2001: 766) offers to view democracy as theoretically 'unrestricted', and the unlimited liberty of 'will formation' enjoyed as a vested right by the 'united citizens'. This unity arises presumably from being in the same political arena. The expectation of liberty emanates from, and arises as, an essential corollary to what Habermas identifies as 'people's sovereign self-determination'. Laws in democracy, Habermas believes, are instances of 'self-legislation' behaviour by the people. On the other hand, constitutionalism (generically, rule of law or human rights) is the self-imposed rules of political behaviour that limit the autonomy of the will of the people (Habermas 2001: 766). Habermas experiences great difficulty in furnishing a legitimate account for why the Constitution (the will of the 'ancient' people – the founding fathers) should restrict the political liberty and free will of the 'moderns'. Habermas's notion of legitimacy, as he urges, flows from either sovereign free will of the people or what we may generically term as constitutionalism or strict constitutional legalism ('human rights' and probably 'rule of law', as Habermas sees it) (Habermas 2001: 767).

This bifurcated origin of 'legitimation' may have crucial empirical consequences: the caretaker system of governance under the Bangladeshi Constitution, for example, made its entry into the constitutional text following an upsurge of popular support. Nevertheless, its introduction could not be fully described as a democratic act. It arose initially as a kind of informal agreement between the various political protagonists to address a particular predicament, namely how to conduct elections which are free, fair and participatory immediately post long-term military rule. However, the paradoxical relation between democracy and the rule of law or will formation and constitutionalism resolves itself in the dimension of historical time, provided one conceives the Constitution as a project that makes the founding act into an ongoing process of Constitution-making that continues over time, and possibly even across generations. The CTG in Bangladesh is clearly an unelected body that governs the State for an interim period – the enunciation of a new dimension to politico-legal philosophy of transition to democracy, and yet is thought to be the outcome of the will of the people/political parties due to the social and political reality of time, despite appearing to be opposed to the politics of electoral democratic principles. Here there seems to be an interesting similarity between the caretaker system of governance and Habermas's paradox of democracy and constitutionalism, albeit its Euro-focused and Eurocentric perspective. Is it, then, still quite impossible to hope for a peaceful co-existence of democracy and constitutionalism? The answer to this question may be deduced from Habermas's idea of evolving constitutionalism, which he terms as the Constitution 'project'. These developmental and evolving notions of constitutionalism and democracy have, over time, as Habermas seems to presume, learnt to co-exist in a mutually reinforcing manner within the space of contemporary notions of democratic constitutionalism. Its compatibility with the broader constitutional scheme and basic democratic values under the Constitution may be proven over time in emerging democratic nations like Bangladesh, transiting to democracy.

In other words, this means to indicate that there is, in theory at least, a direct connection between the discourses in and outside the parliament and public opinion or the will of the people. To that extent, then, the acts of parliament do depend on the opinion of the people or the will of the people. Chapter 4 discusses this issue further, when the CTG structure emerges in the context of Bangladesh. Although it may not be asserted in a straightforward manner that acts of parliament are basically the will of the people, it may not be unsafe (relying on Habermas's opinion) to state that the opinions of the people or the will of the people have a very strong bearing on the acts of the legislature. Whether such theoretical assumptions will hold up in practice in every scenario is, however, an entirely different matter and is a question of empiricism. The abolition of the CTG in 2011, despite the fact that the voting public strongly favoured it, shows that there is something else at play here than merely the politics of democracy. The public space perceived by Habermas is there, no doubt, but the power plays in that space have not been following the idealistic rules that the learned scholar imagines.

In addition, the issue of fair procedure is in principle a question of justice, from which Habermas (1998: 150), according to McCarthy (in Rosenfeld, Michel and Arato, Andrew 1998: 115–153), distinguishes bargaining processes, which aim at a negotiated compromise. In fact, he allows that in complex pluralistic societies, most political processes will involve bargaining of some sort. In line with mainstream theory, he understands bargaining as a form of strategic interaction which includes the use of promises and threats that are based on the parties' access to power and resources outside the bargaining situation. Fair compromise must then be framed by regulations that somehow ensure an appropriate balance of power among the bargaining parties, regulations that could themselves be agreed to by all parties as participants in practical discourse. Compromise can, at most, be fair if it is based on an equal balance of power. But in lived reality, equal balance is probably just a notion. Habermas himself thus also cautions that many intractable ethical political disputes cannot be settled by such means (Habermas 1998: 150). Disagreements about who we are and who we want to be or about the common good or fundamental values are often susceptible to compromise of this sort. This reinforces the suspicion that high-profile theorising of the Eurocentric Habermasian type has tended to overlook aspects of 'living law' that other authors, notably more recent legal scholars, have identified as crucial to understanding how political contests in scenarios of legal pluralism work out. It also feeds the lurking question as to whether democracy really works in a South Asian developing country as it ought to, an important point which this chapter towards the end discusses in more detail.

Before we embark on the discussion about trust in the next section of this chapter, we need to analyse, albeit briefly, the relationship between a State and its people. What does it mean when we talk about the relationship of State and people in the context of Bangladesh? How has that relationship evolved and been shaped since Bangladesh's independence? Contrary to John Locke's Social Contract theory (Locke 1740), where both the government and the citizens have distinct roles to play, in the context of Bangladesh, the role of the citizenry is somewhat rather limited to casting votes during local and general elections.

Despite this limited, albeit important, role of only being able to cast votes during elections, the grassroots of Bangladesh seem to have a clear understanding and acceptance of their significance in the running of a nation. Reflection of this emerges in the recent work of Madsen, Nielson and Skoda (2012: 4) as they indicate that, like democratic formalists, many South Asian people take the vote to be the *sine qua non* of democracy. Although people are also eager substantivists (Polanyi 1944), in so far as the vote is immediately followed by other expectations such as food at affordable prices or perhaps developments of schools and other infrastructures, the vote is a crucial part of an exchange relation, transubstantiating the act of voting into the delivery of benefits. It is a series of hierarchical relations tying locals to people of power. In Arild Engelsen Ruud's (in Madsen, Nielson and Skoda 2012: 45–70) interesting research on electoral politics and democracy in Bangladesh, he takes a closer look at how democracy and the democratic machinery in the everyday lives of people actually work through fieldwork studies in two villages of Bangladesh. Ruud focuses on 'the various locally and culturally embedded meanings that democracy acquires as it is transplanted from a western context of origin into the inhospitable soil of Bangladesh which has witnessed the abrogation of democracy and the dismissal of popularly elected governments on more than one occasion'. He brings out the complexity of democracy's local meaning and significance among his Bangladeshi informants. While the act of voting and the expectation of some kind of material benefit and development to flow from this act emerge as locally defining features, this study shows how democracy is perceived as an appealing and desired form of governance and, indeed, as a citizen's choice. The study revealed that village citizens felt that while everyone can be a citizen, not everyone can be a leader, and that ordinary people do not make good political leaders. Instead, the people preferred leaders in an almost *Kautilyan* fashion. An ideal leader embodied personal qualities like education, wealth, generosity and a proven talent for getting things done. Voters especially preferred candidates who were close to one of the country's supreme political leaders and who could therefore ensure, for the constituency, a continuous flow of patronage from above. Ruud's contribution, therefore, demonstrates that ordinary people in Bangladesh today can cherish citizenship and democracy for the egalitarianism and dignity they offer, while at the same time adhering to strong hierarchical ideas about personhood, leadership and patronage, without any contradiction.

The result of the above research of Ruud offers a contrasting perspective to the perception of democracy and voice of the citizenry of the middle class and higher classes, including the civil society of Bangladesh. This would then show and confirm that the élite in Bangladesh are perhaps influenced more by 'Western' notions. It is the perception of the middle class, including the civil society, that Bangladeshis have been restricted to only casting votes during local and national elections ever since the fall of the military regime in 1990. The nation has not been able to move from the debate over political institutions and freedom of political expression of democratic transitions, let alone focus on the qualitative relationship between the State and the people and the resulting power structure. The rulers, also part of the élite, use this perception of the grassroots electorate to their advantage or to their underlying agenda, on the one hand, and try to subdue the voice of dissent, on the other. In reality, this is often achieved by the State through the tools of government power at many levels, constantly trying to wipe out the opposition, undermine civil society, silence and restrict the media, politicise the bureaucracy and directly and indirectly manipulate the judiciary and law enforcing agencies and intimidate human rights organisations. This rather nervous and somewhat distrustful top-down approach, instead of an integrative approach, has damaged the relationship between the State and the people. Rather than being responsive to the people, the State in Bangladesh has adopted the attitude of an oligarch, which negatively impacts on the level of trust and confidence that people have in relation to the State and its institutions.

There has been no sustained effort on the part of the State to offer consultation, dialogue or participation to its citizenry on major issues of national interest, let alone policy discussions. The role of the opposition is also particularly unhelpful, mainly due to their frequent and long-term boycotts of parliamentary proceedings and their lack of meaningful or participatory roles, whether inside or outside Parliament. It prompts us to ask the all-important question, which is, 'where are the people' in all of this? One can take judicial notice of the fact that, after any election, there is a tendency to explore the percentage of participation of people in that election. Why is this? As Fishkin (2009: 45–46) puts it, the participation of people signals a form of consent. When people participate and approve certain results (whether in an election or referendum), there is a mandate for that outcome or result in question. The idea is that those who are subject to living with decisions should have an actual share in the decision-making process. It engages the bulk of the population in participation which is political. Political participation is meant to be a behaviour on the part of the members of the mass public directed at influencing, directly or indirectly, the formulation, adoption or implementation of governmental or policy choices. Voting has become by far the most widely shared form of political participation, although other forms exist. Thus, when people vote, they are engaging in mass political participation. The extent of mass political participation is a matter of how widely such behaviour is spread throughout the population and how much activity there is per person. More people participating and/or the same people doing more are two ways for mass participation to increase. However, for there to be mass participation, the bulk of the population has to be involved.

But not in all democracies can people's participation be taken for granted. There may be situations where people have to raise their voices to ensure their participation in the political and electoral process or to ensure their voting rights, as in the case of Bangladesh. And it is in these still somewhat initial days of democratic transitions, even after 45 years of independence, that challenging issues of political processes arise.

Transition to democracy: A gradual path

The transitory journey to democracy faces a myriad of stumbling blocks. Although experiences may differ, democratic transitions go through certain processes (Doorenspleet 2006: 19). Whether it is with regard to a postcolonial independent State, a post-military regime democracy, a post-communism democracy, a post-authoritarian democracy or from a democracy-in-waiting to a democracy-in-practice – transition to democracy will follow certain courses and steps, whereupon people will decide and ensure their participatory terms in State functions, be they minimal or substantial. In this gradual process, the experiences of States may vary in terms of their cultures, conventions, laws and peculiar socio-political circumstances. However, such a transitory journey is unavoidable. Bangladesh clearly continues its journey within this transition, hence the significance of this subsection. The country went through, and in some cases is still going through, the processes of postcolonialism, post-military regimes and post-authoritarian democratic regimes, and is at present striving to achieve a basic functional democracy, at least in practice. Democratic consolidation is still an ambition – in fact, probably a distant dream.

Rustow's (1970) article 'Transition to democracy: Toward a dynamic model', cited in Anderson (1999), assumed that the conditions required for the initiation of democratisation were also dictated for the maintenance of established democracies. This assumption, according to Rustow, cited by Lisa Anderson (1999: 2), was mistaken: 'The factors that kept democracy stable may not be the ones that brought it into existence; explanation of democracy must distinguish between function and genesis'. Quite importantly, Rustow (1970) opened up the conceptual space for considering 'democratic transitions independently from democracy'. This analytical notion accentuated a dynamic process of change rather than stability, allowing ample room for violent conflict, struggle and civil competition. At the same time, it aims towards a better democracy, but cannot really afford to use one standard democratic means. This form of transition also underscored the importance of choices by identifiable political actors in crafting democratic institutions. When Rustow wrote his article, transitions to democracy in the 1970s were relatively rare; far more common were transitions from unstable democracies to authoritarian regimes or revolutionary totalitarian systems. But by the end of the 1970s, events in southern Europe and Latin America gave rise to a new sense of hopefulness and Rustow's framework of democratic transitions became more plausible and attractive as a choice. Almost half of Rustow's article is devoted to the rejection of functional approaches that focused on democracy's economic, socio-political and psychological prerequisites. Instead, his emphasis was on agency, progress and bargaining, which broke new ground in understanding the development of democratisation through transitions.

Transition denotes an undefined period in the interval between the dissolution of a regime (authoritarian/military/revolutionary or otherwise) and the installation of some form of democracy, or even to the return of another authoritarian rule or perhaps the emergence of a revolutionary entity. What is significant is that, in between these periods of incremental changes and/or qualitative alteration of the old political regime, there exists a more defined interlude characterised by the governance of the interim government which is committed to hold free, fair and competitive elections within a short stipulated time. To this effect, Shain and Linz (1995b: 7) have noted that

> The interim government usually operates within a context of volatility and political vulnerability marked by uncertainty, anxiety and high expectations concerning the future distribution of power and loyalties. The nature and the action of the interim government are of enormous political moment. The degree of boldness and skill with which it makes certain policy decisions and its willingness and ability to fashion an efficient succession (whether based on continuity or disjunction with the past) can help to determine whether or not the character and conduct of its successors will be democratic. Moreover, interim governments may affect the mere survival of the state by determining the type of its institutional structures, sequence of elections as well as the state's national character.

The above quote illustrates two important points in the context of transitional government: first, although this interim regime functions amid volatility or vulnerability, it is required to deliver an election amid an atmosphere of high expectations from the electorate. Second, its skilful navigation during its tenure or interim period, through its actions and inactions, may direct and determine the kind of elected government a nation is to inherit. All these elements are relevant in the context of a CTG system of a nation, which is why transitions or these periods of regime change are formative or founding moments for a nation.

Why do modes of transition matter to political scientists and lawyers, and how do they matter in the development of democracy? Transitions matter because they generate fairly durable legacies that affect the post-transitional regime and politics. Different modes of transition are likely to have distinct consequences for a country's politics and legal development. The primary challenge is to explain how modes of transition matter by specifying the causal mechanisms and significance of these legacies (Munck and Leff 1999: 195). Social scientists, in analysing democratic transitions, have broadly distinguished between problems of 'transitions from authoritarian rule' (O'Donnell, Schmitter and Whiteheads 1986) and problems of 'democratic consolidation' (Mainwaring, O'Donnell and Valenzuela 1992). The former transition focuses on what undermines an authoritarian regime and will bring it down, while the latter focuses on the broader and more complicated process associated with institutionalisation of a new democratic set of rules for political life (Munck 1994). It is important to understand the most crucial moments through which States evolve in democratic transitions and to better understand why and under what compelling circumstances transitions happen in newly emerging democratic nations like Bangladesh.

Linz and Stepan (1996: 4) pertinently point out that there are two issues in a democratic transition. First, transitions may begin that are never completed, even though a new authoritarian regime does not assume power. Some of the most common examples of electoralist non-transitions are found in those cases, where a previously ruling military regime, though relinquishing direct control of government, retains such extensive prerogatives that the democratically elected government is not even *de jure* sovereign. Second is the need to reach an agreement on the specific institutional arrangement for producing a democratic government. In this regard, we are alerted to decision-making within the democratic political arena. Disagreements over issues may create questions about the legitimacy of the emerging democratic government, the decision-making process and indeed the future of the political system. Such institutional indeterminacy about core procedures necessary for producing democracy may not only leave the transition incomplete but may also postpone any consolidation of democracy.

This does not mean that there cannot be any disagreement about the most desirable democratic institutions early in the transition and in the constitution-making process. Such disagreement is normal. However, deep and continuous confrontation and ambivalence about democratic institutions among the political élite and the majority of the population, with no sign of accommodation to the enacted institutions, is certainly not conducive to consolidation (Linz and Stepan 1996: 4). It is therefore disagreement, not only about the value of democracy, but also about the specific institutions of a democracy that might make consolidation difficult (Linz and Stepan 1996: 4). Introducing a clear standard of what is actually necessary for a completed transition makes it easier for the democratic opposition to point out what additional, if any, indispensable changes remain to be completed.

Such a standard is also extremely useful in circumstances where the old non-democratic regime has collapsed or has been overthrown and an interim government is in power. Such moments are normally replete with elation, sweeping reforms and decrees. We see that at the cathartic moment in Bangladesh in 1990, when the desire to end the military regime was so strong that all parties agreed to hold free and fair elections through an unelected body such as the CTG. However, the agreement to act in such a democratic fashion may collapse the moment the threat of the undemocratic 'other' is removed. In Bangladesh, this would be the case when the first post-dictatorship government had been elected. This shows that, unless there is a rapid and comprehensive, somewhat deeper commitment to completing all the steps required for a democratic transition, a temporary interim government may itself become permanent. In the context of Bangladesh, where such abuses have been faced, there has been serious and continuing disagreement about specific institutions of democracy, including the institution of the CTG, making consolidation of democracy – even at a minimum – difficult, to say the least.

Another perspective highlighted by Linz and Stepan (1996: 5–6) is that 'democratic consolidation is obtained by combining behavioural, attitudinal and constitutional dimensions in which democracy is the only game in town'. Again, Bangladesh seems to be struggling with this theoretical and idealistic perspective as, behaviourally and attitudinally, democratic ethos is not the game in town for the political leaders and their parties. Riaz (2016a: 158) has identified the prevalent ethos and practices of the political parties, such as lack of internal party democracy, concentration of power in the hands of the party chief, familial connection as the means of accession to and continuance in the party hierarchy, predominance of dynastic succession and lack of accountability of the party leadership, as merely some of the characteristics of the major political parties of Bangladesh which make democratic consolidation so challenging in this country. Democracy here is restricted to merely holding ritualistic elections, not necessarily qualitative ones. The objective of many of the main players is to remain in power and to ensure the return to power by any means, and even if not in power, to grab it at any cost.

According to Markovitz (in Lisa Anderson 1999: 45), in analysing democratic transitions, social scientists have distinguished between problems of transitions from authoritarian rule and problems of democratic consolidation. He continues that there are different types of transitions – through transaction, reform, regime defeat, rupture and extrication. The advent of transition is then advanced through a series of bargains between the State and the opposition élite. Markovitz (1999: 45) further stated that

> We cannot assume that 'transitional democracies', that is transitional from authoritarian regimes will automatically, naturally or inevitably become consolidated democracies. What is necessary is the institutionalisation of a new regime type and what the pluralists have called a new set of rules for the political game. How can a new state consolidate a democratic system at least to the extent that the major actors in a society become willing

> to accept the rules, to work within the new system for the advancement of their interests? We still do not know enough about the circumstances under which political actors have the power to break free of supposedly deterministic forces to create their own society. We do however know that institutional settings are crucial elements in this process.

The above quote, in the context of Bangladesh after the fall of authoritarian rule in 1990, confirms that the nation's struggle to attain basic democracy by ensuring regular free and fair elections was not an automatic step. The united movement of all the political parties, with the people's will, secured a non-institutionalised 'caretaker system' for the 1990 election. The formal institutionalisation of this structure occurred only in 1996, not automatically, naturally or inevitably, but due to a series of events that gripped the nation and, after the opposition political parties, with the people's support, broke free from deterministic forces of the elected government of 1990 to create a more permanent CTG mechanism to oversee transition in this nascent democratic State. Although the people's will was not tested in 1996 through any referendum, their overwhelming mandate was plain for all to see.

Trust as a political element

Hetherington (1998: 9) notes that political trust is a concept which people think they understand till they are asked to define it. Although there are numerous definitions of political trust, authors like Luhman (1979) consider it as a commodity which helps political actors to achieve their goals, while others like Warren (1999) conceptualise it as people's willingness to follow the political leadership of others. Fukuyama (1995) defines it broadly as a sense of shared moral community, both political and social, with an agreement on what values a society ought to pursue, thereby suggesting that political trust originates outside the political sphere and is largely determined by how much people trust each other. Hence people living in more trusting societies tend to trust their government more than those living in less trusting societies. While this definition identifies political trust and social trust as distinct entities, it reminds us that in Bangladesh social distrust appears to be a problem equally as severe as political distrust. Hetherington (1998) defines political trust as the degree to which people perceive that a government is producing outcomes consistent with their expectations. This does not tell us how lack of trust may arise, and how it may be alleviated, as this varies from nation to nation.

Vigoda-Gadot and Mizrahi (2014: 3–6) examine the relevance of trust in government in modern democracies. They explore whether trust in the government is a necessary pre-condition for democratic stability and a well- functioning government. Risks and uncertainty are essential conditions for the existence of trust. They differentiate trust from a political culture and a constitutional approach. The political culture approach is about the relationship between interpersonal trust and democracy. Trust encourages moderation in political conflicts and fosters cooperation among citizens. It also strengthens the legitimacy of democratic institutions and may lead the political élite to make the necessary compromises. A political culture approach perceives distrust as a kind of political alienation and as an issue that threatens the stability of the democratic system. Turbulent times are a major source of greater political alienation. The critics of this approach hold that trust is not the most important source of social and political cooperation. They view trust as a symptom of a deeper structural and political problem rather than as a cause or problem in its own right. In Bangladesh, it would be fair to say that the problem of trust, or rather the lack of it, relates deeply to the competing and opposing visions of what the nation should be like as an ideal construct. One could go even as far as identifying a definite contrast and clash between what is seen and presented as the 'secular' vision of Bangladesh and its founding élite, the AL model and a more Islamic vision for the country, as propounded by the BNP/Jamaat alliance. Deep down, the issue of trust in Bangladesh reflects a clash over the basic vision for the nation.

In a democratic structure, opposing trends are to be harmonised as far as possible through democratic processing of discourse and interaction. Margaret Levi (1997), cited in Vigoda-Gadot and Mizrahi (2014: 5), argues that cooperation can be achieved through compliance with government regulations and through transparency and perceived fairness rather than trust. This sounds plausible, and these thoughts create the basis for the constitutional approach theory to trust. According to this approach, a politician does not have to be good as long as s/he is accountable. Trust can be created by ameliorating the means for redress and accountability and providing more openness and better information. However, more openness and better information also help to lay open the unacceptability of 'the other' in this competition of visions about the nation.

Whatever may be the approach, Vigoda-Gadot and Mizrahi (2014: 1–7) conclude that institutional trust is an essential component for a stable democracy. Again, while it sounds theoretically correct, it may well break down in practice if the vision of 'the other' is really not trusted to deliver the common good. Vigoda-Gadot and Mizrahi (2014: 1–7) indicate that democracies cannot operate without mutual trust between the various players and institutions, and more specifically between the electorate and those who put themselves forward for elections. The essence of the democratic State is to solve social conflicts resulting from the lack of trust between individuals by establishing a social contract between citizens and the government (Dunn 1988; Ely 1980). Elections are then a mechanism to test this trust – and again we see that we can identify the problem here, but it is challenging to find the tools to offer a solution out of this impasse for persistent distrust. It has been argued that trust is a fundamental requirement for any kind of cordial cooperation because it is a vital tool for managing risks under uncertainty. Since political relations and public sector decision-making in modern democracies have a great deal to do with risk management and uncertainty, trust is a major component in securing these institutions and mechanisms. Such arguments, however, are de-masked as wishful thinking if there is no basic trust as a mere foundation.

Citrin (1974: 973–975), in interpreting Arthur Miller's (1974) article 'Political issues and trust in government: 1964–70' in the context of the USA, suggests that Miller interprets the persistent decline in the levels of political trust and political efficacy to indicate that a situation of widespread basic discontent and political alienation exists in the USA along with a certain hostility towards political and social leaders, the institutions of government and the regime as a whole, and that there exists a negative orientation towards the political system. The American example, particularly since the much-talked-about 2016 election, is drawn here to portray that the issue of trust is a global phenomenon and a problem that is not restricted merely to developing countries. Basic discontent, divisiveness and deficiency of people's trust occur whether in America or Bangladesh. It could be that people's discontent and mistrust emerge from political decay, political illegitimacy, political alienation – or simply over matters of ideology (currently the rise of the new 'right' across many nations, for example), or public policy, which have deeply divisive effects within a society. No nation can perhaps be immune from such latent challenges.

Askvik and Jamil (2013: 459–476), in mapping the levels of citizens' trust in public and political institutions, addressed the gap between how experts on governance assess the trustworthiness of public and political institutions in Bangladesh and how ordinary people perceive these institutions in terms of trust. While most experts, according to this article, rate the trustworthiness of Bangladesh's public institutions as low, their data curiously suggests that ordinary people in Bangladesh tend to express a high level of trust in such institutions. They have observed that the gap between expert judgments and popular perceptions suggests a case of what trust specialists have referred to as blind trust (Sztompa 1999). They are of the opinion that this may indicate a governance paradox in Bangladesh: the level of popular trust is far above what the experts would predict from their assessments of institutional trustworthiness. This disparity between the popular perception (blind and naive trust, as they term it) and expert judgment (which may also have its share of cynicism and pessimism) may both be the cause in partially contributing to the dysfunctional state of democratic governance system in Bangladesh. Although this analysis is circumspect, given that the EC of Bangladesh is yet to be an independent, reliable, autonomous body, free from executive influence (which is why the country needed the crutches of a CTG in the first place), this may perhaps explain why, despite the non-inclusive, non-participatory, non-representative election of 5 January 2014, the mass public or bulk of the electorate were not immediately on the streets of Bangladesh, attempting to bring the current government down. Viewed from this angle, the analysis provided by Askvik and Jamil indicates that merely looking to élite representations does not capture the entire picture of a country's mood, but worse, confirms that battles of mistrust could be an élite phenomenon. However, it did not seem like an élite phenomenon when the country descended into a spiral of violence in early 2015, when BNP called for demonstrations to mark the one-year anniversary of the controversial election of 5 January 2014, pressing for a fresh new election. The general strikes and country-wide blockade unleashed violence of the magnitude seen in 2015 when the law enforcement agencies were given a free hand by the government to deal with opposition activists, resulting in violence for 91 days and resulting in 138 people dead (Riaz 2016a: 102–104).

Generally, Bangladesh is often cited as a low-trust society (Jamil *et al.* 2013), with its institutions of governance often and typically hierarchic, élitist and exclusive. This reflects a long historical tradition, as most of its institutions were built during the British colonial period, having inherited the remnants of pre-independent bureaucracy and military. As Chapter 3 narrates and explores further, while analysing the history of democracy in the area, the seeds of mistrust became embedded in Bangladeshi culture over a long period of time. In such a culture of mistrust, cooperation is seldom spontaneous and requires an extensive legal apparatus to control and sanction the implementation of formal contracts and public policies. Such apparatuses do not come without costs and in a low-trust society, the transaction costs may be considerably higher than in a society where individuals tend to trust each other.

It is perhaps due to Bangladesh's élite-driven political culture, combined with the absence of a minimum trust required for a functional democracy, that there was an advent of the CTG structure in the political sphere. Its genesis assisted in providing the electorate and the opposition political parties with basic trust; at least there was a better chance that elections would take place freely and fairly through this structure, even if the caretaker structure itself happened to be unelected and undemocratic. The Chief Advisor, heading the CTG, would be a figure of trust, reliability and integrity due to the previous post he or she held: that of a retired Chief Justice of the Supreme Court of Bangladesh, a post believed to command sanctity, impartiality and justice.

It makes one think whether it is really this sole element of having a free and fair national election in Bangladesh which would sow the seeds of a basic functional democracy, when much else has no semblance to democracy or democratic character. Despite the reality of this innate absence of a democratic culture per se, the CTG had nevertheless been the outcome of Bangladesh's political struggle over how to find a way to avoid manipulation of the electoral process. The crisis of creating a congenial atmosphere in holding free and fair elections was created by the political parties, who themselves had come forward with this pragmatic solution for overcoming the same through the constitutional process of a 'Non-Party Caretaker Government'. With such an amendment of the Constitution, institutionalising the caretaker structure, the free will of the people to exercise their fundamental right of casting a vote in the general election was established, which in turn contributed to the establishment of democracy, even if it is at a bare minimum.

Mistrust between the political parties is a more damaging factor than mistrust among the common people. In fact, the common people, when given a chance to vote fairly and freely, are happy to conclude and/or presume that democracy has scored a victory, provided the election is free, fair and participatory. Mistrust within the political realm, which led to the emergence of the CTG structure and its institutionalisation, did not happen overnight, nor was the institution superimposed. It took root in the legal/political sphere of Bangladesh due to the demands and concerted efforts of the political class. Its *raison d'être*, as we know, has therefore been founded on the basis of the 'will of the political class' who indirectly represented the 'people's will', but that could well be a fallacy as a referendum to directly test the people's will did not take place in 1990, right after the fall of the military regime of General Ershad. Neither did a referendum take place in 1996 when the CTG was institutionalised. And once again, neither did it take place when the CTG was abolished in 2011. Therefore, it is officially the people's will which the political class use when they wish to justify an action, but as we shall see, it is also the people's will which they will ignore when it is suitable for them to do so.

Yet, the people's will and the people's voice remain as constants in this process, whether they are skilfully manipulated by the political class or not. And the 'will of the people' for the CTG instrument has been unremitting, as evidenced from the fieldwork survey samples, online polls and stakeholders' interviews conducted in this study. It seems that a part of the Bangladeshi political consciousness realises that this manipulation of trust is an élite phenomenon which the leaders and those below them utilise as and when it suits them. Discussions and seminars among civil society members, various online polls and articles by journalists and academics have echoed the need for some kind of a transitional modality during national elections in Bangladesh, without which the 'changing of the guard' continues to remain troublesome.

It appears that trust in any public institution is not automatic: it is about positive expectations from an institution which grow incrementally provided the institution delivers what it is mandated to deliver. When people assume that those who are qualified to be part of this institution will follow procedures ethically and without manipulation, which will be beneficial not only for the image of the institution itself but also for society at large, that is when trust will in essence proliferate. The EC during any partisan government in power has failed over and over again to be trustworthy. In contrast, the institution of the CTG, as far as the electorate is concerned, remained a body which fostered a modicum of trust: trust in holding a free, fair and participatory election despite an environment of hostility, violence and confusion. Now that the CTG stands abolished in 2017, the need for some other reliable, independent and trustworthy crutch is clearly needed if Bangladesh is to avoid all tension and turbulence prior to the next general election in 2019.

Elections

Elections are not only a political process but also the reflection of democracy and elections as inseparable twins. Democratic institutions ideally are, in essence, a set of arrangements for organising political completion, legitimating rulers and ensuring accountable governance, typically through fair, free and participatory elections in order to determine the composition of the legislature and of the government. They also imply that basic rules of governance will be established by the constitution and the rule of law. Furthermore, democratic institutions are underpinned by notions of common citizenship, in which the rights and freedoms of all citizens are equally protected under the law. Seen from this prospect, an inclusive strategy on the part of a governing ideology would be more conducive to the strengthening of democratic foundations than a divisive approach that seeks to exclude certain sections of the population/electorate. Institutional arrangements are essential for arriving at political decisions in which individuals acquire the power to decide by means of competitive struggles and claim their right to vote. It is the absence of such developed autonomous democratic institutions which, among other things, has caused such difficulties in Bangladesh, particularly when conducting elections.

Democratic politics include, but are broader than, the processes of political contestation which animate liberal modern democracies. They depend upon a culture of participation, including a range of mechanisms – pluralistic views, a vigilant media, an active civil society and competing political parties through which all citizens can, if they want to, acquire a political voice. This voice is most evidently granted at the time of voting in elections every four to five years. It is through adherence to the basic principles of democratic politics that governments and, more broadly, democratic institutions acquire legitimacy, are made accountable to their citizens and can in turn regulate powerful private interests as well as matters of public interest. Mismanagement and/or the failure of such institutions make the existence of democracy questionable and volatile.

Corrupt manipulation of elections is far more intricate than is widely assumed, surfacing sometimes in crude forms, on election days and at times way before election day through election engineering by the government in power. This engineering can extend much more deeply into the political and legal arenas. Together with the politicisation of executive agencies and even to some extent the judiciary, this serves as a severe hindrance to democratic consolidation. It is this continuing problem of election-time governance which led to the formation of the CTG structure.

Elections matter because they are the womb of democracy and are certainly something more than a democratic device, as is sometimes perceived (Kuper 2006). If this is deemed correct, then sustainable democracy necessitates both pre- and postnatal care, which is due care by the election instrumentalities at the prenatal stage in order to facilitate a free and unobstructed birth of democracy. For every democratic nation, one of the fundamental challenges to ascertaining meaningful democracy is to ensure free and fair elections, and hence vital to democratic elections are the election laws. Why do election laws deserve such special attention? Is it mainly because generally, in emerging democracies, it is feared that the outgoing government may be guilty of moulding – or may have the propensity to mould – election laws according to its volition for its own benefit and/or for its return to power? Plainly put, election laws are probably more vulnerable in the hands of a partisan government of an emerging democracy than any other laws, particularly during the waning days of a partisan government's term. Clearly, like birth, this is a crisis – a similarity that may spell disaster in the absence of due care.

Election laws that are supposed to ensure 'a level playing field' may often be manipulated and used as a device for the systematic oppression of political rivals and the suppression of opposition. In addition to any general test for democratic legitimacy, election laws must also pass a higher degree of scrutiny. Such scrutiny potentially means judicial scrutiny and may go far beyond that. For example, even a shrewd, politically motivated and calculated delimitation of the electoral constituencies might pass the judicial test, but not necessarily the political legitimacy ordeal. A pragmatic approach to determining election disputes necessitates applying an even more stringent test of constitutionality during the constitutional review of such suspect election laws due to the significant constitutional overtones and undertones in such election disputes.

Another way of manipulating an election may be to effect a change in the configuration of the election machinery. The outgoing, possibly partisan, government may wish to carefully install its pro-ideology officials in charge of the EC and the local administrations who would conduct the election. Practically, it may be fairly possible to try out some sort of 'election engineering', probably without any effective legal challenge. This is one of the reasons why the CTG was deemed to be such a relevant body for creating a level playing field, within a period of 90 days, for a free, fair and participatory election to take place.

Well-accepted also are the limitations of election as a democratic device. Election laws, as the 'rules of the game', may have a significant role to play in overcoming these limitations and must therefore compulsorily pass both the formalistic test of legality and the more stringent normative test of constitutionality. Although this would appear to suffice for any piece of election legislation to claim the status of 'positive law', it may not necessarily be sufficient to claim 'efficiency'.

But how can we then measure the efficiency of election laws? One probably does not need a performance scale to measure it as such, but for the present purpose, it may suffice to say that efficiency must be measured on the scale of democracy and constitutionalism itself. The material test, perhaps, is how far the laws go to ensure free, fair and participatory elections, promote democratic governance and further the ends of constitutionalism. Election laws are thus purpose-specific – they are supposed to deliver a free, fair and participatory election so that the government elected is legitimate. However, this stereotypical view of election law has experienced major diversification, mostly due to a mounting 'pressure of expectation' from civil society and pro-democratic campaigners. Nowadays, much more is expected from election laws. In Bangladesh, the judiciary, in keeping with the ethos of such expectations, has directed that candidates need to compulsorily disclose certain vital information about their education, occupation and sources of income, which was not the practice previously. Although these steps are very basic in the context of existing global practices, they may be perceived as the dawn of judicial activism in the field of election laws in Bangladesh. However, there is still a long way to go to promote constitutionalism through efficient election laws.

A major expectation of election laws is also that they could be instrumental in installing democratic practices and values in the operation and activities of political parties in a democratic set-up. The dearth of democratic spirit and ideology in the behaviour of political parties may be seen as one of the major impediments to democracy in developing countries, particularly Bangladesh. It may be that, in the near future, emerging democracies – and thus, as we are beginning to see, the voting public – will demand more and more from election laws; the constant efforts to maximise their efficiency must match that expectation and should meet that demand.

The relationship between democracy and free and fair elections can be found reflected and discussed in various judgments in India. In *Mohinder Singh v. Chief Election Commissioner*, it was observed by the Indian Supreme Court that

> Democracy is government by the people. It is a continual participative operation, not a cataclysmic, periodic exercise. The little man, in his multitude, marking his vote at the poll does a social audit of his parliament plus political choice of his proxy. Although the full flower of participative government rarely blossoms, the minimum credential of popular government is appeal to the people after every term for a renewal of confidence. So we have adult franchise and general elections as constitutional compulsions. 'The right of election is the very essence of the constitution' (Junius). It needs little argument to hold that the heart of the parliamentary system is free and fair election periodically held, based on adult franchise, although social and economic democracy may demand much more.

In another Indian case, *Rameshwar Prashad and Others (VI) v. Union of India*, the court said that

> Therefore, the well-recognised position in law is that purity in the electoral process and the conduct of the elected representatives cannot be isolated from constitutional requirements. Democracy and free and fair elections are inseparable twins. There is almost an inseparable umbilical cord joining them. In a democracy the little man that is the voter has overwhelming importance and cannot be hijacked from the course of free and fair elections. His freedom to elect a candidate of his choice is the foundation of a free and fair election.

In *Special Reference No. 1 of 2002*, the Indian Supreme Court again held that

> Free, fair elections are part of the basic structure of the Constitution. Democracy and free and fair elections are inseverable twins. There is almost an inseverable umbilical cord joining them. The little man's ballot and not the bullet is the heartbeat of democracy.

For the judges in Bangladesh who are yet to address such issues to this extent, these snippets from India indicate that in postcolonial South Asian jurisdictions, the necessity for free and fair elections is deeply appreciated and has been monitored judicially, certainly in India. In Bangladesh too, it is appreciated, as Ruud (2012: 53–54; 67–68) demonstrates in his article 'Democracy in Bangladesh: A village view'. When Ruud asked people whether a good government that works for the people but is not elected can be considered democratic, most people answered in the negative and emphasised that 'without election it cannot be called democratic'. The notion of 'democracy as election' seemed fairly well-established to them. Interestingly, they associated voting with freedom and 'if you cannot vote, there is then no freedom'. On asking the reasons why people would spend hours in a queue to vote, people suggested that 'it was their right to vote' and their 'responsibility/duty'. They went as far as to say that 'if there was no vote, it would not make any sense to be a citizen'. In his conclusion, Ruud drew out that people regarded leaders as middlemen who acted on their behalf, whose credentials are what they achieve and who cannot necessarily be trusted, but that they felt that the elected leaders provided for the poor, almost like a service delivery. The distinguishing mark of 'leadership' is class and social hierarchy, which are sustained by democracy and not eradicated. The practice of democracy, even if it is just through voting/election, has been seamlessly adapted to the social customs and mechanisms of an unequal world. To be able to vote is not only a celebratory ritual for the Bangladeshis but a matter of 'dignity' and self-'worth', and this is why free and fair elections matter. The popularity of democracy stems from this.

In his article (in *The Daily Star*, (2016b)), Riaz highlights a popular aspiration of the Bangladeshis which demonstrates a wide and unwavering support for democracy, including elections. He indicates that nearly 62 per cent chose a 'government ruled by democratically elected representatives' as the preferred system of governance in a survey conducted by the United States Agency for International Development (USAID) in late 2003. A decade later, he continues, the sentiment remained the same, as a survey by the Pew Research Centre demonstrated that 70 per cent of Bangladeshis still preferred 'democracy' as opposed to a 'strong leader'. In the USAID survey, democracy received high grades for being the best system for protecting individual's rights and freedoms (79 per cent), ensuring equality of citizens (69 per cent), providing order and security (69 per cent), keeping the country united (68 per cent) and solving community problems because it gives everyone the chance to speak about their concerns and interests (59 per cent). These surveys also revealed what Bangladeshis mean by democracy, as the Governance Barometer Survey Bangladesh (2010), carried out by BRAC University, showed that '80 percent felt that elections were the critical ideal of democracy', followed by free public debate (71 per cent), rule of consent (60 per cent), ability to participate in decision-making (50 per cent) and ability to access information on government activities (40 per cent). In the survey conducted by the International Foundation for Election Systems (IFES) in 2000 on 'how important it is that certain rights be respected in Bangladesh', rural respondents overwhelmingly supported that right as 'one can choose from several parties and candidates when voting', while urban respondents indicated 'honest elections held regularly' as the most important of rights. A similar undertone is found in the survey among young people, Giving Youth a Voice: Bangladesh Youth Survey of 2011, whereby when defining democracy, a wide majority stated that 'elections are a core parameter'. Accordingly, 'the survey reflects that Bangladeshi youths' perception about democracy are mainly defined by having free and fair elections which was given a first priority by 65 percent'. Riaz concludes in the article that

> These surveys taken together provide a clear message: democracy is not an abstract idea to Bangladeshi citizens. Bangladeshis view democracy as a competitive pluralistic political system which holds regular free elections, protects individual's rights and freedoms, and allows citizens to express opinions freely without fear or being persecuted, either by the State or by the non-State actors.
>
> (Riaz 2016b)

While the various South Asian countries have different experiences in this field of democracy and elections, and some countries are more successful than others at managing their electoral systems, the key issue of political management of the most basic foundations of a legal system raises its head everywhere as a major challenge. But this explicitly political process of managing free and fair elections also has other dimensions that need to be further examined theoretically in the next sections before we turn to the more detailed evidence from Bangladesh itself.

The cultural lens

The people of the Indian subcontinent are co-heirs to an ancient civilisation as a result of various races and tribes coming to this region in successive stages and settling down among existing people, sometimes seeking refuge and sometimes coming to rule. Over time, it appears that these various cultural influences were integrated with the patterns of life of indigenous inhabitants of this region, and in the process, a rather hybrid form of civilisation was born. This South-Asian civilisation developed through the ages by the intermingling of various elements, internal and external (Ahmed 2007: 15). The richness and diversity of culture is one matter, while coexisting in this environment and managing conflict is quite another. Although the dominant trend of people's lives has not been of conflict but of harmony, which is reflected in the different facets of South-Asian cultural life, music, arts, literature, dress and manners, religious and social thoughts and in the general outlook on life, there has also been incessant conflict and sometimes warfare in the political arena.

According to Ahmed (2007: 31), if one had to pick three distinct factors which have contributed to the making of the cultural heritage of this region, one would perhaps have to mention the pre-Aryan and Hindu–Buddhist aspect, the Islamic aspect and the European/Western aspect. Each of these have been woven into the socio-cultural fabric of South Asia through a long and tortuous process, beginning with clash and conflict, followed by meeting and compromise and ending in assimilation and harmony. This syncretic and humanist tradition in South-Asian society and social thought has been portrayed by Bangladesh's national poet, Kazi Nazrul Islam (in Sanchita), in Bengali, the meaning of which is as follows:

> I sing the song of equality
> Where all barriers have crumbled,
> All differences have faded,
> And Hindus–Buddhists–Muslims–Christians
> Have come together and have merged.

Quite clearly, the area that is today Bangladesh takes part in and has inherited this multicultural, diversified society as a result of the eras of Hindu/Muslim/colonial/Pakistan rule. How this has impacted on the legal systems in the region is discussed in Chapter 3. Here, we are more concerned with the law-related nature of these rules, having inherited customs, conventions and practices which may have had different and at times conflicting cultural perspectives. In order to keep a harmonious and syncretic society, the people of Bangladesh have over time strived to adopt, whether consciously or subconsciously, a middle ground to create a more nuanced and balanced society. Perhaps this is the reason why no religious political party in Bangladesh has yet bagged a significant number of votes to form a majoritarian government on its own for any extended time, despite Bangladesh having a majority Muslim population. Previous rulers' diverse practices have left their imprint in some form or another on society. As a result, the people, while adapting to the new rules, have not fully rejected old practices. This has resulted in the development of a culture which is inherently used when seeking some kind of balance between old practices and new rules. Consequently, despite the homogeneity of the language, Bangladesh essentially has remained a heterogeneous society – an aspect which did not fully emerge during the country's independence movement in 1971 (when the assertion of the Bengali language and culture against West Pakistani domination was a major element), but which has gradually become more evident.

Today, the struggle, among others, in Bangladesh is over the question of religious versus ethno-linguistic identity. Although religious and ethnic issues were important factors in the colonial period, the only visions that make it to the public sphere of debate today are Bengali ethno-linguistic nationalism, religious nationalism and the more universal Islamist vision (Uddin 2006: 181–185). The AL's ethno-linguistic nationalism is partly successful perhaps because it taps into an affinity for the native language with a rich literary heritage known to Bengalis. The *Shaheed Minar* resonates Bengali nationalism, not only in Bangladesh, but also amid Bangladeshi communities across the globe. Although the practice of Islam is diverse in Bangladesh, and a significant number of the populace wishes to see the nation also uphold its 'liberal' Islamic identity, the Islamists continue to wish to impose their view of 'orthodoxy' on the majority of the country's Muslims (Hasan 2011).

With global (particularly Middle-Eastern) and local support through a political alliance, the Islamists have more leverage to assert a vision of Islam which rejects regional or culturally informed interpretations of Islam. The Islam that they preach and practice is in reality a *Wahabi* version of Islam, which resonates more with the rigid customs of Saudi Arabia than with the liberal Islam which most Bengali Muslims have been practising over many centuries. The existence of these competing nationalisms in Bangladesh today demonstrates the fragile state of competing visions of a society and how they are caught between Middle-Eastern Islam's pull and native ties to the region. Nationalism, be it ethnic or religious, is therefore highly contested because homogeneity seldom exists in any nation. Such tensions lead to violence, so that it is no exaggeration to claim that Bangladesh has had its own 9/11, which has not significantly appeared on the global radar (Hasan 2011), when Islamist militant groups carried out 450 home-made bomb explosions in less than an hour throughout the country on 17 August 2005, killing 30 and wounding 150 more. The victims included judges, lawyers, policemen and journalists. This occurred within a year of the assassination attempt on the leader of the opposition at the time, Sheikh Hasina, on 21 August 2004 during a public meeting she addressed, when a grenade attack took place leaving her injured and 24 dead (Riaz 2016a: 81–82).

As a result of these two competing visions of secularist and Islamic paths, specifically in the arena of constitutional law, the Bangladesh Constitution has been pulled in two diametrical directions. Secularism as a fundamental principle of State policy is one path, and part of the Founding Father's vision for the nation. However, this has subsequently been replaced by the words 'faith and trust in Almighty Allah' and, currently, the official labelling has again reverted to secularism. Interestingly, however, this secular Constitution has retained Islam as the State religion and it has also retained the words *Bismillahir Rahman Ar Rahim* (In the name of Allah, The Most Beneficent and The Most Merciful). These superficially contradictory positions of the State depict the reality of a fierce struggle, perhaps a constant 'balancing act' society has to go through and the State has to manage. Bangladesh hence is an example of a paradigmatic model of a South Asian jurisdiction and a remnant of its complex arena with an old, diversified history. As a Muslim majority nation with a strong consciousness of local hybrid cultural phenomena, it could not follow the Pakistani model, which is one of the reasons why the country's divorce from that nation was inevitable. This separation was hence also brought about as a result of an irretrievable breakdown of agreement over the very basis of the country's culture and identity.

Riaz (2016a: 218) picks up this issue of identity and pertinently adds that the quest for identity for the Bangladeshis does not involve merely 'a contestation between the secularists and the Islamists but comprises multiple contestations' and, accordingly, 'variations within Islamic ideas and constructions of Muslimness are one part of it. The other remains within what is often described as the proponents of secularism.' Not only are the secularists perhaps unsure as to what they mean by secularism, but some opine that the State, viewed as both an instrument of authority and of hegemony, should be a secular institution and that a top-down approach should be adopted. But Riaz cautions as to whether this approach is viable and effective, and asks how a deeply religious society like Bangladesh can be secularised and what such secularisation would mean. These unresolved questions would have to be openly and deeply debated, involving all strata of society, including civil society; whether a workable ground will be reached remains to be seen.

The following sections take a brief look at the initial practices of Hindu and Muslim socio-cultural laws in relation to governance, in order to better grasp the cultural and religious impact these laws have had on this region, particularly their notions of a ruler or a representative government which has influenced and shaped the local society for centuries, but constitutes a history that is apparently not well understood. This is so to a large extent, because religious rivalries have constantly prevented calm analytical reflections among lawyers and politicians, in particular, on how the country's hybrid cultural patterns came to be what they are. Putting the matter this way indicates that cultural scholars may have a better understanding of such foundational matters, but it appears that they are not listened to, in the heat of the argument, over directions in which the nation should be envisioned and developed. In the discourses on Bangladeshi law, it is mostly the lawyers and politicians that dominate the arena, as we shall see again and again, and they seem insufficiently aware of the strong power of the socio-cultural dimension in law-making and the management of the Bangladeshi legal system.

Hindu law

The important aspect of traditional Hindu law, provided we allow ourselves to go far enough back in the history of Hindu law, which many scholars see as beginning only in colonial times, is that the Hindu ruler is and acts as a servant of Macrocosmic Order (*rita*), which is much higher than any human type of law, but is perceived as connected (Menski 2003). The task of the ruler as protector of the realm is to support that higher order and its values. From that, it follows, as Derrett (1968: 162) wrote, that

> The king was traditionally the custodian and also the censor of custom. It was his responsibility to determine if any were repugnant and to cancel or modify customs of proved repugnancy.

Derrett (1968: 163) further wrote that

> The king decided whether his kingdom was to be governed upon orthodox Hindu principles or not. His decision was guided by the temper and inclination of his people or peoples, who would support a rival claimant to the throne if he offended them in this regard. In nothing were the public so tenacious as of their ancient customs and the social system which they upheld.

This, as Derrett goes on to explain, means that the ruler had some say, but ultimately it is the people's cultural preferences that tip the balance when it comes to adherence to the anodyne principles of traditional Hindu law, with their many customary and local cultural manifestations. While this is not democracy in the modern Western sense, since also the ruler, in the first place, was not elected in any democratic form, the interplay between ruler and ruled is obvious. There is ample evidence that a ruler who loses the support of his people will be replaced, sooner rather than later, and if necessary through violent means. Derrett (1968: 164, footnote 3) clearly stated that '[t]he conventional view is that the king might make proclamations and regulations furthering dharma but not incompatibly with them'. He is thus bound by this higher law. Clearly, Derrett (1968: 165) picked this up and elaborated further that, in the mind of scholars, this led to confusions over the nature of these ancient systems of governance:

> Indian scholars have been wedded to the view that the rulers were subject to the law, and when asked to whom law was subject they are forced to reply 'God'. One may assume this is wishful thinking, and unconsciously entertained for the purpose of making unflattering comparisons with the legal systems of the West, which was the motive that sent this doctrine on its way.

What Derrett is saying here, in a basic spirit suspicious of the alleged predominance of 'religion', could also be said for the later Muslim ruler, as God's law is – in the same kind of theoretical approach – also higher than man's law according to *Shari'a*. Derrett could have said that the Hindus were trying to claim to be equal, if not better, than Westerners when it came to obedience of the law, but that is probably not what he meant to argue in the book that he produced in 1968. The more relevant point for this book is that this system as a whole is portrayed as highly idealistic, and presumes that there is a good law in place – some type of higher entity of a natural law, which just needs to be upheld. It does not have to be imagined as an old man with a grey beard, and indeed Islamic law prohibits any kind of imagery of Allah, while Hindus have taken to treating their old authors of *dharmashastras*, like Manu, as God-like figures. This awareness of a higher law, however envisaged, then, restricts the role of the Hindu State as a potentially positivist entity in actually making law. This comes out further in the next passage.

Menski (2003: 71) highlights 'the limitations of political and legal domination by rulers through the concepts of *rajadharma* and *vyavahara*, the latter being often completely informal self-controlled ordering rather than formal recourse to legal processes'. The same point is made by Menski (2003: 111) when he critiques the assertions of modern Indian writers on Hindu law who claim that the Hindu ruler and his officers directly regulated people's daily lives.

Menski (2003: 72–74) discusses Orientalist constructions of Hindu law and identifies the distortions introduced by Western scholarship into our understanding of what 'traditional Hindu law', with all its internal plurality, was about. His key argument is that Hindus' awareness of the higher Order meant that human power, also of the most powerful ruler, would always be perceived as subject to some higher authority, exactly of this macrocosmic or holistic type embodied by what Menski (2003) calls the *rita/dharma* complex. Forgetting that dimension is seen by him as the critical mistake made by secularised Western legal scholarship (and its Indian following), which perceives 'law' merely as State law and has chosen to forget or ignore what in Western legal theory would be called 'natural law', clearly Corner 1 of Menski's Kite of Law model. This illustrates that law always needs to be navigated between four competing corners, namely natural law *and* positivism *and* socio-legal norms *and* international norms. Law, being internally plural, is then its own other all the time, causing constant conflicts and tensions. It puts on the table four different types of law, namely (1) at the top, natural laws in the form of ethics and values, which may be religious and/or secular; (2) on the right hand side, socio-cultural and socio-economic norms, and thus mainly peoples' customs and ways of doing things; (3) on the left hand side, State law and its various kinds of rules, which may of course not have been made by the State, but were accepted by it on various grounds of expediency from the other corners; and (4) in the bottom corner, international law and the various forms of human rights, collectively perceivable as new natural law (Menski 2011a: 13).

Though this has not yet been fully developed in Menski's scholarship of Hindu law, the assertion that even the modern Constitution of India of 1950 can be read as a catalogue of *dharma* rules rather than as a modern Western-style legal document may partly explain why so much of modern Indian law, even in the realm of public law, has remained unclear and undefined, and seems to rely on situation-specific adjustment. Here again, the kite image may be useful in that at any one moment, competing expectations and stakeholder interests would need to be balanced out and negotiated, rather than merely having a legal rule imposed from above.

On this, Menski (2003: 116, 261) shows how public interest litigation today can be read as a form of legal balancing in which rulers are reminded of their duties and obligations, rather than being allowed to claim their rights as those who govern.

Derrett (1968: 169) noted in passing that 'the Hindus retain an ambivalent attitude to legislation which their Muslim compatriots may, or at any rate should not'. The fact that Hindu private law was largely a matter for custom and outside the direct control of the State, meant that the studies we have focus more on politics and governance than on processes of day-to-day law-making within society, and thus, inter alia, Hindu customs.

Menski (2003: 108) reports on how different authors have portrayed the law-making role of the Hindu ruler and shows how Hindu authors like Paras Diwan, in particular, have overstated the positivistic powers of the ruler. All of this of course takes place outside the formal framework of democracy. But Derrett (1968: 169) noted, with an eye to modern India, that

> What Parliament does, cannot bind the conscience where the religious elements of law are confronted. And this dichotomy is nothing new: it was built into the Hindu outlook on law and government, and has a respectable antiquity.

From this realisation arises the inner strength of the notion of *rajadharma*, the duty of the ruler to uphold the order that his people wish to see. Although not democratic, the ruler is still interactive and self-controlled, because he is structurally constrained to respect the self-perceived *dharma* of his subjects. A Hindu ruler, thus, could not ban the killing of animals for meat consumption, nor activities such as prostitution. He would have to respect the right of people and their cultural and religious patterns for continued practice. A quick reference to Menski's Kite is relevant here, in that Corner 3, which is state authority, has at all times to consider the concerns and interests of Corners 1 and 2, and thus in effect also upholds the human rights of everyone (Corner 4). It thus illustrates such a plurality-conscious balancing of competing perspectives, which means that following a kind of Hindu rule of law implies that it is at once cosmic as well as individual, global as well as local, and cultural as well as legal.

Derrett (1968: 175) argues that the king's duty was also to oblige everyone to observe caste distinctions and thus to maintain a balance within society and between different people, based on the wider principles of *varnasramadharma*, the key notion that all people should follow their respective duty according to their caste and their stage of life as well as they might. The history of Hindu law can thus be seen as an illustration of the close connection and partial overlap of law and culture, and law and religion. For a deeper understanding of the current struggles over governance in Bangladesh, such realisations may not be irrelevant, not least because an estimated 9.6 per cent of the population of Bangladesh is composed of Hindus, making it the third largest Hindu state in the world after India and Nepal, consisting of 1.3 per cent of the global Hindu population.

Muslim law

In order to understand the Islamic notion of governance, it is similarly necessary to understand the interconnected nature of Islamic law. We can do so briefly, because within Islamic jurisprudence itself lies the plenitude of answers relating to Islamic governance. The starting point is the Qur'an, which according to Muslim beliefs is the divine words of Allah (God in Islam), revealed to humanity through Allah's messenger, the Prophet. There are also the sayings of the Prophet including his exemplary behaviour (*Sunnah*) as recorded in *hadith* compilations. The texts of the Qur'an and *Sunnah* are the guiding principles, either as direct orders or in the nature of injunctions. These two main textual foundations form the sources of Islamic law, which some refer to as the *Shariah*, while others identify the predominance in terms of scriptural and religious authority of *fiqh* (Islamic jurisprudence) as a product of human endeavour to understand the will of God as well as possible.

There is a challenge here in how Islamic law or Muslim law are operationalised, most clearly identified by Coulson (1969). There are times when these textual sources need human interpretation and reasoning in order to formulate the rules that they were meant to convey. However, the efforts (*ijtihad*) of individual scholars, often referred to as 'jurists', to come to the best possible conclusions have remained contested to this day, and the concept of *ikhtilaf* (tolerated diversity of opinion) is the central bone of contention here. This is clearly the major Islamic notion of 'pluralism', and unsurprisingly it is deeply contested to what extent such diversities of opinion can or should be tolerated. The 'strict' view would be that only God makes law (*ahl al-hadith*), while the more 'liberal' approach admits that human effort is inevitable and should be exercised with a deep sense of responsibility (*ahl ar-ra'y*). Coulson (1969) expertly contrasts these two approaches and identifies the scope for violent disagreement, a phenomenon that marks also the current realities of day-to-day life in Bangladesh.

In general terms, this interpretational human activity is called *fiqh* or jurisprudence, which as a term in practice is extended to the rulings derived by the jurists from the two fundamental texts. Thus, while the Qur'an and *Sunnah* are the divine commands, transmitted by Allah through His messenger, the *fiqh* is a human attempt to identify and elucidate these divine injunctions (Peters and Bearman 2014). It may be seen as a religious activity, a form of legal action, but it is also a manifestation of culture, which is why it is discussed at this specific moment.

Thus, the task of Muslim jurisprudence from the beginning of the advent of Islam was the discovery of the terms of Allah's law for the benefit of society, a society that could be characterised as Islamising, a process that can be said to be an ongoing challenge, specifically in conditions where other religious and cultural traditions are practised in close proximity. Legal scholarship on Islamic law gradually built up a corpus of doctrine, and by the end of the tenth century, *Shariah* had achieved a definitive formulation in legal manuals composed by individual jurists, as noted by Coulson (1968: 58). The focus on doctrines and the swift move towards jurists, who had not been an institutional feature of Islam from the beginning, obscures the role of individual activities, and puts these 'jurists' in the role to act as catalysts in the process of creating an early 'living' Muslim law. In later Islamic doctrines, the terms of Allah's law were to be recovered from the text of the Qur'an by human agents. In that sense, the Prophet himself was the first Islamic jurist, just as he was the first leader and judge. Qur'anic revelation introduced a comprehensive all-encompassing new ethic, a new natural law. It therefore created solid foundations for what Chiba (1986) called 'legal postulates', but not an official legal system by which a State would henceforth govern its subjects, as Menski (2006: 293–294) observes.

The Prophet played a crucial role in the early development of Islamic law because he alone knew directly about the new system of ethics during the long period of revelation. He was closely involved in advising fellow Muslims about legal issues, acting not only as a moral guide, but also as a leader and administrator of justice. He would at times continue using the 'living tradition' (another meaning of the Arabic term *Sunnah*) and declare it to be the correct practice. In other words, these were Islamised good customs, tested and approved by the Prophet, as noted by Pearl and Menski (1998: 5). He also consulted his fellow companions (*Sahabas*) on difficult issues and thus paved the ways for consultation amongst jurists, which later became a cornerstone for the development of Islamic jurisprudence (the principle or methodology of *ijma*, 'consensus', discussed further below). The Prophet's practices subsequently became known as *Sunnah*, as stated previously. Through creating the new *Sunnah*, the Prophet produced authoritative statements on the newly Islamised 'living law' of his people, a process reminiscent of and comparable to common law techniques of judicial restatement.

After the Prophet's death, revelation ceased but the legal traditions in political and legal terms continued. Coulson (1968: 56–57) reiterated that

> The mantle of the judicial authority was assumed by the Caliphs, who succeeded to political leadership, and their decisions together with those of the Prophet, marked the beginning of the growth of a body of law which supplemented and expanded the general precepts of the Qur'an.

A new phase thus began in the development of Muslim law and the task of worldly and spiritual leadership devolved upon the companions of the Prophet

– the next most reliable source of guidance when new questions and conflict situations arose. This process, then, also illustrates the close links between law and culture in Islamic law. In the absence of any explicit Qur'anic source or any direct *Hadith* or *Sunnah* on any point, the *Sahabas* or the companions, out of necessity, guided themselves by their reasoning, having regard to those usages of the community which had not been condemned by the Prophet. An agreement among the companions on a specific matter and in a particular view vouched for its absolute soundness (Rahim 1994: 17–18). It may be important here to note that the first four Caliphs were also elected by consensus of the companions of the Prophet. However, a deeper analysis of Islamic legal history also identifies very soon the fundamental split between *Sunnis* and *Shias*, again to some extent based on culturally motivated differences of opinion and custom over questions of succession to the Prophet.

The concept of agreement or consensus, *ijma*, was later to become a critically important source of Islamic jurisprudence (Hasan 1984: 15). Schacht (1984) reports that this formative period, after the death of the Prophet, was crucial. As the Caliphs turned their attention to secular law, or in other words went beyond the Allah/human relationship (*ibadat*), the focus shifted to Islamising inter-human relationships (*muamalat*) and more attention was given towards administration, developing also more and more secondary rules in the Hartian sense (Menski 2006: 299). Concentrating on such secondary rules, these early rulers made numerous administrative decisions and regulations (Schacht 1984: 15). The road to 'political governance' in the name of Islam (*siyasa shariyyat*), with all its challenges, was clearly laid out.

Under the Umayyads, who ruled after the four Caliphs, the process of legal restructuring began which involved frequent borrowing of legal models from other legal systems. These were legal transplants with Islamic imprints, meaning that they were adapted to the needs of the Muslim population and rulers. During the last days of the Umayyad rule, a proposition was made by a highly placed government official (Ibn al-Mukaffa) that the State should have total control over law-making and thus over religion too. This was the highest attempt during that time to make secular laws by Muslim society.

After the Umayyads, the Abbasids ruled the Islamic empire till the thirteenth century. According to Coulson (1964: 52):

> The Abbasids had endorsed the idea that the Caliph was the servant of the law, not its master; legal authority was vested in the scholar-jurists and not in the political ruler.

This shows that Allah's law remained central and indicates why Islamic jurists became a central agency from the Abbasids onwards (Coulson 1968: 59). This can be seen even today in the practices of Bangladesh. In the decided *Fatwa Case*, it was observed that the judges of the Appellate Division of the Supreme Court of Bangladesh, in deciding the issue of legality of *fatwas* by the Muftis (Islamic jurists), sought opinions from the Islamic jurists on this point as *Amicus Curiae*, in determining this Islamic question of law under a secular Constitution and under a secular legal system. This speaks volumes about the challenges which any form of governance face in this Muslim-dominated space, indicating that a State like Bangladesh should not be seen as contradicting the *Shariah*.

From the fifteenth century onwards, Ottoman Sultans had begun to enact regulations or *Qanun* dealing with land law, and fiscal and criminal laws. These regulations did not replace *Shariah* rules. Rather they supplemented them where *Shariah* was silent or not precise enough. This kind of legislation was always regarded as part of the Islamic legal order and as being not in conflict with *Shariah*. Although the enactment of these statutes did not imply that the State had a monopoly on law-making or that State-enacted law was of a higher order than other laws, the existence of the Ottoman State legislation within a *Shariah*-dominant legal system paved the way for the codification movement of the nineteenth century.

The adoption of the modernist notion that law must come from the State required that the *Shariah* became part of the national legal order – subordinate to national law and operating only by virtue of a legal provision issued by the national legislator, either by codification of parts of the *Shariah* or by referring the judiciary to the *Shariah* for adjudicating cases in certain domains. This drastically changed the rule of recognition in the Muslim world. The criterion for valid legal rules was no longer that they had been derived by Islamic scholars from the fundamental sources according to the principles of Islamic jurisprudence, but that they were grounded on the constitutional rules of each State regarding the composition of the national legal system. The law now could be changed by the legislator. Codification or legislation took place both in regions colonised by Western power and in those that were still independent in the late nineteenth century. This was done to meet administrative needs. As a result, the domain in which the *Shariah* was applied was reduced to family laws or Muslim personal laws (Peters and Bearman 2014). This is, of course, the pattern that we also find in Bangladesh today, with all its difficulties of defining the precise boundaries between private law and public law.

In terms of selecting the ruler after the death of the rightly guided Caliphs, when the Umayyad ruled the Islamic world, they radically changed the electoral consensus to dynastic rule. The Abbasids and the Ottomans continued with the same practice, clearly not a form of electoral democracy. As the early twentieth century evolved, and during and after the break-up of the Ottoman Empire, new Muslim countries evolved. With the advent of these new Muslim countries, the colonial influence and the decolonisation process, these newly established state entities needed to decide on the form of their government. While most of the Middle East was under the influence of Saudi Arabia-created kingdoms, the rest of the Muslim world endeavoured to implant democracy as their system of governance. However, the very term 'Islamic state' was never used in theory or practice in Muslim political science before the twentieth century, as a noted Pakistani scholar (Khan, Qamar-ud-Din 1982: 74), and some Western scholars of Islam (Eickelman and Piscatori 1996: 53), have agreed.

Thus, a modern Muslim country today would seek to encapsulate the norms of democracy or rather adopt a more or less direct Western implant in terms of electing a government. This is theoretically possible because the State sought to design itself to be coordinated with the new world order and not in any direct conflict with the Quran or *Sunnah*. In practice, though, the question becomes which corner of Menski's Kite is now the starting point for all law-related negotiations and balancing acts. In the traditional Islamic system, it was clearly Corner 1, but under the modern democratic system it would need to be Corner 3. The benefit of Menski's Kite model is that it emphasises the inevitable interconnectedness of the various corners of the kite. This means that a good State law in a Muslim-dominated country could politically and socio-legally argue that Corner 3 is the proper starting point, but a fundamentally Islamist position would tend to question and oppose that, harking back to the scenario where Corner 1 is the starting point. This remains, also today, a largely unspoken point of enormous conflict and tension in Bangladeshi law.

Efforts were made early on in Islamic legal history to argue that this dichotomy of 'religious' and 'secular' law posed no contradictions. Islamic modernists called for a selective borrowing of European science, politics and culture, insisting that the Qur'an was fully compatible with modernity (Mishra, 2012: 44) However, in most of the Muslim countries, in addition to applying *Shariah* to personal laws, it is expected that no laws contradicting *Shariah* should be adopted. Although in Bangladesh the same norms are followed, there are emerging contentions that may create fissures between Islam and the secular principles of State, for example, the reservation clause of Bangladesh with regard to the Convention on the Elimination of all forms of Discrimination Against Women (CEDAW) 1995. This of course, in today's world, also involves conflict and tension over Corner 4 of Menski's Kite model.

Shariah has, so far, somehow survived in a secular environment of government and governance, and also where a majority of the population are Muslims. There is a cultural as well as religious expectation that forms of government and patterns of governance should reflect this majoritarian scenario by some kind of adherence to *Shariah* principles. This is still the old expectation of *siyasa shariyya*, even if that is not publicly discussed. The same can be observed in Bangladesh, where the state religion, according to the Constitution, remains Islam, while the country makes an ideological commitment also to secularism. In addition to the family laws, Bangladesh has allowed very recently, under the Bank Companies Act 1991, Islamic banking to be practised in parallel with conventional banking. Again, this shows a constant effort to balance these competing expectations and to please both perspectives as much as possible. One may see the beginnings here of maturing secular Muslim systems of governance of necessity, a deeply contested concept and an internally plural phenomenon.

In Bangladesh, issues of criminal justice, judicial administration of fundamental rights and other political, social or economic rights continue to be governed by secular principles. Apart from substantive personal laws for Muslims, Hindus, Christians and Buddhists (and certain Islamic banking transactions), the whole legal and political system is secularised, including procedural aspects of applying religious laws. This shows that this navigation is not an either/or scenario, but that there is growing awareness that plural arrangements are inevitable in practice.

Further examples can be given to understand how *Shariah* law is applied in Bangladesh and how the State, despite being a secular one, involves itself with religious communities as a whole. In terms of the application of personal laws or any other law where there may be an Islamic element (such as Islamic banking transactions), one has to rely on the secular Civil Procedure Code (1908). Despite identifying itself as a secular nation, the government of Bangladesh, in its annual budget, allocates funds for mosques, temples, churches and monasteries. The main religious events of all religions are public holidays in Bangladesh. Thus, Bangladesh makes elaborate compromises between secular principles and religious diversity, which is rooted historically and connected to practices of the Hindu and Muslim people and their rulers over time, who supported the building of temples and mosques from State funds. In such a deeply pluralist socio-cultural scenario, it does not seem that the critical issue is the toleration of non-Muslim others in the body politic of Bangladesh. It is more about toleration of any other, including the Muslim other. Thus, it is deep down a matter of toleration for *ikhtilaf*, a question of methodological pluralism within Islam/Islamic law, not perhaps a conflict of law and religion, or law and culture.

Schacht (1984: 54–5) opined that a dual system of religious law and secular law-making could coexist. Schacht continued that power over the administration of justice was exercised by the *Qadi* on the basis of *Shariah*, and that the political authorities based their governmental power on the basis of customs, equity and fairness, and governmental regulations.

This dual system, according to Schacht, has survived in practically the whole of the Islamic world. Menski's scholarship has more recently identified this as a type 3 legal system, in which the coexistence of general law and personal laws is a widespread, standard pattern, especially in the Global South. That this current pattern has ancient precedents and builds on old structures is evident. It means, then, that in jurisdictions that are Muslim-dominated, it should not be a significant issue to harmonise religious expectations and cultural concepts. However, where Islam is a minority religion, the pattern may be different, and spokespersons of the Muslim community may need to defend their 'religion' and 'culture' against interventions of the modern nation State. In a Muslim majority nation such as Bangladesh, on the other hand, there should be no need to engage in violent conflict over the hybrid relationship of culture and law.

Pre-colonial India was not an exception to this rule of basic hybridity under the Muslim rulers. For the Muslims of the sub-continent, personal issues of family law, inheritance of property and *hiba* (gifts) were governed by *Shariah* law and were enforced by *Qadis*, who were appointed by the rulers while general issues of State governance, like taxation or commercial transactions were the domain of Secular laws enacted by these same rulers. During the British Raj, the same dual system persisted. In addition, the British Raj enacted The Muslim Personal Law (*Shariat*) Application Act 1937, with respect to Muslim personal laws. Pakistan, despite declaring the State to be an Islamic republic, did not change the continuance of the dual system of laws, though of course it engaged in the Islamisation of laws (Lau 2006).

Bangladesh inherited this dual and deeply hybrid system from its inception and continues to do so till today. Despite being a Muslim majority country, it has adopted secularism as a fundamental principle of State policy in its Constitution. This state ideology is supported by the ruling party in power, the AL, while the BNP/Jamaat subscribes to Islamist notions. One way perhaps of looking at this is Bangladesh's adherence to keeping its cultural balance, which may appear to be an inclination to follow the Turkish model of democracy as far as practicable, for global acceptance, if anything else. What we see in Bangladesh, however, is not so much a struggle between secularism and religious law, which is the smokescreen in front of which battles are being led, but in reality, there appear to be fierce disagreements over the methods by which the cultural and religious principles of Islamic law should be incorporated into the structures of governance of the country. Seen from this angle, the major disagreements and conflicts and tensions, to use the key phrase employed by Coulson (1969) in Bangladesh today, are not between Islamic law and some perceived 'other' such as culture, but arise within Islamic law itself. The conflicts, then, are over the methods by which legal structures and processes should be managed in a culturally plural society and by a State in which Muslims are unquestionably a majority but where there are also minority non-Muslims. Given that this battle has become personalised between two protagonists of two conflicting ideologies, as embodied in the phrase 'Battle of the Begums', the realisation may strike that the governance problems of Bangladesh, and the struggles over managing the country's elections, have less to do with perceived conflicts of culture and are much more down to different, clearly competing interpretations of how to manage a sustainable form of Islamic governance in the twentieth and twenty-first century, on the part of two leading protagonists and the various élite individuals supporting them, including the lawyers and scholars who discuss all these heavily contested issues. Where this leaves 'the people' of Bangladesh is indeed an issue. What this discussion of the cultural lens has brought out and confirmed, however, is that the application of law is, of necessity, influenced by culture.

Socio-legal and legal lenses

Having seen that the idealised theorising of political scientists and theorists is often not turned into political realities, it is now important to adopt socio-legal and legal lenses to examine and understand further the emergence of the CTG in the specific context of the troubled legal history of Bangladesh. It has become evident from the discussion above that law and politics are closely intertwined. Moreover, the analysis has demonstrated that positivism-dominated legal theorising alone will not suffice in understanding the subject examined here. While the present book is not attempting to make an innovative theoretical contribution to knowledge in the field of social or legal theory, some jurisprudential analysis of the key issues will be useful here and hence appropriate lenses need to be adopted to that effect. This strategy should serve as a helpful and relevant device to deepen the analysis of the CTG phenomenon from a variety of perspectives and to create a richer backdrop to the later analyses of Bangladesh's troubles with managing elections.

Living law and Ehrlich

Eugen Ehrlich, who lived and worked at the time of the Habsburg Empire in the early twentieth century, saw law as derived from social facts and more dependent on social compulsions than State authority, recognising that the State possessed certain characteristic means of compulsion, but that these had limited effects in lived reality. Basing his powerful theory of 'living law' on sociological foundations, he said in his preface that any attempt to formulate his basic theory in one sentence would be as follows (as quoted in Menski 2006: 93):

> The centre of gravity of legal development lies, in our time as well as in all times, not in legalisation nor in juristic science, nor in judicial decisions, but in society itself.

This lens clearly identifies Ehrlich as a socio-legal scholar. In Ehrlich's view, the norms which govern life within any given society are only imperfectly and partially reflected in traditional formal legal sources, such as statutes and decided cases. Ehrlich's analysis highlights an inevitable gap between the official law and actual practices, so that living law is not simply the law as practised but comprises an amalgam of the official laws and people's values, perceptions and strategies, constituting a new hybrid entity. This was portrayed by Menski (2006: 92–93) as an example of early pluralism.

Ehrlich (1936) emphasised that understanding the living law of a community necessitates looking far beyond legal manifestations, concentrating instead on how people live in society, thereby downplaying the significance of the State and its legal institutions as a source of law. To him, formal legal State norm was only one factor of social control as other factors such as local, family and group customs, morality and norms of associations contributed much more to the whole of 'law', and this according to Ehrlich was 'living law' (Menski 2006: 94). This interplay of social forces, seen through this lens, yields the clearest early picture of socio-legal reality, where the formal State law is only an official structure, as Chiba comes to call this later.

However, Ehrlich's theorising does not quite fit into the context of analysing the CTG of Bangladesh. Despite his model being a socio-legal one, his concept of living law is merely showing the gap between the formal law and the living law. In order to analyse the CTG structure of Bangladesh, we need a more sophisticated methodological toolkit because the operational difficulties of CTG management are a matter of how to handle the official law and formal processes, and are not merely a question of the interaction of the State's law and 'people's law'.

A more appropriate lens seems to be offered by Chiba's analysis of law as a tripartite structure of legal pluralism, and this is today seen as integral to a globally focused legal analysis (Menski 2006: 97). Official law, unofficial law and legal postulates work better to help explain the complex management troubles in the context of Bangladesh's CTG.

The tripartite model of law and Chiba

Masaji Chiba's tripartite model of a legal system encompassing the interaction between 'official law', 'unofficial law' and 'legal postulates' reminds us that none of these elements ever exist in isolation but interact continuously in a dynamic fashion, as Menski (2006: 119) elaborates. A Japanese socio-legal scholar, Chiba clearly relied on Ehrlich's earlier theorising, but he also seeks to go beyond it. For Chiba, law is always multi-dimensional and internally plural, and it is inseparably rooted in society so as to be approachable by sociological methods. Chiba (1986: 1), cited in Menski (2006: 121), also notes that

> It has become accepted that law must be recognised as an aspect of the total culture of a people, characterised by the psychological and ideational features as well as the structure and functional features of each fostering people, and may therefore be approached by anthropological methods.

Menski (2006: 121) explains further that Chiba views law not as an isolated phenomenon but as a complex social element which may have its own legal characteristics but is 'inseparably rooted in society' and thus not fully accessible through mono-focused legal analysis. Menski (2006: 122) continues:

> In this respect, Chiba (1986: 3) asserts that various Asian philosophies and religions should be seen as comparable to those of the West and that the Asian legal systems found today are an amalgam of all kinds of cultural influences on legal processes and institutions.

While pursuing this argument would stray into the topic of legal transplants, which is discussed further below, the pluralistic view of the CTG structure in Bangladesh can also find a place in Chiba's model of the three-level structure of law. According to Chiba (1986: 4):

> The whole structure of law as an aspect of culture should include all regulations, however apparently different from state law, which the people concerned observe as law in their cultural tradition, including value systems; the very cultural identity of a people demands that we include all of them in a whole structure. Thus, the whole structure of law is plural, consisting of different system of law interacting with one another harmoniously or conflictingly.

The CTG in Bangladesh was the creation of a long-standing demand by the people reflected through political parties. The idea of a fair election in the country was a matter of consensus among the people of Bangladesh, an element of their vision for what their country ought to be like, giving rise to support for a clear and higher value of fairness. People in Bangladesh before and during the 1990s had enough of rigged or improper elections, conducted under the skewed rules of the military and political parties in power. This affected the nation at its core, as local people had always fought and revolted against unfair treatment and inequality from various colonial rulers, only this time, post-1971, the rulers were from within. The high value placed on fairness generates the thrust, political will and reason for creating a viable, trustworthy and workable structure like the CTG, which assured people that through this mechanism, they had elected a government in a fair way, which would have a moral and legal authority to rule.

If we are to view the CTG structure through a socio-legal lens, this perspective seems to be more fitting at first sight. The initiative for change is coming directly from the people, who are dissatisfied with how the official law at the hands of the manipulators works. The remedy for amelioration of the official law is the CTG, but the postulates for its operation in practice are still critical, thus verifying Chiba's hypothesis that law as rules and structures is always connected to values and subjective assessments. We may ask what considerations would motivate the administration of the CTG to deliver free and fair elections to the people and hand over power to the newly elected incumbent government. Although all four CTG administrations, in a span of 20 years, have ultimately delivered free and fair elections, we see the government in power's attempt at manipulating the CTG structure in two ways. First, in 2006, the BNP government manipulated the retirement age of Supreme Court judges so that a particular judge of their preference could be the last retired Chief Justice and could thus act as the Chief Advisor of the CTG in 2006. Second, the fourth military-backed CTG remained in power for longer than the mandate, namely for two years instead of 90 days, indicating that even the CTG structure itself might not be foolproof should the political will to manipulate it exist. Despite a time limit of 90 days, within which the CTG had to provide for elections, those empowered to form the CTG in 2007 found a way, by exercising discretion and/or abusing their power, to stay longer than 90 days on the postulate-based grounds of creating a level playing field – including creating a new voters list and national photo-identity cards for all its citizens. Quite clearly, not complying with the constitutional provision of remaining in power for a maximum of 90 days risked the emergence of a new dictatorship at that time. Although at the end of two years, a free and fair election was conducted and through a peaceful transition power was handed over to the newly elected government, this incident raised lurking fears about power slipping away, even from the hands of the political class, back to a potentially dictatorial oligarchy, leaving the will of the people again on the sidelines.

In this context, the academic work of Chiba has, in my view, been important for further legal theorising, laying foundations for wider analyses of legal pluralism. Chiba (1986: 1) identified the key problem as 'a long-established belief among both specialists and laymen that law is a special mechanism for social control isolated from other social mechanisms'. Chiba's critique of 'traditional, model jurisprudence' (1986: 1), by which he means above all legal positivism, leads him to suggest, firstly, that 'law is so inseparably rooted in society as to be approachable by sociological methods' (1986: 1), as we saw already. Immediately after that, Chiba (1986: 1) goes further in stating that law can also be approached by anthropological methods, which we also covered previously. Both of these strands of argument focus on the cultural factors connected to law. In this context, Chiba (1986: 2) identifies legal positivism ('model jurisprudence') as a product of long Western history, coloured by Hellenistic and Christian views of man and society. It is here that Chiba indicates subtly, but does not develop in depth, a critique of Western presumptions that State-centric legal methodology by itself will lead to satisfactory outcomes in terms of good governance. Chiba was apparently aware at the time of writing that he would be criticised and dismissed as a non-Western voice if he expressed this criticism too openly. As we shall see below, the subtle critiques produced by Chiba resurface, therefore, in his discussion at this point about the interaction between received law and indigenous law (1986: 7–9). This is covered further on, but at this juncture it is important to point out that in his early writing (e.g. Chiba 1986: 7), he talks of 'received law' and does not yet speak about 'transplanted law', as he clearly does in later writing (see 'The problem with legal transplants', in this chapter). Chiba himself has clearly explained that the changed use of terminology reflects his non-Western perspective and a critique of the Western perspective that, as non-Western legal agents, Asians and others would be portrayed merely as the receivers of laws, not the givers of laws. In bringing out these ideological tensions between Western and non-Western laws and their political implications, Chiba (1986: 8) also further elaborates on another key aspect of his theorising, in that he clearly identified the dynamic nature of this process.

Bangladesh's iccher ghuri and Menski's global pluralism

Menski (2006) applied Chiba's tripartite structure of law and turned it into a triangular model to also express visibly (2006: 612) the constant dynamic interaction between the three basic elements of law identified by Chiba (1986), namely official law, unofficial law and legal postulates.

In subsequent work, in particular, Menski (2010) has taken Chiba's model much further with his Kite Model of Law, which is beginning to be seen as a relevant analytical tool in understanding the interactions of law, society and politics, particularly since the emphasis is on the balancing of competing perspectives (Donlan and Urscheler 2014). I argue that it is possible to show that the emergence of the CTG in Bangladesh has been the culmination of many such influences including competing perspectives, as analysed in subsequent chapters.

One of the founding principles, when Bangladesh emerged as an independent country, was democracy which was enunciated as a fundamental principle of State policy in the Constitution. Along with democracy, socialism, secularism and nationalism were also incorporated as principles of fundamental State policies. These reflect an aspiration of a new nation wishing to function in a pluralistic environment, which was denied before as well as post 1971. These aspirations have to some extent had their origins in local diversified history and the experience of Hindu, Muslim, colonial and Pakistan rule in the territory that is now Bangladesh. Interestingly, while the principles of socialism and secularism suffered some form of erosion, with secularism in particular still remaining deeply contested, the principle of democracy as a fundamental State policy, on the face of it, was relatively less tampered with in Bangladesh's Constitution. This reflects that there was an inclination and a clear aim to portray the nation as a democratic one, despite its flaws in practice and whatever may have been this nation's lived reality. Of course, that could simply be interpreted as a matter of strategic convenience, as no country in the world today could simply abjure democracy and hope to escape international disapproval or sanction. However, the troublesome electoral history of Bangladesh depicts reluctance in applying democratic principles in practice, while realising at the same time that a pluralistic lens is needed to encompass the new country's historical, social and cultural diversity instead of a monolithic/unifocal one. The attempt to make a Western transplant of democracy work in Bangladesh, without the appreciation of pluralistic ground realities over all these years, failed till the advent of the CTG. In fact, as already indicated above, even the CTG structure itself was subject to further undemocratic manipulation and almost turned into a dictatorship again.

Before we embark on further discussion here as to why the CTG should be viewed as a pluralistic phenomenon, let us take a moment to explore how Menski views global legal pluralism. Menski (2006: 193), in confirming the reality of global pluralism, observes that

> We are now able to see that no single major legal theoretical approach on its own, whether positivism, natural law or socio-legal methods, can encompass the internally plural phenomenon of law. Their pluralist methodological combination, in ways yet to be analysed and explored, promises a deeper understanding of the complex nature of law but theory will never be able to capture the practically limitless real plurality

> of law. Problems over the acceptance of radical legal realism are clearly exacerbated by insistence on visions of globalising uniformity that fly in the face of plural socio-legal reality and end up in prescriptive normative tyranny.

Menski introduces the Kite (*ghuri* in *Bangla* language) Model of Law as a tool to navigate through competing interests of society and law. In an article specifically directed at a Bangladeshi readership (Menski 2011b), this is explored with specific reference to family law management, but the model is also relevant for wider issues of governance.

At this stage of Menski's theorising, the earlier triangular model of Chiba-based legal pluralism (Menski 2006) has been replaced by a dynamically volatile four-corned structure, represented as a kite, as Menski was evidently aware that he did not want to end up presenting law as a 'black box' in simple square form, reacting to Twining (2000).

According to this revised model, law always needs to be navigated between four competing corners, namely natural law *and* positivism *and* socio-legal norms *and* international norms/human rights. Menski (2011a: 13) explains that law, being internally plural, is then its own 'other' all of the time, causing constant conflict and tension (as explained earlier on page 58). As per Menski's Kite Model of Law, there are four different types of law, namely (1) at the top, natural laws in the form of ethics and values, which may be religious and/or secular; (2) on the right-hand side, socio-cultural and socio-economic norms, and thus mainly people's customs and ways of doing things; (3) on the left-hand side, State law and its various kinds of rules, which may of course not have been made by the State, but were accepted by it on various grounds of expediency from the other corners; and (4) in the bottom corner, international law and the various forms of human rights, collectively perceivable as new natural laws.

Most legal scholars all over the world continue to prefer seeing law as a separate and often totally exclusionary and superior entity, emphasising the official law as being the only kind of law we should be concerned with (see Donlan and Urscheler 2014). This restricted, positivism-centric methodology ends up disregarding the culture-specific, area-specific and religion-specific concerns, choosing to ignore that competing fundamentalisms and globalisations as well as State-sponsored terrorism are in existence, which a plurality-conscious scholarship must learn to unmask and oppose (Menski 2011: 129b). Menski's new model of the Kite allows for a more complete picture of the CTG's legal theorising, as it illustrates that one does not manage diversity – or in the case of Bangladesh, political intolerance and opposition – by denying it, but by addressing the problems that this competitive plurality may generate. By sensing the people's pulse of wishing for a free, fair and participatory election with a smooth and transparent transition of power through a mechanism that the people (through the political parties) have designed, which in this case is the CTG for election management, the sky is opened up for a better electoral system than the country hitherto enjoyed. It is thus seen that the institution of a CTG, despite the many politics around it, offers the potential and hope, as expressed in the *iccher ghuri* symbolism, for safeguarding free, fair and inclusive elections. Conversely, abolishing such a system, as happened, amounts again to dashing people's hopes for good governance and risks crashing the Kite of Law.

According to Menski (2014), legal management is almost everywhere a pluralistic endeavour. Law, this suggests, always needs non-legal or so-called extra-legal assistance to become good law or the right law. Perceptions of the right law constantly change, however, therefore also confirming that law is everywhere situation-specific and dynamic. Menski (2014) reiterates that from the discussions at the RELIGARE conferences, too, it emerges that good State law actually needs the legal others to generate the right law (Foblets in Ferrari and Pastorelli 2012: 1–21). Good governance critically depends on intricate pluralist navigation, therefore it becomes a matter of justice-conscious public interest and not merely self-protection of law to engage in plurality-conscious management. In the context of heavily contested elections in a poisoned climate, as in Bangladesh, the question posed is to what extent the existing government will be willing to listen to other claimants' voices and to ensure the possibility of free, fair and inclusive elections. Instead of banning and/or marginalising discordant voices either through harassment or refusing them a space to voice such discontent, subjecting them to intelligent scrutiny and ensuring plenty of discourse with them may be a sensible and pragmatic way forward. Such a plurality-conscious approach or a pluralist compromise may make constructive integration of the 'legal other' more palatable to State-centric secular or semi-secular legal systems that are prone to disregarding or overlooking either minority claims or claims of others. A State law which blocks reason, forgets history and fails to listen to the voices of others fast loses credibility, not only domestically but also internationally. Cooperating in the spirit of constructive altruism, viable multi-level solutions to long-term issues may be found. However, to reach that level, toleration of the other, including 'the other' within the law itself, is essential, otherwise the subtle four-cornered structure of Menski's Kite will most likely crash.

The need for plurality-conscious management of law

The above posits that legal pluralism approaches are useful in practice to manage all kinds of competitive scenarios. This realisation is strongly reflected in much law-related scholarship in recent years. Cownie (2004: 51) has quoted the Economic and Social Research Council (ESRC) (1994: 1) guidance, which has defined socio-legal studies as an approach to the study of law and legal processes which covers the theoretical and empirical analysis of law as a social phenomenon. Interest in socio-legal studies is characterised as the emergence of a new legal paradigm (Thomas 1997: 19) and socio-legal scholarship is seen as the most important scholarship undertaken in the legal world (Cotterrell 1995: 314). Those who adopt this approach do so because they find the traditional doctrinal analysis inadequate as a way of explaining the truth about law (Twining 1974: 163).

We have seen that enduring centuries of positivist domination has reduced our vision of what law is and what it can do. For example, interestingly, on 30 November 2016, India's Supreme Court ordered cinemas across the country to play the national anthem before film screenings to encourage citizens to 'feel this is my country and this is my motherland' (Safi 2016). The national election in 2014, which elected Prime Minister Narendra Modi – a devotee of a Hindu nationalist ideology and traditionally at odds with India's secular and pluralist political customs – has fuelled fierce debates over the country's character. Critics say that the political ascension of Modi's Bharatiya Janata Party (BJP) has emboldened Hindu supremacists and given voice to a more divisive and narrower definition of patriotism. The Court's imposition of patriotism through playing the national anthem and making the public stand for it in cinema halls before the movie begins seems rather prescriptive and constrictive to many, and while the tension and debate are directed towards why one should not stand during the national anthem, the crux of the matter is not that Indians do not wish to stand to show respect to the national anthem, it is why the playing of the national anthem has to happen in movie theatres. Indians stand for the national anthem when it is played before a speech, or the Republic Day parade, or in schools. But such an imposition at the beginning of a film, many feel, serves no purpose. Many also have the view that they do not have to prove nationalism and patriotism every time they go anywhere. They feel that such unnecessary State imposition is coming into their private spaces and/or their private lives. At a time when reactionary politics and forces are causing so much angst globally, one questions whether these unnecessary and additional tensions and turbulences created by the State or the State institutions are at all useful.

Reverting back to the issue of legal theorising, we also realise that taking a Eurocentric approach to legal theorising is unhelpful due to today's interconnected world. Consequently, over the past few decades, scholars, practitioners and activists have found more space to discuss, exchange and elaborate new theoretical instruments and to conduct empirical studies to overhaul the concepts and devices produced by two centuries of Western jurisprudence, colonised by the haunting presence of the State. The State is now often perceived as a factor holding back informed discussion, particularly in democracies which are yet to reach democratic maturity and consolidation.

It is in this space that scholars, practitioners and activists discuss the mismatch between traditional Western jurisprudential thinking and the global reality, which the juridico-political settings of modern States pose, in the wake of wide-ranging social and political debacles across the globe. It is indeed this space which paves the way for the emergence of legal pluralism. Croce (2014: 167) has questioned what legal pluralism really is: is it an attitude, a style, a method, a conceptual toolkit, a concrete state of things? What type of threat, if any, does it pose to the political stability of Western polities? Is the lesson it claims to be teaching compatible with the cultural and political identity of Western societies? In answering these questions, Croce (2014: 168) concludes that legal pluralism is neither a concrete state of things, whereby differing legal orderings coexist, nor a methodology to approach such a state of things when and if it occurs. He asserts that legal pluralism mainly plays a role in the deconstruction of a narrative that has long supported a limited understanding of law, and that by doing so it has hampered broader investigations into such a constitutive feature of social order. Its main lesson is a plea for a multifocal analysis of the way law works in the social realm, well beyond the traditional, deep-seated boundaries of the various scientific disciplines.

The CTG structure, in a similar vein, is analysed through a multifocal lens in order to understand how law works in the socio-legal and political realm, taking into consideration Bangladesh's historical legacy and the culture of mistrust. The CTG is hence an example or illustration of managing the electoral process and democratic transition, when State-centric legal processes and State-centric regulation of law fail to work on their own. The institution of the CTG is thus seen as a possible remedy for managing failures during democratic transition. It could be seen as a device to ensure fairness and justice, hence more related to natural law theories, or more as a matter of safeguarding human rights and international law principles of fair, free and credible elections at national level. Again, the message is that managing a CTG is not just a matter of State-centric law.

Positivism and its difficulty

As the CTG, as a legal phenomenon, is in practice firstly a matter of election management and thus of administrative law, focusing on relevant rules and procedures becomes important. However, the previous discussion showed that law is clearly more than just a system of rules. This realisation guides us towards the fact that law, as a set of processes of administration and management, involves the constant exercise of discretion by bureaucrats as a central element. This leads our attention to the important older work of Hart (1961), now Craig (ed.) (2012), and his positivism-centric but also socio-legal concept of law.

In the preface to Hart's *The Concept of Law*, Craig (ed.) (2012), Hart stated that his aim was 'to further the understanding of law, coercion, and morality as different but related social phenomena' and that his work could be read in two ways: firstly, as an essay in descriptive sociology in which it can be recognised from the analysis of the language of daily life, the centrality of rules and better understanding of the nature of rule-bound practices; and secondly, the work is also an essay in analytical jurisprudence directed at clarifying the central features of law. Achieving this aim involves working through the idea that law is a 'complex' social reality, constituted of many elements, some of which are more important than others, and distinguishing the contingent aspects of law's life from the central elements of the concept of law. Thus, law's essence is not to observe law through a predictive lens, seeing only the behaviour of people in social institutions – these are rather questions of law's practice (Morrison 2005: 354).

Hart, as a leading scholar on legal positivism or analytical jurisprudence who wanted to go beyond the earlier, basically undemocratic, model of law associated with John Austin as 'the command of the sovereign', introduced his well-known dual model of 'primary rules' and 'secondary rules'. This reflects an implied though still quite reluctant recognition of legal plurality and leads to a much more realistic methodological approach to understanding law's social interlinkedness. Positivists are reluctant to cross the boundaries between what is properly 'law' and what a deep 'plurality conscious global jurisprudence' would need to take into account when understanding law as an interlinked phenomenon (Menski 2006: 158–160). Hart's theory of law, built on analytical jurisprudence and thus restrained by its own positive law methodology, is focused particularly on bureaucrats or office holders and not the general public. However, according to the scholarship of Craig (ed.) (2012), there seems to be a stronger shift in interpreting Hart's work towards recognising the importance of the social elements in a society too. To that effect, Leslie Green (Craig [ed.] 2012: XV–XVI) in his introduction has explained Hart's message that the attitude towards law should be one of caution rather than celebration. Green continues that, according to Hart (1961), there can be no 'pure' theory of law. This renewed debate, too, which goes too far for the present purposes, confirms that a jurisprudence built only by using concepts drawn from positive law itself is inadequate to understand law's nature; it needs the help of resources from social theory and philosophic enquiry.

This leads us to the conclusion that Hart's original methodology, like that of Habermas in political theory, as discussed earlier in the chapter, was clearly too reductionist and restricted, as he did not consider the full possibilities of what might happen in reality and looked too much at the ideal, and at formal elements. In other words, Hart refers to an 'ought to' approach rather than the 'living law' reality of what is the law. However, as can be seen in Craig (ed.) (2012), there is now some progress (and in that sense, more readiness) in seeing law as a plural entity. This is evident in Donlan and Urscheler (2014: 9) when they still refer to apprehensions that comparative lawyers may be comparing apples and oranges, but conclude (2014: 15) that 'various concepts of law are possible and may prove useful in different contexts'. Maybe the time has come to view law more like a basket of fruits rather than as apples or oranges. From that basket, legal actors can select tools to manage processes and handle conflicts. More so than before, in today's global world, that basket may also contain some pretty exotic fruits and not just familiar types! This image leads us now to a brief final discussion of the role of legal transplants in the context under examination.

The problem with legal transplants

In the quest to embark on a separate democratic journey in 1971 and while making adjustments of all kinds to achieve some sort of global approval and acceptance as a viable nation, Bangladesh too, like many emerging democratic nations, portrayed itself as wishing to make some progress in adhering to the ethos of a functional democracy. In addition to discussing the innumerable difficulties that Bangladesh faces vis- à-vis her own brand of democracy and the state of her governance, another way of looking at this entire scenario of the nation attempting to adopt a democratic path in governance is perhaps to examine whether a jurisdiction like Bangladesh, in all its cultural specificity and variety, is able to absorb the ethos of a democratic culture when the notion of democracy, first of all, appears to emanate from a Western context. It is, to that extent, a foreign fruit. Little do some critics and analysts realise that legal transplantation of democracy is a deeply plural enterprise and not a mere mechanical lifting of one tool or concept into another context. The act of transplanting itself has its own teething problems and pitfalls, and a transplant often finds it difficult to readjust to a new scenario. Below, a brief discussion of the work of Alan Watson (1993), in particular, is provided to present some insights into the contested nature of transplant discussions which match the continuing troubles over plurality-conscious debates on law more generally.

While legal transplants – the moving of a rule or a system of law from one country to another, or from one people to another – have been common since the earliest recorded history, we saw in the previous discussions that law is the reflection of the spirit of a people. This means that any form of reception of law or a more formal transplant will need to be viewed as some kind of socio-legal process, not merely a mechanical act of adoption of some foreign or 'other' rule or process. Importantly, scholars have identified inbuilt resistances against adoption of received forms of law. Thus, as long as the Scots are conscious that they are Scots as people, they must preserve their law (Watson 1993: 21–22). Watson's argument challenges the long prevailing notion that there is of necessity a close connection between law and society in which it operates. The most obvious explanation for this would be that a transplant can of course be superimposed onto a society. It would then need to be examined how that particular society reacts to the specific transplant. Watson (1993) suggests that a society's laws do not usually develop as a logical outgrowth of its own experience; rather the laws of one society are primarily borrowed from other societies. While that is primarily an aspect of social theory, the links with legal theorising are necessarily strong. As a result, as we know, most law operates in a society very differently from the one for which it was originally created, and hence law cannot simply be used as a tool to understand society without careful consideration of history and any processes of legal transplants.

Watson (1993: 34) notes three conclusions when analysing the legal transplant of Roman law into Egypt. First, that it may not necessarily be the case that family law is the branch of law which is least open to foreign influence. Although Roman family law may have been conservative and static, juristic interpretation and edicts allowed significant development. Second, gaps or deficiencies in a legal system are not always due to lack of knowledge that there is a deficiency, but illogicality of legal development is also highlighted. Third, legal rules which are unsatisfactory at home appear even less satisfactory when they are transplanted. In this regard, Watson (1993: 35) referred to Jeremy Bentham's (1843) work, which incidentally also speaks about colonial Bengal: first, that the English law is in great parts of such a nature as to be bad everywhere; second, that it appears worse in Bengal than in England (thus an implied critique of the colonial system); and third, that a system might be devised which, while it would be better for Bengal, would also be better even for England. Hence a time of transplant is often a moment when reforms are under discussion and can be or are sought to be introduced. Watson (1993: 116) concludes that transplanting frequently and perhaps always involves legal transformation. Even when the transplanted rule remains formally unchanged, its impact in a new social setting may be different. The insertion of an alien rule into another complex system may cause it to operate in a fresh way. Without saying so explicitly, Watson's theorising is therefore quite conscious of normative plurality, but it remains too general to tell us anything of specific relevance to the CTG phenomenon in Bangladesh.

Shah (2005: 348–361), while discussing Watson, has pointed out that Watson's notion of legal transplant is very narrow and limited and that Watson has not considered it necessary to acknowledge the strong determining role of culture of the 'sending' or 'receiving' society when assessing the fate of such rule. To that extent, clearly Watson was not a legal pluralist, but his own comments indicate that he was aware of cultural diversity in relation to law.

Cotterrell (2006: 109) significantly differs from Watson's notion and argues that the law and community approach together allows a nuanced, realistic analysis of the possibilities of successful legal transplants. He (Cotterrell 2006: 126) notes that

> Power operates not just in and through political systems but particularly in conflicts between sections of society whose unity or identity is given in terms of the types of community. Conflicts over law are often conflicts between expressions of instrumental, affective or traditional community or a community of belief, or between social groups, societies or sections of societies, that in some sense see themselves or are seen as owning or disowning the law in dispute.

Much more could be said about this, but as indicated, the purpose here is not to claim some theoretical innovation. Rather, the task in hand is to chart the progress of realisation among legal scholars that law and society are intrinsically connected, which may result at times in the creation of some 'unconventional structures' which the society needs to assist in the operation of law, as happened with the CTG's emergence. In the context of Bangladesh, if we saw democracy as a transplanted or received legal phenomenon and the CTG as an innovation introduced into post-military Bangladesh to partly assist with the transplanted structure, the interconnectedness of law, society/culture and politics become clearly evident.

While Chiba (1986) indicated that there had been little effort for seriously considering the issue of 'cultural specificity' in a legal system, he embarks on such an analysis while discussing the Japanese legal system (1986: 301–367). Chiba notes that Japan is perhaps the only non-Western country to have smoothly accomplished the required westernisation in many phases of its society including industrial development and legal systemisation. But at the same time, Japan is also noted for retaining its characteristic culture and hence it has preserved its indigenous law along with such an apparently successful modern legal system. The well-adjusted parallelism of the official law and/or unofficial law, received law and/or indigenous law may methodologically seem justifiable, but in reality, the whole structure of Japanese law covers both elements. Chiba (1986: 384–385) asserts that there is a presupposition that a basic legal postulate exists in Japan which maintains Japanese identity in terms of law through their entire historical development, including the reception of foreign law.

To that extent, the introduction of the Western notion of 'democracy' into Bangladesh's Constitution as a fundamental State policy is a transplant that could be compared to earlier Japanese transplants, which copied elements of foreign law (Prussian law, actually to a large extent) into the Japanese legal system without seeking to change or aiming to modify the postulates of the receiving country. Subsequently, the emergence of the CTG is justified and may be viewed predominantly as an instrumental element for the amelioration of the working of the Bangladeshi legal system vis-à-vis holding free and fair elections, providing a basic electoral democracy and thereby assisting in the smooth transition from one elected government to another and not really anything else. This supplementation or adaptation was helpful till the time it began being manipulated by the Bangladeshi polity.

Chiba (2002: 6), in discussing the workability of transplanted law, notes that it was found never to be working without being supplemented or undermined by indigenous law, since non-Western peoples' indigenous law has been integral to the receiving people's cultural heritage. In the process of encountering foreign laws, there has either been peaceful assimilation or destructive struggle between indigenous law and transplanted law. As a result, indigenous law may have sometimes failed to maintain itself or at other times may have succeeded either by rejecting the encountered law or by adapting itself to preserve its cultural identity. This has caused non-Western law to be in a current state or in an ongoing process of self-developing indigenous law, whether successfully or not.

Shah (2005: 6–8) reminds us that, primarily with reference to the transplantation of foreign Western laws into the Japanese legal system in its effort to modernise, Chiba (1989: 155) attempted to identify how it was that the cultural crisis that this process precipitated was managed by the Japanese legal order. Shah (2005: 6), in referring to Chiba, notes that the success or failure of the reception of foreign legal elements, consistent with the maintenance of the Japanese cultural identity, is dependent on the basic legal postulate which enables a people to maintain its cultural identity. It is an attribute which is indispensable to every system of law that wants to remain culturally independent, and it is this which guides people in choosing how to reformulate law and transplanted foreign law in order to maintain their cultural identity.

Clearly, a functioning Western democracy does not need this kind of crutch (CTG) to operate fair and democratic elections. The introduction of the CTG in Bangladesh has been to address the abuses of electoral processes and accompanying corruptions of power and procedures. And since the people of Bangladesh themselves wanted a better system for managing elections, they resorted to this mechanism which arose out of a realisation that better processes would need to be devised to curtail abuses of power by those overseeing the electoral process, particularly the government in the seat of authority/power.

Coming back to Shah (2005: 349), he pertinently points out that in analysing the relationship between Asia and Europe, although there have been connections with regard to enormous advances in knowledge, science and technology in Europe through Asians, there has also been subjugation of large sections of Asia under colonialism, and recently there has been more pressure of globalisation according to Western terms. These challenges, Shah continues, are faced by Asians using their own countermeasures, by reasserting 'Asian values', so that it is unclear whether globalisation always follows Western dictates. Increasingly it appears as if there have been complex processes involving not one way but multiple exchanges and globalisations, including those of peoples, laws and legal traditions.

In this wider context, the transplantation of democratic norms seemed like a natural course of action as soon as Bangladesh was born, mainly due to past negative experiences, especially just prior to the acrimonious divorce from Pakistan. The subsequent experience of independent Bangladesh in maintaining democratic standards posed significant challenges and generated the assumption that Western democratic norms would help create the conditions for economic growth and political stability among other things, but that first of all the starting point would be better self-management of national elections. In practice, however, such assimilation proved to be more challenging than anticipated due to the reality on the ground, legacy of the past and years of cultural mistrust. Since law is inextricably intertwined with and reflective of the particular history, culture and society in which it has evolved, as we saw, it can never be effectively transplanted from one society to another without some adaptations, as observed by Legrand (1997: 114).

While Legrand's (1997) approach may be too negative and somewhat placative, in a recent and most interesting article, Kelly (2014: 331–333) discusses the scholarship of Legrand, who in echoing Foucault's epistemological theories, argues not just that the law is socially determined but also our thinking of law. This debate stresses that the interpretation of any legal concept or rule will depend on the interpretative community, the episteme that one inhabits. Other inhabitants of other epistemes will interpret the exact same rule in ways that are different and completely unpredictable. To that effect, a meaningful legal transplant can only happen when both the propositional statement as such and its invested meaning – which jointly constitute as rule – are transported from one culture to another. Since this is virtually impossible because of the history, culture, language and modes of interpretation which can never be produced exactly in a recipient country, the true meaning of any legal transplant will fail to survive the journey from one legal system to another. The imported legal concept or rule is inevitably ascribed a different local meaning which makes it *ipso facto* a different rule. Kelly thus cautions that legal transplants between different cultures, languages and epistemic communities are just not difficult, but impossible.

According to Kelly (2014), if we were to take Watson and Legrand as representing opposite poles of the legal transplant debate, a middle position, which is rather comfortable and intuitively sensible, is offered by Otto Kahn-Freund (1974: 27), who stresses that the ability to transfer a given rule depends on the social, cultural and political similarities between the transferor and the transferee. The more similar the dynamics of the two countries, the more likely the transplant will take root and flourish. Thus, the success of transplantation depended on the demand within the receiving society. Voluntary legal reforms are likely to be more successful than reforms proposed by outside forces. Kelly also brings forward Gunther Teubner (1998: 11–12), who helped explain the dynamic and unpredictable nature of legal transplants, indicating that transfers of law from one society to another often do not replace pre-existing legal meanings and practices but instead trigger a whole series of new and unexpected events. This will unleash an evolutionary dynamic in which the meaning of external rules will be reconstructed and the internal context will undergo fundamental change.

In the context of Bangladesh, since the operation of the official law of managing free and fair elections through an autonomous EC, which itself can be seen as a Western democratic implant, did not bear fruit, the creation of a CTG seemed to provide a solution. Thus, initially through unofficial law in 1990, this new CTG process worked and made elections possible. After this unofficial law had worked and delivered due results, it was then formalised and hence became an official law in 1996 by being incorporated into Bangladesh's Constitution through the Thirteenth Amendment. At that point in time, and indeed for the next 20 years, the CTG became a facilitating tool to assist with this struggle of adapting to the teething problems and struggles associated with the transplantation of democracy into Bangladeshi soil.

However, as subsequent chapters will elaborate, the practical operation of the CTG was undermined by all kinds of adjustment processes that partly took away the benefits of the intended innovation – the CTG itself became eventually abused. Hence, when the CTG was abandoned in 2011, the government's argument for abolishing it was that this official law was no longer producing the desired result, as in the guise of the CTG, power was being usurped by those who ran the CTG (as happened with the CTG of 2007). But then the question becomes: what is the desired result in the context of Bangladesh's politico-legal realm? The newspaper polls and the fieldwork results which attempted to measure peoples' pulses tell us a different story: a story of a strong public perception that the CTG is required for electoral management so that there are free and fair national elections. This need arises as elections under an existing government are perceived as manipulatable and hence unfair. The 2007–2008 CTG, despite its abuse of staying in power for longer than 90 days, still gave Bangladeshis a free, fair and acceptable election, lauded both by national and international observers. It was also lauded by the Bangladeshi electorate. So there is, perhaps, some weakness in the government's argument. However, it is also a fact that the CTG was undermined to a critical extent by the particular government in power in 2006, thus raising new questions about its long-term viability without an effective reform by concerned stakeholders.

In any view of the matter, adopting, adapting, sustaining and consolidating democracy and democratic norms from the West in Bangladeshi soil, with its historical legacy and its own socio-political and legal reality, is not as simple as it may look. It is not merely a question of transposing democratic values onto an Asian society. In the African context, Kelly (2014) to that effect has aptly illustrated that differences exist across cultures and legal systems and that those differences are worthy of further careful study. At the moment, we have no firm guidance or answer and can only state that legal transplants between societies with differing historical and cultural moorings are extremely complicated, sometimes in ways that are difficult for outsiders to perceive. It is not about simply diffusing universal legal principles but about changing the rules of the game for the recipient country and its people.

At the end of the day, then, jurisprudential analysis of the CTG phenomenon can identify the basic fact of extreme plurality and competitive interactions between different law-related actors and influences. However, the underlying power struggles are themselves extremely complicated and they are, at the end of the day, more about power rather than law. The rather unilateral act of the then-sitting government of Bangladesh to abolish the CTG in 2011 was clearly more than a legal phenomenon or a legal or illegal act. It was a strategy that served other purposes as well, and the answer about what was really going on is perhaps not to be found in theoretical legal analysis, but in the realisation of Chiba's seminal statement, to the effect that any form of official and unofficial law is always connected to legal postulates, which is borne out by the CTG evidence from Bangladesh. But what are the underlying legal postulates that explain the temporary experimentation with the CTG model and its subsequent abandonment? The present jurisprudential analysis cannot fully answer such a question, but there is a need for stakeholders to ponder upon this. The task now is to examine the historical narrative of Bangladesh in order to understand from when did the seeds of mistrust penetrated this country, which over the years reached to such heights and proportions that merely holding a national election has become such a Herculean task.

3

JOURNEY TO DEMOCRACY – THE CASE OF BANGLADESH

An understanding of the State of Bangladesh today could be from three simultaneous perspectives. Firstly, the proclamations of 'state formation' that have been taking place through the pre-colonial, colonial and post-colonial periods portray the establishment of an architectural construct of 'power'. Secondly, the processes of 'nationalism' which involve issues of cultural, religious and political identity could help explore why Bangladesh remains a nation in trouble as far as democratic governance is concerned. Thirdly, the processes of 'democratisation' which have produced not just discourses on rights and institutions, but also a dynamic of fierce and confrontational politics, have led to a situation where the rules of the game are still being negotiated today.

Although the author is no historian, this chapter attempts to merely project those elements of history which acknowledge the impact of the residues of history in this part of the world, and attempts to highlight how the influence of the past has impacted the journey of democracy in Bangladesh, including the complexities of transition to full statehood. State formation must contend with how these residues of history both constrain and enable the making and taking of opportunity by different political agents in attempting to influence State power. This shows us, regrettably, that the theme of mistrust continues to haunt the nation even after all these years of independence. It began first with mistrust of the British, during the colonial era, followed by mistrust of the Pakistanis and their hegemonic efforts to suppress what used to be East Pakistan until 1971. In post-independent Bangladesh, there is ample evidence of blatant mistrust of major forces engaged in ruling this fairly new country, born out of a violent liberation struggle, whose brutal memories have led to fresh violence in the wake of the attempts to bring those responsible for the atrocities in and around 1971 to justice. Since it is not easy to get closure on unaddressed crimes against humanity which took place during the liberation war, the attempt to establish national identity on a more law-abiding footing by setting up, in 2009, the International Crimes Tribunal (ICT) of Bangladesh – a much-awaited domestic war crimes tribunal to investigate and prosecute suspects of the genocide committed in 1971 by the Pakistan Army and their local collaborators, *Razakars*, *Al-Badr* and *Al-Shams*, during the Bangladesh

Liberation War, has led to waves of violence, further schisms and more restlessness within the society. The nation manifestly continues to suffer from a lack of agreement about how it should be run and governed, and one could thus read the historical account offered here as an extended story of the struggles over plurality management in an intensely plural socio-cultural and politico-legal environment. How this relates to the CTG will be explored in detail in Chapters 4 and 5. But for now, it suffices to say that although the CTG structure may apparently seem to be just an indigenous tool to assist in electoral governance, the need for this transitional modality emanates from deep mistrust, the roots of which can be traced way back to the history of this region. This underlying element of mistrust perhaps represents a certain redefined 'other' in the inevitably plural context of Bangladesh. Before we come to more recent events and developments, this chapter attempts to lay out the major historical and socio-cultural foundations in order to appreciate the depth of the problems of 'otherness' facing governance in Bangladesh today.

The colonial era and its impact on democracy

For millennia, the Indian subcontinent was a rich and complex mosaic of cultural diversities which shaped the creative political mechanisms of compromise and collaboration long before the colonial advent which lasted through two centuries (Avari 2007). Before colonialism from Europe took root, a succession of empire builders, Buddhist, Hindu and later Muslim, sought to bring the contours of political India into conformity with those of its vast geographical expanse (Keay 2010). It was, however, only for a very limited time that India's geographical unity actually corresponded with its political unity. Political arrangements were fragmented and constantly fought over. They had to be continually negotiated and renegotiated between diverse people inhabiting the domains of sovereign or quasi-sovereign regional rulers.

Historian Dalrymple, in his article in *The New Yorker* (June 2015), notes that the first Islamic conquests of India happened in 1021 with the capture of Lahore. In 1192, Persianised Turks, from what is now central Afghanistan, seized Delhi from its Hindu rulers and by 1323, established a sultanate as far as Madurai, Gujarat and Bengal. He continues that although these conquests were perceived as having been made by Muslims, medieval Sanskrit inscriptions identified them by their linguistic and ethnic affiliation rather than their religious identity. Within a few centuries, a hybrid Indo-Islamic civilisation emerged along with hybrid languages such as Deccani and Urdu, which mixed the Sanskrit-derived vernaculars of India with Turkish, Persian and Arabic words. According to Dalrymple, in village folk traditions, the practice of the two faiths came close to blending into one with Hindus visiting graves of Sufi masters and Muslims leaving offerings at Hindu shrines. The cultural mixing took place throughout the subcontinent as the Mughal Crown Prince Dara Shikoh, in the seventeenth century, had the *Bhagavad Gita* (central text of Hinduism) translated into Persian and composed a study of Hinduism and Islam titled 'The Minglings of Two Oceans' which stressed the affinities of the two faiths. Dalrymple further notes that

> In the nineteenth century, India was still a place where traditions, languages and cultures cut across religious groupings and where people did not define themselves primarily through their religious faith. A Sunni Muslim weaver from Bengal would have had far more in common in his language, his outlook, and his fondness for fish with one of his Hindu colleagues than he would with a Karachi Shia or a Pashtun Sufi from the North-West Frontier.

Indians were accustomed to foreign rule since the death of the ancient Indian Emperor Ashoka of the Maurya dynasty, as large parts of the subcontinent had been conquered by Turks, Afghans, Persians, Tocharians and Mongols. Though subsequently governed by the *Mughals* and hence Muslims under a legal system based loosely on *Shariah* Law, its millions of non-Muslim subjects, whether Hindus, Sikhs or Buddhists, were allowed the freedom of conscience and custom till the era of the *Mughal* Emperor Akbar ended. Historian Alex Von Tunzelmann (2007: 11) grippingly narrates the condition of the two nations before colonialism took over the Indian subcontinent, referring to India as being a 'vast, mighty and magnificent empire, brilliantly organised and culturally unified' while England was an 'undeveloped, semi-feudal realm, riven by religious factionalism and barely able to feed its illiterate, diseased and stinking masses.' But this scenario in the Indian sub-continent completely changed with the advent of the colonial period as the Indian subcontinent's deeply intermixed and profoundly syncretised culture transformed into something so divisive and eventually so communal, in a matter of a few decades during the twentieth century, that both sides believed that it was almost impossible for adherents of the two religions to live together peacefully.

The colonial period of the British, through direct and indirect rule, sought to turn the Indian subcontinent into a centralised political unity based on fictitious notions of a singular and indivisible sovereignty. This had large implications not only at the level of the colonial legal system and institutional structures, but also on Indian ideology and politics, which in the course of time sowed the seeds of partition in this area (Jalal 1995: 9–10).

The Indian subcontinent was never a stranger to foreign traders. European merchants frequented the overland camel and caravan trails and the maritime sail-rigged routes. However, as with many other trading systems, the middlemen had increasingly taken control of the markets and often had an iron grip on the upward-spiralling prices. The Arab merchants and wholesalers, who acted as middlemen for the important spice trade, were no different, and the European traders were understandably unhappy with them. This 'middlemen' (*dalaal*) phenomenon still exists in Bangladesh (and more widely throughout South Asia) in all aspects of life (Ruud 2014: 304). In the latter half of the century, the

European fleets started to fan out to devise a more stable maritime route under their direct control. For the first time, the Indian subcontinent encountered the imperial power politics of the European courts and the Indian subcontinent's ability to shape its own future started to slip away. The decline of the Mughal Empire (1526–1858) ran almost parallel to the ascendancy of the Europeans in the subcontinent, which witnessed two centuries of strife, not only between the Europeans and the locals, but also among the natives themselves (Chandra 2007: 50–56).

The English East India Company was founded by a royal charter on 31 December 1600 (Bandyopadhyay 2004: 37). Prior to this, between 1591 and 1594 the English Captain James Lancaster completed his voyage around the Cape of Good Hope and established the trade route from India to England. After managing to get more involved in trade in 1611, the British started eastwards towards Bengal and Burma. The East India Company was one among several European trading ventures that sought to tap the riches of the 'East' (Metcalf and Metcalf 2001: 44). The *Nawab* of Bengal allowed the East India Company to trade in 1633. The Company promptly set up factories at Balasore and Hariharpur, and by 1650, Hooghly Factory was established. By 1669, the East India Company was based at Dacca. Metcalf and Metcalf (2001: 51) observe that trade with Bengal had grown even more profitable to the Company as by 1750, almost 75 per cent of the Company's procurement of Indian goods came from the entire Ganges valley. Commercial interests therefore became of utmost importance. The Company's strength is aptly summed up by Von Tunzelmann (2007: 15):

> The Company could mint its own coin, maintain its own army, wage war, make peace, acquire new territories and impose its own civil and criminal law without any accountability except to its shareholders. This private empire of money, unburdened by conscience, rampaged across the sub-continent until the 1850s.

Not only was it guided by market forces, the Company was incredibly successful and brutal at the same time.

In England, however, the Company was not enjoying a free run. The British Government, although keen to profit from the benefits of the Empire, was feeling the need to re-establish some authority over the Company in the face of growing public unease over the lack of accountability of those trading abroad. After all, by 1765, the East India Company had become a local ruler (*dewan*), with now – somewhat alarmingly – dual loyalty to the British Crown and the *Mughal* court in Delhi. The British Parliament tried to regulate the Company's administration from 1773 onwards, as the East India Company had by then become even more deeply involved in the local administration of the subcontinent. By 1784, the Company's civil and military affairs were subjected to parliamentary scrutiny. Metcalf and Metcalf (2001: 55) have pertinently questioned why the Company succeeded so spectacularly in the Indian subcontinent when others did not. Their answer is that Britain, as an island nation, for whom overseas trade was so vital, was fiercely committed to securing its Indian interests at any cost: control of the seas in an era in which export trade brought the greatest profit gave Britain a clear edge over all its rivals.

Given that the British government's focus was on property rather than social welfare, one of the most notable reform initiatives of the Company at the behest of public opinion in Britain and the perceived need to consolidate control was the Permanent Settlement land tenure, the Land Lease Act of Lord Charles Cornwallis, in 1793. In Eastern India, it replaced the traditional local *zamindari* system in which the aristocrats rooted to the land performed the dual role of collecting revenues and meting out local justice. From an anthropological perspective, for many of the Bengali élite, *zamindari* and the behavioural attitudes of being a *zamindar* created an individualistic, self-centred, monopolistic attitude, which has pervaded the political sphere even as far up to today's political realm of Bangladesh. This is one of the reasons why it was felt necessary to go back into local history as far back as the East India Company in order to understand the deeply embedded traits of the political class, which perhaps explains why even today, the political actors act as they do. This individualistic, self-centred, monopolistic attitude seems to have permeated the political and business class of Bangladesh. A variation of the *zamindari* system was also extended into some other parts of the Indian subcontinent so that the *taluqdars* or administrators of Oudh could now become hereditary rulers of the lands where they collected taxes. (French 2011: 7).

The new system, modelled on English land ownership, attempted to auction off the *zamindaris* to the highest bidder. This resulted in the displacement of traditional aristocrats and their supplanting with a nouveau riche merchant class of the cities who had little understanding of farmlands and their operations. The concept of absentee landlordship, hitherto alien to Bengal, broke down the connection between the landlords and tenants, with a disastrous effect on agricultural development. This system of land tenure and the British policies of rent collection and taxation that followed the Permanent Settlement Act produced severe economic distress among the landless and the peasantry, especially in East Bengal, where these classes were mainly Muslims. Hence resentment against the *zamindars* grew since they were seen as the instruments of this exploitation, not because so many were Hindus, but because they were *zamindars*. The resentment was thus more a voice against feudalism, and there was nothing communal about it at that stage, as is clearly echoed by DeSouza: 'This was a class antagonism and not a communal one according to some observers' (2010: 5).

The properties of the *zamindars* were mostly located in Eastern Bengal. Subsequent Land Acts of 1859, 1868 and 1885 produced among these peasants a class of *jotedars* or peasant cultivators/middle-level landholders/tenant farmers who were also mainly Muslims and who emerged in rural Bengal (Hossain 2013: 2). As the surplus from the land began to accumulate, these cultivators acquired aspirations for education and for subsequent access to the structure and opportunities of the colonial State. Such access was up to then largely enjoyed by the Hindu élite, who had been the first to benefit from colonial education. These were the classes that the Muslim League was subsequently able to mobilise for the creation of a separate State of Pakistan during Partition in 1947, when the Muslim-dominated part of Bengal became East Pakistan.

Side by side, the education system underwent radical changes under Company rule. English replaced Persian as the official language. New civil and criminal codes were put in place, based on the English legal experience. Warren Hastings, the first Governor General of the Company's Indian territories, believed that there were distinct and separate codes of family law, in particular, for Hindus and Muslims. This insistence on a fundamental difference between 'Hindu' and 'Muslim' reduced a variety of sectarian communities characterised by distinct customs and practices to merely two, each defined through its textual tradition. In so doing, the practice of seeing these categories as central to the organising of Indian society helped shape how the Indian subcontinent constructed itself and identified itself in later years (Metcalf and Metcalf 2001: 58). Secular education was encouraged and institutionalised. It resulted in creating a different *Babu* class (clerks), a new class of English-speaking Indians with at least a pragmatic degree of loyalty towards the dominant power, subservient to the British rule. Human rights abuses like human sacrifice and the *Suttee* system were banned. The Muslims were resentful of their fall from power with the end of the Mughal dynasty. This resentment was reflected perhaps in their refusal to accept English education in the vain hope that the old days of glory would return. This period of resentment and boycott of Western education, which was rather unhelpful for Muslim progress, lasted nearly a century until the arrival of Sir Syed Ahmed Khan with his Mohammadan Anglo-Oriental College, which subsequently became Aligarh University.

On the economic front, the British did not treat their new-found colony in any other way than all imperial powers of history did. India was both a supplier of raw materials like cloth and saltpetre and a consumer of British machine-made textiles and salt. Craftsmen of East Bengal bore the brunt of cheap imports like British-made muslin. Local and indigenous products suffered. Such exploitations later became a target of protest, connected to the activities of the legendary Mohandas Karamchand Gandhi and his adherents in the 1920s and later.

In the backdrop of large-scale social upheaval and not very welcome social change, parts of the Indian Army mutinied in Meerut Cantonment in 1857. The Sepoy Mutiny was triggered by some Muslim units from Bengal and the soldiers involved in it marched straight to Delhi to convey their allegiance to the Mughal Emperor Bahadur Shah, who would soon become the last Emperor of that dynasty. The main reason for the mutiny was perhaps the enforcement of the usage of cartridges which used cow and pig fat, anathema to both Hindu and Muslim soldiers respectively. However, it can be argued that this was also a violent manifestation of the unease about colonial rule and dreams to resurrect a bygone political order (Metcalf and Metcalf 2001: 56–122). The aftermath of 1857 was that political sovereignty swiftly passed into the hands of the British. This was, of course, not yet a time for democracy. The local people were simple colonial subjects, not yet political actors in their own right.

Though the perception is one of Muslims taking the brunt of the British assault, it was collectively both Muslims and Hindus who witnessed the country going under unadulterated subjugation – a process that would last until 1947. The eminent Farsi and Urdu poet Sir Muhammad Iqbal, also known as Allama Iqbal, has recorded the extremities to which Indians were subjected through the collapse of the Mughal Empire in 1857. The ferocity of the rise of the British was nowhere more reflected than in the crude manner of the trial of Emperor Bahadur Shah Jalal and his subsequent exile to Rangoon (Dalrymple 2006).

It took the British almost 13 months to quell this rebellion and a direct result of the mutiny was the formal annexation of India by the British Crown in 1858, replacing the East India Company. The Governor General of India was appointed by the Crown and was answerable to a member of the British Cabinet, in this case the Secretary of State for India. The Raj finally arrived in India with the Regal Proclamation of 1858. Britain, at that point, had direct control of almost 60 per cent of the land. The rest of the land was ruled indirectly and remained under the control of the 'Princely States'. The British government devised a 'Principle of Paramountcy', which allowed the states limited sovereignty only in internal affairs – defence and international affairs being looked after by Britain. It was a Permanent Settlement on a larger scale, where the Crown reserved the right to intervene in the affairs of these states wherever it was thought fit. The Indian Army was reformed to maintain a safer balance between Englishmen and natives with the proportion of 1:6 reduced to almost 1:2. The British also formulated a theory of the 'Martial Races of India', the principle being that certain groups within India would naturally make loyal mercenaries while others would not, and wherein the Bengalis (who had initiated the 1857 revolt) were considered non-martial (Chattopadhyay 2011: 265–279) and the Punjabis and Pathans (who remained loyal) were deemed to be martial races and given preference for military employment (Chandra 1979: 281–302). This theory, although never officially announced, cast a long shadow over the actions of the Pakistan Army and the treatment of Bengalis as East Pakistanis in the following century. Hence, another layer of a class system based upon ethnicity was introduced which caused further schisms in society in subsequent years, with reverberations to the present day.

The British Crown initiated wide-ranging infrastructural development in India, not only to regulate the economy but also to strengthen its grip over the land. The removal of internal custom levies and transit taxes along with global improvement in communications after the opening of the Suez Canal in 1869 made India a prosperous land with impressive markets and international trade. India became the agricultural hinterland of the burgeoning British industry. Historian Ayesha Jalal (1995: 10) notes that to maintain imperial control over India's political and economic arenas, the British introduced rules and regulations based on Western concepts, that is, contractual and impersonalised sovereignty without precedence and hence no knowledge of consequences. For a nation quite familiar with 'direct, personalised rules', such a cold-hearted and clinically bureaucratic approach may have appeared to have succeeded in providing institutional coherence in greater parts of India. However, the myriad distinctions and divisions within Indian subcontinental society proved to be unbridgeable. This created further mayhem in the multilayered administrative as well as social diversities: a familiar example would be the district collectors – a quintessential British colonial creation – providing a personalised form of patronage and judicial arbitration within the overall context of a rule-bound, indirect and impersonalised institutionalised structure.

Moreover, subtle manifestations of communalism were put in place through Lord Curzon's decisions to partition Bengal (*Bongo Bhongo*) in 1905. The move evoked strong protests from Hindus who refused to accept the idea of a truncated Bengali cultural heritage. On the other hand, influential Muslim groups based in Eastern Bengal and led by Nawab Salimullah welcomed the division. They saw this as an opportunity for Bengali Muslims to develop their own region and at the same time have a say in their own, albeit distinctly Muslim-related, matter. In exerting control over politics, the British divided Bengal into two parts for administrative reasons. Some significant developments such as new institutions for higher learning leading to expansion of opportunities for Bengali Muslims in the areas of public administration, education and business did take place in East Bengal after the 1905 *Bongo Bhongo*. Although Bengal remained divided for only six years, this transformed the social and political landscape of East Bengal. The population of East Bengal, mainly Muslims, saw this as recognition of their uniqueness from the majority Hindus, a recognition which was amiss earlier.

However, the vociferous protests against the partition of Bengal eventually led to an annulment of the division in 1911 – the year in which the British moved India's capital from Calcutta to Delhi. The British, bowing to the continual pressure of the Indian National Congress (Congress), founded in 1885, cancelled the Bengal partition. Though the partition was annulled, the scars remained embedded as communal disturbances had already affected several towns including Jamalpore, Dacca and Comilla, with indirect and sometimes direct support of the government. At times, the administration not only took 'no steps' to suppress the communal riots but in fact 'connived' in the same (Sengupta 2001: 325–328). The 1911 revocation of *Bongo Bhongo* was, however, perceived by the Muslims of Bengal as a further indication of a Hindu/British conspiracy to continue to deprive Muslims of opportunities for advancement. The deep-rooted scars would subsequently resurface in the 1940s with the Muslim League's demand for a separate State for Muslims to be carved out of India as it existed at that time (Sengupta 2001: 432–433). Historian French (2011: 14) remarks that Curzon's failed attempt to split Bengal had provoked an upsurge of nationalist protest, Bengal becoming the focus of constitutional and revolutionary faces of the freedom movement, which is why a baffled King George V once asked a new governor of the province: 'What is wrong with Bengal?' Agitations became so intense that, at one point, the province became ungovernable, resulting in the passing of the Defence Act 1915. This Act made repression easier since it suspended legal remedies by giving unfettered powers to the authorities, led by Charles Tegart, who ran the intelligence branch of the Bengal Police, carrying out crackdowns swiftly and savagely. It appears that the inherent rebellious spirit of the Bengalis of yesteryear has been carried forward even to this century.

The campaign of the Indian National Congress included the famous *Swadeshi* (devotee of one's own country) movement, which urged Indians to boycott British-made goods and encouraged the production and use of Indian-made goods to take their place (Mukherjee 2014: 28–30). Jalal's (1995: 12) analysis of British colonial consolidation efforts over a newly conquered country clearly depicts the interaction between the two key dialectics which are played out 'between centralism and regionalism on the one hand, and between all-India nationalism and communalism on the other'. The British tried to reconcile the requirement of an all-too necessary colonial structure of centralised rule with the need of thwarting any sort of political unionist movement. Jalal (1995: 12–16) explains that the British colonial consolidation effort over a newly conquered country was a simple, classical British tenet of colonialism of 'divide and rule'. In order to ensure their political and economic – as well as to a certain extent, social – control, the British employed skilful manipulation to superimpose geographical unity on the one hand, while fermenting the age-old rivalry between religions and caste systems within religions on the other. This could be explained by the incorporation of the district collectors – a very selective group of people, part of the British administration for collecting rents as well as actively taking part in administration. In such pre-democratic times and in the colonial context, the separation of legislature and executive was not necessary. This in turn enabled the British to manage an easy and economical way of avoiding demands for representation, since for a long time the administrators were *de facto* public representatives.

The clear policy and mantra of 'divide and rule' led to the growth of communalism in India, which eventually also led to the partition of the subcontinent. However, before 1947, serious efforts were made by Indian nationalists such as Chittaranjan Das, who steered the Bengal Pact in the early 1920s, aiming to strike a local balance between Hindus and Muslims regarding jobs in government services. Das's untimely death in 1925 was to prove a setback for Hindu/Muslim unity and the country would inexorably move towards a communal split in 1947.

Jalal (1995: 13) notes that 'the colonial strategy of emphasizing difference in diversity' went particularly well with the Muslims of India, who despite being part of a binding religion were more interested and comfortable with provincial or regional issues. This is evident from the fact that Congress was able to position itself as an all-India institution early in the struggle for independence rather than the Muslim League, a political organisation born in 1906, which came over perhaps more as a reaction to the mistreatment of Muslims by Hindus. The majority of historians regard Mohammad Ali Jinnah's attempt to carve out Pakistan for the Muslims as a direct result, among other things, of his failure to gain significant political leverage in a Hindu-dominated Congress. According to this view, as far as Jinnah was concerned, he found it convenient to assert the 'diversity of communities' rather than follow the Congress-led idea of 'political unity and geographic divergence'. To Jinnah, it appeared to be exactly the opposite of what Congress had in mind.

A different perspective is provided by French (2011), in which he brings forth quite interestingly that the clash between Hindus and Muslims during partition was also about the clash between personalities among the politicians of that period, particularly Jinnah (leader of the Muslim League) and Gandhi and Nehru (the two most prominent leaders of the Hindu-dominated Congress Party). Although Jinnah and Gandhi were both Gujarati and all three men were anglicized lawyers who had received at least part of their education in England, their relationship had grown so bitter and poisonous by the early 1940s that they could barely be persuaded to sit in the same room. French (2011: 17) observes that although Gandhi was the most famous Indian since Buddha and the most influential political campaigner of the twentieth century, with his message of truth, tolerance and peaceful resistance against injustice, it can be a deflating experience to read what critics, like Salman Rushdie (1992: 27), have written about him:

> To make Gandhi appeal to the Western market, he had to be sanctified and turned into Christ – an odd fate for a crafty Gujarati lawyer – and the history of one of the century's greatest revolutions had to be mangled.

French (2011: 17) continues that far from being a wise and balanced saint, Gandhi was an emotionally troubled social activist and a ruthless, sharp political negotiator. As India's transport minister Dr. John Matthai said in 1947, the final failure to reach a satisfactory settlement with the Muslim League stemmed in part from the 'Gujarati mentality' of the Congress leadership – 'i.e. that of a trader, driving a hard bargain' (French 2011: 17).

In Indian-nationalist accounts, Jinnah appears to be the villain of the story. French (2011: 27) further points out that neither side seemed especially keen to claim Jinnah as a real human being – the Pakistanis (though considering him the Father of their Nation) restricted him to an appearance on banknotes in demure Islamic costume although he remained a secularist of sorts till his end.

French's portrayal of these three politicians (Gandhi, Nehru and Jinnah) of the Indian subcontinent, who played important roles in fashioning the destiny of a large chunk of humanity, was not in black and white but in shades of grey, which gives us ample room to reflect why these leaders acted the way they did.

In the run-up to partition in 1947, conditions were exacerbated by the increasingly strident demands of the Muslim League, in defence of a separate State for Muslims. In July 1946, the cabinet mission, after days of brokering negotiations between the Congress and the Muslim League, was able to cobble together a plan that would keep India intact and yet provide a large measure of autonomy to its contingent provinces, especially in the north-west and east of the country. However, the cabinet mission plan, as it had come to be known, received its first jolt when Jawaharlal Nehru told a press conference on 10 July 1946 that the Congress reserved the right to interpret the plan as it saw fit. That was a cause for relief for Muhammad Ali Jinnah, who anyway had been under pressure from his fellow Muslim Leaguers for having accepted the plan in the first place. Nehru's statement led swiftly to Jinnah's backing out of the plan, and partition now seemed inevitable (Brown 2003: 162–164).

According to Dalrymple (2015), Jinnah felt eclipsed by the rise of Gandhi and Nehru as he was booed off the Congress Party stage when he stubbornly insisted on calling his rival 'Mr Gandhi' rather than referring to his spiritual title, *Mahatma* – 'Great Soul'. The mutual dislike naturally grew and by 1940, Jinnah had steered the Muslim League towards demanding a separate homeland for Muslims. Interestingly, much later in August 1947, in his first address to the Constituent Assembly of Pakistan, a secular Jinnah had said: 'You may belong to any religion, or caste, or creed – that has nothing to do with the business of the State'. But it was too late, as by then, the violence between Hindus and Muslims had spiralled beyond control.

The growing nature of communalism had been clearly felt at the end of the 1930s and in March 1940, the All India Muslim League publicly declared for the first time its intention to establish an independent Muslim State structure in India. On 23 March 1940, the League adopted a resolution in Lahore whereby it demanded the creation of independent Muslim States in the north-west and east of India. One might add here that this concept of two distinct Muslim States was later subverted by Jinnah in 1946 when he had the term 'States' replaced by 'State', perhaps a calculated act that would eventually create a single Muslim State comprising the northwest and east of India. Consequently, in 1947, the Indian subcontinental map was changed by the British to reflect borders between India and Pakistan, further creating a geographically impractical West and East Pakistan.

Matters were seriously aggravated during the All India Muslim League's call for observance of Direct Action Day by Muslims on 16 August 1946 in support of the demand for Pakistan. Jinnah did not specify the nature of the Direct Action Day he was proposing or who it was aimed against. The Chief Minister of Bengal, Huseyn Shaheed Suhrawardy, a prominent figure in the All India Muslim League, called for a shut down all over Bengal on 16 August 1946 in deference to Jinnah. Suhrawardy had in the months leading up to Partition in 1947, along with Sarat Chandra Bose, mooted for the 'United Bengal' proposal in an attempt to prevent the partition of Bengal. Much criticism has been levelled against Suhrawardy, who was perceived to be unleashing the Direct Action Day, acting in a partisan manner and ignoring the fact that he was the chief minister of 'all' the communities of Bengal. According to French (2011: 250–251), the initial provocation in Calcutta came from processions of Muslim Leaguers, 'well armed with *lathis*, iron rods and missiles', marching to listen to Suhrawardy. On the way, they were greeted by Hindus throwing stones and bricks. Suhrawardy delivered a fiery speech in support of Pakistan at the Maidan in Calcutta. Once the rally ended, Muslims and Hindus, driven by communalism and heavily armed with lethal weapons, suddenly went into a spree of attacks on shops and homes in the city. Although Suhrawardy may have encouraged violence, the last thing he needed was mass communal unrest which might unseat his ministry. French continues (2011: 251) that, as the violence became serious, Suhrawardy went to the control room of the commissioner of police in Lal Bazar and attempted to interfere in operations in his capacity as the province's home minister. As one British official noted, he 'showed an exasperating preoccupation with the sufferings undergone by members of his own community.' But by then, the communal violence had spread like fire throughout the poorer districts of Calcutta and to the docks. Although the exact course of the Great Calcutta Killings and the precise communal identity and motivation of the killers have never been properly documented, it is certain that both sides suffered terrible violence and loss (French 2011: 250). The four days of communal violence left thousands dead on the streets of Calcutta, with repercussions being felt in Bihar and Noakhali in Eastern Bengal. In the course of the Calcutta riots, the situation became so out of hand that no one really controlled the various League's factions and it was not until Gandhi wisely intervened that the vicious rioting came to an end. The riots had clinched the argument for Pakistan (Ahsan 2014: 3). The consequential partition of India and Pakistan (west and east) in 1947 saw the largest migration in human history.

Emergence of Islam in Bengal

One of the residues of the pre-colonial and colonial past has been the manner in which Islam has evolved over the centuries in the subcontinent, especially in the area now known as Bangladesh. Uddin (2006: 21) notes that Islam spread in Bangladesh not through the edicts and efforts of Muslim rulers – in fact they were regarded as demonstrating little interest in converting indigenous people to Islam – but through a small religious class of Sufis, such as Baba Adam Shahid of Rampal and Shah Sultan Rumi. These men had visited the north-eastern region of the subcontinent before the major Muslim political concepts of the eleventh and twelfth centuries. Other men with varying degrees of, and specialisation in, Islamic knowledge imparted their understanding of Islam to the people of Bengal. Bengali Muslims, in particular those from the Chittagong and Sylhet districts of Bangladesh, claim contact with Muslim Sufis in the early centuries of *Hijrah* – the seventh and eighth centuries A.D. (Khan 1985: 835). Such ideological impact, more through Muslim missionaries than the naturalised political élite, probably explains why the masses rather than the landed élite became the first converts to Islam in Bengal. This is in marked contrast to the conversion resulting from political conquests in the northwestern and north–central parts of the subcontinent. In the latter case, Muslim conquest transformed the large bulk of the indigenous political élite into part of a new Islamic ruling class. Centuries later, the modal difference in ideological conversion between the north-western and north-eastern Muslims of the subcontinent was to lead to a gigantic misunderstanding of the ways and means to attain the objectives and goals of the initially united nation of Pakistan.

Since Sufism as a philosophical system has aspects in common with the *Vedanta* of the Hindus in Bengal, the Islam that evolved locally, according to some authors (Roy 1987: 11–34), had elements of a cultural practice that wore a distinctive locally coloured Bengali personality. It gave it a liberal outlook and a syncretic character, where customs and traditions from Hinduism were assimilated into Bengali Muslim culture regarding dresses, dance, music, festivals and language, hand in hand with practising Islam. This brand of Islam followed by Bengali Muslims, deeply in consonance with the local Bengali culture of the region, has increasingly come under pressure over time from political Islam that has been travelling across the world, particularly from West Asia, with the advent of the new interplay of geopolitics among various powers. There seems to have been a demand to purge these Bengali elements from religious, traditional and cultural practices because they are not permitted in the perceived true essence of Islam (Hasan 2011).

Over the years, in contemporary Bangladesh, this trend of reinforcing Islam minus the Bengali cultural element has acquired a strong political presence. The struggle between political Islam and Islam influenced by Bengali culture has been one of the most significant contentions to take place in Bangladesh post partition and, most particularly, post independence in Bangladesh. Faced with terrorist attacks over the past few years, the situation has often morphed into one where the State had to become involved as the adjudicator – a scene more visible during the military periods, and hence State formation has to be seen in the light of this cultural battle for the soul of Bangladesh – basically about what kind of Muslim nation Bangladesh is to become. Given that the struggle over national identity can broadly be defined as secular nationalists versus religious nationalists, other factions such as the Jamaat-e-Islami (JIB) party have their own agendas (Uddin 2006: 136). This book observes that this cultural tension is significant because the goal of the contending groups is to first inhabit the symbolic spaces of the public sphere, especially the symbolic actions of the State when it goes about its public rituals, and then to create an impact on everyday practices and the world views of the ordinary citizen.

There was a good historical reason for the development among the Bengali Muslims of a separate cultural and linguistic consciousness, which significantly differentiated them from the Muslims of central and north-western India. The thirteenth, fourteenth and fifteenth century pre-colonial era epitomised the peak of Islamic conversion in Bengal. Both the Sufis and the Muslim conquerors converged in the area but the geographical distance from their homelands compelled them to seek maximum *de facto* independence from any central authority. Distance also deprived both missionaries and conquerors of the opportunity to tap the political and scriptural resources of the Middle East to the extent possible by their counterparts in north-western India (Russell 1972: 25). In the sixteenth century, when the numbers of Muslim conquerors and Sufis considerably thinned, necessity dictated that the Bengali Muslim political and religious élite re-emphasised not only the socio-economic egalitarianism of Islam but also Bengali culture and language. This was clearly a response to the challenge posed by a plebeian appeal of Hindu revivalists under *Vaishnavaite* influence. Preachers like Chaitanya and Nityananda came up, as well as the development of a special Hindu system of rituals by the Sapta Goswami (Sarkar 1977: 220–224). Khan (1985: 838) indicated that historically, Muslim rulers at the turn of the sixteenth century had attempted to spread Islam and its egalitarian ideology in Bengal and became the patrons of Bengali literature to expand Islamic influence in Bengal. Muslim missionaries, on the other hand, took great caution for fear of diluting Qur'anic meaning if translated into Bengali. Thus, the missionaries and preachers indirectly contributed to the strengthening of linguistic nationalism among Bengali Muslims, which later developed gradually into full-fledged Bengali Muslim nationalism. Khan (1985: 839) further noted that during the nineteenth and early twentieth century, a section of the Bengali Muslim élite considered Persian and later Urdu as their language despite the erosion of political power under the British rule, disregarding the masses of common Bengali Muslims whose general medium of communication was Bengali. The élite considered Bengali a language to be associated with the Hindu élite of Bengal and thus neglected Bengali literature by urban, educated Muslims as well as folk literature produced by the rural Bengali Muslim masses. Not until the 1930s did poets representing rural Muslim masses, such as Kazi Nazrul Islam and Kazi Imdadul Huq, succeed in competing with the Bengali Hindu literati in their contribution to the Bengali language, thus shortening the distance between the Muslim élite and the masses. It was noted, much later and not until the middle of the twentieth century, that the élite lent their support to the linguistic nationalism that ultimately led to a political movement in the post-partition period, eventually culminating in the emergence of Bangladesh.

Just as most ideologies undergo periods of dormancy and resurgence, Islam too went through a renaissance in Asia during the eighteenth and nineteenth centuries with various movements, among which the Faraizi movement in Bengal had significant socio-political ramifications. Not only did the movement reinforce adherence to the five pillars of Islam, it rejected *shirk* (sinful innovation including the support or joining of Hindu rites and ceremonies), *pir* (spiritual leader) worship and *urs* (following death rituals of pirs). All these were, however, well established in Bengal during that time. This movement, which reasserted Islamic principles of equality and brotherhood of all Muslims, brought fresh converts from downtrodden sections of the local population, posing a threat to those sections of the élite with vested interests in the continuation and increase of social stratification of Bengali Muslim society. Both the Hindu and Muslim landlords openly challenged the Faraizi's new authority and practices which they felt served the interests of Muslim peasantry and the have-nots (Khan 1985: 840).

The political ramification of this movement became more pronounced when the Muslim peasantry did not challenge the authority's severe dictum because they perceived the decisions and actions of the Faraizi authorities as beneficial to their interests. This was especially so in protecting Muslims against both the growing exploitation of a rapidly rising class of Hindu landlords, traders, money lenders and the repressive practices of European indigo planters. There was tremendous support in the authority's success in strengthening the traditional *panchayat* system among the Bengali Muslims. This sought realisation of the Islamic concept of a fusion of religion and politics by seeking to bring the Islamic *Ummah* into the secular realities of day-to-day administration, irrespective of the economic and social classes. Under the aegis of the Faraizi movement, the seeds of Bengali Muslim nationalism, planted in the mid-nineteenth century, began to germinate and the catalytic role of the movement was carried forward by subsequent disciples in the later part of the nineteenth century and the early and second half of the twentieth century. Whether religious or political figures, they were instrumental in raising Bengali Muslim consciousness against exploitation by the colonial and post-colonial industrial entrepreneurial élite (Khan 1985: 840–841). This blending of religion and politics in the growing consciousness of Bengali Muslims in the twentieth century is crucial to the understanding of the political reality, including the history of democracy and its transition in the subcontinent. It also reverberates in the ongoing political struggles in Bangladesh today and the perceived ideological divide between the two major political parties, AL and BNP.

In the late nineteenth and early twentieth century, the predominantly Muslim peasants emerged as a class of small owner-cultivators and gradually began to appear as competitors to Hindu *zamindars*. The partition of Bengal in 1905 gave this burgeoning small owner-cultivator class ample opportunity to take advantage of education and employment and eventually flourish. Although the principal contradiction remained the same, as in the landed class versus the peasants, the former being Hindus and the latter Muslims, Muslim identity became the principal marker of difference and religion became a means of political mobilisation. The annulment of the partition of Bengal not only gave the Muslim landed class and the burgeoning middle class an opportunity to direct resentment against the colonial state but also discontent towards the Hindus who in general were opposed to the partition of Bengal, which was driven largely by economic interests. The Muslim leadership perceived this annulment as an anti-Muslim political project of the Hindus (Riaz 2016a: 190–191).

Muslim political activism spread through the eastern part of Bengal. The Khilafat Non-Cooperation Movement of 1919–1924, joined and strengthened by the peasants, eventually outgrew and outlived the Khilafat Movement itself as peasant politics went hand in hand with the constitutional politics of the urban bourgeoisie, playing a pivotal role in instigating mass consciousness among the people. Although peasants may have initiated civil disobedience, they altered their path, leading to mob violence against the agents of exploitation. This radicalisation brought an end to the movement as it rang alarm bells for the élite of both Congress and the Muslim League, who apprehended an uncontrolled and dangerous mass movement. Congress's abrupt withdrawal of support for the movement further fostered the perception that this was a largely Muslim movement (Riaz 2016a: 192).

According to Riaz (2016a: 192–193), prior to the partition in 1947, there was a fierce debate about community identity as the Muslim middle class began to found literary and social organisations, including publishing journals and periodicals. The issue of the language of these publications was at the centre of debate on whether Urdu or Arabic was to be used as the language of instruction and interaction, as a mark of Muslim identity, or whether Bengali was to be used, as it was the language of the community. This difference also reflected a social differentiation within the Muslim community as those claiming an immigrant ancestry, assumed to belong to a higher class (*ashraf*), suggested Urdu or Arabic while those who were from the middle class (*atraf*) preferred Bengali. The majority of Bengali Muslims were in favour of Bengali as the vehicle of their cultural consciousness, which is why Riaz (2016a: 193) notes that

> The argument that Bengalis of the eastern part of undivided Bengal rejected their Bengali identity and subscribed to the pan-Indian Islamic identity is erroneous.

Dr. Kamal Hossain (2013: 142), one of the framers of the 1972 Constitution, asserts that in post-independent Bangladesh, the spirit of secularism in the 1972 Constitution had the following ethos:

> Secularism stands for the rejection of communalism in all its forms and of the abuse of religion for political purposes ... [It] was very carefully worded so as to make clear that it did not stand for hostility to religion. The constitution-makers were fully conscious that the majority of the Bengali people were practising Muslims. The principle of secularism, as spelt out in the Constitution, was to maintain a separation between the state and religion and to create an environment in which all religious communities could coexist in harmony, free from discrimination and religious intolerance.

However, whatever vision the framers of the Constitution had about secularism, the issue of Bangladesh's struggle between religious nationalists and secularists remains even today, a continual phenomenon.

Thus, in today's Bangladesh, Riaz (2016a: 195) poignantly indicates that there are roughly three trends of Islam: a local syncretic Islam which arose since the beginning of the expansion of Islam in Bengal, whereby the impact of local traditions/customs has influenced religious interpretations and certain practices which remains the mainstay of Islam in Bangladesh; a Sufi variation of Islam which remained strong for centuries despite its differences with the dogmatic creeds of Islam; and an orthodox interpretation of Islam which became institutionalised initially through the *khanqa*'s of the saints but subsequently through institutions such as the *madrasahs*. One can go even further to add that the orthodox interpretation has been further reinforced by the influence of the labour class, whose remittances from earning a challenging living in the Middle East, especially in Saudi Arabia, has had a profound impact on the economy of Bangladesh, but whose families living in Bangladesh find a strong affinity with the *wahabi* customs of Saudi Arabia, which is discernible through their practices and attires.

The discussions on key issues in the preceding sections regarding the emergence and development of Islam in the subcontinent, including the impact that the British reign had in replacing the *zamindari* system and the consequential social metamorphosis as well as the rise of linguistic nationalism, have had an important and lasting bearing on the legal, social and political framework of the subcontinent, including the forming of individual mindsets of leaders. They continue to have an effect in the contextual analysis of the state of democracy in Bangladesh today. Keeping this in mind, we move on to the progression of democracy post-partition, during the Pakistan era, from what was to become Bangladesh in 1971.

Post-partition: Pakistan and its aftermath 1947–1971

The emergence of West and East Pakistan on 15 August 1947 saw the nation facing a number of major problems. Almost 12 million people were moving across the borders towards Pakistan and India (Zamindar 2010). During that time, millions of people perished in communal conflicts related to partition and mass migration. The boundaries of Pakistan were carved out according to the spread of the Muslim population, without considering economic viability. Pakistan did not inherit the elements of a functional State such as adequate personnel, infrastructure, a working capital, institutions and a parliament. Jalal (1995: 5) indicates that India had inherited the colonial State's central government apparatus and an industrial infrastructure, which for all its weaknesses was better developed than in the areas constituting Pakistan.

Partition, while it caused euphoria among Muslims, was also responsible for Muslim miseries given that in the West, large groups of Muslims from such places as today's Uttar Pradesh and East Punjab migrated to the new state of Pakistan. The Urdu-speaking Muslim migrants would, in time, come to be known as *mahajirs* who settled in and around Karachi, then the capital of the new nation (Brown 2003: 175–178).

In the East, similar migrations took place with large numbers of Muslims from Bihar moving to the Bengali-dominated East Pakistan. Conversely, affluent sections of Hindus as well as members of the teaching community made their way to West Bengal in the aftermath of partition. As the years went by, Bihari Muslims who had settled in East Pakistan came to identify themselves more with their linguistic compatriots in West Pakistan rather than assimilating themselves with the majority Bengali population. As they were increasingly seen to ally themselves with the vested interest base in West Pakistan, opposing all Bengali movements for political autonomy and economic emancipation, (Tripathi 2014: 28–30), they continue to face difficulties in being accepted in Bangladesh.

After partition, Muslim banking shifted from Bombay to Karachi. Much of the investment in East Pakistan came from West Pakistani banks. Investment was concentrated in jute production at a time when international demand was decreasing. The largest jute processing factory in the world, at Narayanganj, an industrial suburb of Dacca, was owned by the Adamjee family from West Pakistan. Because the banking and financing sectors were generally controlled by West Pakistanis, discriminatory practices gradually emerged and East Pakistanis found themselves increasingly excluded from managerial level and skilled labour positions. West Pakistanis tended to favour Urdu-speaking Biharis (refugees from the northern Indian state of Bihar living in East Pakistan), considering them to be less prone to labour agitation than the Bangladeshis. This preference became more pronounced after explosive labour clashes between the Biharis and Bengalis in the East at the Narayanganj jute mill in 1954 (Choudhury 2011: 73–161).

In time, a growing sense of political and economic deprivation would alienate Bengalis in East Pakistan from West Pakistan, to a point where the seeds of Bengali nationalism would be sown within a very short period of time. Such disparity would only increase, especially during the decade of rule by Pakistan's first military ruler, Mohammad Ayub Khan, between October 1958 and March 1969. As many as 22 families, all based in West Pakistan, would dominate the national economy and in particular would be seen as symbols of exploitation by Bengalis who constituted 56 per cent of the country's population (Islam 2003: 62–68).

Pakistan faced a severe shortage of trained administrative personnel, as a significant number of the pre-independence Indian Civil Service officers were Hindus or Sikhs who opted to move to India at partition. Rarer still were Bengali Muslims with any past administrative experience. As a result, the high-level posts in Dacca, including that of Governor General, were usually filled by West Pakistanis or by refugees from India who had adopted Pakistani citizenship. In addition, one of the most divisive issues confronting Pakistan in its infancy was the question of what the official language of the new nation was to be. The Pakistani authorities yielded to the demands of the refugees from the Indian states of Bihar and Uttar Pradesh, who insisted that Urdu be Pakistan's official language. Those who spoke West Pakistan languages – *Punjabi, Sindhi, Pashtu,* and *Baluchi* – were unhappy that their languages were given second-class status but they went along with Urdu as the state language (Wolpert 1984).

In East Pakistan, where the dominant local language was Bengali, the feeling was clearly one of growing disillusionment on the language question. It was on 25 February 1948 that a Bengali Hindu member of Pakistan's Constituent Assembly, Dhirandranath Datta, demanded on the floor of the House, that Bengali be adopted as a language of parliamentary deliberations besides English and Urdu. His demand was quickly shut down by none other than Prime Minister Liaquat Ali Khan, who saw in it a conspiracy to divide the people of Pakistan.

The Bengalis, however, constituted a demographic majority of Pakistan's entire population and their language Bangla (then commonly known as Bengali), shares a common ancestor – Sanskrit – with Hindi. Bangla was quite a contrast to Urdu and Persian whose partial ancestry was Arabic. Therefore, Bangla and Urdu have quite naturally two very different scripts and literary traditions (Ahsan 2014: 20–21).

Muhammad Ali Jinnah, the founder of independent Pakistan and its first Governor General visited East Pakistan on only one occasion after independence, in March 1948. He addressed a public meeting on 19 March 1948 and declared that Urdu alone should be the state language of Pakistan. On 24 March 1948, when he reiterated the same statement at a convocation in Dacca University, students protested against his statement and he modified his position on the issue declaring that in his opinion Urdu should be the state language of Pakistan as it would be good for the solidarity of the country (Muhith 1992: 85–86). Jinnah's views were not accepted by most East Pakistanis, but perhaps in tribute to the founder of Pakistan, serious resistance on this issue did not break out until after his death in September 1948. On 21 February 1952, a demonstration took place in Dacca in which students demanded equal status for Bangla, when it became clear that Jinnah's successor Khwaja Nazimuddin would not budge from Jinnah's insistence on Urdu. The provisional government, led by Chief Minister Nurul Amin imposed section 144 of the Criminal Procedure Code (1898), prohibiting gatherings of more than four persons, as a way of preventing any rallies by the students. On 21 February 1952, the students violated section 144 at the University and raised slogans in favour of Bengali. The police reacted by firing mercilessly on the crowd, killing many students (Ahsan 2014: 22–26).

The merciless shootings of 21 February 1952 sent shock waves across both wings of Pakistan. In retrospect, the incidents of the day have been considered as the first step towards the growth of secular Bengali nationalism. The language movement would in time lead to more sustained struggles for greater political expressions. Two years after the incident, the agitation effectively forced the National Assembly to designate 'Urdu and Bengali and such other languages as may be declared' to be the official languages of Pakistan (Ahsan 2014: 22–26).

Initially what perhaps kept the new country, East and West Pakistan, together was the vision and forceful personalities of Muhammad Ali Jinnah, and Liaquat Ali Khan. However, after Jinnah died, the seat of power shifted and Liaquat, who had extensive experience in politics and understood the pulse of the people, asserted himself as an all-powerful Prime Minister (Jinnah was succeeded as Governor General by Khwaja Nazimuddin). As a refugee from India too, he had the additional benefit of not being too closely identified with any one province of Pakistan. A moderate, Liaquat subscribed to the ideals of a parliamentary, democratic, and secular State. Out of necessity, he considered the wishes of the country's religious spokesmen, who championed the cause of Pakistan as an

Islamic State. He was perhaps seeking a balance between Islam and secularism for a new Constitution when he was assassinated on 16 October 1951, by those opposed to Liaquat's refusal to wage war against India. With the swift demise of these early leaders, Pakistan faced an unstable period that was temporarily resolved by military and civil service intervention in political affairs. The first few turbulent years after independence thus defined the enduring politico–military culture of Pakistan (Ahsan 2014: 12–18), which perhaps, to some extent, also seeped into independent Bangladesh.

The inability of Pakistan's politicians to provide a stable government arose largely as a result of their mutual suspicions and lack of trust. Loyalties tended to be personal, ethnic and provincial rather than national and issue-oriented. Provincialism was openly expressed in the deliberations of the Constituent Assembly. In this Assembly, frequent arguments voiced the fear that the West Pakistani province of Punjab would dominate the nation. Ultimately an ineffective body, the Constituent Assembly took almost nine years to draft a Constitution in 1956, which for all practical purposes, was never put into effect.

Besides, there were inherent flaws in the Constitution. In the first place, all the four provinces of Western Pakistan were grouped into a single province known as West Pakistan under a 'one unit scheme'. In the second, the Constitution did away with the majority status of East Pakistan, whose 56 per cent population was now brought at par with the 46 per cent population of West Pakistan in the name of parity. Ironically, it was Suhrawardy, who was now Pakistan's Law Minister and one of the founders of the Awami League, who claimed that the 1956 Constitution had given East Pakistan 98 per cent autonomy. The Constitution would last a mere two years and would be abrogated since Martial Law was declared in October 1958 (Ahsan 2006: 84–88).

Muhith (1992: 61) also reiterates, in similar lines to Khan (Khan, H. 2009), that from the beginning, Constitution-making presented formidable problems to the polity of Pakistan. The degree of commitment to the concept of Pakistan varied greatly between West Pakistan and East Pakistan as mutual sacrifices were not forthcoming and mistrust dominated. While democracy never seemed to appeal to West Pakistan, East Pakistan stood firmly committed to it. The nature of the society in the two regions was also primarily responsible for such a difference in approach and attitude. West Pakistan continued to be a medieval feudal society where all the authority was commanded by an élite group consisting of landlords, bureaucrats and military officers, who were being joined by the nouveau riche. On the other hand, East Pakistan had a somewhat less stratified culture where individualism, egalitarianism, social mobility and also some measure of anarchy and defiance of authority flourished. In view of these fundamental differences, it became difficult to find a meeting point on the basic law of the land (Muhith 1992: 61). Besides the issue of representation and national language, the real question was whether Pakistan would be a democracy where power could at times be transferred to the East Pakistanis because of their clear numerical majority, or would it be an oligarchy protecting the interests of West Pakistani social élites?

Jahan (2005: 66) observes that the Bengalis had to defend not only the right to practise their own language in East Pakistan but also other expressions of their culture – literature, music, dance, arts. The Pakistani ruling élite looked upon Bangla language and culture as too Hindu-leaning and made repeated attempts to cleanse it of Hindu influence. In the 1950s, attempts were made to force Bengalis to substitute Bangla words with Arabic and Urdu words. Beginning as early as 1948, Urdu and Arabic were inserted into the Bengali language, ostensibly to promote what the central leadership defined as Pakistani culture. This led to certain comical situations, reflected in such areas as Bengali news-reading from State-controlled Radio Pakistan.

A major step in the growth of Bengali nationalism was the move by a section of liberal Bengali intellectuals to observe the birth centenary of the poet Nobel Laureate Rabindranath Tagore in 1961. The Ayub Khan military regime put pressure on the organisers to desist from such action but was unable to prevent it when a respected legal luminary, Justice Syed Mahbub Morshed of the East Pakistan High Court, presided over the Tagore celebration. In effect, these celebrations were a clear demonstration of Bengalis moving away from the Two Nation Theory of the 1940s towards the concept of Bengali nationhood in the early 1960s. The fact that the Ayub regime imposed a ban on Tagore in 1967 only spurred the movement on, eventually leading to a full blown nationalistic movement in the early 1970s (Ahsan 2014: 65–66).

The attacks on their language and culture also alienated Bengalis in East Pakistan from the State-sponsored Islamic ideology of West Pakistan and intensified their linguistic–ethnic identity that emphasised a more secular ideology and attitude despite being Muslims. The ethnic divide between the two parts grew more rather than narrowing.

Choudhury (1993: 8–10) notes that the Bengalis' most serious complaint was of what they called the economic exploitation of East Pakistan by the Pakistan central government. It had been said by many impartial economists, American and British that the economic development of East Pakistan was sadly neglected and that something ought to be done about it. Since political power was exercised by a narrow oligarchy which looked at the whole situation entirely from the colonial angle of maintaining law and order, it was futile to expect any imaginative economic programme or plans. At the time of independence, efforts were made to speed up economic growth but tragically the rate of economic growth was much slower in East Pakistan than in West Pakistan. Many figures have been published to illustrate this disparity convincingly demonstrating the extent to which the East's interests were completely neglected (Choudhury 1993: 9). The bulk of the country's revenue was spent in West Pakistan, because the federal capital was there. Moreover, a high percentage of the budget was spent on defence, which was almost all concentrated in West Pakistan. So did a much larger share of government expenditure, as well as foreign aid and loans. East Pakistan earned most of the country's foreign exchange, due to the export of jute, yet most of this foreign exchange too was spent on the industrialisation of West Pakistan (Choudhury 1993: 9).

Whether it was revenue or development expenditure, foreign assistance and loans of foreign exchange, East Pakistan did not get its fair share, though it contained the majority of the country's population. A report made by a panel of experts to the Pakistan Government's Planning Commission in 1970 provides authoritative documentation of the increasing economic disparity between the two regions. The most striking fact in this report was the widening gap between the income of the average West Pakistani and its Eastern counterpart. It was difficult for any East Pakistani, whether a regionalist or a nationalist, to watch this situation with equanimity. The economic disparity or economic exploitation provided their politicians with powerful weapons to win popular support (Islam 2003: 61–76).

It was against such a background of exploitation that a decisive move was made by the charismatic and courageous leader Sheikh Mujibur Rahman, then general secretary of the East Pakistan AL, to demand widespread autonomy for East Pakistan. The Six Points that he publicly announced in February 1966, were as follows (Hossain 2013: 20–21):

1 The Constitution should provide for a federation of Pakistan on the basis of the Lahore Resolution of March 1940, envisaging a parliamentary form of government elected on the basis of adult universal suffrage;
2 The federal government, under the scheme envisaged thus would deal only with the subjects of foreign affairs and defence; all other subjects being placed under the authority of the federating units;
3 Two separate but briefly convertible currencies would be introduced for the two wings of the country or in the event of such a system not coming into place, a single currency for the whole country with the proviso that flight of capital from East Pakistan to West Pakistan and vice versa would be constitutionally prevented, would suffice;
4 The power of taxation and revenue collection would be vested in the federating units but the federation would be entitled to a share in the revenues based on the agreement of the federating units to meet its expenditures;
5 There would be two separate accounts for foreign exchange earnings of the two wings of the country, with the foreign exchange requirements of the central government being met by the two wings equally or in ratio to be decided upon; indigenous products would move free of duty between the two wings, with the federating units empowered to establish trade links with countries abroad;
6 East Pakistan would be empowered to raise and maintain a separate militia or paramilitary force.

Incidentally, Mujib announced the Six Point Plan in Lahore, the very city where the Muslim League had adopted its Pakistan Resolution on 23 March 1940. On 5 February 1966, Mujib revealed his plan at a press conference after his attempts to announce the plan at the conference of Pakistan's opposition leader then in Lahore, were rejected (Hossain 2013: 19).

The response to the Six Points was swift and scathing. Mujib's fellow opposition politicians thought they would lead to Pakistan's break up. President Ayub Khan threatened to use the language of weapons against those who propagated and supported the Six Points. His foreign minister Zulfikar Ali Bhutto challenged Mujib to a public debate on the Six Points at Dhaka's Paltan Maidan. On Mujib's behalf, his lieutenant Tajuddin Ahmed took up the challenge. In the end, Bhutto did not turn up for the debate. Mujib was arrested on 8 May 1966 under the DPR (Defence of Pakistan Rules) and he did not come out of jail till February 1969. That the Six Points resonated with Bengali sentiments was made amply clear on 7 June 1966, when the AL enforced a successful general strike all over East Pakistan (Ahsan 2014: 88).

It was mainly the lack of political participation and exclusion from State power that drove the Bengalis of East Pakistan from demanding participation to demanding autonomy and finally to demanding self-determination and separation from West Pakistanis. Constituting a majority of the population, the Bengalis expected to dominate or at least share the political power in the federal government of Pakistan. In any system of representative democracy, the Bengalis would be in a position to use their majority in parliament to dominate or at least significantly influence the central government. However, this was anathema to the civil and defence officials and their allies among important West Pakistani landed and business class families. So although landlord politicians in the western wing had no intention of becoming junior partners to various non-elected institutions, the need to prevent Bengali domination of the State led them into an uneasy alliance with civil bureaucrats and military officials who were increasingly coming to define State imperatives in terms of their own more narrowly focused institutional interests (Jalal 1995: 50–51). Moreover, the central government of Pakistan did not only have strained relations with its provinces which were hardly conducive for smooth functioning of political processes. It also had to base its reliance on the civil bureaucrats for central leadership to keep the State going. Hence, it was not merely the absence of democratic ideals that spurred Pakistan's political leaders into seeking comfort in bureaucratic authoritarianism.

This alliance of mixed conveniences worked to undermine the role of parliament in the evolving structure of the State. No free democratic national election was held until 1970. Indeed, the country's first general election had been expected in February 1959 but the military coup of October 1958 had nullified that possibility. In 1962, Ayub Khan imposed his own Constitution on the country. It had no room for adult franchise but stipulated an electoral college of 80,000 members, 40,000 each for East and West Pakistan, who would elect the President and members of the National Provincial Assemblies. This Constitution collapsed when Ayub Khan was forced down from power on 25 March 1969 and was replaced by the country's second military ruler, General Yahya Khan (Chowdhury 1993).

As indicated earlier, Constitution making in Pakistan took nine years due to fierce disagreements on how political and financial powers were to be apportioned between the centre and the provinces and whether Pakistan was to have an Islamic or a secular form of government. A parliament elected in 1945–1946, on the basis of restricted franchise under the Government of India Act 1935, acted as both a legislature and constitutional body. Its unrepresentative character, its inability to draft provisions for a constitutional government and the tendency of the executive to bypass it and rule by ordinance, ensured that Pakistan's first parliament lost all credibility, with disastrous consequences for the future of the representative system. Without an effective legislative organ, it is particularly difficult for a political party system to strike roots. The supremacy of the executive over not only the legislative, but also the judicial organ of the State, was established fairly early in Pakistan's history. Without judicial autonomy from the executive, there was no effective way to address the State's infringement of fundamental rights. Undermining the legislative and judicial institutions of the State was intrinsic to the process of strengthening central authority. This suited the bureaucratic–military combined alliance among the dominant classes in West Pakistan to further undermine and neglect the interests of East Pakistan. It can be seen here that both democratic principles per se and fair power sharing between West and East Pakistan were casualties of this wrangling.

Seven years before the first military takeover in 1958, the political process in Pakistan had thus slipped off the rails. A succession of unelected civil bureaucrats assumed elective office between the years 1951–1954. A series of dismissals and curbing of powers during that time accentuated by the unrepresentative character of State institutions set damaging precedents for future relations between the executive and legislative arms of the State. It was judicial complicity with the executive rather than force of popular opinion that determined the outcome of Pakistan's first and most decisive constitutional crisis. In the early 1950s, the Supreme Court dismissed a petition by the speaker of the Constituent Assembly against the dismissal of the Assembly by the Governor General Golam Mohammad. In the late 1950s, Chief Justice Munir validated Ayub Khan's martial law regime by putting forward a so-called 'doctrine of necessity' relying famously on Kelsen's theory of law. Backed by civil bureaucracy and government controlled media, as well as the judiciary's support to this alliance, citing the principle of 'necessity', this brought in an uneasy balance between State formation and political processes in Pakistan. The centre now had all the necessary powers, legislative administrative and financial, to overwhelm the quantum of autonomy granted to the provinces and tear down the façade of parliamentary democracy. According to Jalal (1995: 55), the military and civil bureaucracy of Pakistan followed their international patrons – the centres of international system in London and Washington during the height of the cold war – aimed at depoliticising the Pakistani society on the face of mass mobilisation. The military intervention under Ayub Khan in 1958 unveils the shift from elected to non-elected institutions into the foray of experimentation of governance – some more authoritarian than others. The military regime felt that parliamentary government based on the Westminster model was unsuited for a highly personalised society like Pakistan where patron–client and clan-based ties determined the nature of politics. What Pakistanis needed was some form of controlled democracy, the emphasis being more on control rather than democracy.

The birth of a nation: Bangladesh

Despite the draconian powers which existed during the military regime of Ayub, the nervousness of the authorities resorted to accusing Sheikh Mujibur Rahman, in the *Agartala Conspiracy* case – the allegation being that he was conspiring with India to force the breakaway of East Pakistan. Mujib's imprisonment and subsequent trial served to further enrage the Bengali majority. The Six Points programme for provincial autonomy by the Awami League, justified on account of wide economic disparities between the two wings, as well as the inadequate representation of Bengalis in the services, was further intensified by the conspiracy case. Defiance of State authority in the East, along with labour and student strikes, created an atmosphere more akin to social anarchy than controlled politics.

The Yahya regime acceded to a number of key demands of the Bengali nationalist movement including the holding of the first ever free democratic national election on the basis of 'one man one vote' in 1970, two decades after the birth of the country, resulting in sweeping victory of the AL in the East and the Pakistan People's Party (PPP) in the West. In the 313 seat National Assembly, AL obtained 167 seats of the 169 apportioned for East Pakistan. In West Pakistan, Bhutto's PPP, which he had formed in November 1967 after leaving the Ayub government, obtained 88 seats. Pakistan government's worst fear at this time was that convening the National Assembly in Dhaka would severely diminish its control and would place the armed forces in a precarious position. Given the AL's overwhelming majority, for all practical purposes the East would be under alien control (Sisson and Rose 1990: 81). In a bid to delay transfer of power, the Yahya regime postponed indefinitely the scheduled third session of parliament, which threw the country into another constitutional crisis (Chowdhury 1993). Based on majoritarian principles, the country would now have to have a Bengali-led government. But West Pakistan could not swallow that reality.

Yahya's action came after Bhutto had threatened to boycott the National Assembly session scheduled for 1 March 1971 unless Mujib modified his Six Points programme. The AL responded by launching an unprecedented non-violent, non-cooperation movement which resulted in a virtual standstill of the entire administration including the government bureaucracy of East Pakistan. Bengali nationalists had the full support of the Bengali people, as demonstrated by their support for the *de facto* administration Mujib ran in East Pakistan between 1–25 March 1971.

With the intensity of the movement growing, on 7 March 1971, Mujib stepped onto the dais of the Dacca Race Course in order to announce his next course of action to a massive rally. As a crowd of million people armed with bamboo staves, as a sign of defiance of the Pakistan army, raised slogans in favour of independence, Pakistani military helicopters circled overhead to keep an eye on Mujib and the crowd. There was palpable fear that the army would strike but that did not deter the crowd from the enthusiasm in favour of a declaration of independence. Ahsan (2014: 154–155) vividly describes how Mujib slowly ticked off his demands one by one: the first demand being the withdrawal of Martial Law; second, the withdrawal of soldiers to the barracks; third, the calling for a swift judicial inquiry into the army shootings that had taken the lives of a number of Bengalis throughout the province; fourthly, the regime's immediate transfer of power to the elected representatives of the people. Ahsan (2014: 155) poignantly observes that Mujib's speech was a remarkable indication of the way he manoeuvred his way out of a challenging situation where he strategically avoided an outright declaration of independence to save his people by depriving the military regime of Pakistan of any excuse to launch an armed assault on the rebellious province, hence holding back from directly treading into the road for independence. His directives to the people in the rally were meaningful and crystal clear as he declared most famously that: 'The *struggle* this time is a *struggle* for emancipation; the *struggle* this time is the *struggle* for independence' for 'Bangladesh' – the name being then used for East Pakistan. The wild cheer of the crowd echoed relentlessly. (Tripathi 2014: 64–71).

Although it appeared as if the Bengalis' direct declaration of independence was averted in the rally for now, but the Yahya regime took this as a sign for negotiations and to that effect initiated political negotiations with the Bengali nationalists, yet at the same time shrewdly mobilised the armed forces for military action to crush the Bengali nationalist movement. On 25 March 1971, he abruptly broke off the negotiations and flew back to West Pakistan. Ahsan (2014: 156) remarks that ironically what Mujib tried to avoid quite naively at the rally on 7 March 1971 – an immediate military assault on the Bengali people – could not eventually be averted. That assault was brutally unleashed by the Pakistan army on 25 March 1971 with a massive strike against the Dhaka population, killing hundreds of citizens and arresting Mujib – all in one night (Tripathi 2014: 82–83).

What followed can only be described as a premeditated genocide (Jahan 2005: 68). Initially it appeared like a 'selective genocide' as there was an extraordinarily brutal crackdown on the 'Bengalis as a racial or cultural group' – both the Muslim majority and the Hindu minority were exterminated and/or targeted to be exterminated. There was a racial prejudice between Punjabis and Bengalis, as one would hear snide remarks from the soldiers that these 'Bengali people are less religious, our own little brothers'. Some West Pakistanis even scorned Bengalis, the Muslim majority, as weak and debased by too much exposure to Hindus among them (Bass 2014: 81). So the depth of racial hatred felt by the West Pakistanis towards the East manifested itself through a horrific genocide – although due to global politics at that time, the extent of the massacre did not get its due coverage. On 26 March 1971, excluded from their rightful place in the governance of the country, the Bengali majority decided to part ways with West Pakistan and declared the formation of a sovereign independent State of

Bangladesh. Moments before his arrest, Mujib declared Bangladesh's independence and his declaration was transmitted via EPR's transmitter from Dhaka to Chittagong and the rest of the country (Salik 1997).

In early April 1971, soon after he had crossed over into India, Tajuddin Ahmed met Prime Minister Indira Gandhi in Delhi and asked for diplomatic recognition for the new State of Bangladesh. Mrs Gandhi, aware that no administrative structure yet existed for the new State, advised the Bengali leader to have a government in place first. A provisional government of Bangladesh, the *Mujibnagar* government, was formed on 10 April 1971 by Tajuddin Ahmed with himself as Bangladesh's first Prime Minister and comprising of senior AL leaders who had managed to escape to India (Ahsan 2014: 173–178).

The *Mujibnagar* government recognised the difficulties involved in trying to wage war against the well-equipped Pakistan army. On the one hand, it was in need of Indian material assistance and on the other, it was necessary for it to shape a strategy for military action on its own. It was therefore that the Bangladesh liberation force, or the *Mukti Bahini,* was formed within weeks of the formation of the government.

According to Raghavan (2013: 71), in a broadcast on 11 April 1971, Tajuddin Ahmed had announced the establishment of the military command, naming various sector commanders. However, the relationship between the political leadership and the military officers was not easy as the politicians felt that 'there was a tendency among some army leaders to take up absolute leadership of the movement'. During that time, Major Ziaur Rahman when proclaiming independence on behalf of arrested Mujib also opportunistically declared himself as the leader of the provisional government (Salik 1997: 75), and as a result he had to be pointedly 'instructed not to make any such further announcements'.

The initial reluctance of the Indian government to directly support Bangladesh's independence movement in the early stages of the war was a subtle fear of Bengali nationalism enveloping the state of West Bengal. Such fears were short lived and soon, as early as April 1971, Indira Gandhi was mulling over a war with Pakistan. At a meeting attended by senior cabinet ministers as well as General Manekshaw, the Army Chief, the Indian Prime Minister wanted to know from Manekshaw his views on a possible military conflict between India and Pakistan. As Manekshaw was to relate later, he told Mrs. Gandhi that at that point, the army was unprepared to engage in war and that even if there were any thoughts of an offensive in the monsoon, it will be difficult for the army to handle a situation where much of East Pakistan would be under water. He did not foresee any offensive before the end of the monsoon period (Tripathy 2014).

There was a certain sense of unease as the Indian soldiers thought that the politicians were not doing enough to meet their requirements and assist their military operations (as many politicians were in hiding in India or killed or imprisoned by the Pakistan army) whilst the politicians who acted as activists against the Pakistani regime over a long period of time were weary of the soldiers' approach to the struggle for independence and as a result, 'meetings between the two sets of leaderships tended to have an acrimonious edge. This in turn bred a degree of mistrust among the Bangladesh leaders about India's intentions' (Raghavan 2013: 71–72) which was eventually addressed, as P N Haksar (foremost Adviser of the Indian Prime Minister Indira Gandhi and an erudite and experienced diplomat) reminded Prime Minister Indira Gandhi prior to her meeting with Tajuddin Ahmed that Bangladesh should not suspect India's motives. Much to Indian BSF's (Border Security Force) chagrin, instructions came from New Delhi for BSF to act under the broad directions issued by the Indian army's eastern command with the overall aim 'to assist the government of Bangladesh in rallying people in support of the liberation movement' and to 'raise, equip and train East Bengal cadres for guerrilla operations in their own native land' (Raghavan 2013: 72–73). Indeed, the Indian army had direct orders to help the Bangladeshi rebels, involving India's top generals, as India secretly helped the insurgents buy weapons and ammunitions (Bass 2014: 179).

Indira Gandhi, whilst reiterating the broad contours of military strategy to Tajuddin Ahmed was concerned about *Mujibnagar* government's ability to work with this military strategy, as Awami League showed its 'unwillingness to collaborate with other political parties or individuals without party cards'. Its insistence that 'every recruit should be politically certified' which resulted in the 'rejection of hundreds of eager, able-bodied Bengali youth for guerrilla training' (Bhattacharjee 1973: 38), was countered by Indira Gandhi, as per Haksar's advice, urging Tajuddin that 'every attempt should be made irrespective of political party affiliations to evolve a commonly accepted programme of action on a national level'. This would allow the National Awami Party led by Muzaffar Ahmad, Abdul Hamid Khan Bhashani (a popular Islamic scholar and political leader who remained a rural-based politician renowned for selflessness and solidarity with the oppressed) and the East Pakistan Communist Party to join the liberation movement. It was quite clear that the provisional government would have to raise themselves above the purely party loyalties (Raghavan 2013: 73).

However, it was not until July 1971 that the *Mukti Bahini* was given a structured shape, with 11 sectors under 11 different military officers, being established for occupied Bangladesh as a whole. Between July–November 1971 therefore, the *Mukti Bahini* was able to conduct a good number of operations against the Pakistan army in different areas of the country.

Sisson and Rose (1990: 205) observed that while the Islamic states were unanimous in their rhetorical support of Pakistan, the degree of substantive military and financial assistance to Pakistan was much less than anticipated. India's military intervention in 1971 had almost no impact between New Delhi and the Islamic States. What is also curious, Sisson and Rose (1990) continue, is that while New Delhi gradually developed a well-defined policy on the Pakistani civil war, there were no serious efforts to engage in substantive discussions or negotiations with the Pakistani government with an objective to reach a compromise. Both New Delhi and Rawalpindi were making decisions on the basis of strongly held preconceptions about each other's behaviour and assumed that nothing could be achieved by the meeting of Mrs. Gandhi and General Yahya. Perhaps they were correct (Sisson and Rose 1990: 205).

By the time India entered the conflict directly on 3 December 1971, the situation had been considerably softened by the *Mukti Bahini* and it was rather easy for the joint command of the Indian army and the Bangladesh *Mukti Bahini* to compel Pakistan into surrender on 16 December 1971.

A significant reason behind India's need to see the conflict come to a quick end was the number of refugees it was being compelled to provide shelter to. By the end of November 1971, the states of West Bengal, Tripura and Assam were handling 10 million Bengali refugees, which meant dealing with the inability of the international community to come to their help on a larger scale. The influx of refugees can easily be imagined when as many as 100,000 refugees crossed the border into India on a single day (Tripathi 2014: 113–114).

The Pakistan army's ruthless campaign against Bengali resistance left three million dead according to Bangladesh government figures and generated an exodus of 10 million people into India. 200,000 Bengali women were raped by Pakistani soldiers (Ahsan 2014: 173–178). This and perhaps its volatile relation with Pakistan prompted the Indian government in December 1971 to deploy troops on the side of the Bangladeshi rebels to expedite the disintegration of Pakistan. Another strategic reason for India's involvement in the war is indicated by Van Schendel (2009: 174–175) in the following words:

> One of the concerns that had propelled India into invading the delta and installing a new government was a fear of radicalisation among the freedom fighters. The Indian regions surrounding Bangladesh were politically unstable: in the West Bengal Maoist revolutionaries, known as Naxalites, were active and so were various groups fighting for autonomy in North-east India. During the war many freedom fighters had begun to imagine a liberated Bangladesh not just as an independent State but also as a socialist society. This prospect worried India's policy makers for two reasons: First it might provide the Naxalites and other leftist rebels with strategic cross border links; and second, nationalisation of land in Bangladesh could lead to an exodus of dispossessed landholders to India. Ensuring a non radical government policy in Bangladesh was high on India's wish list, and this is why it threw its support squarely behind the AL leaders who had formed the Bangladesh government in exile in India during the war.

Bangladesh therefore emerged amidst a sacrifice of millions of lives. In elaborating about the atrocities committed by the Pakistan army, Bass (2014: 73) notes that as many as 6000 people were killed in less than a week in Dhaka alone. Nearly 93,000 Pakistani soldiers were taken prisoners and would subsequently be transferred to Prisoners of War camps in India (Tripathi 2014: 152–153). Anthony Mascarenhas (1986), one of the eight Pakistani journalists, taken on an officially sponsored trip to East Pakistan to show in a patriotic way the great job the Pakistan army was doing during the war, saw the extent of the genocide and sent his eyewitness account to the *Sunday Times* invoking for the first time the terms 'holocaust' and 'genocide', transfixing global attention with a single shaft of investigative journalism (Raghavan 2013: 132). Although *The New Nation* in Singapore and the *Saturday Review* in New York were covering the events as 'massacre' 'slaughter' or 'tragedy', none of those publications commanded the prestige of the *Sunday Times* and it is with Mascarenhas's article that global attention began to rise.

The debacle in East Pakistan, now Bangladesh, was the cumulative result of the Pakistani defence establishment's political rather than military failures. The military action in East Pakistan (Bangladesh) followed because of the inability of a manifestly authoritarian regime (West Pakistan) to preside over a fair transfer of power in the aftermath of the country's first general elections held in 1970 on the basis of universal adult franchise. Thus the seeds of peaceful transfer of power were lacking even during the Pakistan era – something which Bangladesh subsequently inherited amidst its already complex social, economic and political situation.

The atrocities of the genocide were not simply to terrorise the population into submission and punish them (and significantly their women) for their resistance, but there were also elements of racism in this act of genocide. The Pakistani army, consisting of mainly Punjabis, had always looked down upon the Muslim Bengalis as racially inferior, as mentioned earlier – a non-martial people (an image created by the British colonialists, which was readily accepted by the Pakistani ruling élite), a physically weak race, not interested or able to serve in the army (Marshall 1959, cited in Jahan 2005: 70). Jahan (2005) concludes that 'a policy of genocide against fellow Muslims was deliberately undertaken by the Pakistanis on the assumption of racial superiority and a desire to cleanse the Bengali Muslims of Hindu cultural and linguistic influence'. But now the Bangladeshis would have to manage their own nation, a much different challenge than many imagined, for the new country was of course not internally uniform, either. The wish-kite or *iccher ghuri* of the Bangladeshis was not going to be experiencing easy flying amidst fresh winds of change.

Post-independence: The Bangladesh era 1971–1990

It was a moment of great emotion and jubilation – 16 December 1971 – when 'Golden Bangladesh' (*Shonar Bangla*) attained its victory against Pakistan after a violent, bitterly fought and painful nine-month liberation war with an official figure of more than three million casualties. Sheikh Mujibur Rahman returned to war ravaged Bangladesh from imprisonment in Pakistan on 10 January 1972. Among the innumerable challenges faced by Mujib post-independence, Van Schendel (2009: 172–174) highlights three immediate issues confronting the young State, which needed attention: the first was how to cope with the collaborators, second, how to rehabilitate war victims and third, how to repair the massive damage caused by the war. Governance somewhat took a backseat at that point in time. Significantly, this list overlooks the management of internal diversities at several levels. Although the Pakistani prisoners of war and civil detainees were mostly taken by India as prisoners of war, there remained two more groups of collaborators to deal with in independent Bangladesh.

One group consisted of collaborators who remained in the country and who were members of paramilitary groups, death squads, citizens' committees, looters and informers, murderers and rapists – essentially those who were against the creation of Bangladesh and who had collaborated with the Pakistani regime (the *Razakars, Al Badr, Al Shams*). Although it was decided to bring these people before a Collaborators' Tribunal, to try them for war crimes in 1972, this simply did not happen. Instead, in a bid to unite the new nation, the government declared a general amnesty in 1973 to all persons except those who were punished or accused of rape, murder, attempted murder or arson. This was done in return for Pakistan's diplomatic recognition of Bangladesh and the repatriation of several thousands of Bangladeshis held in Pakistan. Hossain (2013: 128) notes that one of the considerations of this general amnesty was that it would advance the interests of national reconciliation. In retrospect, the amnesty did not appear to have advanced the cause of national reconciliation since many of the amnestied collaborators upon release, began to undermine the unity that had been attained, by rousing communal sentiments. It was not until 25 March 2010, four decades since independence, when at long last the International Crimes Tribunal Bangladesh (ICT) was created during the AL regime, to try the war criminals under the domestic legislation, the International Crimes Tribunal Act of 1973. The Act was promulgated to prosecute any persons, irrespective of nationality, accused of committing crimes against peace, crimes against humanity, war crimes, 'violations of any humanitarian rules applicable in armed conflicts laid out in the Geneva Convention of 1949' and 'any other crimes under international law'. The war crimes issue had remained live over all these years: political and military regimes came and went by, but the genocide was never dealt with, until the commencement of these trials (Ahsan 2014: 277–278).

The *Shahbag* protest of 2013 was a public demonstration of thousands of people, especially the youth, which began on 5 February 2013 in Dhaka, demanding capital punishment for one of the accused who received a life sentence and all the other accused war criminals of the 1971 liberation war of Bangladesh. The symbolic value of these voices and the manner of their protests are indicative of the collective demand of the people of Bangladesh wishing for the issue of war crimes to be put to rest once and for all. It is a realisation that the consolidation of democracy cannot happen without addressing the overdue issues of trying the war criminals and collaborators, who did not believe in the birth of this nation in the first place. The connection of this issue with one of the political parties in Bangladesh, the JIB, has posed and continues to pose major hurdles in laying this stressful and extremely damaging issue to rest. In the context of Bangladesh's electoral politics today, given that the trials of war criminals and collaborators is finally taking place after 42 years of independence, the perception of many is that only because the AL government is in power that the trial has begun and is continuing. There is serious doubt as to whether BNP, with its JIB alliance, if in power, will see the continuation of the trial. One of the electoral commitments of AL prior to the 2008 elections was the trial of war criminals, which resonated well with today's youth.

Another group which was a source of concern were the non-Bengali Muslims who had migrated after 1947 in Pakistan, where they were welcomed as *Mujahirs*. As a result, during the conflict with the Bangladeshi nationalists in 1971, most of them sided with the Pakistani authorities. Bangladeshis called them *Biharis*, (though all of them were not from Bihar) and they were branded as collaborators as many helped the Pakistani armed forces. Severe retribution followed and though most of these *Biharis* wished to be repatriated to Pakistan, as that is where their allegiance was, Pakistan was not ready to take them in (Hossain 2013).

In addition to the three million Bangladeshi people who died in 1971, there were many others who were maimed, traumatised, raped. Although the State honoured the raped victims as *'Birangana'* (brave heroines), in post-war Bangladesh, there was discrimination and ostracisation of these people, which was a grave issue for the new State. Moreover, the material damage caused by the war was extensive. Whatever little infrastructure there was in Bangladesh had been destroyed, agricultural production suffered – this grim legacy did not help the new nation.

Amidst all of this, the fundamental question remained who was to take charge of the new State of Bangladesh. Although the authority of the Bangladesh government in exile in India during the war of liberation was not acceptable to some freedom fighters who had done the actual fighting and considered the leaders in exile a 'do-nothing group living in luxury in Calcutta' and out of touch with realities in Bangladesh (Jahan 1973: 200; Van Schendel 2009: 175), Sheikh Mujibur Rahman (now known as father of the nation – *'Jatir jonok' Bangobondhu*) on his return to Bangladesh, received a hero's welcome. He seemed the most natural and obvious choice to be the new nation's leader. He therefore assumed unopposed leadership by mere consent of the people and promulgated a parliamentary form of government for the new State. AL's election manifesto of 1970 had spoken of nationalisation, land reform and the abolition of land tax, after the war, so the leadership was under pressure from radical and armed freedom fighters for revolutionary changes. Sheikh Mujib, however, disregarded the appeals to form a national government with representation from all political parties (excluding the pro-Pakistan Islamist rightists who were now banned from Bangladesh politics) including the strong leftist forces (who gained strength from within and outside AL) and instead formed an all-out AL government, relying on his 'legendary and charismatic appeal and his hypnotic hold' over Bangladeshis (Van Schendel 2009: 175) therefore striking a fragile working balance between the conflicting social groups constituting the Bangladeshi political spectrum.

The newly drafted Constitution of 1972 asserted that the People's Republic of Bangladesh was to be based on principles of nationalism, socialism, democracy and secularism. Although secularism was part of the State ideology, in the first few months of independence, secularism was practically defined in terms of non-use of religious symbols in public affairs and in the State-owned radio and television, secular slogans such as *joy Bangla* (victory to Bengal) were used while Islamic religious slogans like *Allahu Akbar* (God is Great) were dropped. The rapid rise in anti-India feeling within the population grew just as the unpopularity of the secular ideology did because the non-use of religious symbols by the grass root was regarded as an anti-Muslim/pro-India, albeit pro-Hindu, ideology (Jahan 2005: 151). Although the Mujib regime started defining secularism by giving equal place to all religions in public affairs, this did not help. Jahan (2005: 151) picks up this issue and notes that whilst secularism was a widely accepted principle pre-independence, when this was adopted as one of the major guiding principle post-independence, it lost support with the masses. She points out two challenges for the new nation in defining its identity: firstly, if Bangladesh was to define its identity ethno-linguistically, then what should be their attitude to the 60 million Hindu Bengalis living in West Bengal? If the identity was to be defined territorially (Bangladesh), then how much emphasis should be placed on the religious factor (Islam) to differentiate the Bengalis of Bangladesh from the Bengalis of West Bengal? Although the 1972 Constitution defined identity in terms of 'ethnicity' and 'language' while terming the citizens as 'Bengalis', the confusion and concern about the identity remained at mass level. Fear of the Indian domination led the population to identify themselves as Bengali Muslims to set them apart from the Indian Bengalis. Secondly, Jahan continues, that the loss of consensus regarding secularism meant alienation between the regime in power and its people. Loss of popular support of the government brought back to the fore the tradition of mistrust of 'governments' and 'officials' since the region has had a history of exploitation over the years. Since secularism was the official policy, anti-secular slogans were used as a mark of protest against the regime and eventually, as a result the nationalist élite bowed down to the pressure of some of the popular demands and began using Islamic symbols together with symbols of other religions in public affairs (Jahan 2005: 152). Little did the Bangladeshis know that even years later, this 'secularism' would continue to remain a point of major contention between the main political parties due to the way subsequent democratic history would unfold.

Since the State institutions were weak and in disarray in the new nation, many senior positions in the bureaucracy and the armed forces lay vacant because their occupants had been from West Pakistan. These institutions and the political parties became arenas of factional struggle between those who had actively supported independence from exile in India and those who physically weathered the storm of 1971 inside Bangladesh. The weak State was confronted with enormous challenges from establishing law and order, running newly nationalised industries, restoring infrastructure in a war-ravaged nation, to encouraging economic development, to emancipating the country from economic exploitation, poverty and stagnation and to becoming a player in international State system (Van Schendel 2009: 177).

There were also deep conflicts over the ideological orientation of the State within AL, splitting the AL down the middle. One segment led by the finance minister Tajuddin Ahmed, revered by Bangladeshis across the nation, wanted to move in the socialist direction with the help of New Delhi and Moscow while another, spearheaded by the minister of trade and commerce, Khondkar Mushtaq Ahmed, was emphatically pro-American and preferred a mixed economy based on Western aid. Although initially the pro-socialist group appeared to have the upper hand, subsequently the commitment to a socialist economy was marred by disagreements within the ruling party and the result was an absence of clear policy directives and utter chaos in economic management (Jalal 1995: 86). Management of the nationalised enterprises was handed over to inexperienced political activists, leading to a sharp drop in production and a sharp rise in managerial wealth. The standard of living of the majority of the population of Bangladesh did not improve. On the contrary, it fell as economic productivity lagged far behind the pre-war level and agricultural as well as industrial production declined. The cost of living increased drastically while real incomes slumped alarmingly (Tripathi 2014: 232–233).

According to Jahan (2005: 122–123) there were also old and new schisms within the party and the administration, making factional tension in the AL more visible in 1972 and quite acute by 1973. Since an acceptable successor of Mujib as the party chief could not be found, the AL council sessions kept being postponed a few times to avoid showing the division and split inside the party. Factional schisms among old AL leaders such as between Tajudin Ahmed and Syed Nazrul Islam and the younger leaders such as between Sheikh Fazlul Haq Moni and Tofael Ahmed went down to the district and sub-divisional levels of the party. These intra party fights could only be contained by Mujib's personal intervention or by the accommodation of the factional leaders in position of power.

Moreover, the dramatic expansion of the public sector did not see the posts being filled with a pool of skilled bureaucrats. Instead, the regime opted to appoint political favourites into the top jobs in the newly nationalised industries while war veterans were discriminately given seniority as recognition from the regime, at the cost of the loss of seniority of the existing bureaucrats. This kind of State patronage, plum jobs, permits and licences through political networks of AL may have been a good consolidation of the regime's support base, but it was a bad recipe for public sector efficiency as well as the morale of the masses that were clearly discontent. The regime's failure to create a professional, politically neutral State bureaucracy that could have implemented State policies plagued the nation from the onset – this politics of patronage continues to dominate the State machinery even today, in a much worse way than before. Jalal (1995: 87) explains some of the challenges that the regime faced at that time:

> The repatriation of civil servants from Pakistan, quislings in the popular mind, lowered the prestige of the administrative bureaucracy further still. Dazed and demoralised, civil bureaucrats proved amenable to the dictates of the elective representatives. Yet the implications of bureaucratic subservience to the political arms of the State were not altogether salutary. Heightening social conflict coupled with rivalries within the AL set the bureaucracy at sixes and sevens along political lines. This made it even more difficult for the regime to carry out its post war reconstruction policies.

Moreover, the dominance of party political considerations forestalled any coherent economic policy then, let alone its implementation. These dynamics exacerbated the economic muddle and prevented the new regime from developing a social agenda (Van Schendel 2009: 178). The bureaucracy was also factionalised on the basis of those who joined the liberation war and those who had not, as well as on the basis of those who had formerly been in a central or provincial service. Substantial sections of the bureaucracy, suffering from a sense of uncertainty about their own positions and alienation from the political government adopted an attitude of *immobilisme* (Hossain 2013: 128). The tension between the bureaucrats and technocrats were highlighted by Ali (1973: 119) in the following words:

> If the members of the Planning Commission adopted an unhelpful attitude on the question of creating administrative cohesiveness, the civil servants also never missed the opportunity of obstructing the work of the Planning Commission, sometimes out of spite and sometimes because their approaches differed.

The present-day reality in Bangladesh, even forty five years post-independence sadly reflects that ruling party loyalists supersede State interest. Rulers use the State to further their party rather than the other way round.

Some members of the liberation army (*Mukti Bahini*) who had fought against the Pakistan army while most of AL leadership had either been jailed in Pakistan or exiled to India, wanted to see itself transformed into a productive army which could contribute to the country's financial resources and not drain it. The suspicion among certain elements in the government was the questionable loyalty of the army, not only because it proved singularly incapable of squaring the interests of the military, but also because some of the army who had fought in the liberation war had been officers of the Pakistan army, and therefore they were ideologically wedded to the so-called Pakistan ideology. Here was yet another curious mistrust. As a result, the regime created its own para-military force, the *Rakkhi Bahini* (National Security Force), membership of which was based entirely on loyalty to Sheikh Mujib and AL. The creation of *Rakkhi Bahini* was a precursor to the growing authoritarian powers, as this force spread fear through intimidation and torture.

An important lesson for Mujib and the AL had been the bad legacy of the Pakistan army dominating national politics and indeed undermining politicians in the 24 years between 1947 and 1971. Mujib's concern was that the military should be under civilian control, as it is in any standard democracy. However, such concerns were negativised by the formation of the *Rakkhi Bahini* and seemed to be contradicting the entire idea of the military being a loyal institution of the State. Ironically, in 1974, as reports of corruption and hoarding of food grains began to appear, Mujib himself ordered the army into action against the corrupt elements. That was the beginning of the army actually entering a role in administration. It went after powerful political elements including influential AL politicians, on the strength of the Prime Minister's directives, but when pressure began to be exerted on the soldiers to go easy on pro-government elements, military dissatisfaction was its consequential result (Tripathi 2014: 229–230).

Another element of mistrust came in with the repatriation of no fewer than 30,000 Bengali military officers and soldiers of the Pakistan army who had been stranded in Pakistan from 1971 until the repatriation in 1973–1974. A basic mistake made by the government was to have all these returnees join the Bangladesh armed forces without any screening because Mujib happened to believe that all Bengalis were loyal to the State.

Many of the returning officers were to find that their batch-mates who had joined the war had been promoted and were now senior to them. This is how the conflict between freedom fighter officers and repatriated officers took roots. Even a senior officer like Lieutenant General Khwaja Wasiuddin had to be retired when he came to Bangladesh and posted as ambassador to Kuwait, because appointing him as Army Chief of Staff would have led to resentment among the freedom fighter officers. It is a travesty of Bangladesh's history that between 1975–1981, a large number of freedom fighter officers would die in internecine conflict while repatriated officers would go on to occupy senior positions in the army (Ahsan 2014: 272–274).

Jalal (1995: 88) is of the opinion that the economic woes were magnified as the State looked to international donor agencies for a way out of an escalating financial crisis. The loosening of the reins on domestic and foreign private investment followed naturally and brought with it the hated hands of American involvement in both the economic and political spheres. Here was the basis of an alliance between external power and a disgruntled army, put off by the *Rakkhi Bahini's* growing share of the annual budget and ascendant capitalist classes, eager to use State power to enhance the processes of private capital accumulation.

Much criticism has been levelled at Mujib and his government over the failure to conduct a stable administration between January 1972 and August 1975. While the incompetence of the government and the corruption of its followers are undeniable, there are also other factors which left the government in a state of deep confusion during the period. The war ended in December 1971, but a very large number of weapons which had gone into the hands of political elements were not returned. It was the extreme left-wing groups such as those headed by

Shiraj Shikhdar and Abdul Haq which continued to wage war against Mujib's government. Abdul Haq who headed what was still called the East Pakistan Communist Party, wrote to Pakistan's Prime Minister Zulfikar Ali Bhutto in 1974 asking for financial and military assistance to overthrow the Mujib government (Wolpert 1984).

Another unforeseen crisis which undermined the government was the sudden rise in oil prices following the October 1973 war in the Middle East. It was a significant factor in pushing Bangladesh to a colossal famine that would take hundreds of thousands of lives in 1974. Besides, the inhuman refusal of the US administration to provide food aid to Bangladesh to cope with the crisis, also became a major factor in the government's inability to handle the situation. Disturbed by Bangladesh's jute trade with Cuba, the US administration even had a ship load of food intended for Bangladesh turned back. This is not surprising in retrospect, given the 'White House's tilt for Pakistan' (Raghavan 2013: 81) during the war and USA's military assistance to Pakistan, which despite a formal military embargo imposed after its attack on India in 1965, still opened up major arms shipments by making exceptions to the embargo (Bass 2014: 108).

Apart from such realities, the constant propaganda in the Middle East against Bangladesh's secularism, inspired by Pakistani assistance, prevented Bangladesh from establishing normal relations with Muslim States in the region. The exercise of the veto on Bangladesh's membership in the UN by China in 1972 and 1973 also stopped Bangladesh from seeking assistance from Beijing.

It soon became quite clear that Mujib was unable to transform his charisma with his followers into an established authority structure. The early 1970s saw a steep erosion of the popularity of the AL, which was quite a contrast to how the same party built its momentum to become an engine of the movement against the Pakistani regime. Although during the first elections of Bangladesh held in March 1973, Sheikh Mujib still retained much of his personal popularity, there was resentment among the electorate vis-a-vis AL, and this was bound to be reflected in the elections. Fearing this setback, AL attempted to secure a total victory of 97 per cent through coercion/rigging, setting the new nation back to the time and tradition of election irregularities in the Pakistan era. Frustration in city streets and village pathways increased. So did opposition political parties' (including leftist groups') woes and in a bid to regain control, the regime passed the Special Powers Act (February 1974) to give itself powers to suppress individual liberty and press freedom.

Against this backdrop, the harsh famine of 1974 ravaged Bangladesh as it took tens of thousands of lives, thereby exposing the government as inept, indifferent and heartless. The regime lost its political credibility amidst this complex socio-political and economic situation which was a serious disappointment against the expectations of the masses. Disenchanted by it all, Sheikh Mujib understood, albeit quite late, that the rapidly emerging nouveau riche of the AL had become thoroughly discredited and a violent opposition to his rule was spreading. As a result, he made another disastrous misjudgement and attempted to install a one-party socialist State by dissolving all political parties and forming a new national party called *Baksal* (Bangladesh Peasants and Workers Awami League) (Tripathi 2014: 236–237).

The idea of a single party system was first sold to Sheikh Fazlul Huq Moni (Sheikh Mujib's nephew and chairman of the *Awami Jubo League*) and to Monsoor Ali (then home minister in the cabinet) by the embassy of the most powerful socialist State. The pressure of the radical opposition, constant prodding by Sheikh Moni, Monsoor Ali and other pro-Moscow leaders and Sheikh Mujib's own proclivity for total power, propelled him into deciding in favour of introducing a one-party system (Maniruzzaman 1976: 119–129). He proclaimed a state of emergency in December 1974, suspending all rights conferred in the Constitution and discarded all the important elements in a democracy: accountability, separation of powers and a multi-party system.

Jahan (2005: 134–135) interestingly notes that the model of politics and governance that the AL regime initially followed was not exactly that of the Westminster style parliamentary democracy – rather it was the Indian model of parliamentary democracy with a single dominant party. This was not superimposed on the Bengali ruling élite but rather was a deliberate and conscious decision on the part of the AL regime, which perhaps emerged in the process of the 25 years struggle against the Pakistani ruling élite, within the AL and the country as a whole. But then the question remains as to what happened to this ethos post-independence? In analysing this puzzle and this contradictory behaviour pattern of the nationalist élite before and after independence, Jahan's (2005: 135) hypothesis is that the nationalist élite pre-independence commitment to the goals of constitutional democracies was more due to tactical considerations than to any strong ideological belief per se. They became committed to this model of parliamentary democracy because of the potential and perhaps the promise of increased participation which was a powerful slogan to mobilise mass support behind the nationalist movement before independence. The unavoidable challenges that emerged post-independence however, particularly holding on to the ethos of regime maintenance, eroded the nationalist élite's tactical commitment to parliamentary democracy. Power, which was a means to an end pre-independence, became an end in itself post-independence. The nationalist élite rejected parliamentary democracy and turned it to an alternative model which promised it a longer stay in power. Hence, she concludes that both the adoption and repudiation of constitutional democracy as a model of government and politics were due to tactical or power considerations.

Much debate has gone on about *Baksal* or the adoption of the Fourth Amendment of the Constitution in January 1975. Critiques have consistently rightly argued that the move was a clear negation of democracy, as discussed above, and hold the AL guilty of undermining the very parliamentary system it inaugurated in 1972 by throwing it overboard and going for a one party system. Sheikh Mujib's argument that *Baksal* was a national front comprising diverse political elements has not logically been supported, given that all other political parties were proscribed and only four newspapers were allowed to be published (Ahsan 2014: 248–250).

It was Mujib's argument that *Baksal* was a temporary measure which has been the defence of his supporters. They also point out that the system did not discourage but in fact was aimed at presenting a choice of candidates before the electorate as a sign of democracy in action. They also note that the national front accommodated not only politicians but also military officers, civil servants, teachers, journalists and therefore *Baksal* could not be termed as anti-democratic! For many critics, such defence is sophistry at best because it led to greater powers for the President, in this case Mujib himself and a pliant cabinet and parliament. Besides, there was a strong feeling that with such a powerful executive, even the independence of the judiciary would be threatened.

The point is generally made that the 15 August 1975 coup when Sheikh Mujib along with almost his entire family were brutally assassinated, was a consequence of *Baksal*. The reality, however, is that planning for the coup actually began towards the later part of 1974 and only speeded up following the imposition of *Baksal*. All said and done, *Baksal* was a failed experiment in that it did not enable Mujib or his government to establish themselves on a stronger footing in the country. In fact, the move remains an Achilles heel for the AL which has not been able to offer any credible defence of the system because there was none. *Baksal* came to an end in September 1975 when Khondkar Mushtaq Ahmed issued a decree to that effect. No tears were shed at its passing.

Jahan (2005: 165) stresses that by January 1975, Sheikh Mujib had succeeded in alienating most of the support groups of the regime. The extent to which the regime weakened itself was to be seen in the growing rift between Mujib and Tajuddin to a point where the latter was asked to leave the government in October 1974. Clearly Mujib did not appear to go along with Tajuddin in the latter's socialistic principles and had come to the conclusion that a re-orientation of foreign policy, in favour of the west was the need of the hour. In the end, Tajuddin's removal would turn out to be a mishap from which Mujib would not recover. His authoritarian personal rule was still accepted as inevitable because he was the only source of authority in a faction-ridden polity. In a country where institutions were weak and divided, Sheikh Mujib held together all the feuding groups. He was the sole arbiter and mediator of factional conflicts. Therefore, despite the inefficiency, corruption and authoritarianism of his regime, he was regarded as indispensable. There was no alternative institution or leader capable of either controlling or managing the feuding factions in the government and politics of Bangladesh.

However, 15 August 1975 saw the violent assassination of Sheikh Mujib and the annihilation of his entire family, except two daughters who were abroad at that time. The cherished dream of popular democracy for Bangladesh had turned into a nightmare, first due to the civilian autocracy of AL and now 15 years of military rule by General Ziaur Rahman and Hossain Mohammad Ershad (1975–1990) began, gripping the country into their undemocratic and authoritarian clutches. Sheikh Mujib's minister for trade and commerce, Khondkar Mushtaq Ahmed, told the nation over radio that in response to the 'historic necessity' he had assumed the post of President of Bangladesh. The element of 'necessity' in the context of the CTG is discussed in chapter 5. But here we have something called 'necessity' in the wider context of history.

15 August 1975 was thus not a sudden happening, as many observers have indicated (Al Khatib 1981). As early as March 1975, the majors and colonels who would lead the coup began to establish contacts with Khondkar Mushtaq Ahmed, Tahiruddin Thakur among others about their plans. Surprisingly, they were neither discouraged nor reported. At one point, these officers met with some mid-level officers of the US embassy in Dhaka and were told that their plans would not be supported. The US unsurprisingly did nothing however to discourage them or report to the government. The only warnings came from the Indian government, but Mujib dismissed such fears. As Khatib (1981: 50–56) reports that in the three days preceding the coup, Mushtaq, Thakur and Mahbub Alam Chashi and the NSI (National Security Intelligence) Chief A B S Safdar were in Comilla but early on 15 August 1975, they returned to Dhaka.

Ironically, the news of the assassination of Sheikh Mujibur Rahman was first broken to the world by the State Department in Washington, and Pakistan was the first country to recognise the Mushtaq government only a few hours after the coup. The role that external powers/geo-politics played in Bangladesh was apparent from the early days and this influence continues to grip the nation even today.

The events of the three months following the coup after Sheikh Mujib's assassination, especially the power struggle in the week of 3 November 1975, have also shown that it is easier to change a government than to establish and maintain an effective administration (Jahan 2005: 166). Eventually General Zia emerged as the *de facto* military ruler, altering the State system in Bangladesh. Syed Sirajul Islam (1984: 556–573), with that sentiment, notes that:

> A new State emerged which seemed to follow a pattern that had been set in pre-liberation Bangladesh; a marriage of convenience between civil and military bureaucrats, similar to that existing in Pakistan before its collapse in 1971, evolved in Bangladesh after the November 7 coup.

As a commentator (Maniruzzaman 1976: 129) poignantly adds:

> To sum up, at the end of 1975, Bangladesh entered into a period of greater uncertainty than was the case under the Mujib regime.

Within days of the coup, China and Saudi Arabia, which had desisted from recognising Bangladesh, accorded recognition to the country. Under Zia, Bangladesh underwent a radical change in its foreign policy. It turned away from its earlier alignment with India and the Soviet Union and towards warmer ties with the US,

China and the Middle East. Internally, the regime engineered a shift away from secular to Islamic politics, measures which were welcomed by the right-wing elements in the country. While it is true that it was Zia who opened the country to multi-party politics again, it is equally true that he allowed the political parties and politicians who had opposed Bangladesh's liberation from Pakistan to re-enter politics. The Zia regime, in its bid to keep secular forces at bay, scrapped the Collaborators Act of 1973, making things easier for the religious right. It was on Zia's watch that leading collaborators like Golam Azam of the Jamat-i-Islami (JIB) came back to Bangladesh and would not be prosecuted or even go back to Pakistan.

The new regime of Zia banned all the political parties and cracked down on the leftist party Jatio Shamajtantrik Dal (JSD) which had inspired radical soldiers' revolution in the army to carry out the last coup (planned as a soldiers' revolution in the service of the oppressed classes). Although this regime marked a decisive break in the country's economic policies and set the country on a course of liberalisation, it also marked a decisive break in another sense: the emergence of military dominance in post-independence Bangladesh from which the nation has not been fully freed. The army has never really gone back to the barracks and continues to loom large, as the life or death dispensing power behind any throne of successive civilian governments up until the present day (Van Schendel 2009: 194).

The impact of the military in the politics of Bangladesh

The remit of this section is not to assess why the military intervened in Bangladesh politics as numerous scholarly articles have been written in this regard. The focus is more on the impact military interventions have had in the country's journey to democracy from 1971–1990.

Jalal (1995: 115–121) notes that unlike the Pakistani army which has preserved the hierarchical and rigid discipline of its colonial counterpart, the Bangladesh army's involvement in a war of liberation had weakened the structural grip of the high command over the middle and lower ranks of the army. To date all military takeovers in Pakistan have been led by top-ranking generals. At no time has the decision to intervene been challenged from either within the army or the two other services. The institutional coherence of the Pakistan army together with the overall organisational structure of the defence establishment has provided safeguards against breaches in the ranks. Par contrast, the Bangladesh army has been slit with divisions and consequently, shown itself to be more prone to bloody coups led by men other than the commanding officer. The legacies of the liberation struggle – a structurally unstable army, an infirm and divided bureaucracy and a generally more politicised society – have tended to give more scope to opposition parties in Bangladesh than in Pakistan.

Upon being faced with the urgent task of restructuring the administrative framework of the new nation, Mujib felt that his policies were dictated by the civil and military bureaucracies, which were the two inherited State apparatus which he perceived as a potential threat to political rule. Distrustful of the military establishment, suspicious of its colonial heritage and apprehensive of a potential military threat to political rule, after independence Mujib not only decided against a strong military but also attempted to impose complete civilian control over the State institutions. He retained the post of defence minister and consciously adopted a policy restricting the size and strength of the military in the formative phase of Bangladesh (Haider 1999: 65–68). The creation of *Rakkhi Bahini* (National Security Force) composed of freedom fighters, as discussed in the previous section of this chapter, as a counter force to the military did not go well to foster trust between these two groups. The unfettered power of arrest or search without warrant of *Rakkhi Bahini*, the deliberate absence of the provision of appeal in courts for actions of the *Rakkhi Bahini*, the slim allocation of budget/funds for the military and par contrast large allocation on purchasing weapons for the *Rakkhi Bahini* whose patriotism was questioned by the military, increasing the strength of the *Rakkhi Bahini*, rapid promotions of the *Rakkhi Bahini* to fill the gaps of the command structure – making them senior in ranks to more experienced repatriated officers, were some of the fundamental reasons for the discontent. The anti-Indian sentiment grew amidst the armed forces belonging to the liberation army as they perceived that the Indian army stole the show, during the war of independence, by joining nearly towards the end of the war, when the Bangladeshis had already finished the work. Within three years of independence, the circumstances had become such that Mujib declared a state of emergency, feeling threatened by both civil and military opposition. But by 1975, the young officers of the army began to openly express their displeasure whilst the senior officers accused the Mujib government of neglecting the armed forces. Eventually, Mujib was cruelly assassinated.

Jalal (1995: 115–116) narrates that after Sheikh Mujib's assassination in a military coup, the pro-American politician, Khondkar Mushtaq Ahmed, had briefly served as president and the country was placed under martial law. A pro-AL counter-coup on 3 November 1975 led by Brigadier Khaled Musharraf, the chief of general staff, collapsed four days later when Zia came into the limelight. At this time, the entire AL political leadership, including the left-leaning ex-prime minister Tajuddin Ahmed, were ruthlessly murdered in Dhaka prison on the night between 2 and 3 November 1975. The new regime faced early challenges from the Revolutionary Peoples' Army led by Colonel Taher, who had been instrumental in organising the 7 November 1975 coup and freeing Zia from house arrest, within the armed forces, which had close links with a left-wing political party, called National Socialist Party.

During 1976, the regime spent the better part of its energies parrying assaults from within as well as outside the military. Taher and a number of JSD figures were arrested by the Zia regime at the end of November 1975. In a subsequent secret trial before a military court, Taher was sentenced to death and hanged on 21 July 1976. Threatened by all sides, the regime perked up the expenditure on defence and internal security and doubled the size of the police force. This helped strengthen the position of Zia who had become the chief of army staff in 1975, but did not formally take over as president until April 1977. Zia opted to consolidate his hold on State power by restoring the positions of civilian bureaucrats and military officers who had been denied the fruits of State patronage during the Sheikh Mujib period (Jalal 1995: 116). Almost the entire period of Zia's rule from November 1975–May 1981 was dominated by his constant warding off as many as 18 abortive coups. Zia succumbed to the 19th while on a visit to Chittagong on 30 May 1981.

Jalal (1995: 116) further points out that the original 1975–1976 defence budget accounted for only seven per cent of the national budget, but this was revised upwards so that it reached 20 per cent of the entire budget. The size of the army grew from 60,000 in 1974–1975 to 90,000 in 1976–1977. Many of the special privileges enjoyed by the army personnel during the Pakistan period were reinstated. Expenditure on civil administration was also increased and bureaucrats were given more clout in Zia's cabinet, the central secretariat as well as the divisional and district levels of the administration. Former members of the CSP (Civil Service of Pakistan) were put in charge of twelve out of the nineteen districts. Bureaucrats also controlled the National Economic Council, the Planning Commission and 38 major public corporations. The Zia era 'witnessed the ascendancy of the military and the civil bureaucracy over the politician element in the regime's tri-institutional structure of state power' (Bertocci 1982: 995–996). In a similar tone, Syed Serajul Islam (1984: 561–562) highlights that:

> The state apparatus in Bangladesh was dominated by civil-military bureaucrats and thus the Zia regime was fundamentally a resurrection of the 'administrative state' under Ayub Khan in Pakistan; as Anderson points out, 'there was a striking resemblance between Bangladesh after the 1975 coups and East Pakistan before its collapse in 1971. A similar marriage of convenience existed between the military and the civil service'. And like their forbearers, in the administrative state of Pakistan, the civil-military bureaucrats in Bangladesh as an exclusive administrative group have been deeply imbued with a 'guardianship' orientation.

The Zia regime in Bangladesh, as Jalal (1995: 116) continues, initially relied on the support of Saudi-funded Islamic political groups. While 'secularism' had been one of the four principles of *Mujibism*, Zia made 'Islam' the centrepiece of his regime's political ideology by dropping the principle of 'secularism' from the Constitution and replacing it with the words 'absolute trust and faith in Almighty Allah', as well as with added emphasis on unity, sovereignty and independence. There was also a shift in foreign policy towards a closer alignment with the Muslim countries and Western powers. During the Sheikh Mujib era, Islamist politicians whose main political vehicle was the political party Jamaat-e-Islami (JIB) (founded by Maulana Maududi in 1941 in favour of a theocratic State) were discredited and mostly fled to Pakistan. The Bangladesh government during the Mujib era had banned the party for collaboration with the Pakistan army. In 1978 however, Zia not only allowed these leaders of Jamaat to return to Bangladeshi soil but also allowed them to resume political activities. The unpardonable and disastrous effect that this has had on Bangladesh politics and democracy, ever since, is something worth researching further (Hasan 2011). Jamaat is widely thought to have ties with underground activists who aim for a Taliban-style Islamist revolution in Bangladesh. Bangladesh history subsequently portrays in the 1990s what radical Islamism is capable of doing. It is quite evident that in the sub-continent, there is a clear connection between military rule and Islamism. Just like Ayub Khan of Pakistan did, Zia too used Islamists to prop up his own power, thereby politically validating an austere and intolerant version of Islam among the Bangladeshis.

Importantly, Zia also drew a distinction between 'Bengalis' and 'Bangladeshis', accentuating the religious dimension of the birth of the nation in 1971 and emphasising the nation as essentially a Muslim one. The notion 'Bangladeshi' proved attractive to many at the more conservative and religious minded end of the political spectrum and as a result *'Bangladesh Zindabad'* ('Long Live Bangladesh') became a challenge to the *'Joy Bangla'* ('Victory to Bengal') that had been the standard rallying cry during the liberation war.

Neither Islamic nor nationalist rhetoric could however provide Zia's regime with an adequate social base of support or a modicum of legitimacy. So Zia moved towards the formation of village councils in 1976 which were renamed self-sufficient village governments in 1980. These local governments were controlled by the bureaucracy. These were village governments rather than union-level governments. Winning over the leaders of local society through the extension of State patronage and development funds was a safe way of establishing control over the political system. This is why local body elections preceded those to the higher levels – giving the regimes plenty of opportunity to gauge political trends before taking the big step of holding elections to their national parliament. Jalal (1995: 117) further notes that in April 1977, Zia held a referendum on the basis of a nineteen-point policy programme promising to succour the private sector and achieving self-sufficiency in food production by instituting measures of population control and promoting agricultural development. Claiming 99.5 per cent support and an 85 per cent voter turnout, Zia felt confident enough to try and assert complete control over the State apparatus. In June 1978, in a presidential election closely monitored by the civil bureaucracy, Zia declared himself the victor despite the fact that he was still a serving officer in the army.

He eventually created a new political party, the Bangladesh Nationalist Party (BNP), which was designed to hold a majority in a parliament to be set up in 1979. Parented by military–bureaucratic State structures, the BNP and the Pakistan Muslim League, the main component of the Islamic Democratic Alliance (IDA), share some common birth marks. Apart from being congenitally anti-Indian, both claim to be firmly set against secularism and socialism. If not for the differences between the Bangladeshi and Pakistani social structures, the BNP and IDA might pass for fraternal twins. Despite an industrialist as prime minister, the IDA in Pakistan had been predominantly agricultural in composition. When it was formed, one-third of the central executive committee of the BNP was composed of businessmen and less than 12 per cent were agriculturalists. In parliamentary elections held in February 1979, the BNP won 41 per cent of the votes and two-thirds of the seats. Outside parliament the AL and the National Socialist Party remained the most trenchant political opponents of the regime (Jalal 1995: 117).

It proved relatively easier for Zia to conveniently manipulate the political process than to confirm his authority over the Bangladesh army, remarks Jalal (1995: 117). And indeed, it was instability within the army which led to Zia's downfall. According to Bertocci (1982: 996), sorting out of affairs seems to have gradually occurred within the military. First, there was the outright physical repression of military dissenters who had taken arms against the government at various points and/or represented a similar threat to the Zia regime. By the time of Zia's assassination, reportedly 400 officers had been executed. Second, there was a constant reshuffling of the top officer ranks. Third, as mentioned earlier, Zia relied increasingly on Pakistan-returned officers, who were well qualified, to whom he assigned the helmsmen's posts at the top of the services. By the time of his death, only two or three of the top fifty army officers were freedom fighters. Although Zia himself had been a freedom fighter, by 1981 only two of the fifty major generals and brigadiers were men who had fought with the *Mukti Bahini* (The Liberation Army) in 1971. The rest were all repatriates from West Pakistan. Only 15 per cent of the soldiers consisted of freedom fighters, 25 per cent were repatriated and 60 per cent were new recruits, which is why perhaps Zia had faced as many as nineteen abortive coups between 1977 and 1981 (Jalal 1995: 117). Then, on 30 May 1981, Zia was killed in Chittagong, allegedly by a faction of freedom fighters. Zia's death and the almost instantaneous killing of his alleged assassin removed the only two remaining veterans of the liberation army.

The main benefactor of these developments according to Jalal (1995: 118) was General Ershad, Chief of Staff of the Bangladeshi army, who had been repatriated from Pakistan in 1973 and became the second dictator of Bangladesh in 1982. Van Schendel (2009: 207) points out that:

> After General Ershad usurped state power in 1982, he went a step further than Zia and used Islamic symbols and contacts even more freely than Zia. To widespread protests from secularists and applause from Islamists, Ershad amended the Constitution, abandoning state secularism and declaring Islam the state religion.

The parallels with Pakistan at the same time and General Zia are perhaps worth a mention.

In what was symptomatic of the precarious nature of the military institution, Ershad like his predecessor managed only gradually to consolidate his power and deferred the assumption of presidential office until 1984. Taking his cues from the military rulers in the sub-continent, Ershad too began building his base of support by strengthening his hold over the lower levels of the administration. The second tier of local administration – the *thana* – was raised to the status of *upazila* or sub-district and endowed with enhanced administrative functions, thereby becoming the primary locus of the civil and judicial court system (Bertocci 1985: 155–168). Ershad went even further than Zia in establishing rapport with the business community by handing over 33 jute mills, 25 textile mills and 31 other industrial units to the private sector in 1984. He initially formed his own party, the *Janadal* (the People's Party) in December 1983. Elections were promised according to the established military tradition, first at the union and the sub-district level, to be followed by farcical parliamentary and presidential elections.

The AL eventually led by Sheikh Hasina, daughter of Sheikh Mujib, and the BNP led by Khaleda Zia, widow of General Zia, provided an intense challenge to Ershad's political engineering. Perhaps one of the very rare times that AL and BNP worked together with the other political parties and protested against the regime's intention to hold elections under martial law. They demanded at this moment the immediate restoration of fundamental rights and the holding of free and fair parliamentary elections before the local ones. But Ershad refused to budge, accusing politicians of creating conditions which had 'necessitated' martial law. Local elections were deemed to be the first step to the genuine empowerment of the ordinary citizen, not fundamental rights of citizenship which no one really understood.

Jalal (1995: 118) narrates that amidst a rising crescendo of protests and general strikes spearheaded by AL and BNP, Ershad managed to get his way. By holding local body elections first in 1984, Ershad was able to use the newly elected councillors to secure the government's victory for the parliamentary elections. In such a tightly controlled setting and sustained election engineering, Ershad's Janadal, now the Jatiya Party (JP) naturally won a majority. AL bagged more than a third of the seats but refused to enter parliament, charging the regime with widespread rigging. Ershad's JP had now replaced Zia's BNP as the main political vehicle for the distribution of State patronage. A second round of *upazila* elections held in 1989 further consolidated Ershad's support in the rural constituencies. One of the main grievances of the political opposition was Ershad's attempt to include military and bureaucratic officials as members of the local councils. This amounted to giving 'the military bureaucratic state' a suffocating hold over the lowest levels of the political system.

Jalal (1995: 119) concludes that Bangladesh under Ershad shared some of Pakistan's antipathy towards India and also supported the cause of the Afghan Mujahedeen. But its relative lack of importance in geo-strategic terms at that point in history spared it many of the devastations which military rule, combined with regional and international pressures, wreaked on the intricate weave of Pakistani society under the rule there, at roughly the same time, of General Zia. Economically, Bangladesh under military rule remained far worse off than the strategically more exposed Pakistan. Bangladesh's mainly stagnant and aid-driven economy was vulnerable to foreign intervention which inevitably extended to the political domain. With the changed calculations of the 'military–bureaucratic state', the phenomenal movement for democracy in Bangladesh reached an altogether new pitch during the 1990s. While the demonstration effect of other democratic movements may have been a factor, it was the excessive corruption of the Ershad regime which contributed to its isolation and eventual fall in 1990.

The Bangladesh history demonstrates just how difficult it is to reverse the phenomenon of military authoritarianism and deep-rooted election engineering by the party in authority. The 'military–bureaucratic state' utilises its powers of patronage to co-opt significant segments of dominant socio-economic élites and localise political horizons in a manner reminiscent of the colonial State. Jalal (1995: 120) reflects that if proof is needed that the effects of political engineering under military rule linger on long after the formal collapse of the regime, the seats that were secured by Ershad's JP (35 seats in parliament) is not at all bad statistically, showing 12 per cent as its share of the popular vote in the subsequent national election which took place in 1991.

Ahmed (2005), cited in Datta (2009: 47–50) observes that the military has been an integral part of Bangladeshi history and politics and as seen above, it has been rooted from early years after liberation. The fact that a large number of officers and *jawans* threw aside their professional norms and indignantly broke the canons of military discipline and chain of command and rose against the establishment in West Pakistan and joined the war in erstwhile East Pakistan, was itself a revolutionary step. Under normal circumstances they would all have been court marshalled, but after Bangladesh's independence they were all war heroes and greeted with warm-hearted glee and pride by the new nation. The war of independence removed the distance between the civilians and armed forces personnel and made them aware of the weaknesses in political leadership and fragile political institutions. This process was entrenched further, following the assassination of Mujib and the introduction of military rule. Ahmed (2005, cited in Datta 2009: 50) has provided interesting statistical data regarding the infiltration of the army in the various institutions of the country as the following paragraph demonstrates:

> On 1 March 1979, 25 of the 625 officers in the senior policy responsible for policy making in the secretariat were military officers; of 101 chairmen or managing directors of public corporations in June 1980, 42 were military officers or retired servicemen; 22 of the 40 district superintendents and additional superintendents of police were army officers. Moreover, 50 retired military officers were employed in industry, indenting business, foreign trade and supply and contracts under the patronage of the government; quite a few military officers were allotted residential plots in the developed areas of the city and were even granted liberal loans for building houses by the House Building Finance Corporation.

Beginning with Zia and continuing well into the Ershad regime and beyond, the military also made inroads into the diplomatic service with senior military officers being appointed ambassadors in various global capitals. Additionally, military officers were sent to the missions abroad to man the defence and consular wings of the embassies. The practice of appointing generals as ambassadors was to continue under the civilian elected governments of Khaleda Zia and Sheikh Hasina.

This has not only 'civilianised' the military but also bridged the gap between the armed forces and the general masses. It echoes years later, what the chief of army staff during the fourth Caretaker Government (2007–2009) Moeen U Ahmed alarmingly said in this context: 'Army is always with the government like police or civil administration. It can't remain isolated from any government' (Datta 2009: 47–67). Datta also highlights that besides high profile commercial ventures such as the Radisson Hotel in Dhaka, built on land owned by the army, the Rifles Square Mall belonging to the army, the armed forces also annually contribute US Dollars 600 million to the Bangladeshi economy (Datta 2009: 50–51). The country's army today is an important component of UN peacekeeping forces around the globe.

Van Schendel (2009: 197) observes that to enable more popular participation in parliamentary democracy, many citizens of Bangladesh ignored the military influence on judicial and legislative branches of the State, particularly post-independence during 1975 and 1990. In this particular period, civil rights were severely curtailed resulting in more popular demand for returning to at least certain semblance of political democracy.

In conclusion at this point, the coverage of this chapter as a whole has elaborated and substantiated how and to what extent the culture of mistrust is part of the historical legacy of Bangladesh and contributes to serious deficiencies in democratic management. This deficiency has its roots in British colonialism where by the 1940s, the Indian National Congress and the All India Muslim League demonstrated a clear lack of faith in each other about the future. The creation of Pakistan in 1947 led to a new period of mistrust, this time the entrenched political classes of West Pakistan and the deprived population of East Pakistan. It was mistrust at its highest that impelled Pakistan's ruling circles into refusing to hand over power to an electorally triumphant AL in 1970.

Thereafter, in independent Bangladesh, the legacy of mistrust has continued with the civil-military bureaucracy unwilling to acknowledge the superior position of the political classes in the administration of the State. Among themselves, the major political parties, have over the years, demonstrated intolerance to a level where today mistrust happens to be the underpinning of their relations with each other. Indeed, political mistrust in Bangladesh has created conditions where general elections are not considered credible unless they are supervised by a neutral entity even if that neutral entity happens to be a non-elected caretaker system comprising of retired chief justices and individuals from different professional areas who have no overt and preferably no covert political affiliations.

It was the people of Bangladesh who made the return to democracy possible in the 1990s. But an important lesson was learnt over the years since independence: The all-penetrating mistrust was not only against military regimes engineering elections, but was also pervasive amidst the political parties AL and BNP/JIB themselves, due to the historical baggage they were each carrying. It was clear that the ritual of voting (although an important element in democracy) was not to be confused with attaining substantive or consolidated democracy resting on social and economic rights of citizens. Nonetheless, this ritual needed to be carried on if Bangladesh was to follow any semblance to basic democracy. The ground reality was that the political processes in the country remained hostage to highly inequitable State structures and institutions. The continuing imbalances within these State structures as well as between the State structures, the political spectrum and the civil society foreclosed the chance of a significant freely balanced reapportioning of real political power in the near future.

The only way to circumvent this imbalance and mutual suspicion/mistrust was to create some sort of an 'umpire' which would see that at least the rituals of voting through free and fair elections are conducted by way of transition, and executive power is eventually transferred to the elected majority. The present chapter thus grounds the development of the unique institution of the CTG in Bangladesh, which forms the major subject of this book and is discussed in depth in the following chapters.

4

THE CARETAKER GOVERNMENTS (CTG) IN BANGLADESH

Elections under party governments in many developing countries, do not always reflect public opinion and nor do they offer a guarantee or an opportunity to confer legitimacy on those who wish to rule. Bangladesh provides an interesting example where centrally controlled electoral fraud and deeply embedded mistrust between political parties had become so entrenched in the system of governance that the political parties themselves, with the mandate of the people, decided in 1990 to introduce a new mechanism to oversee the conduct of national elections, through the caretaker government (CTG).

In the case of Bangladesh's CTG, an advisory council with eleven advisors, led by a retired chief justice (CJ) as the chief advisor (CA), governed the country for 90 days before an elected government took over. The CA, once appointed and sworn-in, enjoyed the privilege and status of a prime minister and it is in him/her that the executive authority of the Republic was vested, according to the Thirteenth Amendment to the Constitution of Bangladesh. The ten advisors that the CA appointed were personalities and professionals of repute and were usually, on the face of it, non-controversial, which instilled an atmosphere of neutrality in delivering a free and fair national election. During the 90 days tenure of the CTG, people had mostly enjoyed peace, tranquillity and security and had breathed in freedom (Ahmed 2008: 117).

The advisors, who had no experience of politics or political government, discharged their duty as an interim government, carrying out routine functions of the government unless it was necessary to take policy decisions. The main mandate of a CTG had been to give the Election Commission (EC) all possible aid and assistance that may be required for holding a general election peacefully, fairly and impartially. Usually the political parties were seen to assist a CTG (for the first three CTGs) and the support and confidence of the people had been the main strength of a CTG. The law and order situation was reviewed by the CTG, who issued directives to the law-enforcing agencies to make efforts to recover illegal arms and maintain complete neutrality, and the law enforcing agencies' preparedness, activities and achievements were also constantly reviewed during this period. Ensuring and entrusting these law enforcing agencies with independent authority and freeing them from politics and political interference during that time (Ahmed 2008: 118–119) indicates that transition with good governance is still possible, provided there is a will for it to happen.

The CTG mechanism since its inception was beyond any constitutional framework of Bangladesh. However, we will see how the stakeholders, namely the political parties, the civil and military administrations, and civil society at that time endeavoured to create a mechanism within the Constitution in order to carry on the legacy of constitutional rule. Although the structure of the interim government that was created was not purely democratic, it reflected a consensus among all the parties, including the people in general, to submit to this mechanism.

This chapter examines the genesis of the CTG system as a mode of transition in Bangladesh and as an expression of this nation's quest to institutionalise basic democratic order through a free electoral process. It evaluates the four CTG regimes of 1990, 1996, 2001 and 2006–2008 to see whether this indigenous law or this 'home grown plant', as described by Ahmed (2004: 3), played any effective role during the transition between two governments, through its neutral caretaking role, and whether it assisted the country's quest to achieve democratic consolidation. In doing so, this chapter first discusses the circumstances in which the CTG emerged and evolved, critiquing each CTG regime, not only in terms of its mandate and efficacy but also dwelling on the policy decisions each CTG regime had undertaken over the years and the shifts therein. It therefore discusses its gradual metamorphosis, while its demise is elaborated in Chapter 5.

The First Caretaker Government: 1990

The dominant political dilemma facing Bangladesh from 1989–1990 was the issue of a free and fair election of a democratically elected government. This issue arose from the charges made by the opposition parties (AL and BNP) that the parliamentary elections, which were held in March 1988 under the dictatorial regime of General Ershad, were massively rigged by his government, with zero participation in the elections by the political parties and less than 10 per cent voter participation. Moreover, direct and indirect international pressure, particularly persuasion from the United States urging both the government and the opposition to put a free and fair election process in place, was evident as the Foreign Aid Authorisation Bill of 1989–1990 reflected on the urgency to reconstitute the EC and to take meaningful steps to ensure genuinely free and fair elections, including specific indicators of democratisation such as freedom of the press, an independent judiciary and an effective local government.

Proposals to provide different perspectives on holding free and fair elections were also floating around domestically. But there were also several grave problems which needed to be considered. First was the issue of the likelihood of AL and BNP participating in any election, as the former was advocating a parliamentary system of governance while the latter favoured a presidential one. Since no agreement on this particular issue was reached, the differences between these two political parties and their relative strengths and weaknesses made the matter further complicated and difficult to resolve. Second, given the nature of fragmentation in the political system, a free and fair election was not an end in itself but only a means towards democratic decision-making. Serious concerns and questions had been raised regarding intra-political party democracy and the lack thereof. Third, opposition unity was necessary for achieving any success against the authoritarian regime of Ershad. Since unity between AL and BNP was an issue, both parties were apprehensive of either side getting an edge over the other, secretly negotiating with the Ershad government and working out a joint election strategy with him.

The personal nature of the conflict between Sheikh Hasina of AL and Khaleda Zia of BNP (widely termed 'the battle of the Begums') did not help the situation either. Serious mistrust between them and between the two parties was clearly evident then and continues to this day. Lastly, the strength of the principal political parties and their alliances in terms of winning an election and forming a viable government needed careful analysis. Despite AL's organisational strength and grassroot followers (amid factionalism within the party), its image was tarnished due to its participation in the 1986 parliamentary elections (during the Ershad regime), and thus open dissent about this could lead to its breakup. Similarly, internal divisions within BNP itself along with weak grassroots organisational support did not instil confidence in the electorate. These, coupled with constitutional amendments, the role of the bureaucracy and two insurgency movements, the Chittagong Hill Tracts issue and the strained India/Bangladesh relationship, influenced and somewhat shaped Bangladesh's political system during 1989–1990 (Rahman 1990: 150–155).

The first election in 1973, during the Sheikh Mujib era, had witnessed the dominance of the AL regime despite the unpopularity of its policies and strategies. Although AL could have won a majority in fair elections, some leaders were found to have engaged in irregularities in order to prove their popularity (Huque and Hakim 1993: 249). Together with the introduction of a single-party system by Sheikh Mujib, Bangladesh witnessed another blow to its first steps within democracy. During the Zia regime, after Zia's rehabilitating and rewarding of the rightist political forces, his civilian support base was unnaturally strengthened. The dual objective of weakening political opposition and acquiring legitimacy prompted Zia to hold a referendum in 1977. However, the inflated percentage of voter turnout and affirmative votes in the referendum backfired, as the resulting figures were clearly absurd and could not support his claim to legitimacy. He then sought further legitimacy by holding presidential elections in 1978. In order to civilianise his military rule, he formed BNP and held the second parliamentary elections in 1979, a contest which he won (Huque and Hakim 1993: 251–252).

Another party, Ershad's JP, which won the third (1986) and fourth (1988) general elections, also manipulated the electoral process. The scale of rigging, however, surpassed all previous records during the third elections under Ershad, when foreign election monitoring teams considered the election as 'a tragedy for democracy' and 'a cynically frustrated exercise' (Ahmed 2004: 14–15). The credibility of the entire electoral process in Bangladesh was now circumspect and the election system was more or less wiped out due to the violent strategy adopted by Ershad's JP, including musclemen capturing polling stations in various constituencies and terrorising voters. As a result of this dysfunctional electoral history of Bangladesh, it became apparent that no elections held under Ershad would be free and fair, as the government was certain to use State machinery to rig them in its favour. It was therefore agreed in principle by the political parties that some kind of special arrangement was needed to force Ershad to quit and to subsequently hold free and fair elections to bring about a transition to democracy.

The third parliament had been dissolved prematurely under opposition pressure while the fourth general elections were boycotted by all in 1988. The All Party Students Unity (APSU), comprising 22 student organisations affiliated with major opposition parties, began exerting pressure on Ershad to resign from October 1990 onwards. In November 1990, the three alliances ('left of centre' eight-party alliance led by AL, the 'centrist' seven-party alliance of BNP and the 'leftist' five-party alliance) announced a 'joint declaration' specifying the modalities for the transfer of power. Ahmed (2004: 15–16) reiterates the *modus operandi* and spirit of the declaration which was: a) the opposition would not only boycott elections under Ershad but would resist them; b) Ershad must resign and hand over power to a neutral, non-partisan caretaker regime: the CTG; c) the CTG would restore credibility to the electoral system and assure franchise rights to all citizens; and d) this interim government (CTG) would hand over power to a sovereign parliament elected through free and fair elections. The concept of CTG was thus born.

Fakhruddin Ahmed (1998: 9) believes that the importance of the joint declaration of the opposition lies in the fact that for the first time in 8 years of Ershad rule, the opposition was able to broadly agree on a constitutional formula for Ershad to step down and hand over power to a neutral and non-partisan CTG. Although Ershad rejected the CTG formula, calling it absurd and impractical, it was this mechanism created out of 'necessity' which paved the way for democracy to return to Bangladesh after 19 years.

When General Ershad resigned on 6 December 1990, as a result of the mass upsurge against his dictatorial regime, he handed over power to the then CJ Shahabuddin Ahmed, whom he had appointed as vice president and who was the consensus choice of all the major parties to set up a CTG with a team of advisors. Gowher Rizvi (1991: 157) notes that the actual transition, following weeks of chaos, was remarkably orderly and constitutional. To ensure the neutrality of the government and to prevent the advisors from succumbing to temptations of office, thereby ensuring non-partisan roles, the CTG passed a self-denying resolution which made its members ineligible for contesting the election or accepting political appointment under the newly elected government. The December 1990 CTG of Justice Shahabuddin Ahmed CJ (who was now also the acting president of Bangladesh) announced that the nation would go to the polls on 27 February

1991 and repeatedly expressed the government's firm determination to make the parliamentary elections free and fair, as per the aspirations of political parties and the people.

In doing so, the CTG took several measures to re-establish people's confidence in the electoral process. In response to a long-standing demand of the political parties, the EC was reconstituted with three sitting judges to ensure free, fair and impartial polls. It was empowered to suspend returning and presiding officers for election offences. All government and semi-government officers and employees deployed for election work were put under the jurisdiction of the EC. The CTG felt the necessity of giving the Union Parishads (the lowest tier of local government) and Pourashavas (municipalities) certain special responsibilities to maintain law and order within their respective jurisdictions with the help of an ordinance. The Union Parishad and Pourashava (Special Responsibilities) Ordinance 1991 was promulgated to this end (Hakim 1993: 52). This ordinance required that these local bodies resist all activities directed against the holding of fair election; resist any attempt to harm or destroy any office, symbol, poster, or banner related to the election; and resist any attempt at violating election laws and rules on the day of the election and extend the necessary assistance to the concerned authorities in the enforcement of such laws and rules. It empowered the CTG to suspend or dissolve any Union Parishad or Pourashava where peace was disrupted. Such firm actions had not been taken during military governance in previous years, and those in power during erstwhile government transitions had therefore failed to create an atmosphere conducive to the holding of free and fair elections.

Hakim (1993: 52) reiterates that the Shahabuddin CJ CTG, in consultation with the representatives of almost all political parties and the EC, formulated a 16-point code of conduct to be complied with by the political parties and their workers. This laid down, inter alia, that the participating parties must be respectful to mutual democratic rights; that tension must not be created for disrupting the congenial atmosphere of election; that everyone must refrain from indecorous slogans and comments, meetings, rallies; and that other campaign activities could not be obstructed. The code of conduct lacked adequate political sanction and its success depended fully on the goodwill of the political parties concerned. Nevertheless, its value in creating a sense of moral obligation and helping to cultivate mutual trust, respect and tolerance among the political parties and between political parties and the citizens could not be underestimated at that point in history. The People's Representation Order 1972 was amended and, in most cases, punitive measures for election offences were expanded. Regular law enforcing agencies as well as military and paramilitary forces were deployed on election day to maintain the law and order situation. The Arms Law was amended in order to resist electoral violence, and regarding the use of illegal fire arms, while the maximum punishment for possession of such illegal arms was now raised to life imprisonment. Moreover, the CTG launched a countrywide drive to recover illegal arms and ammunition. The Election Law was also amended so that the maximum amount of money that a candidate could spend was fixed at Taka 300,000, in an attempt to reduce the influence of black money on the election process. Finally, each candidate was asked to submit an account of his/her election-related expenditure to the EC within two weeks of the election.

As a result of these initiatives, which may seem like exhaustive measures (but in reality are basic measures that any government conducting a fair election may naturally take), and under the aegis of Shahabuddin Ahmed CJ's CTG, the 1991 elections were held throughout the country in an atmosphere of unprecedented peace, except for some stray incidents. They were generally hailed as 'the most free and fair', not only by local observers but also by foreign observers, who were unanimous about it. The four-member election observation team of the British Parliament, the Japanese team and the four country SAARC (South Asian Association for Regional Cooperation) team visited many polling stations throughout the country on election day and found the polling to be 'free, fair and impartial'. Although the role of foreign observers in granting seals of election approvals only on election day itself is perhaps an issue worth further study, for the purposes of this chapter and at this juncture of Bangladesh's history, it is important to note that such approval rated and continues to rate highly in the mindset of Bangladeshis, among both its political leaders and the people. As the election under a CTG was the first of its kind in Bangladesh during the Shahabuddin CJ CTG period, it generated unexpected enthusiasm among the voters. Since the CTG was not a party to the election, by fairness and neutrality this government could create 'trust' among the voters and between political parties. The voters exercised their voting rights in the election, unlike all previous elections, in an unfettered way and the nation sensed a 'revival of democracy' as this election was contested and participated in fully and freely by all political parties and alliances (Molla 2000: 8). To the surprise of many, BNP won the election and its win was a difficult pill to swallow for AL, but they had to, as the election was unanimously endorsed as the most free and fair.

Origin of the caretaker government movement

During the fifth parliament (after the elections conducted by Shahabuddin Ahmed CJ CTG), with BNP in power and AL as the opposition, the Eleventh Amendment of the Constitution was passed in August 1991, legalising the actions taken by the CTG of Shahabuddin Ahmed CJ, since that particular government was still extra-constitutional in nature. The amendment allowed Shahabuddin Ahmed CJ to resume his duties and responsibilities as the CJ of Bangladesh after handing over the charge of presidency to his successor. Although this arrangement of a CJ returning to his work in the Supreme Court did not posit a wave of discontent among the people, it raised certain concerns as to the propriety of this act from a constitutional legal perspective, and perhaps further study is warranted in this area. Specifically, it raises a concern about how far it is appropriate for a sitting CJ to serve as the head of a neutral CTG and then become re-assimilated in the judiciary of a freshly elected political government. But the euphoria of having a free and fair election, after years of military subjugation, was far more overwhelming for the political players and the people of Bangladesh at that juncture of history than the questioning of the passing of the Eleventh Amendment to the Constitution or the details of the position of the CJ. In the same spirit and during the same time, both the government and the opposition worked together in parliament to pass the Twelfth Amendment to the Constitution, providing for a parliamentary form of government in Bangladesh and changing from the presidential form. Political freedoms were somewhat restored and the restrictions on the press were removed to a certain extent. But the national radio and television remained under State control. In economic, social and external fronts, the new government followed a cautious centrist path, continuing the old policies started under the military rule of Zia and Ershad. One point of departure from democratisation during the BNP tenure was the abolition of the *upazila* system, which created a vacuum in local governance as the government did not introduce any alternative system (Jahan 2005: 286).

The restoration of parliamentary democracy and the assumption of power by Khaleda Zia in 1991 brought to the fore, once more, the conflicting dynamics of the Mujib and Zia political lineages. The bitter past came to dominate their relationship and polarised society, and with it the polity, to a large extent. Not only did personal animosity during this term assume political colour, but also frequent boycotts of the parliament and *hartal* (strikes and total shutdown of normal life and economic activities) came to mark the new democratic political order. The lack of democratic practices and non-cooperation between the two major political parties seriously hampered the consolidation of democracy (Pattanaik 2006).

This trend of personal animosity, polarised society, lack of democratic practices and non-cooperation between AL and BNP and violence would continue, even 27 years later, as we presently observe in 2017. Given the culture of mistrust, it appears that there will remain a need for a transitional modality of some kind to oversee elections, even if it is not the CTG per se. Dr. Iftekharuzzaman, CEO of Transparency International Bangladesh (TIB), pointed out three features during an interview with the author about the nature of Bangladesh politics and clearly proposed that Bangladesh still requires a transitional mechanism for elections given this scenario:

> Firstly, politics has become a business as there is an investment involved in the form of electoral costs. Secondly, there is a strong extraordinarily confrontational politics, which is based on historical legacy, especially post 1975 and there is tremendous distrust gravely affecting the nation. Thirdly, the politics is of a zero sum game. Since leadership is concentrated on one person and the mindset is individualistic, this affects trust and the entire socio-political sphere. We have structures but no democratic governance as it is politics of force which prevails in Bangladesh. There is lack of trust, not only between politicians and political parties but also in the rule of law, in the institutions, in the administration. In

> this atmosphere, a transitional mechanism is needed otherwise, there is no democracy.

In similar lines, during an interview with the author, jurist Dr. Kamal Hossain emphasised how the absence of trust impacts on the various strata of society as it does not only affect the democratic culture of Bangladesh but democratic culture anywhere. This, according to him, is because

> Democratic culture presupposes a certain amount of mutual respect and understanding among citizens, among those who deal with each other, among those who govern and those who are exercising power in different institutions and those who are affected by the exercise of power.

This mutual respect of the 'other', however, is completely non-existent between AL and BNP and looks unlikely to change in the near future.

Hakim (1993: 17) highlights that, notwithstanding the general recognition that the CTG provided a better alternative to a party government in holding elections to the parliament, there was no serious attempt in the initial years of the fifth parliament to institutionalise the experiment. Neither BNP nor AL showed any interest, in this respect, after the 1991 elections by the Shahabuddin Ahmed CJ CTG. Nor, however, was there any public demand for such an arrangement at that point in history. Although the Jatio Party (JP) of General Ershad had opposed the concept of the CTG since its inception, the idea of the CTG had been launched in 1983. At that time, it did not appeal to the main parties, AL and BNP, or the left fronts, who were intensely engaged in anti-Ershad agitation programmes in the streets, aiming to remove the dictatorial regime as that was clearly the focus then. Jamat-e-Islami (JIB) submitted a private members' bill in December 1991, seeking a permanent arrangement for holding all future parliamentary elections under the CTG. The bill proposed that the prime minister (PM) would resign on the day the election schedule was announced. Following the PM's resignation, the president would form an advisory council and those included in the council would not belong to any political party, nor would they contest the elections. The council would automatically be dissolved after an elected cabinet took over the charge of the government.

Almost two years after JIB's bill, AL submitted a CTG bill on 28 October 1993, considering the successful Shahabuddin Ahmed CJ CTG as a model and reiterating that the CTG could be headed by the incumbent CJ to oversee the conduct of parliamentary elections. The reported rigging and malpractices in the by-elections at Mirpur in 1993, under the aegis of the BNP government, undermined the credibility of the EC as well as of the BNP government itself. It was under these circumstances, given the prevailing mistrust and suspicion, that the institutionalisation of the CTG to conduct free and fair elections was conceptualised and demanded by AL. The AL Bill also provided that the CJ would perform the duties of the head of the CTG as an additional responsibility. The JP bill was submitted in November 1993, providing that the president would appoint, at his own discretion, anyone as the head of the CTG after the incumbent PM resigned, following the dissolution of the parliament. Hakim (1993: 18) points out that the three bills (of AL, JP and JIB) submitted to parliament about the CTG had more similarities than differences, the main difference revolving around the aspect of the head of the CTG. While the AL bill restricted the choice of the president by requiring him to appoint the CJ as the head of the CTG (perhaps with the intention of limiting the power of a partisan president and allowing a non-partisan Supreme Court CJ to lead the CTG, thereby narrowing the scope of manipulation and minimising the issues of mistrust), the other bills of JP and JIB granted some discretion to the president in this aspect. In all other aspects, the three bills incorporated the main elements of the transitory CTG. BNP however, strongly opposed the idea of the CTG during the process of institutionalising it. In retrospective, it seems that, from very early on, the three political parties (minus BNP, who opposed the concept initially) differed in the mode of appointing the head of the CTG. This is an aspect which, in subsequent years, as seen later in this chapter, brought the country into a constitutional crisis.

Unsurprisingly, the nascent democracy of Bangladesh had its share of trials and tribulations. Since BNP came to power in 1991, four BNP members had been appointed mayors of the four main municipalities of Dhaka, Chittagong, Rajshahi and Khulna. Under previous electoral rules, city mayors were named by ward commissioners, who in turn were directly elected by the people. But in response to the demand by legislators, the Bangladesh parliament passed a new law providing for the direct election of mayors. Opposition parties, in the interest of free, fair and clean elections, demanded the resignation of the appointed mayors before they could participate as candidates. Based on the recommendations of the Ministry of Law, the government asked its appointed mayors to resign, and they did so and proceeded to contest the polls. The major political parties also fielded their candidates and the result was that the government (BNP) lost in two important cities to the opposition: Dhaka and Chittagong went to its arch rival, AL. The elections were reported to be free and fair although six people, who were identified as AL supporters, were killed in Dhaka in post-election violence. Golam Hossain (1995: 171–178) identifies that while the defeat of BNP was mainly due to internal conflict and poor performance in office, the AL victory probably reflected the voters' expectation of a balance of power between the two major political parties at the national and local levels. It seemed quite clear here, at this juncture of history, that the Bangladeshi voters are more politically alert vis-a-vis the balance of power than what the general perception indicates. For example, Akhtar Hossain (2000: 508–529) characterised Bangladeshi voters as 'uneducated, politically ill-informed and possess[ing] unsophisticated character traits, vulnerable to manipulation of one form or another by politicians' – which clearly may not be the only picture painted here. BNP's loss of the two mayoral posts was a great blow, particularly in Dhaka, where it had won all eight seats in the municipal area in previous parliamentary polls.

Although the issue of the CTG remained dormant in the initial years of BNP rule, this matter arose in the Mirpur 1993 by-elections and subsequently during the Magura-2 by-elections in March 1994. Jahan (2005: 286) identifies that the initial constructive engagement between the two major political parties, AL and BNP, began to evaporate within 2 years of BNP rule. The major contested issue became free and fair elections. Jahan (2005) portrays that the two parties clashed, often violently, over several municipal and parliamentary by-elections. The most significant event in 1994 was the continuous boycott of parliament by the opposition parties, particularly AL, as they pressed their demand for a constitutional amendment that would provide for holding all future elections under a neutral CTG. This demand reached its peak when the opposition parties alleged that electioneering in the Magura-2 by-elections in 1994 had not been free, fair and clean, due to the government's blatant interference and use of government machinery to win the seat. The by-election result galvanised the opposition to demand the creation of a neutral CTG to run the parliamentary elections of 1996 (Kochanek 1996: 707). Hossain (2000: 508–529) explains that the concerned seat of Magura was vacated due to a death and was for several terms occupied by AL, and its loss to BNP led to complaints of large-scale vote rigging. Several media reports also noted unfairness, and some observers thought that BNP was trying to regain the image lost in the mayoral elections just a few weeks earlier.

The opposition parties complained, however, that there could not be free and fair elections under a BNP government and declared that they would not participate in any election except under a CTG regime. The deep-rooted 'mistrust' between the government and the opposition along with the confrontational politics of the two major political parties became more and more embedded and evident. The issue also aroused a national intellectual debate, with the opposition parties pressurising the government by calling nationwide strikes, organising mass rallies and street agitations. The government in response termed the demand of the opposition undemocratic and unconstitutional, and passed a bill in parliament to strengthen the much-forgotten EC. This new law was called the Representation of People (Amendment) Act, 1994. It empowered the EC to issue identity cards to each voter as well as entrusting the EC with the authority to stop polling at any polling station, at any stage, if it was certain that elections could not be held fairly because of malpractice.

The opposition did not reject the law outright but considered it inadequate to check the level of election fraud and rigging. It thus re-emphasised the demand for a neutral CTG, adopting a three-pronged strategy to exert pressure on the government. At the heart of the strategy was their determination to continue with the boycott of the proceedings of the parliament. A second strategy was to exert extra-parliamentary pressure by resorting to *hartals* and *gheraos* (surrounding government offices forcibly), blocking rails and roads and enforcing work stoppages in public and private sector organisations. Ahmed (2004: 23) identifies that in the first nine months of 1995, the opposition parties called 44 *hartals*, with some ranging from six hours to 96 hours. In November 1995, they called for a six-day continuous *hartal*, thereby seeking to paralyse the government and administration which already had the difficult task of handling the economy of the country. The third strategy used by the opposition MPs was to resign 'en masse' from the parliament. This they eventually did in December 1994, when 147 MPs of the opposition handed over their resignation letters to the Speaker of the 300-seat parliament.

Ahmed (2004: 24) is of the opinion that the reaction of the public was that they were not initially enthused about such wrangling to the extent that the politicians expected, and it would even be fair to say that it caused disillusionment among them. Matters were made worse when all the tactics of the opposition were challenged in the court through a writ petition in June 1994, alleging that the opposition MPs were not fulfilling the pledges they had made to their voters in their respective constituencies by staying away from the parliament. It was further observed in the allegation that although the MPs did not attend the parliamentary sessions, they were still seen as illegally drawing salary and allowances and enjoying other facilities, without doing their duty, causing financial losses to the people and the country.

The opposition MPs angrily stressed that not only did the petitioner not have '*locus standi*' to file such a writ petition, as the petitioner was not an aggrieved person, but that even the court did not have any authority to direct the opposition MPs to attend the parliament session. The High Court division of the Supreme Court delivered its judgment in November 1994, declaring the continued abstention of the opposition MPs as illegal and unconstitutional and held that the salaries and benefits they were drawing were also illegal due to their absence from parliament. The court therefore directed the opposition MPs to return to parliament when it was next summoned and ordered that the financial benefits absentee MPs drew were recoverable by the appropriate authority under the due process of law. Ahmed (2004: 25) further elaborates:

> This ruling almost sent death blow to the absentee MPs who argued that the court judgment interfered with the sovereignty of the parliament and the privileges of the legislators and that the judgment clearly reflected a partisan outlook. The Appellate Division stayed the execution of the verdict until 15 January 1995 while the three opposition leaders of AL, JP and JIB filed an appeal against the High Court judgment. A subsequent attempt by the government to vacate the stay order on the judgment was rejected by the Appellate Division. The opposition leaders argued that vacating the stay would defeat the very purpose of the appeal. They also observed that the impugned judgment and order contained opinions on largely political issues: hence any attempt to vacate the stay would create more tension and disharmony between the ruling party and the opposition parties and lead to further constitutional crisis.

Ahmed (2004: 25–26) continues that the other two strategies adopted by the opposition parties were also challenged in court. For example, on the eve of the 72-hour *hartal* called by the opposition, the High Court issued a *rule nisi* upon the leaders to show cause within two weeks under 'what' authority of law they had called the *hartal*. Since the High Court did not pass any order to the prayer for injunction, the *hartal* took place as scheduled. A further *rule nisi* was issued upon the leaders of the opposition to show cause as to 'why' their decision to resign en masse would not be declared illegal. Simultaneously, another *rule nisi* was issued upon the Speaker of the parliament, asking him to explain the 'reasons' for the delay in disposing of the resignation letters which were handed to him by the opposition parties. This, according to Ahmed (2004: 26), precipitated a crisis between the legislative and judicial organs of the government. However, notwithstanding the intervention by the court, the anti-government agitation by the opposition parties continued unabated. Since the MPs lost their stake in the maintenance of the legislative system due to their en masse resignation, they demanded the dissolution of the fifth parliament and the resignation of the government, none of which was ceded to by the latter. The decision of the Speaker to defer his ruling on the resignation letters helped the government withstand the pressure to dissolve the parliament for a little while longer.

Jahan (2005: 286–287) identifies that civil society and the international donor community stepped in at this point as referees to break the continuing political deadlock between the two major political parties. Civil society groups urged the government and the opposition, especially AL and BNP, to settle their differences through dialogue and constitutional means. The international community became significantly vocal, trying to mediate the conflicts between these two parties. The Commonwealth Secretary General's nomination of the former Australian Governor General, Sir Ninian Stephen, is notable in this context. His intervention to facilitate dialogue between the government and the opposition failed, despite three alternative proposals to resolve the impasse during that time. At least 11 initiatives and 21 formulae had been advanced to end the crisis during this period. One of the first proposals that Sir Stephen put forward was for an 11-member all-party interim government to be headed by the incumbent PM with an equal number of members from the government and the opposition. A neutral person would be included in the cabinet to look after the sensitive ministries, such as the home, information and establishment ministries, particularly during elections. The ruling party agreed to the first proposal and suggested that the cabinet members should have no portfolio and that the PM should have no executive power during the transition. But the opposition was not willing to allow the incumbent PM to lead the interim government during the elections principally because of the issue of 'trust', and emphatically reiterated that the PM must resign.

The second proposal was for an interim administration headed by a ruling party MP other than the incumbent PM, while the third proposal was to empower the president to lead the interim administration, which would however require a constitutional amendment, but the MPs had already resigned. These efforts brought no results, despite several attempts to bridge the gap between the ruling party and the opposition by the Commonwealth Secretariat as well as by Dhaka-based ambassadors and a local eminent persons' group.

What was also intriguing was the 'intra party conflict' within the ruling party. This became apparent when the opposition MPs resigned en masse with their demand for a neutral CTG, which caused 'major tensions' in BNP according to Ahmed (2004: 28–29). He pointed out that the then information minister, in an interview with a national daily, expressed the opinion that future elections should be held under a CTG headed by the CJ. This observation seriously conflicted with the official policy of the ruling party (BNP), which still found the idea of a CTG a wild proposition. The information minister was immediately removed from the cabinet. Subsequently, two other BNP MPs also spoke in similar lines and all three were served with show-cause notices and asked to explain why disciplinary actions should not be taken against them. Although the replies of two of the MPs were subsequently accepted by the BNP Standing Committee (the policy-making body of the party), one MP's primary membership to BNP was suspended and it was combined with filed cases from the Bureau of Anti-Corruption. Such are the dangers and risks associated with adopting an independent line of thinking within a political party. It is quite clear that the only voice of the party, whether BNP, AL or any other political party, is that of the head's, and there is no scope for any member to have an independent voice or to not listen to the party head. There is no inculcation of intra party democracy, whether at the central and local level, in any shape or form, within the political parties of Bangladesh and no scope for meaningful pluralistic existence (Institute of Governance Studies, BRAC University 2006).

Institutionalising the caretaker government system

Amid this scenario of continuous boycott of parliament, the public image of parliament and politicians was gravely affected due to the clear failure of the politicians to solve their differences and conflicts even within a period of two years, despite serious diplomatic and other initiatives. This not only affected the public image of the politicians but also seriously questioned their ability to run the country and their commitment to the interests of the nation. In the meantime, a major dilemma was faced by the government after the Speaker declared in August 1995 that the opposition MPs had lost their membership of parliament from June 1995 for unauthorised absence during 90 consecutive sitting days of parliament. Following this deliberation, the government was confronted with the difficult task of deciding whether to hold by-elections for the vacant seats of the parliament or to dissolve the parliament altogether. Clearly both these options posed risks for the government.

According to Ahmed (2004: 32–33), on balance, the government found the dissolution of the parliament a politically more viable option than the holding of so many by-elections. Holding both by-elections and national elections soon thereafter would have cost implications and was likely to cause serious cynicism among the public, not to mention violent opposition. Amid this scenario, the government dissolved the fifth parliament on 24 November 1995, four months before the expiry of its five-year term, and decided to hold elections to the sixth parliament, arguing that this was needed to ensure continuity in constitutional rule and to enable it to enact a bill for the CTG. The opposition threatened that it would resist the elections at any cost under the government as the element of 'trust' had already been gravely compromised. As a result, none of the major political parties took part in the elections held on 15 February 1996. The scale of violence during this election reached serious heights, which was quite apparent because elections could not take place in ten constituencies due to massive escalated violence. The rate of voter turnout was, as expected, very low. BNP unsurprisingly won a landslide victory, causing a serious 'legitimacy' crisis for the sixth parliament, headed by Khaleda Zia.

It is perhaps fair to say that every government that has come to power since the birth of Bangladesh has had to face challenges to its 'legitimacy' at some point. The military regimes of Zia and Ershad adopted identical strategies to perpetuate and legitimise their rules. Military leaders, in addition, need a support base in the civilian sector along with the solid backing of the armed forces. Rulers, whether military or civil, have held elections only when they were confident that 'managing' the results of these elections in their favour would not be difficult. Although the 'legitimacy' obtained through an 'arranged' election is circumspect and unacceptable to the people, it enhances to some extent the bargaining capacity of the rulers in negotiating with opposing political forces (Huque and Hakim 1993: 260). This bargaining capacity is further strengthened if the election is held by a neutral, non-partisan CTG.

Kochanek (1997: 136–142) narrates that the opposition response to the results of the managed vote was to call a three-day *hartal* on 24 February 1996 followed by a 36-hour *hartal* and a decision to launch an indefinite non-cooperation programme beginning 9 March 1996, which would continue until its demand for new elections under the CTG was met. The non-stop strikes brought the entire nation to a standstill as banks, ports, factories and shops closed and all transportation and communications ceased to function. On 10 March 1996, in the midst of this total paralysis, the president of Bangladesh intervened and called upon the government and the opposition to enter into talks to resolve the crisis. When the talks broke down, the president invited the BNP leader Khaleda Zia to form a new government and opened the first session of the sixth parliament. The opposition responded by staging violent protests and on 20 March 1996 the government deployed the army in an attempt to restore supplies and transportation within the country.

Kochanek (1997) further notes that, meanwhile, as the economic paralysis and political deadlock persisted, social groups within civil society intervened directly in the political process in a desperate effort to end the crisis. The Federation of Bangladesh

Chambers of Commerce and Industry (FBCCI) issued a 48-hour ultimatum to the president to invalidate the February elections and set a date for free and fair elections under a CTG. The FBCCI also took steps to mobilise urban interest groups in an effort to create a *third force* that would attempt to compel the political leadership to behave in a more responsible manner. The response was overwhelming, and as a result the business community was joined by teachers, journalists, doctors, lawyers, trade unions and non-governmental organisations (NGOs) in public rallies demanding the immediate resignation of the government, the dissolution of parliament and new elections under a CTG. For the first time in the country's history, the business community had openly – and successfully – intervened in the political process.

It was quite clear that the opposition, the media and the people considered the sixth parliament illegitimate and demanded its immediate dissolution. Political crises escalated economic turmoil and the government, under pressure, decided to move on a constitutional amendment bill providing for the future holding of parliamentary elections under the CTG.

On 21 March 1996, the sixth parliament approved the bill granting constitutional status to the CTG under chapter 2, part A of the Bangladesh Constitution which stated that the non-party 'neutral' CTG would be collectively responsible to the president. It would be headed by a CA and would consist of ten advisors. Article 58(C) clauses 3, 4 and 5 read basically as 'The President shall appoint as CA the person who among the retired CJs of Bangladesh retired last and who is qualified to be appointed as an advisor'. It also lays down that 'if the retired CJ is not available or is not willing to hold this office, the President should appoint as CA the person who among the retired CJs of Bangladesh retired immediately before the last CJ'. As an alternative, 'if no retired CJ were to be available, the President could appoint as CA the person who among the retired judges of the Appellate Division retired last and in case even if he is not available or not willing, the President shall appoint the retired judge of the Appellate Division who retired immediately before the last such retired judge'. If the two most recently retired Chief Justices or Appellate Division Judges are not available or are not willing to hold office, the President shall appoint as CA, a citizen, after consultations with major political parties.

Thus, the Constitution provided five options in total for appointing the CA. Only if all other options failed could the president serve as the head of the CTG in addition to his presidential duties. The Constitution also stipulated that, during the tenure of the CTG, the ministry of defence would be under the president's control as normally the president is only a ceremonial head of the State. Riaz (2016a: 79) reminded us that since political expediency was the driving force behind the inculcation of the CTG, the long-term implications of adopting this structure in the Constitution were not carefully thought out which, perhaps, is why many important details and factors between various relationships remained unexplained, which, as we shall see, subsequently came to haunt the nation.

Thus, the bill provided for the CTG to hold general elections, incorporating an administrative and constitutional framework significantly different from the CTG framework of 1991. Under the 1996 framework, the CTG was held accountable to the president and was also given complete jurisdiction over the defence of the country. The system and the relevant laws were built in such a way that the power of the unelected government was restricted. Since there was no other clear mechanism to hold them accountable, certain limits to their authority were fashioned. One such limitation arose under article 123(3) of the Constitution of Bangladesh which obliged the CTG to hold the parliamentary elections within 90 days of handing over power to them, while under article 58D (1), the CTG was stripped of any power to make policy decisions. Further, an emergency provision was included to emphasise that in case of a state of emergency, like war or a war-like situation, the immediate past parliament was to resume authority (article 72 (4) of the Constitution). The will of the people was argued to be the basis for creating an unelected, though legitimate, government in a transitional democracy.

With the CTG institutionalised through the Thirteenth Amendment of the Constitution, the opposition further intensified its street agitation programmes, demanding the immediate resignation of the government so that power could be handed over to the new CTG. The civil service set a deadline for the government to resign, failing which they threatened to defy government orders. Rashiduzzaman (1997: 262) aptly remarked that

> When the anti-government protests reached a boiling point, a Dhaka based diplomat commented that since key bureaucrats abstained from work and many openly changed their loyalty to the opposition, it was only a question of time before the BNP cabinet was obliged to quit. Maligned for its perceived sloth and inefficiency, the Bangladeshi bureaucracy is a politicised institution and in the hartal dominated political culture, government officers are not immune to polarising agitation.

Civil society and NGOs, along with the civil service, expressed solidarity with the intensified movement which made it impossible for the BNP government to function. As a result, Khaleda Zia resigned on 30 March 1996 and requested the president to form a CTG. The president appointed the most recently retired CJ, Habibur Rahman, as the CA of the CTG and transferred all executive powers except defence to him, unlike under the 1991 framework. To the dismay of the opposition parties, the CTG was formed by the BNP-nominated president and not through a participatory decision-making process involving all major political parties, as was the case in 1991.

Khan (1997: 589) presented that the issue of constitutional amendment to provide for a non-partisan CTG for the specific purpose of holding a general election every five years or when necessary could yield positive results in terms of building the needed infrastructure to nourish democracy. But democratic aspirations are being confronted by the political reality of the incumbent's propensity to use the powers and resources of the State to ensure electoral victory. The ruling party's gestures of good intention, such as strengthening the EC, may not be enough to allay the fears of opposition parties about government-instigated electoral violence and vote fraud. In addition, Riaz (2016a: 78–79) makes the observation that

> One cannot but agree with the Bangladeshi analysts who stressed that the system of caretaker government 'does not provide credit to the uprightness of politicians or of the government'. It manifests one simple fact: that the politicians have no trust in each other. It palpably implies the absence of a healthy political system in the country.

This is precisely why the Thirteenth Amendment to the Constitution mandating CTG-held general elections every five years was overwhelmingly endorsed by most parties, both government and opposition.

The second caretaker government: 1996

The tenure of the Habibur Rahman CJ CTG was limited to 90 days, within which a general election was to be held. Given the level of difficulty in preparing for a politically acceptable, safe, free and fair general election, limiting the tenure of the CTG to 90 days was found to be insufficient to satisfactorily complete the electoral preparatory process. Despite the time constraints and a power struggle within the military, culminating in a failed rebellion by a section of the army, the June 1996 elections under the CTG were acclaimed by both local and international poll observers as basically free and fair (Khan 2007: 158–163). Molla (2000: 13) observes that, while the CTG of 1991 was the outcome of political consensus, the CTG in 1996 became a constitutional reality in order to accomplish a constitutional as well as a historic necessity.

This particular CTG concentrated on three major areas besides the running of the day-to-day government: firstly, to create a stable, peaceful environment for holding a free and fair parliamentary election within the stipulated time; secondly, to streamline the civil administration by reinforcing law and order and by exposing the incidents of governmental corruption and incompetence; and finally, to project a national image before the global community, highlighting the fact that 1) public will had triumphed over the quasi-authoritarian rule, signalling once more the restoration of a democratic electoral process; 2) the CTG was based on the consensus reached by major political parties; and 3) genuine efforts were being made by the people of Bangladesh to sustain a democratic system achieved through struggle and sacrifice (Khan 2007: 160–163).

Khan (2007) remarked that, based on the 1991 CTG, the 1996 CTG took some constructive measures. Firstly, it constituted an impartial EC headed by a senior civil servant. In his Bengali book *Tattabodhayak Shorkarer Daibhar*, CJ Habibur Rahman himself stated that the CTG was relieved to have appointed qualified and experienced civil servants as the chairman and members of the EC (Rahman 2010: 85–86). It deviated from the previous CTG of CJ Shahabuddin

Ahmed to the extent that the former EC consisted of three Supreme Court justices, with the senior-most justice serving as its chairman. The EC was authorised to carefully verify voters' registration and make enforceable a code of conduct for a free and fair election. The previous EC under the 1991 CTG regime had already reduced the number of total voters by 16.1 per cent for false registrations, including non-existent and mostly underage persons. Secondly, it ordered an inter-district transfer of all career district administrators, preventing them from being influenced by vested interests. Thirdly, it ordered a strict enforcement of 1972 electoral rules which imposed serious legal and administrative sanctions on officials and workers at the polling centres for impropriety and fraud. And finally, it invited election monitoring teams from various quarters, ranging from a British parliamentary delegation to SAARC teams, to delegates from the European Parliament, to a Washington-based National Democratic Institute (NDI) team and a Japanese parliamentary delegation, among others. To minimise the incidence of voter fraud and subsequent violence, USAID offered to help the administration with computerised voter registration and the necessary training for election personnel.

In order to enhance its operational effectiveness and political accountability, which could conceivably improve the framework for future CTGs, as well as the process of transferring power and hence the overall democratic transition, CJ Habibur Rahman and his CTG team sought to apply interactive decision-making/implementing strategies such as maintaining unobstructed two-way communication with the leaders of the major political parties; holding frequent brainstorming meetings with the advisors of the 1991 CTG; establishing liaison with leaders of professional/occupational associations and labour unions; conducting periodic sessions with student leaders from all political parties; carefully organising public hearings on selected national issues; engaging interested intellectuals in probing into the possible structural and procedural reforms needed for political stability; accelerating the ongoing training of the EC personnel in the development and application of the computerised voter identity and registration system; initiating a national debate in order to build a consensus for the reform of the legal system, which still carried the anti-people baggage of the colonial rule; and negotiating with all political parties for the continuation of a strong, autonomous EC as established under the CTG framework during the tenure of an elected government. The latter step would alleviate the problem of violation of electoral rules, routinely faced in mayoral contests and parliamentary by-elections. The 1996 CTG, unfortunately, lacked the time and political support base to vigorously pursue its agenda for consensus building. One constant support to this CTG was that it did benefit in terms of receiving support from the head of the 1991 CTG of Justice Shahabuddin Ahmed CJ – an individual revered by most sections of the political spectrum and the people of Bangladesh due to his impeccable integrity, honesty and personality.

As analysed by Rashiduzzaman (1997: 264), AL leader Sheikh Hasina termed the CTG a 'democratic triumph' of 120 million people, but the victory had come through months of agitation, chaos and widespread violence. The anticipated voting, supervised by a non-political authority, generated a new wave of optimism for AL, while for the JP it renewed hopes for the release of its leader Ershad from jail. With a stopgap neutral executive replacing the BNP government, the opposition parties no longer had a common enemy to attack and no burning issue except for the election itself. Their earlier solidarity now waned as each party followed its own electoral goals. The demand for a CTG in 1996 was thus, on the face of it, a well-thought-out strategy that brought definitive advantages to the electoral process.

Rashiduzzaman (1997) concludes by posing some important questions about the CTG and replying to the same: Could the CTG satisfy all the contenders for power? Was it the middle path, bridging the brawling leaders and facilitating a smooth succession? Was the non-partisan executive accepted as neutral? Not while the political leaders were unwilling to cooperate with the advisory cabinet, not when the parties nurtured their respective armed gangs, and certainly not when one party charged the CTG advisors as being 'tilted' towards the other.

The first burst of anger came from Khaleda Zia, who claimed that the CA was not impartial in dealing with BNP. To allay fears of bureaucratic bias against BNP, the CA asserted that civil servants could not support any group except an elected government, but his impartiality was questioned for his failure to take any action against civil servants who had openly sided with the opposition during the March upheaval. BNP continued to challenge the CTG's neutrality and utility, although its own legislators had earlier created (albeit under pressure from AL) such an entity as a permanent electoral supervision and power transfer device. However, despite all the drama, election for the seventh parliament was held on 12 June 1996, peacefully, with AL forming the next government after winning the election under the aegis of the second CTG. The election was deemed to be free and fair according to both national and international observers. It was once again a difficult pill for BNP to swallow, that AL had actually won this election, but it had to concede to this reality.

The third caretaker government: 2001

Kochanek (1998: 135–136) projects that the honeymoon enjoyed by the AL government, elected in 1996, lasted a little over a year and came to an end in the closing months of 1997, as by then Bangladesh's opposition parties once again took to the streets in familiar efforts to topple the elected regime. Like AL in 1991, BNP never accepted defeat at the polls and had been searching for an issue that could be used to launch a sustained anti-government movement. The strategy adopted by BNP was similar to that of AL during the previous BNP rule: general strikes, walkouts and boycotts of parliament and politics in the streets which would lead, as hoped by BNP, to the resignation of party MPs and a call for new elections. But for that to happen, a potent issue was needed. Although the initial year of the AL government produced some achievements (the controversial Ganges water-sharing agreement, repeal of the Indemnity Ordinance, election of the president), it soon began to counter a series of domestic problems and a gradually resurgent opposition. Poor political management, growing economic problems and a series of self-inflicted wounds suffered by AL's efforts to settle old scores with BNP together brought a renewal of opposition movement politics causing instability, aggression and restlessness in the country.

As a result, months before the third CTG was formed, the opposition BNP chairperson began to urge the elected government of AL to step down before the expiry of its term and hand over power to a neutral CTG. While Khaleda Zia charged the AL with attempting to restore the authoritarian cult of *Mujibism* and selling the sovereignty of the country, particularly to neighbouring India, Sheikh Hasina accused BNP of trying to topple her legitimately elected government simply to protect the killers of Mujib. One sees here, too, reverberations of the simmering post-war atrocity issues, which have until recently led to even more violent repercussions. These accusations and attitudes of the *Begums* certainly have not ameliorated the culture of mistrust.

In the meantime, the economy remained stumped, law and order deteriorated and the country faced a mounting failure of administration (Kochanek 1998: 141). Interestingly, the newspaper articles during those times projected an optimism that both the major political parties had about the system of the CTG, having before them two instances when the CTG system had successfully worked for Bangladesh in delivering free, fair and inclusive elections. In one such news item, the PM – while speaking to the diplomats in Dhaka – said that 'if elections could be held in quick successions, people would be used to exercising their franchise in a fair environment and elect a government of their choice, which would help establish a healthy election culture in the country'. What was striking, however, while sifting through the newspapers of the month of March 2001, was the thick evidence of widespread political tension due to the confrontation of AL and BNP on the issues of the resignation of the government and the fixation of the poll dates. The element of mistrust, deeply entrenched in the mindsets of the two major political actors, was embedded to such an extent that whether or not an elected government would hand over power to a CTG or when it would do so to the government in transition plagued the thinking and actions of the political stakeholders.

The most recently retired CJ, pre-election time, at this juncture, was Justice Latifur Rahman CJ (2002: 63–75), who noted in his autobiography that during his farewell on his last working day as a CJ he was somewhat surprised by the tone of certain lawyers at the programme arranged for him by the Supreme Court Bar Association. Pro-BNP lawyers of the association spoke in a way that the outgoing CJ should discharge his responsibility as a CA justly and properly. CJ Rahman felt the need to counter those speeches by stating very firmly that he was pledge-bound to discharge the responsibility of the CA with fairness and neutrality. Nevertheless, he was gently reminded in some speeches that despite having a reputation as a simple and soft-hearted man, he had to do the job very firmly. He noticed that the tones of the pro-BNP and pro-AL lawyers were different, the latter clearly stating that he was capable of holding a fair election and that they had full faith in him. But the hesitation of the pro-BNP lawyers was obvious as they even expressed their doubts about his future role. He remarked, sadly, that the way the politicians have been so blinded and overpowered by their political outlook in Bangladesh means they could never judge a person properly and fairly by rising above such narrow parochialism. According to him, and in line with awareness of the effect of politicisation, the Supreme Court Bar Association is unsurprisingly divided into two camps: BNP and AL. The pro-BNP lawyers erroneously and baselessly identified Justice Latifur Rahman CJ as a silent supporter of AL, perhaps for two reasons: the first was because he had expedited the hearing of the *Bangabandhu* murder case, and the second was because of the non-appointment of Justice K M Hasan as a judge of the Appellate Division during his tenure as a CJ (Rahman 2002: 65–75). Such is the level of bipolar political schism in the socio-political realm of Bangladesh.

The ordeal awaiting Justice Latifur Rahman CJ as the CA of the CTG in 2001 was pre-empted in newspaper articles, highlighting the difficult areas of work he was to face in the following words:

> After accomplishing the onus of picking up the members of the advisory council, the toughest tasks for the interim administration rest with the urgent measures to ensure an atmosphere, which in the analyses of all parties, would be conducive to holding free and fair general elections. The two main political parties have gulf of difference on how to conduct a free and fair voting, to pull the electoral balance in one's favour – political analysts say. Presumably their stands will leave many odds for Justice Latifur Rahman CJ and his short-lived colleagues. The major challenges lie with the issue of law and order situation including recovery of small and light arms and hunting of the terrorists, guaranteeing equal and fair opportunities for all parties, making the EC acceptable to all and helping it to bring necessary reforms, settlement of the contentious issues of deployment of the army with power of magistracy during elections and allowing the local observers in the polling booths and the likes.

Amid this edgy situation, Justice Latifur Rahman CJ took oath as the CA of the third CTG of Bangladesh on 15 July 2001, with the responsibility to conduct the election to the eighth parliament session within 90 days. He appointed ten advisors, about which arose controversy from AL with regard to two of the advisors. According to Ahmed (2004), one such objectionable recruitment was the appointment of barrister Syed Ishtiaque Ahmed, who was a lawyer to the BNP leader Morshed Khan, in a case relating to the Public Safety Act. AL asked whether the judgement in the case would not be influenced, now that Ahmed was in government (Ahmed 2004: 53–54). But the CA nonetheless went ahead with the appointment as the suggestion of this particular advisor's name initially emerged from the head of the first CTG, Justice Shahabuddin Ahmed CJ, with whom Justice Latifur Rahman CJ shared a very good rapport and consulted often with regard to various matters.

Another objection raised by AL was the appointment of Mr. Hafizuddin Khan, a former Comptroller and Auditor General (C&AG), as an advisor in the CTG, on both legal and political grounds. Referring to article 129 of the Bangladesh Constitution, that a former C&AG was ineligible for further office in the services of the Republic, a writ petition challenging the legality of the appointment was also filed in the High Court division of the Supreme Court. AL also referred to a newspaper article to substantiate its argument that the former C&AG had an anti-AL bias. But the CA refused to pay heed to these insinuations, stating that in this case, firstly, the previous appointments of university professors as advisors to past CTGs were then also not legal, but those appointments nevertheless went ahead in previous CTG administrations; and secondly, the appointment of a former C&AG in the elected government cabinet of 1991 was never raised as an issue, hence this particular appointment should also be without reservation. Regrettably, these two appointments remained problematic and raised serious comments from the AL head Sheikh Hasina in the following words: 'the neutrality of the present CTG naturally came under question when the people saw that allegedly partisan persons were inducted in the non-party CTG administration' (*The Bangladesh Observer*, 24 July 2001). The same article continued with Sheikh Hasina citing measures that the CA took upon his assumption of office, such as the abrupt transfer of 13 top bureaucrats, appointment of two controversial advisors and prevention of the broadcast of *Bangabandhu's* historic remarks. She suggested in the same report that it appeared that the CTG considered AL as its opponent. Other criticisms of this CTG included (*The Bangladesh Observer*, 24 August 2001):

> After the mass transfer for both at the highest echelon of bureaucracy and at, as low a level as the sub-inspector of police, its appetite for this particular prescription seems still voracious; not only does it give the impression that it is obsessed with transfer but a few questionable decisions in other areas have made its role no less controversial. One wonders what purpose the transfers in areas not even remotely connected with the process of electioneering will serve. If the administration's liking for transfer has turned almost into an obsession, its more compelling agendas have been relegated to the back burner.

One can sense here, with the benefit of hindsight, simmering doubts in the mind of the AL leader as to whether the CTG was really such a useful institution after all. It may be too simplistic to just dismiss her criticisms as oppositional politicking. Despite strong criticisms, the CTG went ahead with reforming electoral laws through an Ordinance (Representation of People Order (Amendment) Act 2001) amending the election laws of 1972, empowering the armed forces during the election to arrest without warrant and make seizure – a duty usually performed by the police. The law also authorised the EC to take punitive actions against members of the law enforcing agencies if they failed to discharge their election duties without giving any explanation.

Another major development was that election disputes would now be settled by the High Court instead of the election tribunals to make the process faster. Furthermore, a maximum permissible limit of Taka 500,000 was raised from Taka 300,000 as election expenditure (*The Bangladesh Observer*, 9 August 2001). The CTG also gave more powers to the EC, having authority over the entire district administration in line with the Constitution and exercising electoral laws with the announcement of the election schedule (*The Bangladesh Observer*, 21 August 2001). It also announced seven priority tasks for the administration (*The Bangladesh Observer*, 20 August 2001). These included that the civil and police administrations would extend all-out cooperation to the EC and perform with total neutrality their duties, including: the recovery of illegal arms, checking illegal use of legal arms and intensifying the security system to prevent the capture of polling booths, the snatching of ballots and false voting; stopping terrorism, extortion and hooliganism – armed terrorists, extortionists and lawbreakers would be arrested and controlled with an iron hand; taking strict actions against the move to foil meetings and rallies of the opposition and attempts to unleash panic and violence; ensuring a congenial atmosphere so that a voter can cast his or her vote without fear or favour; taking all measures so that female voters can exercise their franchise freely and without any disturbances; and taking all-out measures so that peace during and after the polls is not disturbed at the polling centres in minority and tribal areas, in order to ensure free exercise of franchise.

Despite being under pressure from various political quarters on the polling schedule and severe criticisms regarding being 'bipartisan' (*The Bangladesh Observer*, 21 August 2001) and being an 'invisible force working within CTG', (*The Bangladesh Observer*, 11 August 2001), the business community leaders opined that the CTG should not be disturbed by any means (*The Bangladesh Observer*, 25 July 2001). The media also lent its support to the CTG, with its editorials criticising the two political parties' unhelpful approach to the CTG. AL had gone as far as to say that the CTG administration considered AL its rival, while BNP accused the CTG administration of replacing pro-BNP officials with another set of officials having allegiance to the AL (*The Bangladesh Observer*, 26 July 2001). The CTG was clearly under constant pressure from all sides and had, unsurprisingly, a challenging task. The international community, however, gave its support to the CA. The former US president Jimmy Carter, after an exhaustive meeting with the CA on the forthcoming general elections, said that 'many countries around the world are looking forward to the forthcoming election in Bangladesh and many countries are also thinking of following Bangladesh's model of CTG to conduct free and fair elections' (Statement of the NDI/Carter Center Pre-Election Delegation to Bangladesh's 2001 Parliamentary Elections, 2001). Not only did Carter praise the administrative actions taken to date by the

CTG, he also stressed quite poignantly the importance of major parties accepting the election results and the role of the opposition in the next elected parliament.

The 1 October 2001 election was held peacefully, freely and fairly, as opined by national and international observers, with BNP winning and forming a government for a five-year period. Accepting defeat was not a graceful matter for AL and the allegation of *shukhkho katchupi* (tacit/subtle rigging) was again in the air, just as BNP could not graciously accept its defeat in the election of 1996.

The October 2006 crisis and analysis

After a full term, when PM Khaleda Zia demitted office, the situation was such that neither the government nor the principal opposition party, AL, could agree on a candidate for the position of CA to the CTG administration, which would conduct the elections to the ninth parliament session. The government and the opposition once again had unbridgeable differences over a number of key issues concerning elections and neither side, unsurprisingly, was prepared to compromise. They were locked in their familiar struggle, seemingly to death, over reform of the laws governing both the elections and the CTG that would oversee them. Perhaps such a situation came about due to a host of political and partisan moves Khaleda Zia's government made during her tenure, which undermined the office of the CTG and jeopardised its neutrality. Moreover, the impartiality of the EC to fulfil its constitutional obligations continued to be in question. This is because, as Sobhan (2006: 3275) has analysed,

> The Chief Election Commissioner (CEC), M A Aziz was still in place despite his manifestly poor performance with respect to everything from his flouting of judicial orders, to his testy relationship with the press, to the compilation of a voter list that had 10 million more voters than is even mathematically possible given the last census figure. Senior members of the government had even publicly expressed their reservations regarding him, but there was no indication that the CEC was going anywhere. AL had categorically stated that it will not consent to elections under the present dispensation but it is also the general consensus of the media, civil society and most independent observers that he was too compromised to credibly oversee elections. The impasse seemed intractable. The root problem is and remains that the stakes are extraordinarily high for both sides and neither is inclined to give ground.

So the demand for ousting the CEC loudly echoed through the sentiments of the majority of the public. Although election commissioners cannot be sacked but must resign or go on leave according to the Constitution, it becomes doubly challenging to get rid of one, if the person is politically biased or incompetent and not ready to leave. The CEC and the three deputies, accused of being BNP sympathisers, had still not been removed by the government.

Another political tempest was the unexpected commotion that developed with regard to the presidency. There was growing uneasiness among the BNP government with regard to the loyalty of the president, Iajuddin Ahmed, who was sufficiently subservient and pliant to the wishes of the government but had succumbed to an understandable infirmity on health grounds. As a result, the Speaker of the House became the acting president. But there seemed to be a nefarious scheme on the part of the government to keep President Ahmed out of office when he returned from overseas treatment. It could perhaps have been that Khaleda Zia herself wanted to take over the presidency, although that plan was shelved as a result of the ensuing commotion. Another plausible explanation could be that BNP preferred the more pliant and loyal acting-president and barrister Jamiruddin Sircar (Speaker of the House) in place, as unobtrusively as possible. The reason why the identity of the president is such a major issue is because the president takes on a significant – or at least potentially significant – role during a CTG, as according to article 58(C) (5) of the Bangladesh Constitution, it is the president who more or less single-handedly gets to appoint the CA after consultation, as far as practicable, with the major political parties. Under article 58(C) (6), he is, as discussed above, even empowered to appoint himself to the position of CA if the previous clauses cannot be given effect to, for whatever reason. Therefore, the need for the government to be able to ensure the absolute loyalty and servility of the president, who also controls the defence of the country, becomes paramount.

A further source of discomfort for the BNP government was perhaps their understanding of the provision of the Constitution, which was contrary to popular understanding: according to article 58(B) (12), 'the CTG shall stand dissolved only on the date on which the PM enters upon his/her office after the constitution of a new parliament'. Thus, if it is not possible for the CTG to hold elections due to either boycott by the opposition or unrest in the streets, the CTG is constitutionally mandated to remain at the helm. Thus 'who' will constitute the CTG adds tremendous weight to the entire constitutional/political debate.

Devin T Hagerty (2007: 107–108) examines three trends in Bangladeshi society which provided a deeper context to the endemic political turmoil of 2006. First was the continuing and massive corruption in all sectors of society, which was endorsed by Transparency International Bangladesh's (TIB) rating of Bangladesh as the world's most corrupt nation. Second, everyday politics continued to be played out amid chronic stagnation of citizens' political rights and civil liberties. Third, a contextual trend was the continued rise of political Islam at this time, as a salient phenomenon for many Bangladeshis, which was quite alarming (Hasan 2011).

Rampant corruption and institutional decay in recent years had created a widening socio-political vacuum into which JIB and *Chhatra Shibir* (the student wing of JIB) had nimbly stepped. The BNP–JIB alliance of the 2001 election, which gave the fundamentalist JIB (consisting of leaders who were collaborators and war criminals) 18 seats but the two very important portfolios of agriculture and social welfare in an impoverished agrarian society, shows the party's electoral importance. Its organisational capacity and political shrewdness and maturity meant that it had built huge networks of social, educational, informational and economic institutions, in effect creating a state within a State, with infusions of funds from oil-rich Middle Eastern countries like Saudi Arabia and Kuwait. This produced explosive growth in the construction of Islamist schools and mosques in Bangladesh. The return of migrant workers to Bangladesh from the Gulf each year, imbued with conservative, often *Wahabi* Islamist doctrines and flush with remittances that gave them influence at home, reinforced Islamist trends. This allowed JIB to favourably juxtapose its institutions with the corruption and inefficiency of the Bangladeshi government. The year 2005 saw the rise of Islamist militant groups and terrorist organisations such as Jamaat-ul-Mujahideen Bangladesh (JMB) and Harkat-ul-Jihad al-Islami Bangladesh (HUJIB) carrying out suicide attacks and well-coordinated nationwide bombings for the first time in Bangladesh's history, which the BNP government chose to blatantly ignore and failed to control (Hasan 2011 and Harrison 2013). Riaz (2016a: 81) notes that although some of these organisations were clandestinely organising themselves in the last days of the previous AL regime, they found a favourable and hospitable environment under the BNP/Jamaat alliance and began to engage in violent activities, which the latter did not strictly control or address. In addition, the gradual Islamisation of society is pronounced in the education sector, and up to four million children are educated in 19,000 *madrasahs* in Bangladesh at a primary level. The surprising aspect is that there are almost as many girls as boys in Bangladesh's *madrasahs* which perhaps indicates that the Islamic forces at play in Bangladeshi politics have a strength and strategy that goes beyond mere electoral achievement (Harrison 2013: 15). The population of Bangladesh finds itself confronted with the narrow exclusivist Islam of the Islamists, which shows little tolerance for those who think and practice an Islam alien to local history, culture and society as we saw in Chapter 2, one that many argue has crept in with individual remittances and national aid packages from the Arabian Gulf countries. Those seeking to fight this strand of Islam may find that the most effective strategy is perhaps not so much to undermine religion, which is rooted in peoples' lives, but to highlight the differences between the Islamist brand of Islam and the broad inclusive Islam, long practiced in rural Bangladesh, generally accepting the different beliefs, practices and dress both within and outside the Muslim community (Shehabuddin in Riaz and Fair [eds.] 2011: 110–111).

The political scene remained unsurprisingly dominated by the virulent rivalry of the two major political parties during this time. Amid the boycotted parliament, clashing personalities and display of street muscles, Khaleda Zia stepped down from power in October 2006 at the end of her five-year term. However, the resignation of the PM was not followed by the inauguration of the CTG. In this situation, President Iajuddin Ahmed 'queered the pitch when he chose to join the fray. Without adequately exploring the various options enshrined in the

Constitution through the Thirteenth Amendment, he concurrently appointed himself as CA to the CTG. A single individual concurrently holding two constitutional positions led to weeks of political chaos, public protests and an impending civil war situation' (Datta 2009: 7). This continued until January 2007.

Between November 2006 and January 2007, the turbulent, violent and chaotic ten weeks which paralysed the nation were the result of the excessive politicisation of various institutions in the country which undermined their effectiveness and authority. These institutions and the government failed to intervene when they were required most. The political uncertainty quite naturally also underscored the serious and fundamental crises facing democracy in the country. If one were to identify or analyse the principal players whose failures and short-sightedness were primarily responsible for such a crisis in Bangladesh in 2006, they would be the PM, the EC, the president and, to a certain extent, the opposition (Datta 2009: 7–8).

When a PM demits office in Bangladesh, according to the provisions of the Constitution, the formation of a neutral CTG to supervise and conduct free and fair elections to the parliament within 15 days of dissolution of the latter, designating the most recently retired CJ as its head, is the norm. This arrangement worked effectively in the 1996 and 2001 CTGs. In an apparent bid to influence this procedure, in May 2004 Khaleda Zia's government suddenly increased the retirement age for Supreme Court judges from 65 to 67 years. This goes to show that unless there is a genuine political will for the party in power to play fair during elections, no system or State institution, however effective or foolproof, can work. This two-year extension and straightforward manipulation meant that Justice K M Hasan (Khaleda Zia government's preference) would be the most recently retired CJ when the government completed its term in October 2006, thus qualifying him as CA for the next CTG. This led to the opposition (AL) accusing the government of partisanship, of politicising and compromising the neutrality of the CTG with fears that elections under Justice Hasan could be manipulated in favour of the BNP-led coalition. Despite opposition protests and movement, the government remained adamant about its projected choice of CA for the next CTG and was not prepared for a compromise candidate acceptable to all parties. This stalemate precipitated a political crisis as the government term came to an end. Although Justice Hasan finally declined the position, violence continued, taking 12 lives in one day. This uncompromising attitude on the part of the government brought the army into Bangladesh's civil governance through the back door, as the nation was eventually gripped by a military-backed CTG from January 2007–December 2008.

In addition, a number of measures taken while the government was in power further nurtured the feeling of mistrust between the government and the opposition. One such measure was that from 2005 onwards, around 700 members of BNP and its coalition supporters were recruited as election officers at district and sub-district levels. Secondly, the BNP government succeeded in manipulating a pliant Justice M A Aziz, who became CEC, on a number of critical issues concerning elections as well as appointing BNP loyalists as commissioners of the EC – the EC secretariat is directly under the PM's office. Thirdly, the government undermined the judiciary in the sense that despite a Supreme Court directive in 1999, the judiciary remained under executive control. Disregarding a High Court order to the contrary, the government enabled the CEC Aziz to publish a voters' list which was potentially inaccurate. At a much wider political level, the government was accused of impeding the functioning of the opposition by preventing them from raising issues in parliament, creating inordinate delays in the formation of parliamentary standing committees overseeing various ministries and by their failure to control religious extremism, which was on the upswing.

There was also the clear impression both within and outside the country that the government was in league with Islamic militants. Although the coalition with JIB may have been strategically useful for BNP, it certainly did not facilitate the impression the BNP government projected both at home and abroad. Between 1999 and 2005, Bangladesh witnessed over 30 major bomb blasts and most of these were attributed to militant groups or individuals (Datta 2007: 167–168 and Hasan 2011). The persistent denial mode of the BNP government did not assist, especially when official investigations were left incomplete and ineffective. They were not yielding any result, despite assassination attempts on the leader of the opposition (Sheikh Hasina), the assassination of a senior opposition leader (Ivy Rahman) and nationwide coordinated bomb blasts, all between 2004 and 2005. At one level, the citizens saw a clear failure on the part of the government to restore law and order. On the other, the government's subversion of key institutions through political manipulation and partisan decisions was evident. According to Hagerty (2007: 112):

> Although warnings of an imminent descent into Taliban-style medievalism are overheated, many of the country's political trends point in a potentially dangerous direction. Both major political parties, not only BNP (though BNP has gone as far as making JIB an alliance), have at times played with fire by courting Islamists to increase their own power. Democracy's survival in Bangladesh rests upon the re-invigoration of political institutions and the rejection of politics as usual. But whether the country's leaders are up to this task is doubtful.

The opposition, in its part, had its share of blame too. Following the electoral debacle in October 2001, Sheikh Hasina periodically resorted to boycotting the parliament, on numerous occasions preventing the smooth functioning of this institution. The absence of dialogue/communication/discourse between the government and opposition and their intolerance towards each other was unhelpful to the survival of any democracy. The non-acceptance of the election results of 2001, despite the elections being led and duly conducted by a CTG, was seen by people as immaturity, arrogance and not conducive to democratic progression. During the BNP government tenure, AL boycotted the parliament for 13 months. Despite the two sides exchanging eight letters over a period of six weeks about forming a committee for electoral reforms, very little was achieved by either government or opposition. The inability to engage in political dialogue for the sake of the nation primarily arose from AL and its 14-party alliance's refusal to sit with JIB members on the committee, as JIB was not only against the birth of Bangladesh but many of its important leaders were war criminals and/or collaborators during the war of Bangladesh's liberation. With the EC announcing the election dates in September and in the absence of any political dialogue, the opposition announced a 23-point common minimum programme and resorted to street agitation leading to violence and the further hardening of positions on both sides. AL's subsequent signing of the Memorandum of Understanding (MoU) with radical religious groups created serious dissention within the AL alliance, and hence its endeavour to woo the Islamic block by choosing to sign a MoU did not go down well with its allies. Although in the face of severe criticism, especially from her own party, Sheikh Hasina was forced to terminate the agreement, this action of hers created sharp fissures among the opposition alliance members, with scepticism and confusion among the electorate.

The immediate provocation for the October 2006 crisis came from the president himself when he assumed the position of the CA without fully exhausting the provisions of the Constitution for selecting the CA. The manner in which he appointed himself CA to the CTG led to a major crisis of confidence among both the opposition political parties and the people. As per the Constitution, if none of the alternatives were available, as stipulated under article 58(C)(3)(4)(5) and under extreme circumstances, the president was supposed to assume the functions of the CA of the CTG in addition to his own functions under article 58(C)(6). Therefore, only under exceptional circumstances and where all other alternatives had been fully exhausted could the president take this step. For reasons still unknown, the president did not follow all the procedures of the Constitution completely and ended up wearing both hats – that of the president and of the CA – and found an opportunity in the impasse. As Huda (2006) remarked:

> [The] President is now perhaps uncomfortably wearing two hats. He is head of the government and head of the state. He is the functioning executive and also the superintending authority. In other words, he is answerable to himself only, a not very tenable position from the point of view of the conduction of state affairs. How we landed in this rigmarole may not be satisfactorily explained but as of now, it is a fact that the nation has to live with. Concerned observers agree that the assumption of the office of the CA by the President may not strictly be illegal but is definitely an irregular feat in the face of objective situation. In such a process, there are chances of stumbling, as few necessary steps have not been taken before resorting to ultimate action. The future course of events will testify to the veracity of such a premonition.

Jurisprudentially speaking, the appointment of President Iajuddin Ahmed as the CA only served the purpose of the left-hand side of Menski's Kite, the State corner. This meant that it only kept intact the formal/State law in place without having the elements of fairness, as all the constitutional steps were not undertaken by him in order to appoint a CA from the judiciary to follow the spirit of the law of Chiba's 'legal postulates' (the top of the Kite). The trust of people in the CA to be appointed according to appropriate procedure (the right side of the Kite) and the international recognition element (the bottom corner of the Kite) were amiss because the international community was reluctant to give support to President Iajuddin's administration. This was positivist manipulation in action, and clearly not good for the plain sailing of a nation's *iccher ghuri*.

Having appointed himself as CA, the president then appointed a ten-member team of technocrats to assist him effectively in his CTG. The opposition, which initially took a 'wait and watch' approach, soon developed further misgivings over the neutrality of the president-led CTG administration. The president's subsequent actions, such as his refusal to negotiate with the Grand Alliance (AL/JP/LDP), his rejection of an agreement with the political parties negotiated by some of his advisors, the appointment of two BNP loyalists as new election commissioners, and the deployment of the army without consulting with his advisors, demonstrated anything but neutrality per se. The opposition therefore soon accused the president-cum-CA of merely pursuing the policies of the BNP government instead of acting as a neutral administrator. Meanwhile, the CEC announced the election date (22 January 2007) amid public protests over the current situation. The president's refusal to remove the controversial CEC raised doubts over the credibility of the scheduled elections. Moreover, the president did not exercise the power granted by the Constitution whereby the matter could be referred to the Supreme Court for an opinion if he felt 'a question of law has arisen or likely to arise, which is of such a nature and of such a public importance' (Article 106 of the Bangladesh Constitution). This could have provided a way out for the president to delay the elections in the light of widespread opposition.

The media also reported differences and disagreements between the president and his advisors. There were also external pressures and warnings over the manner in which the president was handling the situation. Matters escalated further when four CTG advisors out of ten resigned in protest as the president-cum-CA's neutrality was bitterly criticised by the people, including civil society and the diplomatic corps. Soon opposition groups were clashing, ensuing killings and massive violence. Bangladesh was again on the verge of a civil war with heightened violence and the kite of hope/dream/aspiration (*iccher ghuri*) was beginning to crash. A stubborn EC decided to disqualify Ershad from becoming a candidate and almost the entire opposition eventually withdrew their nominations on 3 January 2007. Clashes between the law enforcing agencies and the opposition activists became such regular phenomena that economic activity, education and business practically ground to a halt, but despite such unrest and international concern, the EC, CTG and BNP/Jamaat alliance were bent on completing the unilateral polling exercise (Riaz 2016a: 84). Amid these domestic developments, the international donor community, including the UN, announced the withdrawal of its agency monitoring the proposed elections. Western powers such as the United States, the United Kingdom, the EU and Canada were urging the president to undertake significant reforms before holding credible elections. The 'Tuesday Group' consisting of foreign diplomats from seven major powers was constantly engaged in attempts to bring about a truce between the government and the opposition. The president-cum-CA rejected the call to defer the election date on the constitutional pretext that a CTG cannot be in existence for more than 90 days.

Eventually, the president was pressured and forced to relinquish the post of CA, the cabinet he appointed was dismissed and the election scheduled for 22 January 2007 was cancelled with the support of the armed forces. This was followed by three major developments in the country: first, an internal emergency was declared in Bangladesh which curtailed all political activities, media coverage and popular gatherings; secondly, a new CTG headed by technocrat Dr. Fakhruddin Ahmed was installed; and thirdly, the military was given power and responsibility for maintaining law and order in the country. The outcome was that Bangladesh was now in an emergency situation.

The caretaker government: 2007–2008

A modicum of political stability, although unnatural, was restored on 11 January 2007 (popularly termed as 1/11) when the noted economist and World Bank official (who also once headed the Central Bank of Bangladesh) Dr. Fakhruddin Ahmed was appointed as head (CA) of the new CTG with ten new advisors. Under his leadership and that of the chief of army staff, General Moeen U Ahmed, Bangladesh navigated through one of its most difficult political crises since 1991 to eventually hold free and fair elections after almost a two-year period in December 2008. The long delay indicates the massive turbulence which gripped the nation, yet its journey to electoral democracy continued up to that point. Hagerty (2008: 178) explains that

> Most Bangladeshis initially appeared to support the declaration of emergency, believing that it would prevent sharply escalating instability and perhaps even civil war. However, with the passage of time, concerns have grown about the army's long term political intentions and the sincerity of its pledges to restore Bangladesh's democracy. As 2007 dawned, Bangladesh's democratic political institutions appeared to be broken. In the words of a senior US State Department official (John Gastright, Deputy Assistant Secretary of state for South and Central Asian Affairs), Bangladesh was 'fast becoming a democracy in name only, where money, cronyism and intimidation increasingly dictated the outcomes of elections, the parliament could not function, the electoral

> winners vanquished the losers and the opposition's sole focus was on bringing down the government at any cost'. From its inception, the military backed CTG attempted to do much more than simply fix a defective electoral system. With ample domestic and international support, it embarked upon a wide ranging effort to repair the very institutional foundations of Bangladesh's democracy. At the heart of the CTG's reforms was a sweeping anti corruption drive.

Hagerty (2008) continues that the army had been calling the shots from behind the scenes, partially to help protect its valuable international peace-keeping role, which brings it money, prestige and on-the-job training. European, American and UN diplomats had warned the army prior to the emergency not to acquiesce in a rigged election or to intervene directly by imposing martial law. The army therefore compromised by wielding power quietly, yet firmly, but allowed the CA (and the new CTG administration of ten advisors) to be the public face of the government in Bangladesh. Ironically, this political change, despite the suppression of fundamental rights, received sufficient public approval as by now, the people were so disgruntled with how the politicians had paralysed the nation for months without any justification or respite.

Naik (2007: 3540–3541) reiterates that this strategy of technocrat-led military government appeared to work smoothly for the first few months and the euphoria following the takeover was real. It was based on the hope and aspiration that there would be more freedom, and not less, and that those who had taken Bangladesh for granted would get their comeuppance. The administration was viewed as neutral and capable of making the necessary political and institutional changes for an effective or renewed democracy, although there was the lurking fear among some that long military rule akin to that in the 1975–1990 period may have returned to Bangladesh or even that the intervention of the military in politics may prove counterproductive to Bangladesh's democracy (Riaz 2016a: 86).

But in the meantime, within ten days of the formation of the CTG regime, the controversial CEC Aziz was made to submit his resignation along with members of the EC. Reconstituting the EC became an urgent priority for the new CTG. A retired and well-accepted bureaucrat, ATM Shamsul Huda, was appointed as the CEC with Mohammed Sohul Hussain and Brigadier Muhammad Sakhawat Hussain appointed as the other two members of the EC. Three other members' posts were withdrawn. The preparation of the voter list for the new EC became a new priority as the High Court had earlier declared that the voters list prepared under Aziz was invalid and reiterated the earlier directive of the Supreme Court to update the voters' list prepared in the year 2000.

In the six months following the proclamation of emergency, the nation's military-backed CTG morphed from caretaker to an aspiring 'lord of the manor'. The suspension of democratic rights; the negative impact this CTG had on the observation of human rights, democratic values, norms and procedures, curtailing freedom of expression and any rights of the media; and the army's influence in key State institutions fundamentally put a halt to any step the nation had taken towards democracy since 1991. Yet, despite these damaging effects, the CTG pledged to push a string of reforms in order to attempt to put 'democracy back on track', not only by holding free and fair elections, but also by reshaping the political culture of the nation and freeing State institutions like the EC and the Anti-Corruption Commission (ACC) from partisan influences (Riaz 2016a: 86).

Although there was widespread public approval in seeing corrupt and audacious political figures, who kept abusing their power with impunity, behind bars, somewhere within the military running the show from behind the CTG were tensions between the various factions of the army. There were senior groups within the army who were pro-AL, pro-BNP and even pro-Islamist, and conflicts between them regarding which way to direct the nation apparently surfaced. Eventually, people began to get slowly disillusioned about not only the absence of a clear 'roadmap' from the CTG but also the commitment and ability of the regime, for a number of reasons. One such reason was the massive anti-corruption campaign in which 200,000 people were arrested under charges of political or financial corruption. Although hailed initially as a success, the electorate soon understood that this anti-corruption cleansing had no structured plan or focus. It became widely perceived as an instrument of terror.

Riaz (2016a: 86) notes that extensive change regarding detention, confiscation of property, bail and trial were made, providing the caretaker administration with enormous power. Naik (2007: 3541) examines that the preventive detention laws, such as the Special Powers Act (1974), were widely used to target political opponents by the previous AL and BNP governments. It ensured unquestionable authority by enacting emergency laws and arresting 95,825 persons under the Bangladesh Emergency Power Rules of 2007 between 12 January and 12 March 2007. The Emergency Powers Rules (2007), provided under the Anti-Corruption Commission Act (2004), states that if a person is suspected of possessing property disproportionate to his/her 'legitimate' income, he or she must provide a statement listing all movable and immovable properties within 72 hours of receiving a notice to this effect from the ACC. If the information is not provided, the ACC may bring charges against the detainee within 45 days. In some cases, the time limit was breached, with suspects remaining in detention for months.

Naik (2007) further notes that the ACC's remit was shockingly vague. When asked about the working methods of the commission, its secretary was unable to explain the basis on which the list of suspects was prepared. The potential for abuse by the nature of this arbitrary determination is even more disturbing. Although the initiative proved exciting at first, as everyone loves a clean-up and witnessing influential politicians behind bars was newsworthy because no one dared touch these influential politicians before, nevertheless the subsequent crackdown by the CTG demolished any illusion of there being a clean break from the past. A few voices pointed out, in the *New Age* newspaper, that just as we do not support unabated crime and corruption under a jungle law in the guise of rule of law, of which some of the arrested have been frequently accused, we do not also subscribe to any persecution in the name of prosecution under cover of a State of emergency!

Thus the anti-corruption drive, which was headed and coordinated by serving and retired military personnel, quickly ran into trouble because of numerous due process and fundamental rights violations as well as the selective nature of the corruption prosecutions. In monetary terms, the anti-corruption drive unearthed over Taka 12 billion. But at the heart of the drive was an attempt to break up the two main political parties in the country, AL and BNP, which were held responsible for the dysfunctional nature of the country's democratic and political culture (Sobhan 2008: 8a). The CTG regime not only tried to capitalise on the popular discontent against political leaders, it also wanted to put an end to the mindless squabbles exhibiting the political parties' inability to govern. For this purpose, the CTG pursued what is popularly known in Bangladesh as the 'minus two solution', designed to permanently sideline AL leader Sheikh Hasina and BNP leader Khaleda Zia, the two politicians whose mutual loathing knows no limits. Initially the regime tried to exile the 'two Begums' but eventually resigned itself to arresting them and confining them to the idle parliament building where they remained till they were eventually released (Hagerty 2008: 179).

According to Momen (2009: 67–68), Sheikh Hasina was formally charged with having committed extortion when she was PM in 2000. The High Court challenged the legality of trying her and ruled that the CTG government could not prosecute past offences under present rules because this would violate the Constitution. The CTG appealed the order but the Supreme Court ultimately stayed it and Sheikh Hasina was finally set free by an executive order signed by the CA, though the CTG government reserved the right to revoke this order at any time. The ACC also filed a formal case against Khaleda Zia on graft charges. Her sons were also arrested on corruption charges and imprisoned but were all eventually released on bail (after significant closed door negotiations between the CTG regime and Khaleda Zia/BNP) on health reasons, and permitted to go abroad for medical treatment. The ACC did not file further cases because it could not find significant discrepancies between the wealth statements submitted by the former PMs and the actual value of their assets, even after a prolonged inquiry. Attempts to exile the two political leaders in order to clean up the political environment and keep them out of politics also failed because of a lack of alternative viable leadership within either political party.

Consequently, the probability of a 'third force' emerging in Bangladeshi politics seemed as far off the horizon as ever, despite trying to launch the Nobel Laureate Professor Muhammad Yunus 'by capitalising on his international acclaim and clean image. While banning all political activities, the military-led CTG allowed Yunus to form a new political party namely *Nagorik Shakti*'. (Datta 2009: 29). In an interview with the author, one of the interviewees, wishing to remain anonymous, regarding this particular issue, reiterated that closed-door negotiations failed as Yunus apparently claimed that he needed a period of 10 years to clean up the political spectrum of Bangladesh and the CTG could not mandate such a long tenure. Datta concludes that this twin strategy – of propping up new leaders and exiling the old ones – was supposed to offer an alternative stream of politics as the people of Bangladesh were let down by the national parties over and over again. The failure of such a move clearly reflected a lack of understanding within sections of the civil society about the grassroots support base that these two political parties commanded, despite the violence, corruption, manipulation or inefficiency. Poor ground-level support for Yunus's new political party, as an alternative political party, disproved the popular belief that Bangladeshis, particularly at grassroots level, were weary and fatigued with the existing political parties and were seeking other political alternatives. A parallel may also be drawn here with Imran Khan's political party in Pakistan, Tehreek-e-Insaf. Despite having emphasised an anti-corruption policy, he was unable to win the 1997 general election in Pakistan, and despite his celebrity base and perceived clean image, he did not manage to cultivate enough grassroots support for the party to become a viable third force in Pakistan's political sphere.

Therefore, having failed to exile 'the two Begums', i.e. having failed in the 'minus two' strategy/formula, having failed to imprison them indefinitely on the grounds of corruption and having failed to bring in a new political player, the CTG worked strenuously to convince Bangladeshis and the international community that it truly intended to return the country to democracy during the second half of its tenure. It announced plans for continued electoral reforms, staggered local elections in early January 2008 and national elections in December 2008. It eased emergency restrictions in September 2008, allowing political parties to resume indoor meetings, and also opened talks with the major political parties about reforms concerning funding, codes of conduct and the eligibility of candidates (Hagerty 2008: 179). According to Momen (2009: 68–69), the EC engaged in an electoral reform dialogue with various political parties in February 2008, resulting in new ground rules to ensure financial transparency and accountability while also raising the ceiling of poll expenditures. These rules also aimed to permanently bar war criminals from contesting parliamentary elections. In response, AL proposed a major restructuring of its nomination process in order to make it more democratic. BNP agreed to curb the power of its party chairperson, while JIB recognised the liberation war in its party constitution (since JIB opposed the war of liberation from Pakistan in 1971, it was forced to change its ideology on paper to recognise the separation of Bangladesh from Pakistan). Thus, the EC partly succeeded in pressurising the various political parties to adopt some democratic measures at that moment in history, but the extent of the impact, in retrospect, is seriously questionable in 2017.

The military-backed fourth CTG, with the help of the army, managed to achieve five major tasks which helped strengthen electoral democracy: firstly, it completed the world's largest electronic database of voters, which included over 81 million names. For the first time, the EC registered 160,000 Urdu-speaking Bihari Muslims who were born in the country. Furthermore, 32 per cent of the enlisted voters were first time voters, of which about 52 per cent had just attained the voting age. Secondly, for the first time, the nation had photo identity cards issued to its citizens, a worthy albeit time-consuming endeavour which even countries in the West struggle to achieve. Thirdly, as mandated by the Constitution to undertake this exercise after every decennial census, the EC went ahead with the delimitation exercise. Meanwhile, a challenge by a BNP functionary was set aside by the High Court. The new arrangement had a more equitable distribution of voters: the process affected 133 out of 300 constituencies and left each constituency with about 267,000 voters (Datta 2009: 20). Fourthly, the EC regulated campaign costs for elections and introduced some electoral/political party reforms in line with democracy to be followed by the political parties. Lastly, the CTG strengthened the judiciary by freeing it from the clutches of the executive. Despite popular demand and a Supreme Court directive, the judiciary always remained under the control of the political bosses and was subjected to political interference and manipulation. The CTG amended the Criminal Procedure Code Ordinance and formalised the independence of the judiciary from the executive. It also called for the formation of a separate Bangladesh Judicial Service Commission in November 2007, despite opposition from the bureaucracy (Datta 2009: 27–28).

However, the CTG was severely criticised for two reasons: first, its incompetence in organising relief after Cyclone Sidr devastated large parts of the country in 2007. Although it arranged for the movement of people to high ground and saw to it, as a result, that the casualties were kept relatively low, it refused to recognise the enormity of the physical damage wrought by the cyclone and was inept in relief management (Bakht 2007: 8). Second, 'in the name of cleaning up corruption or criminal activity, emergency and repressive measures were being used to institutionalise a cycle of disregard for human rights in general and for abuses against human rights defenders in particular. A cycle for impunity for human rights violations which has prevailed in the country over its decades-long existence is becoming a daily affair' (Sharma 2007: 3294). Despite these criticisms, the actions of the CTG received little international criticism. Reactions ranged from cautious optimism, 'eastern style', to hushed encouragement for illusory roadmaps, 'western style' (Naik 2007: 3542).

Other criticisms from commentators (Alamgir 2009: 51) include that

> The [CTG] administration misdiagnosed the root problem by blaming the democratic system as a whole. The ills that tore at the country's political life sprang from semi-authoritarianism and electoral manipulation specifically in the mid-1990s and after 2001. The problem was not democracy but rather its subversion.

Furthermore, the wish to reshape the political culture cannot be prescriptive, and the time that the CTG had was far too short to try to bring about any such change. The CTG also underestimated the popularity of the 'Two Begums' at grassroots level and to that effect they also underestimated that their 'Minus

Two Formula' would not only cause a backlash but would potentially fail, as Bangladesh is yet to have a popular democratic third choice which is entrenched enough and accepted at a grassroots level.

Therefore, the period between January 2007 and December 2008 proved to be critical for CTG and democracy in Bangladesh. The 23-month tenure of the CTG far exceeded the 90-day limit mandated by the Constitution. The constitutional propriety of a number of measures taken by the CTG remains uncertain. Many of its ordinances were not ratified by the parliament within the stipulated 30 days after it was constituted and hence their legality is questionable. Moreover, for the entire duration of the CTG, Bangladesh remained in internal emergency, with most fundamental rights suspended. There were severe restrictions upon political activities and the media remained censored. A number of prominent politicians, bureaucrats and members of the business community remained incarcerated. Despite these drawbacks, the CTG headed by Dr. Fakhruddin Ahmed introduced a number of political reforms and far reaching anti-corruption measures and strengthened key institutions in the country.

In pursuing its reform agenda, the CTG enjoyed the unqualified support of the military. Normally such an active collaboration between the military and an unelected government would have been domestically unpopular. Internationally, it would have led to the condemnation and isolation of Bangladesh. This time, it did not happen. Though unable to endorse the prolonged delay in holding elections, the international community did not isolate Dhaka over its transgression of democracy. Their faith in the CTG was vindicated when the elections to the parliament were held on 29 December 2008. The elections were free, fair and transparent and enjoyed universal approval and endorsement. Riaz (2016a: 87) indicates that although by the end of two years, the great expectations of the Bangladeshis who saw this as an unprecedented opportunity to bring about qualitative changes in Bangladeshi politics remained unfulfilled, he continues that 'even staunch critics of the CTG acknowledged that although its goal of reforming politics remained unmet, the CTG delivered credible elections and a peaceful transfer of power'. The tenure of the CTG thus ended when the 14-party coalition headed by Sheikh Hasina secured a landslide victory to form the government on 6 January 2009. The BNP again did not accept the defeat with grace.

The CTG headed by Dr. Fakhruddin Ahmed posed a number of challenges for Bangladesh. First and foremost, its prolongation and extra-constitutional functioning were perhaps inevitable. In the past, political parties driven by bitter personal rivalry often paralysed the government. Much of the opposition's activities were conducted outside of parliament. On its part, almost every government of the day treated the opposition as enemies. Over the years, principal institutions such as the EC and the judiciary had been politicised, manipulated and denuded of their credibility during various regimes, including civilian regimes. Democracy, however flawed in Bangladesh, urgently needed a course correction and hence the Bangladeshi public tacitly accepted the large-scale suspension of fundamental rights during the fourth CTG regime. These are indications of the public's awareness of the crucial importance of 'higher public necessity'. The survival of the nation was clearly at stake. For a country used to frequent street protests and stoppage of work, strike politics took a long holiday during the fourth CTG regime and Bangladesh largely remained free of political violence. This acceptance of the CTG was most likely because day-to-day living amid mindless political aggression and deadlock, which took place prior to the fourth CTG takeover, suffocated people to an extreme extent and deprived them from going about their daily lives, with educational institutes closed for weeks, businesses badly affected and city life paralysed due to these horrific non-stop strikes and killings. The loss of life in political battles has become the norm. The value of life is taken for granted.

Intriguingly, unlike in the past, the Bangladesh military showed a greater degree of maturity this time. It was aware of public anger and disappointment with political leaders as well as the unpopularity of direct intervention by the army in the form of military coups. While the country needed far-reaching reforms, the army viewed itself as the instrument of change. However, rather than taking over the reins of power as it had previously in the 1970s and 1980s, it settled for a lesser role on the face of it. Resolutely supporting the reform agenda of the technocrat-led government, the army resisted the temptation of direct action. Despite some expectations and not-so-subtle suggestions, the men in uniform eventually avoided active intervention and settled for wielding influence from behind the scenes. For its part, the technocrat-led CTG was conscious that its survival and reform plans rested on the unqualified support of the military. Thus, the CA Dr. Fakhruddin Ahmed and Chief of Army Staff Moeen Uddin Ahmed worked in tandem throughout the 23-month tenure and ultimately succeeded in chaperoning a new election, albeit with much delay.

In retrospect, it may be said that a CTG mechanism after the 1991 elections would have indeed been unnecessary if Bangladesh had had a neutral and powerful EC to oversee elections. But such an EC was absent from the beginning of Bangladesh's history – a total contrast to the Indian story, where the EC was made powerful and independent from the early days of India's independence. Such a reliable and autonomous EC is yet to emerge despite the lapse of 27 years from the time of democratic governance, after the fall of the Ershad regime. To that effect, former CTG Advisor Dr. Akbar Ali Khan observed, during an interview with the author, that 'during the last [more than] twenty years, the political parties could not agree on the neutrality of any EC'. Under elected governments, he continued, 'The EC is usually highly politicised. All people are controversial and the polling and presiding officers are themselves highly politicised'. So, he asked: 'If you appoint a partisan EC and it is rejected by the other political party, then what will be the use of strengthening it?' According to him, it was indeed in the absence of a neutral and powerful EC that the Thirteenth Amendment was passed in 1996 to institutionalise a CTG mechanism.

More widely, it can be said that the CTG mechanism arose, as we know, because there was a lack of confidence in the general population in politicians conduct of elections'. This particular proposition is also borne out in the fieldwork of the research. When those surveyed were asked whether they agreed with this proposition, 62.5 per cent overall replied in the affirmative and only 18.5 per cent replied in the negative.

The prolongation of the fourth CTG beyond its mandated tenure, however, underscored the urgency for political reform in Bangladesh, a problem now even more open for all to see. A CTG should certainly be a temporary arrangement. It had been widely recognised that the failure of Bangladeshi leaders to reform and democratise their polity was perhaps an invitation for military intervention and the next time around, it was feared, the army might be more ambitious than during the tenure of this particular fourth CTG. And it is this fear – that played around in the minds of the polity and caused another action – which had a series of repercussions in the political/legal realm of Bangladesh. But for now, the military-backed fourth CTG had nothing more up its sleeve and was looking for nothing more than an orderly and securely negotiated exit with its honour intact after holding a free, fair and inclusive election. The honour (*izzat*) of the nation was saved once again. The kite of law remained in the air and had not crashed, despite severe turbulence. The CTG had once again proved its usefulness as an institution, however much contested.

5

GOVERNMENT TRANSITIONS IN BANGLADESH

Critical contextual analysis of the CTG mechanisms, their performance and their assessment

This chapter evaluates how Bangladesh was able to progress from the flawed electoral process of earlier elections to one that most observers agree met with the basic electoral standards, acceptable nationally and internationally, through the caretaker government (CTG) system. In doing so, the progression and metamorphosis of this 'constitutional innovation' of the CTG, as some commentators brand it, is analysed and its contribution to the process of State formation and democratisation assessed.

But before moving forward, there have been certain developments with regard to the CTG which need to be flagged as they have affected the way this analysis was developed. After successfully conducting four national elections within a span of 20 years, Bangladesh was just getting comfortable with a system of regular electoral governance, through the CTG mechanism, which was holding free, fair and inclusive elections. But the rushed Fifteenth Amendment to the Bangladesh Constitution, under the aegis of the AL government on 30 June 2011, completely threw the electorate off-guard because this saw the demise of the CTG, among other things. While the AL government has insisted that a CTG is no longer necessary in what it sees as a maturing democracy, the electorate in Bangladesh – including members of civil society as well as the opposition – have been alarmed and disgruntled by this unilateral act of the government. Once again, we have watched a simmering political deadlock turn into something quite critical on the eve of the 2014 election. Although the election on 5 January 2014 took place in an atmosphere of heightened political drama and violence *sans* the CTG, Bangladesh neither saw the participation by BNP-led opposition, since it boycotted the election, alleging the risk of government manipulation, nor did it receive complete acceptability nationally and internationally due to poor voter turnout and non-participation of the opposition, thereby seriously questioning electoral credibility. Bhaumik (2014) asserts that Sheikh Hasina was aware of this limitation when taking over as prime minister (PM) for the third time, as she promised a dialogue with the opposition and fresh polls as soon as a consensus was reached. The United States rubbished the January 2014 elections as 'less than credible', and its envoy called for fresh dialogue and mid-term polls to 'let

Bangladeshi people express their will freely'. The EU and the Commonwealth also dubbed the polls 'one-sided' and called for fresh elections. Bhaumik concludes that only India backed Sheikh Hasina, as expected, saying that the polls were a 'constitutional necessity'. Subsequently, within a week of the election, Russia too came out in support of Sheikh Hasina's government, which was yet another Kremlin assertion in a major Asian issue. Although China had maintained equidistance in the 'battles of the Begums' and called for a dialogue between AL and BNP prior to the January 2014 election so that 'wisdom prevailed over violence', a message from the Chinese Premier that China was keen to 'join hands' with the new government in order to 'advance the Sino–Bangladesh comprehensive and cooperative partnership to a new height' came as little surprise (Bhaumik 2014). There was no mention of election in that message, let alone the serious credibility of the election issue itself. Fresh polls hence never took place and Sheikh Hasina continues her term, and is at present on the verge of completing her second consecutive term in office. With this, we can clearly see one corner of Menski's Kite at play: the impact that the international community or global politics has upon emerging democracies like Bangladesh.

In view of this somewhat changed ground reality of an abolished CTG, we move forward to understanding the dominant rationale in favour of abandoning this mechanism, despite the deep animosity and culture of mistrust prevailing and manifesting itself in the major institutions of the country. We also explore the workings of all CTGs over a span of 20 years, which delivered four successful general elections.

Given these developments, the first section of this chapter deepens the analysis of the CTG system by discussing the element of 'necessity', which has been used expressly and/or tacitly. We then proceed to a discussion of the doctrine of 'basic structure of the Constitution', which was used at various times in order to justify the usurpation of power and/or amendments to the Constitution. For a meaningful evaluation, the CTGs have been grouped into two: the first three CTGs have been placed into one group, and the military-backed CTG falls into the second group. The impact that the policies undertaken by the CTGs have had on democratisation is crucial, hence a major section of this chapter is dedicated to analysing that aspect. There is also a section on the Thirteenth Amendment case, which abolished the CTG system altogether, and the resultant constitutional amendment is added in order to understand how this structure was brought down, creating more uncertainty than before for future democratic transitions in Bangladesh. Finally, the last two sections discuss Bangladesh, post-CTG abolition, and the effects of the election of 5 January 2014 *sans* CTG, including where Bangladesh stands today with an impending election in 2019.

The element of 'necessity' and the 'basic structure doctrine'

The Constitution of Bangladesh provides that, except in the case of 'necessity' for the discharge of routine functions, the CTG shall not make any policy decisions.

In the absence of a description of the ingredients of 'necessity' in article 58(D)(1) of the Constitution, it can be assumed that the Constitution assigns this responsibility for the determination of what entails 'necessity' to the CTG (Rashid 2001: 27).

The doctrine of necessity was first used in the subcontinental context of justifying military governance in Pakistan, in *Dosso*'s case. This well-known case upheld the declaration of martial law by General Ayub Khan, basing itself on Kelsen's pure theory of law, whereby 'necessity' was shown as a reason to hold power upon successful revolution. In the subsequent *Asma Jilani* case, which overturned the decision of *Dosso*'s case, it was held in unequivocal language that *Dosso*'s case had come up for decision during the regime of General Ayub Khan and it was decided therein that a successful revolution was entitled to the support/allegiance of the courts of law. The decision was based on what the learned judges thought was Kelsen's theory of jurisprudence. This theory was interpreted to provide the legal justification for the acceptance by the domestic court of the success of an internal revolution within the State. It was thus not borne in mind, as it should have been, that Kelsen's was a 'pure theory of law', as distinguished from 'law' itself. Overlooking this obvious position caused basic fallacies in the *Dosso* judgment. Kelsen himself was aware of the fact that this theory did not form part of any legal system. Furthermore, the court had assumed that there was a revolution and that the revolution had succeeded. Both of these questions were questions of fact and were required to be decided upon evidence, and upon issues raised before the court. There is nothing to show that there was any rebellion or insurrection. The Proclamation of 7 October 1958 by President Iskandar Mirza made no mention of any rebellion or insurrection. It is thus evident that the very foundations upon which the decision in *Dosso*'s case rested did not exist.

The court in the *Asma Jilani* case should have made it clear that the validity or otherwise of an existing order could only be determined with reference to the laws of Pakistan and not to any theory of international jurisprudence. It is also necessary to state firmly (as was done in the *Asma Jilani* case) that the questions of the existence of a revolution or of its success are questions of fact, which can only be decided upon evidence and not assumed. This would remove, once and for all, the temptations that have been placed in the way of an adventurer seizing power illegally and destroying an existing legal order.

Despite this ruling, Pakistan has time and again allowed a dictator to continue in power with judicial acquiescence and even approval, citing the principle of 'higher necessity', which is basically a public interest argument to the effect that judicial refusal to recognise a *fait accompli* would throw the nation into turmoil, and thus is not appropriate. To continue with the kite image used earlier, the kite of the nation would crash if the judges did not support and endorse the usurpation of power by the new leader. Unsurprisingly, Pakistan has regularly faced deep trouble over transitions of power and governance in general.

In the context of Bangladesh, the Fifth Amendment Act was passed by parliament on 6 April 1979. The effect of the amendment on the legislature was that all amendments or repeals made in the Constitution from 15 August 1975 to 9 April 1979 (inclusive) by any proclamation or Proclamation Order of the Martial Law Authorities were deemed to have been validly made and could not be questioned before any court, tribunal or authority. The Fifth Amendment had given legitimacy to military governments by a constitutional blanket cover after the 1975 assassination of *Bangabandhu* Sheikh Mujibur Rahman in a military coup. The proponents, however, argued that the successful coup of 15 August 1975 was not a simple murder case by any account, but a victorious case of necessity! The proponents further argued that the Fifth Amendment was made not arbitrarily but in the duly elected parliament in 1979. In addition, the Seventh Amendment Act was passed on 11 November 1986 during the Ershad regime, which among other things provided that all proclamations, proclamation orders, Chief Martial Law Administrator's orders, martial law regulations, martial law orders, martial law instructions, ordinances and other laws made from 24 March 1982 to 11 November 1986 (inclusive) had been validly made, and could not be called into question before any court, tribunal or other authority.

The cumulative effect of these two constitutional amendments made under military regimes gave the notion that Bangladesh applied the doctrine of necessity – even 'higher necessity' justifying the political realism of those military eras. It appears that it is the same story or the same argument as far as military regimes justifying their political dominion is concerned, whether in Pakistan or Bangladesh. It seems that all along Bangladesh, too, has simply hidden behind this method to bow down to the new strongman.

However, the Supreme Court of Bangladesh, in the *Constitution Fifth Amendment* case in 2006, long after the amendments made by the military regimes, declared all the regimes from 15 August 1975 headed by Khandaker Mushtaque Ahmed, Abu Sadat Mohammad Sayem and Ziaur Rahman as 'illegal'. The court held that the usurpation of State power through the proclamation of martial law was 'unconstitutional'. Hence, although it may appear that various leaders played these power games, the Bangladeshi courts dared to defy them. In reality, it is not always so. Over the years, politicisation of the High Court has seeped in and the tacit exertion of power by the executive through the judiciary has been an emerging trend. The courts sometimes speak the language of the executive or, more precisely, that of the PM. It works well for the political governments – and perhaps on occasion rightly so – to have an upper hand over the military regimes; in both the *Constitution Fifth Amendment* and *Seventh Amendment* cases, this has been clearly demonstrated. In citing *Anwar Hossain Chowdhury v. State*, the judgment of the *Fifth Amendment* case provided that a parliament cannot legislate in any manner that actually infringes the supremacy of the Constitution. This is akin to the basic structure doctrine, which is particularly strong in Indian law.

The doctrine or principle that there are basic features in a Constitution which cannot be amended made its official debut in neighbouring India in 1973 in the case of *Kesavananda Bharati v. State of Kerala*, whereby an amendment made by the Indira Gandhi administration was challenged in court. This led to the Supreme Court developing the idea that parliament's amending powers were not unlimited but were restricted when it came to certain basic features. The doctrine crossed the border into Bangladesh in 1989, when Ershad's Eighth Amendment setting up four High Courts around the country was challenged and the Supreme Court held that the amendment was an affront to a basic feature of the country's Constitution. In the process, the apex court made a list of features which were found to form the basic structure of the Constitution, although over the years strains on this basic structure doctrine have appeared, with additions and deletions to the list. The main premise upon which the basic structure doctrine stands is that parliament cannot have unlimited powers to amend the Constitution. So, in adopting the doctrine, the courts have assumed the role of overseeing amendments and striking them down if they are found to be contrary to the basic features of the Constitution. But there is neither a conclusive list of basic features nor are there strict interpretations attached to these features to guide the courts. In such a situation, the basic structure doctrine does not simply restrict the unlimited powers of the parliament, it also has the effect of handing over the unlimited and potentially unwarranted power of striking down amendments to the courts, when the courts were never meant to do this job in the first place. It is, however, typical of South Asian jurisdictions that courts ultimately have enormous power, even if at times it appears that strong leaders rule the roost. Usurpation of power, as the Bangladeshi events clearly confirm, is first in line, and only later do the courts have a say. Perhaps this is one reason why the CTG mechanisms keenly involved former chief justices (CJs), who have in their professional lives encountered the deep turbulences that abuses of governance can generate.

Whatever may be the state of the basic structure doctrine in Bangladesh, it must be emphasised here that the argument for basic structure in the context of the CTG is not tenable, as democracy has been held and understood to be one of the basic structures of the Constitution, having survived numerous amendments to the Constitution. The CTG was brought forth primarily to ensure the functionality of one basic and fundamental component of democracy, which is the holding of free and fair elections. Therefore, notwithstanding the fact that certain unelected people administered the country for 90 days, this does not change or affect the basic structure of the Constitution, since this apparent deviation is only a superficial observation, narrow interpretation and convenient point of criticism for those uncomfortable with the powers that a CTG possesses. The CTG gradually became a reliable institution, despite its setbacks, delivering what it was mandated to deliver: free, fair and participatory elections. The CTG, therefore, as an element of 'higher necessity', has been from its inception the result of popular movements, and the constitutional change institutionalising the CTG in Bangladesh is reflective of the 'will of the people'.

The Supreme Court held in the *Fifth Amendment* case in 2000 that since martial law proclamation was in itself against the nature of the Constitution, when any change is made in the Constitution through this proclamation, it creates double illegality. So, a parliament cannot ratify such acts as it is not within its authority. Although, legally speaking, parliament cannot just ratify, confirm or validate any act which is unconstitutional and which has destroyed the basic feature of the Constitution, in reality the Bangladesh parliament does so at times, depending on who is in power: the military, AL or BNP.

The judgment in the *Fifth Amendment* case was stayed by the Appellate Division on 1 September 2005 and was subject of a leave to appeal until 4 May 2009, when the attorney general of Bangladesh moved a petition for withdrawing the leave to appeal petition. In January 2010, the Appellate Division of the Supreme Court observed that parliament did not possess any authority to suspend the Constitution and proclaim martial law and hence it could not legitimise the actions of martial law regimes. Thus, the doctrine of 'necessity' was officially discarded as a means of taking power or continuing in power. The struggle in the Bangladeshi courts over this very issue and its eventual clear stance may have been because of three reasons: first, that the courts have become more emboldened than before and it may be seen as an example of judicial activism; second, senior judges might not have managed to fully remain above political influence, as there is much more evidence of politically appointed judges than in the past; and third, that the courts may be more emboldened as a matter of precaution, after observing what happened in Pakistan in 2007 in the battle between President General Pervez Musharraf and the CJ of Pakistan, Iftikhar Muhammad Chaudhry, who had reacted promptly to the emergency declaration of Musharraf, convening a seven-member bench which issued an interim order against the president's action and directed the armed forces of Pakistan not to obey any illegal orders.

Although the Bangladeshi courts may have formally discarded the notion of 'necessity', the fourth CTG clearly made a case for it when Chief Advisor (CA) Fakhruddin Ahmed addressed the nation on 21 January 2007, reiterating that

> You are all aware under what circumstances we had to take this difficult responsibility. I am sure that my countrymen will agree with me that none of us would have wished for this path. But the difficult reality remains that our dear motherland finds itself in the midst of a serious crisis. Despite repeated calls for caution from the honest and sincere segments of our society, their message has not been heeded. Hence the time has now come when we must work together to pursue the goal of establishing a solid foundation for our country. For our efforts to succeed, it is essential for us to unite as a nation and work together with a common sense of patriotism.

It is quite apparent here that the military-backed CTG regime of 2007–2008 wanted some seal of approval to justify its hold on power. To that effect, the CA went on further to add that

> Any general election becomes meaningless if the essential rules and regulations of the election are not followed. Therefore the most important responsibility of the present government is to create a transparent, peaceful and congenial atmosphere for conducting a truly democratic election. It is therefore the responsibility of this government to undertake the 'necessary' electoral reforms to ensure a free, fair and universally acceptable election with participation from all parties as soon as possible (speech added as annexure 6 in Datta 2007: 138–140).

We must note here that the somewhat dangerous keyword 'necessary' is even used by the technocrat CA.

Fakhruddin and Moeen's CTG made its case to the electorate by staying longer in power than the stipulated 90 days, as per the constitutional provision, on the pretext that it needed to give the country a free and fair election, 'conditions' which were not present in late 2006 due to the intensified, violent, virulent and irresponsible conflicts between BNP and AL. So, this is again, very clearly, a 'necessity' argument being placed to Bangladesh. The 'conditions' – a level playing field for all participants and the establishing of rules of the (election) game –needed to be created, which required a certain amount of time. Since this CTG had inherited a compromised electoral system, an overhaul was necessary in the form of a reform of the electoral system, the creation of a new electoral roll, the introduction of a national photo identity card for each citizen, the strengthening of the autonomy of the EC and the reorganisation of other supporting agencies such as the police and the courts.

However, this explanation, although palatable to the electorate initially, was not an easy pill to swallow for the political parties or for the proponents of democracy. So while the idea of an emergency situation was anathema to the supporters of democracy, positive public opinion regarding the legitimacy of Dr. Fakhruddin's CTG initially showed how politically pathological the preceding period of flawed democracy had been with regard to the law and order situation, rampant corruption, heavy-handed use of force, poor governance, alliances with Islamist parties that allowed extremists groups to expand their space, politicised administration and dysfunctional State institutions. Marred by internal party divisions, a faction which was controlled by the PM's son Tarique Rahman ran what many close observers within and outside the party reportedly termed as a 'parallel government' with his entourage at *Hawa Bhaban*, antagonising many BNP parliamentarians and some sections of the party leadership. It is this politically pathological period of defective or flawed democracy, leading to mindless violence, that this CTG relied on in order to justify its *raison d'être*, under the cloak of 'necessity'. Indeed, it interpreted the constitutional provision of the word 'necessity' according to its own roadmap. It justified its length of stay or its overstay to create 'a level playing field', perceived as a 'necessity' despite the 90-day time limit as per the provision of the Constitution. However, the notion of a 'higher necessity' had not been phrased as loudly as in Pakistan. Neither had there been any debate about it. There is understandable reluctance to connect back to the Pakistani jurisdiction from the pre-1971 period. It may have been implied, but there is curiously a virtually complete silence about it. While use of the word 'necessity' appears in the context of serious crisis, emergency or even semi-emergency, nobody speaks of 'higher necessity', even though the facts speak for themselves.

Interestingly, though, for the first time, the CTG structure appears to have been a method to prevent a new strongman from appearing in 2007. Perhaps, in the context of Bangladesh, we could go as far as saying that the CTG system echoed some principles of democracy, as expounded by John Morison, in that everyone affected by a decision has a right to participate in decision-making, reinforcing the idea of a society as a 'collectivity' and not merely as a ruler/ruled equation. Elections are clearly the key to basic democracy and not strong individuals as rulers without adhering to elections. The two 'Begums' and their entourage perhaps see this otherwise, of course, hence the discomfort of a ruling party with regard to the CTG mechanism, which was seen as acting as a 'higher authority' than the executive authority. Clearly it is problematic for any other entity to be a 'higher authority' than the executive authority, i.e. the power of the PM.

Most Bangladeshis initially appeared to support the declaration of emergency in 2007, believing that it would prevent the sharply escalating, incomprehensible violence (and perhaps even a civil war) that had plagued the nation for quite some time then. But the overstay of the CTG soon became a cause of grave concern, anxiety and uncertainty as far as the intention of the irregular interim regime was concerned.

CTG system: Progression and metamorphosis

Let us recap that the driving force for the creation of the CTG system in Bangladesh was the constant need for a free and fair election, to ensure fairness in the election process and to create 'a level playing field' for all the relevant parties to participate in credible elections, thus fitting specifically into the corner of the natural law component of Menski's Kite Theory. Then there was the issue of the modality of giving power to someone who is deemed to be neutral/apolitical and who would be able to hold the election fairly, according to international norms and practices. This combines Corners 3 and 4 in Menski's Kite Theory: positivist law and respect for international legal norms. The socio-economic-political reality of Bangladesh at the time when the CTG was created supported the idea of bringing the CJ into this position as the CTG head. The rationale behind this is perhaps that, during those times, no one ever questioned the integrity of justices of the Supreme Court of Bangladesh. Justices lived almost a life of seclusion and were mostly apolitical. Hence, the office of the CJ was regarded as ideal for this position. It can further be argued that, at that time, there was hardly any other office or person upon whom the people of Bangladesh, as a whole, could rely on or have such a level of confidence in to hold a neutral and fair election than the office of the CJ. This was the people's voice and people's way of tackling or encountering the problem of neutrality and for making a Western transplant of democracy work on Bangladeshi soil, which is bedecked with its historical legacy including the issue of mistrust and the ground reality of having dysfunctional State institutions. This also takes into account Menski's right-hand side of the kite, namely the socio-cultural and socio-economic norms – Bangladeshis' normativities and ways of doing things.

The first three CTGs, following the well-balanced constitutional mandate, had Supreme Court judges as CAs. The fourth CTG, however, as we know, was headed by a technocrat. Since the nature of this CTG was different from the earlier ones, it makes sense to categorise and evaluate the four CTGs of Bangladesh into broadly two groups: the CTGs of Shahabuddin Ahmed CJ, Habibur Rahman CJ and Latifur Rahman CJ may be placed into one group, with Dr. Fakhruddin Ahmed's CTG in the other. The reasons for doing so are simple: the first group consisted of former CJs acting as CAs, as stipulated by the Thirteenth Amendment of the Bangladesh Constitution, while the second group consisted of a military-backed CTG headed by a technocrat CA, not according to the proviso of the Constitution. The first group conducted the elections within 90 days as per the Constitution, while the second group violated the constitutional provision of 90 days by remaining in power for two full years on the pretext of requiring time to create 'a level playing field' for elections to take place. While there is no doubt that there were severe problems at the time when the fourth CTG took power, this argument constitutes a sophistication of the 'necessity' rationale, as we saw. Although the mandate of the CTG appears to be quite limited, as it essentially acts as an interim administration, all the CTGs had in fact taken policy decisions contrary to article 58(D) of the Constitution, which provides that the CTG shall carry on with the routine functions of the government with the aid and assistance of persons in the services of the Republic.

The first group

Ahmed (2004: 49) observes that, theoretically, Justice Shahabuddin Ahmed CJ enjoyed greater freedom than the Habibur Rahman CJ's and Latifur Rahman CJ's CTGs in making policy decisions. Although the 1990 Joint Declaration of all political parties provided some kind of guidance to the CTG, yet ruled out the making of policy decisions by it, the declaration categorically observed that the government would run only routine administration. But despite this provision, Shahabuddin CJ took two major policy decisions.

First, the University Ordinance promulgated by the Ershad regime to neutralise the movement of All Party Students Unity (APSU) was draconian in nature, as it empowered the government to close down educational institutions such as the universities under emergency situations. There was also a provision in the ordinance debarring people from speaking against it, and this seriously antagonised the student and teacher community, who decided to defy it by reopening the universities. But the Ershad government found it impossible to avenge the actions for fear of further violence. Following the fall of the Ershad regime, the CTG found it convenient to repeal the ordinance, as it was in conflict with certain fundamental rights guaranteed by the Constitution, and hence the Shahabuddin CJ CTG repealed it so as to restore due order.

Second, the health policy undertaken during the Ershad regime, decentralising the health administration and bringing it under democratic control, was cancelled by Shahabuddin CJ CTG. The Bangladesh Medical Association (BMA), the national medical association of the country, representing 34,000 physicians across the nation, being the highest professional body of doctors (a platform controlled by the two major political parties AL and BNP), had demanded its cancellation as soon as the policy came into existence. As part of the BMA's strategy to exert pressure on the Ershad government to repeal it, medical professionals, especially doctors, went on a countrywide 18-hour strike, denying hospital and medical services to the people and setting a deadline for the repeal of this policy. Although initially the Ershad government refused to accede to the demands of the BMA, it eventually was compelled to negotiate with them to formulate a new health policy acceptable to all stakeholders. However, since the Ershad government had set up a new committee with the communication minister to finalise the draft of the new health policy, the BMA considered this a serious breach of agreement, threatening to go on renewed strikes. But before the dispute between the BMA and the Ershad regime could be resolved, the anti-Ershad movement reached its height and the BMA immediately lent its support to the political leaders who were leading this new movement. The political leaders in turn agreed to lend their support to the demands of the doctors.

The policy then remained in suspension until Shahabuddin CJ CTG decided to repeal it, probably under pressure from the BMA. The BMA president was one of the advisors of the Shahabuddin CJ CTG and perhaps may have exerted some pressure from within to repeal the policy. Ahmed (2004: 51) is of the opinion that the health policy did not generate any serious public controversy and could perhaps, if properly implemented, have heralded a new beginning in providing basic health care services to the people. Yet the Shahabuddin CJ CTG cancelled it, perhaps to appease the resentment of doctors nationwide. This portrays the extent to which politics has pervaded into various institutions, organisations and even professional associations in Bangladesh from the early days of democratic awakening. The lack of trust exists not only in the realm of party politics but has also trickled down and fully pervaded the wider institutions.

In addition, quite curiously, advertently or inadvertently, Islam-based religious education was undermined, as Ahmed (2004: 52–53) interestingly notes that the policy decisions by the Habibur Rahman CJ CTG to reduce the marks for the course of Islamic studies from 100 to 50 at secondary level for the 1998 session seemed to somewhat attempt to secularise the religious education system. This, and the decision to celebrate 17 April, the day the government in exile was formed in 1971, could be considered as a deliberate attempt to promote a certain kind of ideology – an ideology akin to secular and pro-liberation thought. Though both decisions caused political controversy, critics argued that neither of the policies was related in any way to the holding of elections in an impartial manner.

Ahmed (2004) continues that the Latifur Rahman CJ CTG also took major policy decisions with regard to allowing the US government to use Bangladesh air space, fuelling facilities, airports and seaports in the backdrop of 9/11. But this policy, despite the criticism, was not taken unilaterally as it was evidently a significant foreign policy and defence decision. The CA had consulted the president, the leaders of the main political parties, senior bureaucrats and heads of the three services before going forward with the decision, as a result of which this element of policy-making did not draw irreconcilable controversy.

However, the attempt to separate the judiciary from the executive by the Latifur Rahman CJ CTG was considered by many as a policy decision, as was the controversial decision to set up a committee with a High Court judge as its head to assess the cases filed by the outgoing AL government against its political opponents – this initiative was perceived to be non-neutral, with the CA's tilt towards the BNP camp. The controversial mass transfer of civil administration was severely criticised by AL and the media, as it seemed 'over the top' with many such transfers seen as unnecessary, although the CA defensively justified them on the basis that, as a result of these transfers, the administration became more neutral.

Generally speaking, despite the critiques, the different election-related activities taken by the first three CTGs have been more positive and successful than otherwise and they have been broadly grouped together and appear to have constructively played a role in a) improving the overall law and order situation of the country, b) reforming the EC, c) modernising election laws, d) reorganising the administration, e) educating the voters and f) providing access to State-run electronic media.

The second group

The fourth CTG of Dr. Fakhruddin Ahmed constituted an important interregnum in Bangladeshi political history since it emerged from a complex socio-political situation prevailing in the country. With ample national and international support initially, this CTG embarked upon a wide-ranging effort to repair the basic institutional foundations of Bangladesh's democracy, although this was not really the constitutional mandate of a CTG. After taking power, the CTG quickly passed the Emergency Powers Ordinance (EPO) and the Emergency Power Rules (EPR), which laid out the ground rules of the regime and gave it the tools to pursue a zealous anti-corruption agenda aimed at removing the extant political class from the helm of the State. These promulgations gave the army and the CTG unprecedented authority to detain and try citizens on potentially unverified charges. This kind of an emergency scenario helped to justify the military-backed

CTG's emergence as it conveniently placed the State in a quasi-emergency situation. Several related issues are highlighted in the subsections below to provide a necessary scrutiny.

The ordinances' dubious role in democratisation

Among the 122 ordinances that this CTG passed in a period of two years, several related to elections. But there were also many policy decisions which had no direct relevance to holding free and fair elections. However, the ordinances altogether can be seen as a contribution to both the process of State formation and of democratisation. This is perhaps an irony that an unelected CTG, in a state of emergency, when fundamental rights are suspended, deliberately passed ordinances that seemed to deepen and improve the quality of democracy or good governance (DeSouza 2010: 12–18) – possibly also an irony of necessity and proof of an awareness of a 'higher public interest'.

The Institute of Governance Studies (IGS) of BRAC University, in its State of Governance in Bangladesh Report (2008: 51–52), explained this contribution to the process of State formation and democratisation in the following words:

> A number of efforts were taken to bring about qualitative changes in the functioning of the political parties. Amendment of the Representation of People Order (RPO), 1972 allowed important measures to ensure free, fair and credible elections, including mandatory registration of the political parties intending to contest elections, and disclosure of certain information by candidates. These changes in electoral laws had a positive impact as candidates with comparatively cleaner images were selected by the political parties. This momentum continued during the first session of the Ninth Parliament. For the first time in the history of parliamentary democracy in Bangladesh, all standing committees have been formed within the first session of the parliament and with two chairman positions (of standing committees on ministries) being held by opposition party members. This 'empowerment' of the opposition in parliamentary procedure is a very welcome change.

Seven sets of ordinances were expected to have had a further impact on democratisation. As an example, the impact of some of these ordinances is highlighted. At the heart of the CTG's reforms was a sweeping anti-corruption drive through the Anti-Corruption Commission (Amendment) Ordinance 2007 and the Prevention of Money Laundering (Amendment) Ordinance 2007. Both resulted in a public discourse on corruption that had not only made it a part of the electorate's political imagination, but had also influenced the imagination of the political parties who, during election time, kept such factors in mind when selecting their candidates. These corruption ordinances altered the perception that politicians were above the law, since the prosecutions targeted all politicians irrespective of their party status, including its top leaders, which was quite inconceivable for both the polity and the electorate. Fakhruddin Ahmed CA appointed a former army chief as the chairman of the reconstituted Anti-Corruption Commission (ACC). This move could be interpreted as a signal of the military's control over the anti-corruption agenda. It gave the impression to the electorate that the ACC was transformed into an independent and credible organisation with extraordinary powers to investigate, arrest and seize the property of suspects without any official permission.

The history of setting up an ACC goes back to 2004. Under pressure from the international community, the BNP government at that time agreed to set up an independent ACC, but establishing an effective ACC proved to be difficult. There were concerns as to whether it would ever function independently as the chief commissioner of the ACC was appointed by the president and the ACC's organisational structure and budget were decided at the discretion of the government. It has always been alleged that there was clear partisanship and bureaucratic interventions and that thousands of cases were pending and remained unaddressed due to the absence of rules and procedures for the operation of the ACC. But during the fourth CTG regime, this was different. The ordinance to this effect disallowed any legal remedy from any higher court until corruption cases were resolved in a trial court. Backed by the CTG government and the army, the ACC arrested hundreds of political figures, business persons and former bureaucrats accused of acquiring disproportionate wealth, extortion and misappropriation of relief goods.

The two leaders of AL and BNP were no exception, for the first time in Bangladesh's political history, and consequently were arrested under extortion and graft charges (Datta 2009: 24–27). The sons of Khaleda Zia were also arrested and imprisoned on grounds of corruption. Since it was public knowledge that Khaleda Zia's regime saw an increase in unbridled corruption and manipulation, the news of the arrests of the political leaders and their heirs hit the politicians hard, sending a clear message that the agenda of the army was to cleanse the polity of corruption and to showcase the new CTG's power and control over the State, which was a nationalist and legitimate move for the greater good of the nation, perhaps indirectly using the 'higher necessity' argument.

Robinson and Sattar (2012: 737–779) note that, amid this anti-corruption blitzkrieg, on 5 February 2007 the CTG announced that Bangladesh would sign the UN Convention Against Corruption, providing additional legitimacy to its far reaching anti-corruption activities. These initiatives were already broadly supported domestically and backed up by the international community. According to the Human Rights Watch Report on Bangladesh (2009):

> Several international donor agencies such as Asian Development Bank, United Nations Development Programme and the World Bank are providing support to the government's anticorruption efforts. They have rarely raised publicly any concerns about abuses resulting from the campaign.

According to the Human Rights Watch Report on Bangladesh (2008):

> The international community was generally supportive to the military backed regime as no international actors publicly called on the army to return full powers to a civilian government. Transparency International also worked closely with the CTG as an advisor on its anticorruption efforts, hoping to make the most of what it saw as a potential opportunity to strengthen anti-corruption institutions during the emergency. During periods of rule by elected governments, these initiatives are not plausible as each institution of Bangladesh is manipulated and politicised.

According to Robinson and Sattar (2012), central to the reformulation agenda was its 'minus-two' strategy (a ploy to get rid of the two Begums of AL and BNP) to send into exile former PMs Sheikh Hasina and Khaleda Zia. This plan failed as the army underestimated their grassroots political support base and encountered international resistance against their potential exiles. After arresting the two Begums and a large number of powerful political leaders from the major political parties, generally on allegations of corruption, many were held in custody for months without formal charges being framed against them. In cases of accusations of corruption, the problem had been producing evidence in court against those charged. This was where the major problem lay, as it was a serious challenge for the fourth CTG to bring forth the required evidence within the stipulated time.

The fourth CTG had taken on far too many issues at hand without a clear strategy in place, and with both internal and external pressure mounting with time, it proved a real challenge to duly address all the issues. Given the levels of corruption in Bangladesh, the US state department described many of the ACC charges as 'credible'. But as the anti-corruption drive continued, increasing numbers of Bangladeshis and outside observers began to view the detention of these leaders as politically motivated, over the top and out of balance. Fuelling this suspicion was the fact that several high-profile politicians, who were widely perceived as corrupt but who had supported the CTG and the military's intervention, were simply not prosecuted.

According to Sobhan (2008a: 8–9), at the heart of the CTG reform was not the elimination of corruption but an attempt to break the deadlock between the two main political parties in the country, AL and BNP, which had alternated power since the restoration of democracy in 1991 and which were held responsible for the dysfunctional nature of the country's democratic and political culture. Since the leaders of both major political parties were tainted by corruption charges and forced into long incarceration, the CTG had hoped that this would result in their marginalisation and even their eclipse. The unsuccessful twin strategy of propping up new leaders and exiling the old ones reflected the lack of understanding within sections of the technocrats/civil society and the army about the grassroots hold that these political parties had on the electorate. As a result, the CTG was neither able to implement the 'minus two' formula nor did it manage to bring forth a 'third force' through the Nobel Laureate Muhammad Yunus's new political party *Nagorik Shakti*, which tried to capitalise on his international acclaim and clean image. Against the backdrop of continued pushback by the courts, the military-backed CTG came under increasing domestic and international pressure to hold elections, which were eventually scheduled for December 2008. By this point, Dr. Fakhruddin's CTG had failed to actualise its plan to remake Bangladesh's political parties or reshape the nation's political landscape. It could also not make the State institutions function in an autonomous way, which seemed one of its goals. It was now faced with a situation in which the nation's leading politicians were in jail in the run-up to the elections. It was due to this inability to remodel the political landscape that ultimately led to the release of the hundreds of politicians charged with corruption and other offences under the EPR 2007. As negotiations between the military and political parties continued, politicians started to be released from jail one by one. The ACC had rushed to prosecute so many, and so fast, that it had often not followed all the required procedures and the defendants used these irregularities fully to their advantage. As a result, the ACC's investigations during the emergency regime, regardless of their actual merits, were discredited as politically motivated. This proved counterproductive in two ways: first, the politicians, upon their release, were even more confident that Bangladesh's political landscape needed them and that they were indispensable; and second, the politicians' release was apparent proof of their so-called clean image.

Regrettably, the ACC in Bangladesh today remains as compromised and ineffective as it was since the military attempted to replace it when it came to power during the emergency of Dr. Fakhruddin's CTG.

The role of the High Court

Since most political leaders were detained on corruption charges at that time, the silent battle between the military and the politicians was fought in the judiciary. The High Court division of the Supreme Court dealt with some of the first and most visible blows against the legitimacy of the army-backed CTG's 'good governance coup'. The ACC either hired many of the best-known senior lawyers of the Bangladeshi bar on retainer so that they would not be available to defend politicians or threatened them into not representing those facing corruption charges. Despite this situation, the High Court provided a constant source of aggravation to the military government during the emergency, consistently offering limiting interpretations of the government's emergency powers. The judiciary seems to step into such scenarios, as it perhaps strengthens their powers in the process too, but it could also be that the court felt it necessary, in fact almost an integral part of its job description, so to say, to play an active role to avoid the nation slipping into a new form of dictatorship.

Hence, on 26 February 2007, the High Court declared illegal the detention order against a former AL MP and three others, observing that the power of the

High Court which allowed it to issue directions could not be curtailed by the EPR. This outspoken decision was prominently covered in the media and was among the earliest and most visible defiances to the government's claim to broad emergency powers to remake Bangladeshi democratic institutions (Robinson and Sattar 2012: 756–757). The CTG provision in the Constitution of Bangladesh was meant to be merely a transitional tool for 90 days in order to hold free and fair elections which the earlier three CTGs had successfully delivered. But this military-backed CTG was of a different fabric and seemed to be more akin to an 'alternative emergency' through an unconventional military coup, with a techno-crat-military nexus, pretending to apparently do greater good to the nation than the political class. The speaker of parliament at that time referred to the CTG as an 'irregular' administration and not an 'illegal' one.

Robinson and Sattar (2012) conclude by explaining that throughout the period of emergency, decisions of the High Court, including its controversial position regarding the bail matters under the EPR, provided a rallying point for those who opposed the military government's attempts to use the crisis to restructure or cleanse Bangladeshi politics. These decisions carried great symbolic weight. Declaring the CTG's actions as illegal significantly undercut the military's claims that its intervention was 'necessary' to promote good governance. For most of the emergency period, however, these judgments usually remained merely symbolic as the Supreme Court's Appellate Division stayed or overruled the High Court Division's most assertive decisions.

We note that the High Courts are often left to sort out the mess and do the unpleasant work in these kinds of situations. There seems to be orderliness in this mess, however. The far greater willingness of the High Court Division to challenge difficult situations could be because of a number of possibilities: it could perhaps be due to the different personalities of the judges, or perhaps because the High Court judges knew that their judgments could be later overruled in the Appellate Division. Hence, they attempted to test the waters and assert their judicial powers more strongly against the executive; it could also be that the executive was simply less successful in capturing the opinion of the lower levels of the judiciary than in the Appellate Division. Alternatively, one may ask whether the High Court Division might have been pressured by the political parties to support their leaders, as the judges are mostly recruited during political governments' regimes and have an indirect, soft allegiance to the respective political parties. Whatever may have been the reason, the Bangladeshi experience of having a High Court Division that is more spirited and more proactive than before has protected to some extent encroachments by non-political, unusual executives or usurpers of power during an emergency.

Reviving the institutions

Several institutions which are important components in consolidating democracy have suffered during the regimes of both military and political governments. In a bid to revive them, the fourth CTG took a few initiatives, which on the face of it looked promising. But eventually the issue became one of sustainability and propriety: sustainability in the sense that whether there was clarity of plan to genuinely revive these institutions and whether such revival was sustainable in the long run; propriety in the sense of whether it was deemed proper for a CTG to undertake initiatives beyond its constitutional mandate.

Whatever may have been the case, during the tenure of the fourth CTG, the National Board of Revenues (NBR) became active against tax evaders. In addition, the Truth and Accountability Commission (TAC) that the CTG appointed was to unearth 'ill-gotten wealth' and enabled people to voluntarily admit their corruption wealth to the exchequer and seek pardon. In return for amnesty, individuals charged with corruption were barred from contesting local or national elections for a period of five years. Such persons were also barred from holding any public office or executive position in public associations or financial institutions. For some time, there were uncertainties regarding whether such persons could resume political activities and contest the next elections, but the issue was resolved when the High Court declared the TAC unconstitutional (Datta 2009: 26–27).

Datta (2009) also examines that, despite the setbacks facing the TAC, it met with some success in its fight against corruption. In monetary terms, the drive unearthed Taka 12 billion and secured the conviction of 116 politicians and businessmen. It also approved a proposal to manage the illegal assets that had been confiscated from individuals charged with corruption. Importantly, it also promulgated the Abandoned Property (Control, Management and Disposal) (Amendment) Ordinance 2008 with the State objective of better management and control of abandoned property in the event of confiscation of such property by the courts. The ordinance subsequently lapsed due to non-ratification by the elected parliament in 2009.

The real implication of all of this has to be seen within a larger context. The accomplishment of this CTG has to be viewed against the backdrop of Bangladesh's dubious track record of large-scale corrupt practices. As noted, between the years 2001–2005, the anti-corruption watchdog Transparency International Bangladesh (TIB) ranked Bangladesh as the most corrupt country in the world. In 2006, it was the third most corrupt. The CTG could only pursue the anti-corruption drive up to a certain point due to the widespread public revulsion against corrupt politicians. The prolonged acceptance of the internal emergency by the people of Bangladesh – a country known for its agitational politics – indicates its people's feelings of anger, frustration and helplessness towards elected governments' corruption and manipulation. The prolongation of the CTG seemed partly justified due to its ambitious anti-corruption drive. However, Sobhan (2008a: 8–9) notes that the drive, which was headed and coordinated by serving military personnel, quickly ran into trouble because of numerous due process and fundamental rights violations and the selective nature of the corruption and tax-related prosecutions.

The establishment of a National Human Rights Commission, Consumer Rights Protection Ordinance and the Right to Information Ordinance have been significant in the eyes of civil society. But what caught the attention of the electorate were the local government ordinances that have foregrounded the importance of introducing or at least strengthening decentralised government in a political system that had hitherto been quite centralised. The strength of a decentralised government is the way forward since it brings the government closer to its people. Local politics also becomes a training ground for political leaders, including women, who aspire to national representation (Zaman 2012). It also helps to defuse local issues and tensions, reducing compliance costs since it disperses power and creates multiple points within the polity, where disputes can be attended to and resolved by local leaders.

Separation of judiciary from the executive

The ordinances separating the judiciary from the executive were clearly important to re-establish and strengthen the rule of law. The separation of the power of the judiciary from the executive has been a long and arduous journey and did not happen in one go. Datta (2009) notes that despite popular demand, the judiciary had always remained under the control of the political bosses and was subject to political interference and manipulation. When in opposition, both BNP and AL endorsed the independence of the judiciary, but once in power, both strived to retain control over it. In December 1999, Bangladesh's apex court, the Appellate Division of the Supreme Court, gave a landmark judgment in *Secretary, Ministry of Finance v. Masdar Hossain*, reaffirming the principle of independence of the judiciary from the executive, elaborating on the constitutional position and practice regarding the separation of the judiciary from the executive, and laying down 12 declarations and directions for implementation by the government in this regard.

The decision originated in a constitutional challenge brought before the High Court by 218 people in the judicial service, including one Masdar Hossain, who argued that the subordinate courts were part of the judiciary, and therefore that persons in the judicial service could not be included within the Bangladesh Civil Service (Reorganisation) Order 1980. Neither could they be controlled as though they were a part of the Bangladesh Civil Service, as defined by the Bangladesh Civil Service Rules 1981 (the BCS Rules). The High Court division held in favour of Masdar Hossain, the appellant. After the government appealed this decision, it lost, as the Appellate Division affirmed the High Court's judgment. In this judgment, the Appellate Division affirmed that a separate judicial service should be established, distinct from the executive and administrative cadres of the Bangladesh Civil Service. It also noted that this separate judicial service should include both persons in judicial service and magistrates exercising judicial functions. It stated that these two categories formed a class distinct from other services of the Republic and that they could not be treated alike, merged or amalgamated with any other service except a service of an allied nature. As a result, the court held that the government's inclusion of judicial officers within the Bangladesh Civil Service (Reorganisation) Order 1980, as the Bangladesh Civil Service (Judicial), was beyond the terms of the Constitution. The historic judgment identified therein five key characteristics of independence of the judiciary: first, security of tenure; second, recruitment to the judicial service as permanent and through a transparent Judicial Service Commission; third, security of emoluments including pensions, et cetera; fourth, institutional functional independence of the subordinate judiciary from parliament and the executive; and last, financial autonomy over the funds allocated.

However, despite the passage of time, the government did not fully comply with the *Masdar* directions and full implementation of the same was postponed as many as 20 times. In addition, a number of actions taken by the government detracted from the letter and spirit of the *Masdar* judgment and have themselves been the subject of questioning and further constitutional challenge by lawyers focused on ensuring compliance with the judgment. One such case concerns the transfer of judicial officers without the consent of the CJ (Hossain and Alam 2006). However, what the fourth CTG did was to create a baseline for an impartial judicial system.

The original 1972 Constitution of Bangladesh gave the power to the president in order to appoint the CJ and provided that judges of the Supreme Court would be appointed by the president after consultation with the CJ. But this constitutional requirement of consultation was removed in 1975 and remains absent even today. The power of appointment at present is effectively exercised by the PM since the president acts in accordance with the PM's advice under article 48(3) of the Constitution. However, a recent decision of the Appellate Division has reasserted the requirement that consultation with the CJ is necessary and that noncompliance with the CJ's requirement is a violation of the Constitution (*Idrisur Rahman v. Bangladesh*). The military-backed CTG established a 'body' for making appointments to the High Court and the Appellate Divisions of the Supreme Court for the duration it was in office.

Within days of assuming office, the fourth CTG also amended the Criminal Procedure Code Ordinance and formalised the independence of the judiciary from the executive. It also called for the formation of a separate Bangladesh Judicial Service Commission. Despite some opposition from the bureaucracy, this came into effect in November 2007. Meanwhile, a number of incidents have highlighted the growing independence of the judiciary and its favourable impact on Bangladesh.

Electoral laws reloaded and limits of the law

Lastly, a significant set of ordinances concerning the electoral system have not only produced an electoral system that is qualitatively of a higher order than was the case earlier, thereby guaranteeing a freer and fairer election, but have also created the opportunity and space for political processes to evolve. The concept of 'reforms' within political parties and 'inner party democracy', civil society engagement with the asset disclosures of candidates, restricting criminals from contesting elections, and increased confidence among the silent majority to participate without fear, attempted to improve the quality of democracy in Bangladesh (DeSouza 2010: 14–16). The impact of these collective ordinances in the short term contributed to the democratisation process of Bangladesh in at least three manners: a) they added significantly to the institutional density of the polity; b) they impacted on the political discourse, particularly on the issue of corruption, which has become an important part of the vocabulary of politics, especially those of the street; and c) they began to stem the tide of disregard for the rule of law that defined the previous political culture (Datta 2009: 27–28).

Unfortunately, the effects of such ordinances disappear when political governments are in the driving seat again. As a result, some of the ordinances promulgated by the CTG were subsequently rejected by the courts; examples include the TAC, the Muslim Marriage and Divorce (Registration) Amendment Ordinance of 2008, and the Contempt of Court Ordinance of May 2008, among others (Datta 2009: 27–28). This is perhaps because the courts wanted the CTG to have only a 'governance and an election focus' instead of deviating to other policy decisions and getting involved in routine law-making. It could also be because all these elements that were introduced after international and human rights activist pressures perhaps went a bit too far. If that is indeed the case, we have here an example of judicial awareness of the limits of law (Allott 1980), recognising that State involvement in family law matters, in particular, is not necessarily going to lead to acceptability or better results among the electorate.

Finally, the judicial reactions could also be explained and interpreted as a reassertion of national sovereignty, as the fourth CTG was possibly too influenced by international agents and human rights lobbying. Disregarding the ordinances expressly or in spirit is an expression of a renewed hold on power and position of authority, and now with the people's mandate, as the vast majority of parliament seats were won in the elections of December 2008 by the AL government.

The unconventional CTG

The civil/technocrat-military relations have been a contest between military encroachment upon politics and popular opposition to authoritarian trends. Over a significant period of time in Bangladesh's history, the military prevailed and took over the reins of power and established authoritarianism. There were occasions when popular opposition and disapproval kept the military within the barracks. According to Riaz (2016a: 140), despite the transition to democracy, the ruling élite connected to the previous military regimes maintained significant prominence and returned to power within a short time. Not only did BNP, a product of the military regime, emerge as a major party, JP too – which was founded by General Ershad – became a kingmaker. As a result, within the electorate and the polity, there has generally always been a lurking anxiety and malaise whenever the army took over, especially during turbulent phases of politics and confrontations. For its part, AL finds it difficult to admit that their introduction of the one-party system in 1975 was a colossal mistake which paved the way for institutional authoritarianism. Authoritarianism today not only resides in political institutions, working its way through the mechanisms of governance; there is also the socially rooted authoritarianism which has remained unaddressed in the democratisation process of Bangladesh (Riaz 2016a: 140). However, despite the authoritarian flavour of the fourth CTG, what the October 2006 crisis in Bangladesh resulted in was an unconventional dimension not seen at play before: a civil society/technocrat-military government working in tandem towards political reform.

Datta (2009: 53), in relying on the words of the editor Matiur Rahman of the Bengali daily newspaper *Prothom Alo*, after the fourth CTG takeover, remarked as follows:

> The political leaders have not been able to show us any path; the problem is only increasing. It is the military today that has saved us from falling deep into a crevice; we would not have been able to solve our own problems ourselves. It is the stark reality now we are at such crossroad where we think that it is impossible for any political leader to solve the problems by themselves.

This, as we know, paved the way for the army to use the notion of 'necessity' to intervene when faced with a collapsing political administration. As the chief of army staff Moeen U Ahmed (2007) clearly stated:

> The country had three options in front of it: the first was to go for elections scheduled on 22 January 2007, the second was to proclaim martial law and the third option was to protect the national existence through establishing an acceptable CTG by quickly promulgating the state of emergency. Everybody in the world including Bangladesh at that time was apprehending that martial law was imminent. But we decided not to follow the footsteps of our predecessors as the third option was adopted.

Such a decision, then, does not seem to have erupted out of the blue or on the pure basis of sheer nationalism on the part of the army. One can also discern the international factors which influenced such behaviour. The UN was categorical in its opposition to military rule, pulling out its election monitoring team from Bangladesh. It warned the army about being party to any sham election. Consequently, the EU and the Commonwealth also cited that the conditions for holding national elections were absent and suspended their election observation missions.

The UN then went one degree further in threatening to remove the Bangladeshi army from UN peacekeeping duties (which are highly lucrative in several respects) if they took part in sham elections. Its threats to disallow blue helmet responsibilities deterred the army from engaging in any move akin to a coup. This was a powerful instrument, because Bangladesh between 1988–2006 had contributed more than 40,000 soldiers to various UN peacekeeping operations throughout the world. In early 2006, Bangladeshi peacekeepers were operating in over 30 missions in 12 countries, spread across three continents, and were therefore the second largest contributor to global peace-keeping operations. This brought home US$200 million annually. The pride and international prestige that was brought to the Bangladesh army as a result of this involvement was not something that the army could just throw away, and now the army's role in political reforms through the fourth CTG also became a matter of pride and prestige. Moeen U Ahmed (2007) further remarked, in espousing democracy, that:

> I reckon Bangladesh will have to construct its own brand of democracy, recognising its social, historical and cultural conditions with religion being one of the several components of its national identity We have tried both the presidential and parliamentary forms of government and now the people will judge which is better I believe the aspiring democratic process of search for new direction for Bangladesh, the current transition period will allow us an opportunity to develop a new concept and find a new sense of direction to the future politics of Bangladesh.

He clarified on various occasions that the army was subservient to civil authority; that the army had no intention of taking over; that the army was to restore democracy, law and order and eliminate corruption; and that the army had come to the aid of the civilian government. It seemed rather odd that the army and the technocratic team of the fourth CTG worked in harmony, as there were no public or known disagreements between the two during its rule, despite rumours about tensions of ideologies inside the army. Besides holding free and fair elections and reshaping politics, other issues such as fighting crime and maintaining public order – including dealing with Islamic militancy and corruption – became the top priorities and the *raison d'être* of the army during the fourth CTG regime. The CTG was successful in demonstrating another dimension of its control and power play: the interplay between civil society, the army and the international players. This did not ring well with the polity, as for the latter, two more groups of players came directly onto the political scene: civil society and the international players.

This prolonged CTG rule did not at all reduce the prevailing culture of mistrust in Bangladesh. It may have accomplished three objectives vis à vis the political parties: first, for a very brief period, the political parties during the fourth CTG seemed tacitly united against a common enemy – the enemy being the civil–military alliance. It was understood that it was possible for this alliance to deliver better governance than the political regimes had done in the past. So, in the minds of the politicians, such future alliances ought to be nipped in the bud. Second, there was a renewed suspicion about the military and a fresh bargaining technique had to be reinvented between the political parties and the military, mainly any incumbent political government and the military. Third, any emerging force interested in governance from civil society had to be immediately crushed. Besides the usual aggression between AL and BNP, these were the newer dimensions of power play in Bangladesh.

On many counts, the 29 December 2008 election delivered by the fourth CTG was a milestone in Bangladesh both in terms of the high voter turnout and the unprecedented result. The election campaigns were violence-free, all candidates more or less adhered to strict electoral rules, the election-day atmosphere was festive, and the election was free, fair and inclusive and – most importantly – credible. The holding of a successful election and the peaceful transfer of power from the technocrat-military-backed fourth CTG to the new civilian government was applauded both at home and abroad. The electorate almost overlooked the suspension of democratic rights, including the freedom of expression and the troubled human rights records during the two-year, military-backed CTG takeover. The AL-led alliance secured a landslide victory with four-fifths of the parliament seats, while the BNP and its allies recorded its worst ever electoral defeat. JP regained its position so as to have a better prospect of negotiating with any of the major parties. JIB experienced a setback (Riaz 2016a: 88).

At present, with the potential 'higher authority' – the CTG – abolished, there is even more uncertainty, turbulence and violence in the country's political and electoral sphere than before, with barely any check or balance subsisting between the all-powerful executive and the other organs of the State.

The demise of the CTG mechanism

Despite the CTG's wide popularity among the electorate, almost to the astonishment of the nation and within months of being in power through a free and fair election held by the military-backed CTG, the AL government began treading on the entire issue of the CTG provision of the Constitution of Bangladesh. This was on the basis of a writ petition which had originally been filed in January 2000 (when the AL was in power) and heard in 2004 (when the BNP was in power), challenging the Thirteenth Amendment to the Constitution. During that time, in 2004, the BNP-led government's attorney general and AL's advocate both backed the system. The High Court upheld the amendment in 2004 but gave the petitioner leave to appeal to the Supreme Court, which heard the case seven years later, in March 2011.

It based its argument on the fact that the CTG, which was brought in through the Thirteenth Amendment of the Constitution, distorts the principle whereby the Republic will be governed by an elected government. The Supreme Court thus ruled that the Thirteenth Amendment violated the constitutional principle of people's sovereignty by giving unelected people control over the State for 90 days. Conceding that the CTG enjoyed political and popular support, however, it allowed the parliament to retain the mechanism of the CTG for the next two national elections. This crucial time, a window of ten years, could have been used to address the loopholes that the law regarding the CTG provided and could have been an opportunity to improve the CTG system overall. But the AL government did not pay heed to the initial ruling of the Supreme Court which approved keeping the CTG mechanism for the next two elections. Instead, the government hurriedly went for its abolishment before the full judgment was written and before an alternative arrangement for holding free and fair elections was set up. According to the International Crisis Group report (February 2015):

> Instead of building consensus for a new model with the opposition, the AL government abolished the system through the fifteenth amendment in June 2011, justifying this on the Supreme Court judgment and abuses of power during the military-backed CTG. The BNP believed that this was done to improve the AL's re-election prospects, given the advantages of incumbency, particularly control of the law enforcement apparatus. These perceptions were reinforced by the failure to introduce electoral reforms to prevent executive interference and strengthen the autonomy of the Bangladesh Election Commission. TIB warned this would likely "jeopardise the level [electoral] playing field."

In a country which is already plagued with mistrust and hostility in its political sphere, the repercussions of both the Supreme Court order in 2011 and the consequential amendment to the Constitution in parliament through the Fifteenth Amendment have had far-reaching consequences, the effects of which are piquantly felt even in 2017. It is important that we zoom in to the details of both events.

Supreme Court order on the CTG

In the brief verdict, the seven-member Supreme Court panel, headed by CJ ABM Khairul Haque, pronounced first the short order of the judgment, which provided that the Constitution Thirteenth Amendment Act, 1996 (Act 1 of 1996) is prospectively declared void and *ultra vires* the Constitution. The Appellate Division ruling further said that the parliament in the meantime was at liberty to bring in necessary amendments excluding the provisions for making the former CJs of Bangladesh or the judges of the Appellate Division the head of the CTG.

Briefly, the fact of the case is that the Thirteenth Amendment of the Constitution, which institutionalised the CTG structure, is against the basic structure of the Constitution and hence illegal. And since a CJ is the head of the CTG, this has also curbed the independence of the judiciary of the nation, which is also another basic feature of the Constitution. So, the Thirteenth Amendment should be declared illegal and abolished on the above grounds. Israfil Khosru (2012) remarked that

> If our politics is not confrontational enough, it seems we are quite adept at scoping out new sources of confrontation and agitation. On

> May 10, 2011, The Supreme Court declared a fifteen-year-old constitutional provision illegal. In other words, the Thirteenth Amendment with which the system was put to place officially in 1996 was declared unconstitutional. Furthermore, in the same verdict the apex court also stated that the system, although it has been deemed illegal, can be practiced, for another two parliamentary elections for the safety of the state and its people.

The confusion regarding this initial ruling was widespread. It raised four major questions in the minds of the electorate: first, why was the 15-year old constitutional provision for transition suddenly declared illegal and *ultra vires* the Constitution? Second, if it is so declared, then under which law may the nation hold two more parliamentary elections under the CTG structure, as suggested by the Supreme Court? Third, if the court is of the opinion that due to 'necessity' two more parliamentary elections can be held under it, then why is there such a rush to declare it illegal now? Last, instead of addressing the loopholes within the CTG structure, why was the entire system scrapped without providing a viable alternative to the electorate?

This decision initiated heated discussions and debates among the populace – civil society, political parties and the media. Eight notable *amici curiae* were consulted on the issues in the court and seven of them were in favour of the CTG, as the system was hailed as appropriate for Bangladesh because the nation had a history of bitter political hostilities and mistrust prevailing and had its own brand of democracy – managing elections and balancing transitions has always been problematic. Such opinions, however, did not have any bearing on the matter and, as expected, the Supreme Court's ruling clearly reflected the intention of the government in power. The biggest criticism of the ruling was that the Supreme Court tried to solve a political issue in court. It also managed to further divide an already politically divided nation. Once a consensus choice of all major political parties, especially the AL, the CTG provision now stands abolished despite the High Court declaring at an earlier time that the Thirteenth Amendment was valid.

Constitution Fifteenth Amendment Act, 2011

The AL-led government did not wait to get the copy of the full text of the judgment. Rather, on 30 June 2011, within six weeks of the short judgment of the Appellate Division, it speedily scrapped the CTG system by amending the Constitution (Constitution Fifteenth Amendment Act of 2011). In its opinion, 'an illegal system cannot be kept in the Constitution' (Liton and Sarkar, 2012a). PM Sheikh Hasina asserted that the elections to parliament in the coming days should definitely be held in accordance with the established norms, practices and constitutional legacies of a parliamentary system of government. It also noted that all possible doors to the usurpation of power by the defence forces in the wake of any political catastrophe or deadlock had meanwhile been closed by article 7(A) of the Constitution (Fifteenth Amendment) Act, 2011. The article basically states that if the process of the Constitution is stalled (if anyone abrogates, repeals or suspends the Constitution or attempts or conspires to do so) by anyone, such persons shall be liable for sedition, which is punishable by death. It implies that any military adventure/intervention becomes risky for persons who throttle the constitutional supremacy with any possible argument of 'necessity'.

The Fifteenth Amendment also restored 'secularism' but retained 'Islam' as the State religion. The basis of this amendment was perhaps an earlier case, the *Fifth Amendment* case, the judgment of which was released in July 2010, whereby the Supreme Court, in strong terms, not only denounced extra-constitutional methods of acquiring State power but also restored the 'secular spirit' of the original Constitution of 1972. The links to these two aspects were reflected in the following two pronouncements of the Court in the *Fifth Amendment* case:

> We are putting on record our total disapproval of martial law and suspension of the constitution or any part thereof in any form. The perpetrators of such illegalities should also be suitably punished and condemned so that in future no adventurist, no usurper would dare to defy the people, their constitution, and their government, established by them with their consent.

While on 'secularism', the court observed that

> Martial law proclamations by omitting secularism, one of the state policies from the constitution, destroyed one of the basis of the struggle for freedom and also changed the basic character of the Republic as enshrined in the preamble as well as in Article 8(1) of the Constitution.

In reaction, the editorial of a mainstream English newspaper (*The Daily Star*, 30 July 2010) seemed to reflect public sentiment when it wrote:

> The judgment of the Supreme Court nullifying the Fifth Amendment to the Constitution must be considered one significant means by which history can be restored to its natural course or must be made to move in a direction that will uphold the interest of the nation. Apart from a return to unfettered democracy, we also have the opportunity today, thanks to the landmark Supreme Court verdict, to have our secular spirit as a nation restored in the constitution. Secularism has never been and can never be a negation or abandonment of religion. It is a much higher principle, the one that promotes and ensures the equality of all faiths and the right of all citizens to practice their religion in their individual ways.

Perhaps as a pragmatic compromise, which is a balancing act that this region has had to do over the years, the judgment made no mention of the Eighth

Amendment which had declared Islam as the state religion, thereby retaining it. This was therefore not a radical step, opening the court to challenges of overstepping its limits, but was nevertheless a highly significant judgement, designed to strengthen and highlight the plural composition of the Bangladeshi populace. That this would not go down well with adherents of political Islam was abundantly clear (Hasan 2011). Neither did it go well with the proponents of secularism who did not see any reason to retain Islam as the State religion as that, according to them, defeated the ethos of secularism.

Coming back to the bill for the Fifteenth Amendment to the Constitution: it was passed by division vote with a majority of 291–1 for PM Sheikh Hasina's ruling alliance. However, amendments moved by two ruling alliance leaders opposing Islam as the State religion and religion-based politics were rejected. The Constitution, however, formally upholds equal rights and dignity for people of all religions. To prevent the misuse of religion, a ban has been imposed on terrorism and militancy. This is a sign that the government declared terrorist activity in the name of Islam as 'intolerable' (Twining 2009: 218).

The Fifteenth Amendment Bill was passed amid protests from various quarters including the BNP-led opposition, which had been boycotting the House since the current session began. The BNP, which had been opposing the annulment of the CTG system, was asked by the ruling alliance to put forward an alternative but did not do so. The constitutional changes incorporated strict provisions against military takeovers, stating that capture of State power and suspension or staying the operation of the Constitution would be treated as treachery and a subversive act. Parliament had been empowered to hand down the maximum penalty to those usurping State power, which was a clear warning signal to the military with an eye to Pakistan.

Following the horrific Bangladesh Rifles (BDR; a paramilitary border security force under army command) carnage on 25 February 2009, the army morale was at an all-time low, after 57 talented officers of the Bangladesh army had been brutally killed by assailants through a conspiracy which is believed to have had a foreign hand in order to purposefully weaken Bangladesh's military. The BDR mutiny was provoked by longstanding grievances over pay and facilities and resentment among the BDR's rank-and-file officers over the corruption of army officers. The gap between the haves and haves-not was wide, and it did not take much of an effort to add fuel to fire. Military-AL relations had not been too comfortable in the past and Sheikh Hasina's decision to negotiate with hundreds of rebelling soldiers on that ill-fated day, despite high-command pressure to use force, caused intense resentment within some military circles that even accused her of complicity in the plot. Several senior officers were dismissed and scores were sentenced to imprisonment. The military trials and even government reports of what actually transpired during the carnage remained classified information and hence kept away from public knowledge. In 2010, five officers were convicted of trying to murder Sheikh Hasina's nephew, an AL parliamentarian, for involvement in the negotiations that ended the mutiny. Since that massacre, there have been further grudges of the military vis-à-vis the AL government which have apparently been dealt with ever since. In January 2012, the military announced that it had foiled a coup attempt by mid-level officers. The AL government since then has adopted a carrot-and-stick approach. It purged the military of AL critics, BNP/JIB supporters and officers who were in close contact with Pakistani counterparts and were critical of India. Simultaneously, the military now is overcompensated by salary increases, creation of more top posts, support for new divisions and cantonments and allocation of residential land to senior army officers to name a few. The constitutional changes perhaps guard against any future military/civil society nexus in governance, as was seen during the fourth CTG. In May 2014 it was announced by the government that personnel in the military's main intelligence agency (Directorate General of Forces Intelligence, DGFI) would receive a special monthly allowance of 30 per cent of their salary. The AL government's understanding with the military also saw its support of the military's growing business interests, awarding its entities major infrastructure and other governmental contracts, insurance businesses, power plants, gas stations, hotels and so forth. Given the government's current relationship, it is unlikely that for now it will pursue any policy that contradicts the military's interests.

Eminent citizens and civil society members urged that a 'people's commission' be formed comprising jurists and civil society leaders to resolve what they termed a 'crisis' that arose following the controversial Fifteenth Amendment. Sharply criticising the amendment, particularly with regard to the abolishment of the CTG, eminent jurist Dr. Kamal Hossain and former director of the Bangladesh Legal Aid and Services Trust Dr. Shahdeen Malik both opined that the government had committed a 'despicable offence' by going against the fundamental rights of the people. They observed that the latest amendment created instability in society and that another unconventional military coup like the 1/11 situation might be created in the country if the crisis was not resolved. Online polls conducted by the media to test the reactions of the populace gave a clear message, indicating strong public support for the CTG system. The fieldwork survey results also corroborate this sentiment.

The verdict of abolishing the CTG system through the Fifteenth Amendment to the Constitution also triggered mixed responses among lawyers with some calling it contradictory, some disapproving it and very few hailing it. Some of the reactions from senior and well-known legal personalities include the attorney general Mahbubey Alam's opinion that the verdict was 'right in principle' and that the next two parliamentary elections would be held under CTGs to avoid political instability. Senior advocate Rafique-ul Huq and Khandker Mahbub Hossain, president of the Supreme Court Bar Association, termed the Supreme Court verdict as 'self-contradictory', saying that the Supreme Court declared the Thirteenth Amendment illegal but suggesting holding the next two parliamentary elections under this law. Senior advocate M Amir-ul Islam said that parliament had to play a responsible role in finding an 'alternative' to the CTG system. However, senior advocate M I Farooqui, who stood for the petitioner, expressed satisfaction over the verdict, saying it was 'good for the nation and the Constitution'. Of the *amici curiae*, Mr. T H Khan, Dr. Kamal Hossain, Mr. M Amir-Ul Islam, Mr. Mahmudul Islam and Mr. Rokanuddin Mahmud gave opinions in 'favour' of the CTG system. Two jurists, Rafique-ul Huq and Dr. M Zahir, also supported the transitional modality, but suggested alternatives to the system. *Amicus curiae* Ajmalul Hossain QC along with the appellant's counsels M I Farooqui and Mohsen Rashid placed arguments against the CTG system.

Constitution Thirteenth Amendment Act case

Originally, a civil appeal had been brought in the Appellate Division of the Supreme Court of Bangladesh in 2005, reiterating that the Thirteenth Amendment Act 1996 was *ultra vires* of the Bangladesh Constitution as it was passed by the Sixth Parliament of Bangladesh, introducing the concept of non-representative and undemocratic government through the system of CTG in violation of the basic and fundamental concept of democracy and also in violation of the mandatory provision of article 142 (1A) of the Constitution. Accordingly, as indicated earlier, it was the contention of the appellant that the impugned amendment could not be justified as it had changed the meaning or modified the basic structure of the Constitution, either in its effectiveness or by keeping the basic structure in abeyance temporarily or permanently. The impugned Act, in effect, has amended the preamble and other articles, including those requiring reference of the bill to a referendum.

It was also stated that the independence of the judiciary, which is a part of the basic structure of the Constitution, was also affected and impaired by the impugned Act and that the president had assented to the Bill without referring the question to a referendum, as mentioned above. The petition also elaborated that such legislation was fraud under the Constitution and that the parliament had transgressed the mandatory provision of constitutional law in disguise and indirectly. It was further submitted that the induction of the CJ and other judges into the office of the CA seriously impaired the independence and dignity of the Supreme Court of Bangladesh. Quoting Shahabuddin Ahmed CJ in the case of *Anwar Hossain v. Bangladesh*, it was noted that '[o]pening up of opportunities for appointment after retirement may serve as a temptation and temper with judge's independence during the concluding period of his service'.

For that reason, there is a total bar on holding any office of profit under the original Constitution, which has been explained in the case of *Abdul Bari Sarkar v. Bangladesh* in the following words:

> The purpose behind this prohibition was that the high position and dignity of a judge and of the Supreme Court should be preserved and respected even after his retirement. Further, that if any provision was made for holding of office, after retirement, then a judge while in service of the Supreme Court might be tempted to be influenced in his decisions in favour of the authorities, keeping an eye upon a future appointment.

It was further pointed out that, as the president is not responsible to the CA, the nation would remain under the governance of double executives. Mr. M I Farooqui, the counsel for the appellant, also submitted that the concept of two executives, that is, a 'diarchy', had been injected into the Constitution whereas the framers of the Constitution had conceived of only one executive, to be headed by the PM, and this also added to the destruction of the Republican character of the Constitution. He also argued, with reference to article 58(C), that succession to the office of the CA starts from clause 3 thereof and if the succession fails, eventually the president takes over as the CA. He then has a chance to become autocratic and, in that case, the democratic character of the Republic shall totally be destroyed and on that count the Thirteenth Amendment does not stand up to scrutiny.

The Thirteenth Amendment concealed the truth to divert the public mind from the issues which mattered in as much that events do not wait on decisions. Least of all in matters of foreign affairs, finance and war, there is no scope for practically controlling the area of operation for an unrepresentative government to carry out routine functions. In addition, this amendment has also provided the scope for the unrepresentative government to take decisions, even in policy matters. However, the *amici curiae* of the Court, Mr. T H Khan, Dr. Kamal Hossain, Mr. M Amir-ul-Islam, Mr. Mahmudul Islam and Mr. Rokanuddin Mahmud, quite succinctly clarified their submissions in court for keeping the CTG system in place, as discussed below.

Mr. T H Khan reminded the court that before striking down the Thirteenth Amendment, the 'history' behind it must be taken into consideration as to why, in the first place, CJ Shahabuddin Ahmed was approached to become the acting president in 1990, when elections could not be held or trusted to be held under the autocrat leader Ershad. He also submitted that the Constitution of any country is not a revelation and is 'amendable to amendment to suit the need of the people and the State' (echoing perhaps Habermas's concept of an ever-evolving Constitution) and that the Thirteenth Amendment to the Constitution was brought to strengthen democracy and not to destroy it. He referred to a well-known saying of Sir Winston Churchill:

> At the bottom of all tributes paid to democracy is the little man, walking into a little booth, with a little pencil, making a little cross, on a little bit of paper; no amount of rhetoric or voluminous discussion can possibly diminish the overwhelming importance of the point.

Hence, it is clear that the concept of CTG had been brought into the Constitution by the Thirteenth Amendment to ensure the right to vote of the 'little man of Churchill'. He continued that people, by participating in CTG elections on a large scale, elected their representatives to form the government and thus accepted the system. After each such election and a smooth transition of power, a new government took oath, obviously accepting the election results. So the question of declaring the Thirteenth Amendment *ultra vires* of the Constitution does not arise at all. He also submitted that the provisions made in the Thirteenth Amendment, making the retired CJs of Bangladesh and the retired judges of the High Court division eligible to be the CA, had in no way impaired the independence of the judiciary, as article 96(2) of the Constitution had ensured that no judge shall be removed from his office except in accordance with the provisions stipulated in that article. Therefore, the tenure of a judge being fully secured, the CJ or judge of the High Court division, who is supposed to become CA after retirement, has no reason to be apprehensive of his office and as such there is no reason to be influenced or allured to perform the judicial function as a sitting judge in favour of the authorities, keeping an eye upon such future appointment. He stressed that the CTG is a must for sustaining democracy, which is a basic structure of the Constitution.

Dr. Kamal Hossain submitted that the court has a special role to play as a guardian of the Constitution. In interpreting any provision of the Constitution, the court should not approach any matter in a mechanical way and should keep in mind that the constitutional process is carried on and that extra-constitutional force does not get a chance to intervene in the matter. He also reiterated that the Constitution is a 'living document' (echoing perhaps Ehrlich, Habermas and Granville Austin as well) and must be durable, and at the same time, it has to be responsive to the needs of the people, keeping intact its basic structures, and thus interpretation has to be given life to it. He reminded the court that because general elections under party government had lost all their credibility in the name of election, what had happened could not be said to be any election. The sole motive to pass the Thirteenth Amendment was to hold free, fair and impartial general elections so that people could choose their representatives, who in turn would form the government; thus the people's supremacy as enshrined in article 7 of the Constitution would have been ensured. Successive elections have already been held under the new dispensation and thus people have accepted the CTG mechanism. He concluded that the issue raised by the appellant that the Thirteenth Amendment to the Constitution created diarchy and gave dictatorial powers to the president is tendentious and shows lack of understanding of a constitutional mechanism adopted by consensus to meet the widely shared concern of supplementing the EC's capacity to ensure free and fair elections. He finally emphasised that the Thirteenth Amendment had not in any way impaired democracy, the Republic character of Bangladesh or the independence of the judiciary as well as the separation of powers.

Barrister M Amir-ul-Islam remarked that merely holding an election cannot give legitimacy to the result of the election unless the 'process' of such an election is transparent. Past elections have shown that elections held under political governments were not free and fair. People, who are the supreme authority to decide their representatives, could not exercise their right of adult franchise because their votes were hijacked by muscle power and money. The Thirteenth Amendment was passed as a consequence of the 'people's movement' and then on the basis of 'consensus'. He pointed out that, like the Constitutions of India and Pakistan, the Bangladesh Constitution too has provisions (article 72 clause 3) for interim government to carry on the administration for the period between dissolution of parliament and the successor's entry to office, on the basis of the next election of parliament. After the dissolution of parliament, the tenure of the elected government expires and then the elected government, which remains in power, ceases to have been elected and to have a representative character. So, there is nothing wrong in the mechanism of the CTG being manned by unelected people for 90 days. The objection raised by the appellant against the system was a mere technicality and the introduction of the CTG in the Constitution had not in any way destroyed democracy, which is anyway a basic feature of the Constitution. By the Thirteenth Amendment, the boat of democracy was rather salvaged and people's right to vote freely and fairly had been restored. So, in effect, the democratic right of the people had been protected rather than destroyed. Certain improvements might be made in the CTG system in the light of the experiences of the previous three CTGs, but that too must be on the basis of 'consensus' among the political parties as was reached in 1996.

Mr. Mahmudul Islam reminded the court that the circumstances came to such a state that rigging of elections by the party in power became the rule rather than the exception, and that the Magura by-election in 1994 offered an example of the worst form of rigging. Although the Thirteenth Amendment suspended the representative government for a short interregnum, it ensured the operation of democracy in the country. He submitted that in social engineering, there is no panacea which can cure all political maladies in all places and at all times. What suits Great Britain may not suit Bangladesh and vice versa. In the present context of political maturity of the Bangladeshis, there is no alternative to holding elections under the CTG in order to preserve the democratic character of the Constitution of the country, and democracy had to be suspended for a little while for its ultimate survival. He concluded by emphasising that in the recent past, the power to constitute a CTG had been abused. But merely because of this abuse, the Thirteenth Amendment could not be held unlawful. Rather, measures were needed to be taken to prevent future abuse instead of abolishing the system introduced through the Thirteenth Amendment altogether. Reform of the provisions of law to prevent its abuse is the combined function of the executive and legislature and not of the judiciary.

Mr. Rokanuddin Mahmud stated that the Thirteenth Amendment was the outcome of the emotion of the entire nation. If article 7 of the Constitution is read with the preamble, it will appear that people are supreme and that all powers belong to them, and the Thirteenth Amendment is based on article 7 as it has ensured people's participation in general elections to select their representatives in a free and fair election, which was previously an impossibility under any political government. He also showed that it is not correct to say that during the CTG, the country will be run totally by unelected people. After all, the president to whom the CTG shall collectively be responsible is an elected person, and therefore neither the Republican character of the country nor democracy will be absent during the 90 days. As a result, the question of declaring the Thirteenth Amendment as *ultra vires* the Constitution does not arise at all.

These strong, valid legal arguments, however, failed to convince the court to take into account the socio-political reality and, particularly, the absence of trust between the political parties and between people and the political parties which prevailed in Bangladesh and which necessitated the inclusion of the CTG provision through the Thirteenth Amendment in the first place. Despite the lapse of 16 years since the institutionalization of the CTG, the nation remains deeply divided and the element of trust between AL and BNP governments in gifting a neutral, fair and participatory election to the nation is completely absent. Notwithstanding this ground reality, the Supreme Court declared 'illegal' a 15-year-old constitutional provision that mandates an elected government to transfer power to an unelected non-partisan caretaker administration to oversee a new parliamentary election upon completion of its term. In the same verdict, the highest court said the voided system may however be practiced for another two parliamentary terms for the sake of 'safety of the state and its people'. The court also asked the parliament to amend the Constitution to make sure that former CJs or any other Supreme Court judges are not chosen as heads of CTGs, in case the system is kept for another two parliamentary elections. A seven-member SC panel, headed by CJ ABM Khairul Haque, reached the verdict on a majority vote. It rejected a 2004 High Court ruling that upheld the Thirteenth Amendment to the Constitution which provided for a ten-member non-partisan CTG to take over, following the dissolution of parliament and resignation of an elected government on completion of its term.

The dissenting opinion of Justice Md. Abdul Wahhab Miah reiterated that the Thirteenth Amendment was neither illegal nor *ultra vires* the Constitution and did not destroy any basic structures of the Constitution. He did not agree that the CTG system had become unworkable due to the improper exercise of power of the president which had led to the unnatural and unconstitutional state of affairs in 2007. He also did not agree that in order to avoid recurrence of such a situation, the mode of setting up the interim government by whatever name it may be called was to be replaced by another system. The Thirteenth Amendment was passed to preserve and ensure democracy and effective participation of the people in the affairs of the Republic. He found that it was incorrect to say that the exercise of government power for the interregnum period, as envisaged by the impugned Act, was destructive of democratic values. There was no illegality in holding the last general election and as such the question of condoning it or legalising it under the doctrine of 'state necessity' does not arise. The petitioner was trying to unsettle settled issues which may create commotion in the polity and in such a situation, it is clear that this petition had not been made *bona fide*. Due to the introduction of the CTG, the fragile democracy of Bangladesh had survived. The concept of the CTG was introduced to protect and safeguard democracy. It was designed to be an aid to democracy and not to its destruction.

It was a popular demand. People had accepted it. It was for the greater interest of the public good of the country. The petitioner had filed the application with the *mala fide* intention of destroying the democracy of the country.

Justice Muhammad Imman Ali, in his dissenting opinion, also stated that each losing party which had been in power up to the dissolution of parliament lost the election held by the CTG and claimed that the election was subtly rigged (1991), manipulated with the help of civil administration (1996) or crudely rigged (2001), or that even the election was fixed by the CTG and EC with backing from foreign powers and engineered with the help of digital means (2008). Rare is the occasion when the losing party gracefully accepts defeat in any election, local or national. He continued, importantly, that it must not be forgotten that the CTG system grew out of the political parties' distrust of one another. Continuation of that system had progressively increased and hardened the level of that distrusting mentality to the extent that one party now accuses the other of establishing a certain election-engineering mechanism to choose the next head of the CTG. There is doubt as to whether this mentality will be outgrown in the foreseeable future. Hence there has to be a means of achieving at least a 'minimum level of neutrality' in the election period for democracy to sustain. He concluded:

> Thus it is quite clear that the amendment was enacted by parliament through the will of all the people of this country, both those represented by the party in power and those represented by the parties in opposition. Such an act of parliament can be said to be extraordinary, in as much as it reflects not only the will of the majority under a democratic system, nor just the will of the two thirds of the House of Parliament which is required for amendment of the constitution, but in this case the amendment was a reflection of the will of the whole nation. Hence the [thirteenth] amendment cannot be said to be unlawful. When the whole of the nation demands passage of a particular provision, it cannot be said to be undemocratic.

He further concluded that:

> The CTG system worked to a great extent for two terms. For reasons which are alluded to above, the system became unworkable. Again the people must be allowed to decide the solution to the problem. That can only be done through dialogue in parliament by their elected representatives. The suggestions made above are mere suggestions. The Supreme Court or the judges do not make law and it is not their mandate to do so. The Supreme Court has the authority given by the constitution to declare any law to be *ultra vires* the constitution. The court may travel to the extent of recommending that parliament should consider enacting a particular legal provision to cater for a given problem which has been brought to its notice, but that does not extend to law making power.

In an interview with the author, former CTG advisor Dr. Akbar Ali Khan reiterated, that politicians in Bangladesh are not expected, once in power, to allow themselves ever to be voted out of power. He contrasted the situation of Bangladesh with that of Britain in 1945 when PM Winston Churchill, despite leading the nation to victory in the Second World War, lost office in the general election and promptly went home. Referring to Bangladesh, Dr. Akbar Ali Khan said: 'In order to have democracy the ruling party must be willing to accept defeat if they are not elected. In Bangladesh when the ruling party is in power, they do certain things which are controversial, as they think that they cannot leave power. So they are not willing to accept defeat. It is not democracy as no one wants to give up power'. This predicament or pattern is echoed by another former CTG Advisor, Dr. Wahiduddin Mahmud, in an interview with the author: 'The government in power will never think about going out of power, and this is combined with another element: democracy deficit, which is due to the fact that Bangladesh started with extremely weak institutions'. The EC, which should be critical to the holding of an election, is among those weak institutions.

Notwithstanding these issues, in a judgment issued in short form on 10 May 2011, the Supreme Court's Appellate Division under then CJ Khairul Haque struck down the Thirteenth Amendment to the Constitution, which in 1996 had instituted the CTG mechanism, but allowed the next two general elections to be held under the existing system following the age-old principles that suggest 'that which otherwise is not lawful, necessity makes lawful', 'safety of the people is the supreme law' and 'safety of the state is the supreme law'. The full judgment was completed after Justice Khairul Haque CJ's retirement on 17 May 2011 – a whopping 16 months later on 16 September 2012, which did not provide any scope for retaining the CTG in the next two general elections as purported in the short judgment or even until the EC was neutrally strengthened or another viable alternative transitional mechanism was established. Meanwhile, on 30 June 2011, the Thirteenth Amendment was removed from the Constitution by parliament through the Fifteenth Amendment.

Post CTG abolition

Anam (2011) insightfully remarked that all political problems of Bangladesh stem from 'our peculiar and specific political culture', whose hallmark as we know is the complete 'lack of trust' between the ruling and the opposition parties. In his view, this is the root of all political problems. He continues that there is an instant 'no' from the opposition to all suggestions of the government, regardless of which party is in power and irrespective of how good and beneficial the proposal is. Parliamentary boycott is a norm for both BNP and AL. The economy-destroying *hartal* is condemned by the party in power and practised by the opposition, again regardless of it being AL or BNP. Thus, there is a total lack of morality in their respective positioning which is filled with only political opportunism. The

CTG was proposed by AL in the mid-1990s because of mistrust. The only acceptable way to hold elections, AL repeatedly demanded at that time, was to create a neutral, non-partisan body, a caretaker body. And so, it was done. The question is, has that situation changed? Has trust been forged between the two sides? Has the practice of dialogue between the two major parties about any matter, let alone national interests or political goodwill, begun? Has the animosity between the two major parties lessened? In fact, it is the contrary. Will BNP ever accept an election under AL government? Would AL have accepted an election under BNP? Unfortunately, such a chain of reasoning does not move beyond rehearsing the discouraging story of long-established mistrust.

Israfil Khosru (2012) aptly summarised the matter in the following words:

> The CTG system can be fine-tuned to add provisions to prevent illegal take-over of power (as the military backed 2007–2008 CTG had done) but its overnight abolishment has created a field for probable confrontation and chaos. It should also be mentioned that several credible civil society platforms and personalities have already voiced their opinion in support of the CTG. Apart from the previously mentioned panels of illustrious *amici curiae*, noted individuals like Sir Fazle Hasan Abed, Professor Yunus, Professor Muzaffar Ahmed and Barrister Rafiqul Haque were outspoken in their opinions supporting the continuation of the system. While there were no calls for abrogation of the CTG system from the civil society and the opposition, the government's decision to pursue the annulment of the system can only be labeled as unilateral and politically motivated. While several civil society members felt that there might be some room for reforms to the system, almost none felt that there was any need to do away with the system entirely by virtue of the Fifteenth Amendment. It is clearly evident that although the Supreme Court judgment has divided the nation, it has made the ruling AL a minority within that division. Certain voices of reason within the AL also felt it was rather premature to do away with a proven system before a viable alternative has been decided. While the AL hardliners can be found incessantly praising the cancellation of the CTG system, the nation is undoubtedly heading towards a grave situation, which eventually the government has to take responsibility for. Single-handedly pushing for constitutional reform of national importance without building consensus can only lead to further alienation of the people and that is not desirable for the ruling party.

People's opinion, on a small scale, was gathered by the author after the CTG abolition in July 2011, well before the full text of the Supreme Court's judgment was published. The abolition led to widespread politically inspired shutdowns and violence. The respondents during the author's fieldwork had predicted that such a toxic political atmosphere would prevail when 61 per cent agreed that the opposite standing of the political parties on the issue of the CTG would lead to future political crisis, while 28.5 per cent did not think so.

Referring to how elections were held under CTGs, former Election Commissioner Brigadier Sakhawat Hossain opined that 'the CTG regime fostered transitional good practice. The CTG period brought some confidence in people. Even if it is for a very small period, the parochial administrative nature goes under the carpet' (from a research interview with the author). Retired Lieutenant General Masud Uddin Chowdhury, who was a key member of the military during the events of 2007–2008, referred to the anti-incumbency factor present among voters at the end of a political government's term and observed that 'The fact that no party in power came back again during elections is an indicator that elections have been free and fair during CTGs as there has been no influence of the party in power during elections' (Research interview with the author).

That CTGs have delivered fair elections is borne out in and confirmed by popular perception. Again, during the fieldwork, when respondents were asked to look back at past elections, 70 per cent of those surveyed said that CTGs had been the most successful at delivering fair elections, as opposed to only 16 per cent who said that political governments had had the most success. When respondents were asked about what kind of government they would like to see for future fair and neutral elections, 62 per cent preferred the CTG as opposed to 19.5 per cent who favoured a political government, while 18 per cent remained silent on the issue. From these two sets of data, there was a clear perception that past CTGs had resulted in an increase in fairness in the election process, and it was a strong preference of the respondents, as voters, to see the CTG carry future elections, as it was deemed necessary to ensure fairness in elections.

Former CTG advisor Hafizuddin Khan was unambiguous about the continuing need for some kind of caretaker arrangement. He observed that since the situation for which the CTG was established is continuing or rather has been aggravated, there could not be a fair election without a CTG. One of the reasons is that the 'bureaucracy and all other socio-political institutions have been totally politicised and with a politicised administration, an election [that is fair] under a political government is impossible' (Research interview with the author). This is a perception that again is widely shared. During fieldwork, 68.5 per cent said that it was essential for there to be a CTG to ensure fairness at the next election, which took place on 5 January 2014 *sans* CTG and hence was boycotted by the main opposition. Just 21 per cent thought that the CTG was not essential. This level of support for the caretaker mechanism is particularly impressive despite the fact that a) the last CTG which took office on 11 January 2007 overstayed its mandate of 90 days, thereby not leaving office until 6 January 2009; b) the last CTG was to a large extent a façade for the military that brought about its installation; c) there were increasing violations of due process and human rights as its tenure proceeded; and d) the Supreme Court had ruled that the Thirteenth Amendment was passed unconstitutionally.

Noted economist Dr. Wahiduddin Mahmud observed that 'norms of democratic behaviour develop only during those brief periods when CTGs are in power: i.e. they are absent during elected governments' (Research interview with the author). Reflecting on widely held perceptions as to how politicians behave in government, barrister Manzoor Hassan OBE, head of the Institute of Governance Studies at BRAC University, reiterated that 'politicians behave in such a way that they give us the impression that once they get power, they can do anything. It is a kind of arrogance. It does not go well with the whole idea of democracy and tolerance' (Research interview with the author). Hence one criticism that could be made about the CTG mechanism was that although it succeeded in producing fair elections, it did not necessarily succeed in consolidating democracy. But then, that was not the mandate of the CTG. The CTG's main role was simply to assist in electoral governance and to oversee a smooth democratic transition, which it did, despite the turbulences and manipulations it faced.

Hence, when asked as part of the survey whether the CTG system was contrary to democratic values, a large minority of those surveyed assented – 38.5 per cent. This was not a much smaller proportion than those who felt, on the contrary, that the CTG system was compatible with democratic values – 42.5 per cent. The greater level of such acceptance in Dhaka than in Dinajpur, as the survey indicated, may be reflective of a greater degree of political sophistication in the country's major urban centre compared to that in a provincial area.

When asked whether it was possible to hold fair elections under a political party, however, the percentage agreeing diminished to 33 per cent, whereas 55 per cent thought this was not possible. Those supporting the proposition may perhaps be composed of those supporting the AL – the current ruling party – and/or those reluctant to ignore the possibility of a fair election under a political government because they recognised the non-democratic nature of the CTG mechanism.

Subsequent developments indicate that this rushed and unilateral measure of abolishing the CTG caused fresh trouble for an already plagued nation with ongoing multilayered challenges. One wonders whether all of this means that politicians have some kind of strange interest in stoking the fires of distrust and trouble for their political gain. Or is this phenomenon simply a manifestation of the never-ending acrimonious relationship between the two major feuding political parties?

January 2014 election and its aftermath

The experience of alterations in power in the previous 22 years and the potential for losing the forthcoming election, in conjunction with the dominant party mindset, perhaps led to the annulment of the CTG proviso in 2011 (Riaz 2016a: 156–157). Or perhaps one could go even further in saying that the door for any unelected force, whether the military, civil society or both, as seen during the fourth CTG era, which relied on the crutches of the CTG mechanism to alter the political landscape of Bangladesh, was forcefully shut by the AL government so that in future such incidents would be prevented from recurring. In consolidated democracy, it is not the norm for civil society to seek power and its strength is the sum total of the neutrality, independence and high moral ground it occupies, but the 2007 adventurism severely damaged that credibility of civil society since the message given as a result of the latter's involvement in politics seemed to have been that civil society also wants a share in power. This has been quite damaging as the political class governing at present not only has the military to be vigilant about regarding usurpation of power, but also perhaps civil society. Whatever may have been the motive behind the abolishment of the CTG by AL, it certainly caused the fragile democracy practiced in Bangladesh since 1991 to have taken a turn for the worse.

Following the Fifteenth Amendment to the Constitution and the resultant CTG abolishment, the opposition parties kept arguing for the reinstatement of the CTG and threatened to boycott the forthcoming election should the government not pay heed to this demand. After weeks of unprecedented violence and scores of deaths, the opposition finally announced, on 2 December 2013, its boycott of the January 2014 elections. Despite the involvement of the UN Assistant Secretary General for Political Affairs on the need to have inclusive, credible elections and for attempting to break the deadlock between the government and the opposition, the initiative of the UN still failed to enunciate any consensus between them. PM Sheikh Hasina eventually proposed 'an all-party' CTG rather than amending the Constitution against the judgment of the Supreme Court, suggesting that 'an all-party cabinet' could be sworn in, with her as the head of the cabinet. She offered the opposition any ministry that it wished to have, keeping her as head of the government and urging BNP to join the election within the present constitutional framework. BNP refused to join any election under a government headed by Sheikh Hasina. Meanwhile, the EC had announced the election schedule which the government refused to change.

Civil society, seeing a stalemate yet again, took the active initiative and sought postponement of the election so that the government and the opposition could reach some sort of consensus for the sake of national interest in order to hold a participatory, credible election and, to that effect, a citizens' dialogue jointly arranged by various organisations such as CPD, SUJAN, ASK and TIB themed 'Bangladesh in Crisis: Citizens' Concern' was held in Dhaka. More than 60 civil society, academic and business community members participated and agreed overwhelmingly that the 5 January elections ought to be postponed so that some sort of political agreement could be reached for an all-inclusive democratic election to subsequently take place. The main demands of that meeting were stopping the mindless political violence immediately, postponing the scheduled election of 2014 and continuing dialogue between the political parties for bipartisan participation in the election. The government, however, held on to their argument for the 5 January 2014 election date on the basis that parliament was already dissolved, despite legal opinion reaffirming that elections could be deferred up to 90 days, even after the dissolution of parliament under the existing constitutional framework (Khan 2015: 9, 14).

Regardless of these efforts and advice from various sectors of society, the AL government did not budge from the scheduled election day. The BNP opposition declared a series of strikes and *hartals* leading up to the election day itself. The violence that BNP perpetrated, along with their murky stand on the war crimes trials, lessened their popular appeal both at home and abroad. Aisha Gani (2014) reports that 5 January 2014 was the most violent election day in Bangladesh's history, with 21 people killed as they headed to the polls and in the run-up to elections and night raids in the homes of opposition supporters. The situation was depicted by a medical college student in Gani's article in the following words: 'My friends are afraid and nobody wants to come into college', as it was not safe for her or her friends to travel, given the violent clashes between protesters and police on the streets, strikes and road blockades, and buses being petrol-bombed. The medical college girl in Gani's article continued that 'Bangladesh is very dangerous at the moment. People did not want to go out during election time. There is horror every day'. In a similar vein, Asia director Brad Adams of Human Rights Watch, in its 2014 Report, noted that 'these were the bloodiest elections since independence and unless concrete steps are taken to address what happened, the situation in Bangladesh is likely to worsen'. The Bangladesh authorities, according to the article, were urged to prosecute members of law enforcement agencies found responsible for unlawful killings, torture and other human rights abuses. Leaders of the main political parties were also urged to make clear and unambiguous public statements opposing violence by their supporters and also to end the reign of impunity enjoyed by Bangladesh's security forces. To date, no such steps have been taken.

The violence that resulted from the new turn of events, which was the abolishing of the CTG, caused 500 people to lose their lives by the end of 2013. Usually elections under CTGs are festive affairs, with people lining up from the early hours to cast their votes, raising up their ink-stained thumbs in triumph, but this time 'the sense of disappointment was palpable, the city eerily quiet and JIB was on rampage targeting schools that had been turned into polling stations' (Anam 2014). Tahmina Anam's (2014) article provides that

> It is easy to say that both parties have irreparably damaged Bangladesh's nascent democratic institutions. But this would be a mistake. This government made a grave error in abolishing the caretaker administration and allegations of corruption and cronyism have subsequently damaged its credibility. But the opposition has unleashed a campaign of violence that has undermined any claim it could have had to victimhood.

Anam concluded that, like her fellow citizens, she felt robbed of her fundamental right to determine the fate of her country, as 153 seats were won uncontested with some polling stations seeing no voters at all. There were also allegations of vote stealing. The story was written without her this time and the millions of others who wait to make their small mark on history every five years.

What is particularly a cause of grave concern since these developments is the trend that this is setting on the nature of democracy and democratic legitimacy in

Bangladesh. The AL government's uncontested second term in office and BNP's boycott of the 2014 elections denote various ironies. Mahfuz Anam (2016) notes that one such 'irony' is that the autocrat, General Ershad, against whom all the political parties marched in 1990, is now a special envoy to the PM with the rank of a minister and his party, JP, is the formal opposition in parliament, led by his wife and with three of its members occupying ministerial positions. He continues that 'this makes us the only parliamentary system in the world where the so-called opposition party is also part of the government'. Second, BNP, the second-largest political party in Bangladesh, 'cannot hold party events without the government's permission, cannot hold public rallies without the fear of police repression'. Its executive and grass roots 'leaders run from pillar to post appearing in cases lodged in various parts of the country and most alarmingly, whose members have simply disappeared'. Thus Anam (2016) concludes that 'the regime that was toppled from power as an enemy of democracy in 1990 is now an integral part of it whilst the party that assisted in toppling the autocrat side by side with AL, is now labeled as an enemy of democracy'.

Assuming that this is democracy at work, what stares at us glaringly, however, is the severe lack of political space for dissent and the failure to agree on basic standards for multiparty democratic functioning. While AL believes that it is the sole author and custodian of Bangladesh's liberation, BNP claims to be the guardian of Bangladeshi nationalism. The AL government needs to understand that the marginalisation of the opposition BNP from mainstream politics may encourage antigovernment activism to find more radical avenues, especially more so because of its own increasingly authoritarian tendencies (International Crisis Group Asia Report No. 264; 9 February 2015). The AL government needs to stop behaving as if it is in power indefinitely, as it is the electorate and the electorate alone who decides who is to assume power, provided people have a free, fair and inclusive election. The opposition, BNP, for its part would benefit too if it undertook internal reorganization to strengthen its lower ranks and reinvigorate the middle and even higher leadership, as well as abandon its alliances of convenience with violent Islamists groups and revive a set of basic standards for multiparty democracy. Despite being away from the parliament, BNP could adopt a shadow cabinet that formulates and communicates constructive policy proposals as a government-in-waiting instead of resorting to unconstructive rhetoric, agitation and disregard for the human and economic costs of violent protests which meet with disapproval and rejection from the electorate and which undermine its image as a responsible democratic force, and stop persuading the army or negotiating with foreign powers for its return to power at any cost. Both the government and the opposition need to look at the greater national interest and inculcate long-term visionary politics, otherwise violent fundamentalism will take its opportunity and build its roots in this Muslim-dominated nation. This has already manifested itself, not only in the Holey Artisan Bakery massacre in a Dhaka café, killing 22 people – mostly foreign nationals – on 1 July 2016 (Dearden 2016) by Islamic State of Iraq and Syria (ISIS) recruits, but also in Shibbari, Sylhet on 25 March

2017 when at least six people, including two police officials, were killed and about 40 people were wounded in 'two time bomb blasts' near a militant hideout that was raided by commandos (Mahmud and Islam 2017). The explosions in the northeastern district of Sylhet came a day after a suicide bomber blew himself up at a security checkpoint near the country's main airport in an attack claimed by Islamic State.

Amid this delicate state of affairs, there is every possibility that the forthcoming 2019 elections will be marred with even more aggression and violence because the stakes this time are so much higher. The crux of the matter remains the direction in which the identity of the nation will be pulled. Carefully balancing Menski's Kite Model, which for Bangladesh is its *iccher ghuri*, will be most crucial, otherwise there is every risk that the nation will be torn apart if one corner is pulled way too harshly. In this context, balance would be needed between every aspect of the nation's culture, religion, positive law and international norms. It is not prudent to wish to get rid of any one corner of the kite because that would defeat the essence of the pluralist society that Bangladesh is. One can discern from the pattern of politics in Bangladesh that the 2019 election may not only take unaccounted lives but may also halt the lives of the citizens who become unwilling hostages in the battlefield clouded with the toxic and destructive political culture of AL and BNP. The only way to prevent this is to initiate an effective dialogue in order to set the institutions in motion for having a fair and functional electoral democracy at the very least, perhaps with an agreed transitional framework – any mutually acceptable, renegotiated modality – which can act as an umpire and stop the political point-scoring and revenge-seeking agenda, focusing instead on unity and working within Bangladesh's pluralist society to offer the electorate a national election which is transparent, inclusive and credible. Bangladesh does not have to go back to being 'Kissinger's basket case' (Anam 2014), especially as the nation has steadily progressed in its economic, social and development domains in recent years.

Between December 2016 and January 2017, President Abdul Hamid held talks with 31 political parties for the reconstitution of the EC, since the tenure of the Commission expired on 8 February 2017, pursuant to article 118(1) of the Bangladesh Constitution which provides that there shall be an EC and that the appointment of the CEC and other election commissioners shall be made by the president, subject to the provisions of any law made in that respect. Out of the 27 proposals he received, 20 of the political parties proposed the enactment of law on the appointment of the CEC and other election commissioners, as a specific law in this regard was never formulated in Bangladesh. Perhaps this was because the absence of such a law gives the government of the day the required manoeuvrability to have an EC of their choice, with an eye to influence the election. Most countries in South Asia, especially within the SAARC region, have such a law – except for India and Bangladesh. The track record of India's EC since its inception, even in the absence of such a law, is highly commendable and surely to India's credit, as the Indian executive provided the space for the Indian EC to develop into an autonomous institution from the beginning. Over the years, the Indian EC has thus earned public confidence through its consistent performance, which has made the institution credible, powerful, reputed and prestigious. Bangladesh's EC has neither law nor credibility as it was never allowed to flourish as a separate independent institution by any government, whether dictatorial or democratic. There is also the added scepticism that even if there is a law enacted for the purpose of selecting the EC, CEC and other commissioners, there is no guarantee that this law too will not be tampered with, as happened with the provision of the CTG.

Whether the demand for a new law is met or not in future remains to be seen but in the meantime, on 25 January 2017, President Hamid formed a six-member Search Committee, headed by a Justice of the Appellate Division, for the reconstitution of the EC as the tenure of the latter will come to an end. The Search Committee also included a Justice of the High Court division of the Supreme Court, the comptroller and auditor general of Bangladesh, the chairman of the Public Service Commission, a Dhaka University English professor who is also a trustee board member of TIB, and a Chittagong University pro vice-chancellor. The panel was asked to submit its recommendation with regard to the composition of the new EC to the president within ten working days. At its first meeting, on 28 January 2017, the panel had asked 31 political parties to propose five names each for the posts of CEC and commissioners by 31 January 2017. It had then shortlisted 20 names out of the 128 suggested by 26 political parties. Unlike previous Search Committees, this panel had held meetings with various civil society members, seeking their views on EC formation. The panel then had finalized ten names, from which the president appointed former secretary and freedom fighter KM Nurul Huda as the new CEC and four election commissioners, including a woman, for the first time, who was a former District and Sessions judge. The background of the CEC is that he had joined the civil service in the administration cadre, serving as a deputy commissioner of Comilla and Faridpur. When the BNP-led alliance came to power in 2001, he was a joint secretary who was then forced into retirement. He fought a legal battle against the BNP government but by the time the verdict appeared in his favour in 2008, he had already retired in 2006. When AL came to power in 2009, he was made secretary with retrospective effect. Other new commissioners include a former additional secretary who was a war hero with experience working with Sheikh Mujibur Rahman and President Abu Sayeed Chowdhury, besides being a novelist; a former secretary who had worked as the additional secretary at the EC secretariat; and, finally, a retired brigadier general who was a director of the 'Preparation of Electoral Roll with Photographs and Facilitating the Issuance of National Identity Cards' project during the tenure of the last CTG. BNP expressed dissatisfaction, as several BNP leaders felt 'frustrated' and 'aggrieved' over the newly formed EC due to the potential AL affiliation of the CEC and some commissioners. However, members of civil society had mixed reactions ranging from clear disappointment to optimism. Those civil society members who did not see the reflection of their recommendations to the Search Committee were sceptical about the selection criteria because, according to them, unless the entire process of selecting the EC candidates was transparent, any confidential process would raise many questions and subvert accountability which would not assist with the issue of mistrust that exists at so many levels. There were also those who refrained from commenting on the selection as they would rather observe how the new EC carries out its functions over the coming months. AL, as expected, supports the choice of the new candidates in the EC.

These intervening developments in Bangladesh, where the political situation remains precarious, have reinforced the key case made in this book that the CTGs or neutral administrations are more and not less necessary in a country driven by periodic political deadlocks caused largely by deep-rooted mistrust of other parties. The concluding chapter takes this discussion further, as we shall see next.

6
THE CTG AS AN INTERMEDIARY STRATEGY OF RESPONSIBLE GOVERNANCE IN BANGLADESH AND THE UNCERTAIN KITE JOURNEY AHEAD

What has been presented so far insinuates that there are serious democratic deficiencies at various levels of Bangladeshi society, politics and law, even after 45 years of independence. These deficiencies threaten to affect the implementation of desired agendas and visions (symbolised by the *iccher ghuri* image) as it comes to transition from one government to the next at the critical liminal phase of national elections every five years. The intensity and wrath of the culture of mistrust have created a political mess and even endangered the very survival of the nation as an electoral democracy, and therefore it is about time Bangladesh learnt from all of this in order to understand itself better. The nation is urged to develop the tools to empower itself for a sustainable future, based on a fundamental democratic ethos and principles. The key issues which have emerged all too prominently are repeated and consistent abuses of power, failure to implement good governance and risks to the management of fair elections without the support mechanisms of the CTG or any other neutral institution as a constitutional safeguard. Even at the time of writing this book in 2017, the situation vis à vis creating a reliable institution or finding a mechanism for holding free, fair and participatory elections remains amiss and the modalities for having a new one are yet to be negotiated.

The absence of the CTG is in fact an unstated presence – the realisation that the CTG was most useful at a certain period of time during the country's first steps to democracy, after its extended military regimes. Although the mechanism after three elections could not protect the eventual safe sailing of the *iccher ghuri* for a variety of reasons, it did nevertheless deliver a free, fair and participatory fourth national election. Instead of addressing the reasons or weaknesses in the mechanism itself or further strengthening the CTG, the unconstructive government decision to abruptly dismantle an established institution, insisting that the election commission (EC) was suddenly fit to hold credible elections under the aegis of a political government, destabilised the only democratic practice the nation had. This has taken Bangladesh quite a few steps back as far as basic electoral governance is concerned, since there is no autonomous institution, free from government influence, which can assist in offering credible periodic elections. This, in the first place, had been the most important point of contention over the years for all the political parties. Placing trust on a political government in power to run elections is not yet a plausible and workable option for the nation as the government is yet to reach that stage. The current situation, which is the absence of a CTG or a neutral institution or a neutral election-time government, along with the absence of an effective trustworthy EC, deepens the issue of mistrust and increases tension and uncertainty for the future of electoral governance and eventual democratic progression.

We know that the newly independent country in 1971 wished to hold on to the notions of Western models of democratic governance, because from its inception Bangladesh had included 'democracy' in its Constitution as a fundamental State policy. This was done without testing the waters as to the suitability of electoral laws as received or transplanted laws. Predictably, the nation suffered, particularly during electoral governance, given its politico-socio-cultural realities wrapped in a cloak of distrust. To circumvent these gaping anomalies, the polity eventually came up with the CTG modality as a solution to the problem of electoral governance. The CTG's key role in seeking to hold periodic free and fair elections during the second phase of democratic awakening in 1990, in a nation where the democratic institutions are not fully built, gave the nation an opportunity to experiment with its own way of dealing pragmatically with election-management issues through this mechanism. Thereafter, the CTG became a subject of critical national interest as well as an issue of constitutional importance. However, it became evident that even the best possible 'neutral' legal institution still remains subject to manipulation by the human actors that manage it. Hence, this book, among other things, exemplifies that the Hartian concept and image of law as a legal field may be subject to the activities of social actors, indeed prominent bureaucrats, who are agents of the executive. But this tension also plays out on a wider field, certainly not removed from the general public and its volatile observances of and reactions to what those 'in power', especially governments, do with existing institutional structures. It also shows that in a prevailing climate of suspicion at various levels, even an innovative institution such as the CTG has limits to its usefulness, despite being a popular mechanism among the people and other stakeholders. In fact, it may even assist in the return of an electoral result which may not be favourable to the perceived safe future of the country. That this is a matter of competing perspectives regarding the identity of this young State has become abundantly clear.

The preceding chapters have indicated that the disputed matters are not merely about a CTG instrument, but concern a host of other issues which are so embedded in the nation's socio-anthropological beginning, its hybrid cultural structures, its historical legacy and disrupted progress of democracy that it will take much more than only a caretaker instrument to address these issues. But a caretaker instrument has been a beginning, at the very least, agreed upon by all concerned, to get rid of the much-resented electoral manipulation that prevailed in Bangladesh. The CTG mechanism was therefore the commencement of a journey of dealing with deep-rooted distrust at all levels of society, particularly during election time – during the nation's 'changing of the guard'. One of the conclusions which emerge from this work is that the CTG had indeed served a useful purpose during the time that it was in operation, despite the attempted manipulation in 2007–2008, and it has certainly reinforced the argument about the need for an umpire or election-time neutral institution of some kind to ensure free, fair and participatory elections.

There is also a realisation that wider solutions need to be found to oversee electoral democracy and democratic consolidation. Bangladesh needs a credible modality which will not only oversee free, fair and inclusive elections but will also assist the feuding political parties and the electorate to rely and place their trust upon such a reinvented and renegotiated instrument. It will be a challenge to reach an agreement regarding this new modality before the next national election in 2019. At the very least, the much-needed discourse and negotiation between the government and the polity need to begin at once. The call for bringing the government and the opposition for constructive dialogue regarding election-time modality has been a consistent stumbling block over the past decade to the extent that there has been a public interest litigation in the High Court to explain why the two Begums should not be directed to sit across a table for talks to end the ongoing political impasse since 2013. Unless all the parties can genuinely agree to something akin to a 'citizens charter for good electoral governance' or 'an agreement to establish free and fair election modalities', this problem of holding free, fair, participatory national elections will continue to remain a recurrent crisis. Having said that, one is reminded of the promises that the political parties had once willingly made to the people after the fall of the Ershad military regime back in 1990, and how over the years, everyone moved away from those promises. What was known as *Teen Joter roop-rekha* (The Joint Outline by the Three Alliances), comprising the 15-party alliance led by AL, the seven-party alliance led by BNP and the five-party alliance led by the left leaning parties, had set out a very clear outline for a democratic and egalitarian society committed to the welfare of the people, especially through good governance and building a corruption-free society (Anam 2016). The focus was to have a legitimate government, meaning one that came through the people's vote expressed through a credible election. So sincere was the intention of *The Jote* to make the election truly free and fair that they voluntarily prepared a code of conduct to ensure that the election was truly reflective of the 'will' of the people. This is reflective of Habermas's theory whereupon he emphasised that legitimacy of democracy depends on 'finding arrangements for collective will-formation through discourse' (Warren, 1993: 211), and it is this discursively meditated consensus which is needed for making collective decisions. He stressed the need for a connection between discourses in parliament and the public opinion or will of the people. That code of conduct in 1990 looked promising. Some points that all the political parties included in that code were that a) they would follow general democratic norms of mutual respect and tolerance of others' views in their electoral statements and activities and try to instil democratic spirit in their workers; b) they would refrain from publicising slander or making derogatory remarks about other parties' patriotism and religious beliefs and would not support communalism but would resist communal propaganda; c) they would pledge to shun confrontation in carrying out electoral activities; d) they would not try to influence the administration or law enforcing agencies for their own electoral interest and also uphold the neutrality of the administration; e) they would ensure that the mass media could play an independent and neutral role; and f) they would take forward the democratic process of Bangladesh by accepting people's mandate given through elections.

It seems quite impossible to believe today that the political parties had willingly agreed to these codes. Not only were the codes voluntarily proposed and accepted by all the political parties and their alliances but they reflected the extent to which the polity was committed to the idea of a genuinely representative government to run the affairs of the country at that juncture of history. Had the polity stood by those promises, Bangladesh would perhaps have progressed to significant democratic consolidation by now. As the 'common enemy' at that time, which was the military, was removed from the scene and the first free and fair election took place after the restoration of democracy through a CTG, this political unity began to wither and, regrettably, partisan interests overtook national interests (Anam 2016). Democracy-building or democratic progression halted once and for all. It is this democratic ethos which needs to return and be restored within the polity today.

The discussion on 'democracy' under the 'political science lens' in this book indicated that the idea of 'power sharing' and processes of 'participation' by stakeholders, which is the basic democratic interactive functioning, is not a lived reality in Bangladesh, as the nation finds it difficult to follow this ideal model. Whether this is due to the negative consequences of expressing public resentment or critiquing elected powers or whether it is perceived as a form of exclusion by the losing side, parliamentary democracy in Bangladesh, through the eyes of the opposition, is seen as a way of challenging the government's management of decision-making. While this is a correct starting point in principle, in practice this is often done in an extremely adversarial and destructive way. Regrettably, the Bangladeshi political élite, ever since the second phase of democratic awakening, have not been able to offer an ideology that provides moral and intellectual leadership to the people. The ideologies do not provide any substantive solution to the daily struggles of the people or uplift the people for a common cause. The political parties' incessant bickering over the role of their deceased leaders, rewriting history in a narrow partisan manner, and their inability to provide a futuristic vision to the 60 per cent of citizens who are young people under the age of 25 years have not helped them to become visionary leaders. Yet these leaders yield enormous influence and exercise a significant amount of power over their citizens and their respective parties (Riaz 2016a: 141). The presence of such powers undermines the authority of the democratic politics making the elected representatives, whether of the parliament or local bodies, subordinate to the wishes of their top leaders/masters. The top leaders' unbridled power, zero accountability and absence of checks and balances as they play with State institutions creates defective democracy. Often leaders have been elevated to leadership positions due to their family lineages or their claim to the foundation of the party. This establishes dynastic rule within the parties and their unrestrained powers are exercised 'legitimately' as they are institutionalised in party constitutions and reaffirmed through regular practices. In such a situation, where no intra- or inter-party democracy is exercised, at least for the sake of electoral governance, a free and fair ritualistic election by a neutral government becomes even more necessary.

The CTG structure has thus provided some remedy as far as addressing the 'participation' issue is concerned by creating a 'level playing field' where the electorate can participate in exercising their basic right to vote without fear of manipulation or violence before, during and after elections. Over the years, the CTG has fostered considerable trust as far as the credibility of holding elections is concerned. CTG-held elections therefore had minimum issues regarding the 'elected' being legitimate, as the CTG put a halt to the system of election engineering which took place years before the actual day of election.

The discussion earlier in the book also included the contrasting perspective of the perception of democracy between the grassroots and from the middle class upwards, including the higher classes and civil society. The grassroots still tend to have what some authors describe as 'blind trust' in political institutions, while the experts' perception of institutional trustworthiness is far more cautious and sceptical. Such disparity may both contribute to the dysfunctional state of democratic governance in Bangladesh and provide partial answers as to why, despite a non-participatory and very low voter turnout election on 5 January 2014, the mass public did not immediately take to the streets. The scenario, however, slowly shifted by mid-January 2015, a year later, as BNP's nationwide transport blockade and strikes showed peoples' participation amid serious violence. Whether such participation is merely politically motivated or spontaneous, and how sustained it would be in the future if an alternative modality of holding credible and participatory elections is not negotiated, remains to be seen. But one must bear in mind that peoples' spontaneous participation undergoes a setback when law enforcing agencies are fully controlled by the executive and can go to any extent if unleashed by the latter. Since AL came to power in 2009, human rights organisation *Odhikar* has identified over 325 people who were picked up and secretly detained for various degrees of time, allegedly by one of the country's law enforcement bodies, including the Rapid Action Battalion (RAB). After weeks or months in unlawful detention, the men were then either 'shown arrested' or killed. Out of more than 90 people secretly detained in 2016, 22 dead bodies have been found. In relation to extrajudicial killings (which occurred in even greater numbers under previous governments) since 2009, *Odhikar* reports nearly 1,300 deaths. In a Swedish radio recording, an unnamed senior RAB officer divulged the gruesome manner in which men were picked up and tortured, stating among other things that the fate of the men so captured and killed was decided by 'high ups' (Bergman 2017). These snippets indicate the extent to which the executive can go in having any form of dissent suppressed.

The section on 'transition to democracy' depicted that these limbo scenarios were times of volatility and vulnerability. For Bangladesh, such a phase had been when the CTG was expected to deliver a credible election amid an atmosphere of high expectation and considerable latent tension. The skilful navigation of any transitional tenure, through its action and inaction, determines the type of elected government the nation is to produce which is why transitional periods usually manifest themselves as founding moments for a nation.

Examining the relevance of 'trust' pointed to two different approaches to trust: the 'political culture approach', which speaks of inter-personal trust and democracy, where compromises can be made by the political élite and where distrust, which is a kind of political alienation, threatens the stability of the democratic system; and the 'constitutional approach', which focuses more on accountability, openness and better information. Institutional trust's importance cannot be understated as it is essential for a stable democracy. In the context of Bangladesh, the problem of trust – or rather the lack of it – additionally relates to the competing and opposing visions of what the nation should be like, as an ideal construct, and here the *iccher ghuri* symbolism resurfaces. The CTG provided a modicum of trust as far as the electorate, the global community and, to a great extent, the political class is concerned, in holding credible elections notwithstanding the environment of suspicion, hostility, violence and confusion.

The importance of 'elections' was seen not only as a political process but also as a reflection of trust therein. Since the democratic awakening of 1990, elections in Bangladesh have been a method by which rulers are legitimised for a period of five years. It is the only time power comes as close as possible to the people. Although election laws may be manipulated and used as a device for the systemic oppression of political rivals and suppression of opposition when such elections are conducted by the political government in power, the CTG elections offered a change in the configuration of that election machinery. The CTG in charge did so by creating 'a level playing field', which was trusted by both the electorate and the political parties at play, as long as the CTG CA and his team were untainted individuals, as far as their honesty, integrity, neutrality and credibility were concerned.

The 'cultural lens' reminded us that the various cultural heritages of pre-Aryan and Hindu-Buddhist aspects, the Islamic aspect and the European/Western inputs were integrated with the patterns of life of the indigenous inhabitants of this region, creating a rather hybrid form of civilisation. Over time, through a process of clash and conflict, this saw 'meeting and compromise' as well as 'conflict'. The syncretic humanist tradition of this region, although at times adopted as a middle ground, still meant that underlying tensions and conflicts remained. This tension surfaced, despite the homogeneity of the language, in the form of a struggle in 'identity' at one particular level, which is not a central focus of this book: between a secularist versus an Islamic direction of governance. On another level, the struggle is also over the 'methods' by which legal structures and processes should be managed in a culturally plural society such as Bangladesh, which has a majority Muslim populace. This section focused briefly on the initial practices of Hindu and Muslim socio-cultural laws in relation to governance in order to better grasp the cultural/religious impact these laws have had upon this region, particularly their notions of a ruler or a representative government, which has influenced and shaped local society for centuries. Although cultural scholars may have a better understanding of such foundational matters, it appears that they are not consulted or listened to during discourses of legislators in the course of framing laws.

The 'socio-legal and legal lenses' further explored the various relevant aspects of the jurisprudential basis for the CTG system in Bangladesh as a mode of transition of power. This was done by discussing some relevant theoretical insights, mainly from Chiba (1986, 1989) and Menski (2006). Ehrlich's earlier theorising of 'living law', despite being a socio-legal model, did not quite fit in the context of the CTG of Bangladesh, as a more sophisticated methodological toolkit was needed. This is because the operational difficulties of managing the CTG are matters of how to handle official laws and formal processes and not merely of handling the interaction between State law and peoples' law. To that effect, Chiba's (1986) 'tripartite model' fitted better, as law must not only be recognised as an aspect of the total culture of the people and hence approached anthropologically, but also seen as an amalgam of all kinds of cultural influences and value systems on legal processes and institutions.

The first unofficial and informal birth of the CTG took place because Bangladesh was dissatisfied with how the official law worked with regard to elections and how it could be manipulated in the hands of the government in question. People clearly wished for an amelioration of the official law and ways to stop that manipulation. The aim was to let a neutral body conduct free, fair and reliable elections instead of the government in power, given the history of manipulation. This verifies Chiba's (1986) hypothesis that law as rules and structures is always connected to values and subjective assessments. Despite delivering four elections as mandated, even this indigenous structure, the CTG, was not infallible, as not only did the fourth CTG stay far longer than its 90-day mandate, it brought with itself the military in the guise of a technocrat government, through the back door. This caused fresh unease and fear for the newly elected (AL) government about the future of the political class, as power may slip again in the future to another dictatorial military/technocrat class, should the mechanism of the CTG remain constitutionally and allow these elements to take power. But most people saw that the major issue was not with the CTG system. It was lying elsewhere: it was the manipulation of the CTG structure by the political actors, which led to a politics of extreme violence between the AL and BNP, resulting in a deadlock which seemed unbridgeable. It was those extreme circumstances which led to the entry of the military in the garb of a technocrat CTG.

It was argued that Menski's (2011) pluralist *iccher ghuri* allows for a more complete picture of analysing the CTG as it illustrates that one does not manage diversity and political intolerance and opposition by denying it but by addressing it. The CTG, which was the aspiration of the political class and the will of the people, to deliver electoral governance worked, despite the turbulences it faced, giving the nation the desired results of free, fair and inclusive elections. Good governance, during elections and thereafter, will depend on the intricate pluralist navigation and is indeed a matter of justice-conscious public interest and not merely achieved by self-protection of law to retain power and ensure a return to power. The section on 'positivism and its difficulty' critiqued that relying merely on Hart's original methodology to assess the CTG would give a reductionist and restricted result and hence would not do justice to this mechanism. Pluralist analysis clearly yielded a deeper and more interdisciplinary, connected understanding of the malaise and its remedies.

The section on the problems with 'legal transplants', in providing a completely different perspective as to why it is difficult for the notion of Western democracy to work on Eastern soil, analysed the complexities of the problem in relation to such transplants, especially democracy as a transplant, and brought in discussions of Chiba, Watson, Cotterrell, Shah and Kelly. In the context of Bangladesh, the difficulty in adopting, adapting, sustaining and consolidating democratic norms from the West is a greater challenge than the country has been able to gauge. Given the nation's historical legacy and socio-political and legal reality, in a climate of embedded mistrust, such journeys of democracy are full of turbulence. Although the CTG assisted in part in this journey of giving the nation acceptable electoral governance structures, which were nationally and internationally acceptable, the underlying power struggles that have been witnessed are more about 'power' than 'law'. This is something which must again be taken up by the political actors so that another workable modality can be found in order to have inclusive, free, fair and legitimate elections which would defy the larger-than-life 'culture of mistrust' in the future.

The 'history of democracy' of this still fairly young nation from the British period to the Pakistani era until post-independent Bangladesh in 1990 was charted in this book. It has been discussed how the residues of history have deeply and at many levels influenced the journey of democracy, including the complexities of transition in this country. The impact of an emerging syncretic Islam in Bengal was portrayed as a central element in this context and hence a section discussed how this syncretic Islam evolved in the region which makes up Bangladesh today, in order to better comprehend how this has affected the ideology of the people. Religion and culture as much as law and culture are perceived to be deeply connected with the local patterns of life that developed as a result of what Chiba (1986; 1989; 2002) would call 'indigenous laws'. These then face challenges from various forms of 'received' normative patterns, both religious and explicitly legal, that may challenge established local patterns. The ongoing confusions in Bangladeshi legal discourse over the meaning and implications of 'secularism' are the clearest indication of such deep-rooted and pervasive tensions.

Independent Bangladesh had to confront its hybrid cultural identity, which explains the dichotomy of Bangladeshi society today, and which in turn also explains some of the major divisive effects to the ongoing challenges of governance. The bipolarity of the AL–BNP contest is clearly not only a matter of personalities ('the battle of the Begums') but goes far deeper into the extent of understanding the role of Islam in the entire system of culture and governance of Bangladesh. While it is not a major focal point of the analysis here, it needs to be explicitly mentioned that tensions over the 'religious' nature of Bangladesh are manifested in this complex battlefield of election management.

The influence of the 'military' as a key actor, since it has been an integral part of Bangladeshi history and politics, cannot be overlooked. It has been rooted in and involved with governance from the early years after liberation. The political system that evolved in Bangladesh between 1975 and 1990 was one in which the judicial and legislative branches became hostages to military-controlled executive power. Indeed, the depth of mistrust which existed from the colonial period only worsened during the military regimes. In a sense, and to a large extent, the emergence of a perceived need for the CTG can thus be related back to a post-crisis scenario of desperately seeking to end a string of military rules in independent Bangladesh. However, having said that, the nature of the Bangladesh army has meanwhile seen a change in its mindset. The military between the years 1971–1990 and the military in 2009 – or for that matter, in 2017 – is not the same. The gap between the military and the general masses has been reduced. Army presence is seen in various civilian structures and institutions; their international reputation and the resulting revenue from being the second largest global peacekeeping corps, is something that they are unlikely to compromise on by voluntarily wishing to usurp power from an elected political government and earning national and internal disrepute and unpopularity, unless perhaps there was a grave humanitarian emergency. The political government most comfortable with the army historically was the BNP, but lately there seems to be a better rapport between AL and the army too. For now, at least, after the BDR massacres of 2009 which left 57 army officers slaughtered, it appears that the army is content with its riches and benefits (currently furnished by the sitting AL government), thus taking a back seat as far as coming to the immediate helm of power is concerned.

The second phase of democratic awakening from 1990 to 2008 demonstrated and traced the trajectory of the emergence of the CTG structure so as to appreciate the extent that the political class and the electorate went to in order to innovate a way to ensure credible, participatory elections. The CTG's institutionalisation in the form of the constitutional Thirteenth Amendment and its progression during the tenures of the four CTGs of Bangladesh were traced in depth. Each CTG era was discussed in terms of how it emerged, the issues faced, and how the CTG conducted elections. Although some policy decisions were undertaken by the first three CTGs, some of which were outside of their strict electoral remit, the fact that they held credible elections was what mattered to the electorate.

The political crisis and deadlock on the eve of the controversial military-backed fourth CTG merited a separate section which highlighted the toxicity of the culture of mistrust among the political class, necessitating emergency action. It also showed how the unusual CTG structure, whose acceptability rested on the bedrock of popular legitimation, had assisted in the country's quest for democratic consolidation in a scenario of mistrust, which continues to dominate the socio-political and legal milieu of the nation. However, this was also not without troubles in the process of implementation. It is quite possible that those implementation troubles gave rise to deeper thoughts about how to manage the continuing multilayered crisis of identity and governance that has been engulfing Bangladesh for decades.

A further section deepened the analysis of the CTG and its role, leading to the period of its eventual abolition. The CTGs were divided into two groups. The first group analysed the first three CTGs together, as their nature, composition and deliverance were similar. The second group included the fourth CTG, whose emergence, composition and overstaying of its mandate needed separate analysis. This demonstrated that although the Bangladeshi courts have formally dismissed the notion of 'necessity' when abolishing the 20-year old CTG, the reality remains that the CTG structure appears to have been perceived and used as a method to prevent a strongman from dominating the electoral processes. In discussing the policies of the CTG elaborately, particularly those of the military-backed CTG of 2007–2008, it emerged that the ordinances they promulgated have intriguingly played a role in democratisation, even if this was only in the short term – something which the political governments failed to do over the years, due to their preoccupation with power, manipulation and election engineering. The segment concluded that the unilateral and rushed constitutional amendment abolishing the CTG structure in 2011 may not have been a pragmatic or altruistic approach for electoral governance, dislodging whichever format electoral democracy was working in the country. The subsequent sections highlighted that there are other, probably more important considerations in addition to the basic adherence to electoral governance standards – maybe a results-oriented approach could take the analysis further. This is necessary, given the toxicity of mistrust at various levels. In any view of the matter, the ultimate opinion of the CTG is determined by the people, whose will ought to matter most in concluding whether the CTG as a neutral entity is needed to oversee electoral transition or not.

Through the CTG, Bangladesh cultivated principles of holding credible elections by which the nation adhered to the rudimentary norms of electoral democracy. The CTG had, at critical times, the support of leading political powers and clearly was a reflection of the people's will which created the law of non-party and neutral CTGs under which elections were to be held. Free and fair elections gave legitimacy to an elected government through which the nation could claim that it adhered to the nationally and globally agreed ethos of electoral governance. Figure 6.1 depicts the above discussion:

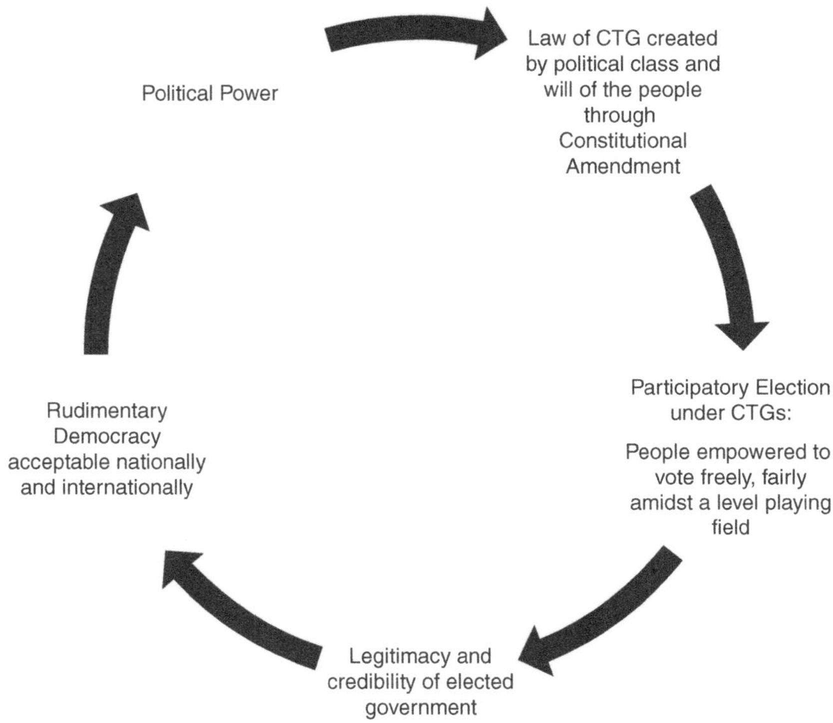

Figure 6.1 Circle of rudimentary electoral democracy in Bangladesh during CTGs

However, the abolition of the CTG ended this rudimentary circle of electoral democracy. What transpired between the abolition of the CTG and the holding of the January 2014 election was a series of indescribable sufferings that the electorate were subjected to by the clashes of AL and BNP. Anam (2012) described this situation regarding BNP's *mohashomabesh* march for change, demanding elections under a CTG or any ad-interim government, in the following words:

> When does a government strangulate its capital city by preventing all modes of transport from reaching it? When does a government bring to a virtual halt almost all internal city movements? When does a government create such a panicky situation that traders do not open shops out of fear of vandalism? When does a government prevent its own citizens from carrying out their day to day activities? When do government leaders tell blatant lies on television while the truth is clearly the opposite? When does a ruling party let loose its goons upon normal citizens on suspicion that they might attend the opposition rally? When does an elected government adopt the most oppressive measure to prevent the opposition from holding a public rally? Only when it is unsure of itself. A party confident of its popular base, sure of its public support, certain of the efficacy of its policies and

> surefooted about its public record would never have done what the ruling AL did yesterday to prevent BNP from holding its public rally [this] reveals a political party frightened of the strength of the opposition and loathe to allow it to show it. In its massive show of strength, AL looked at its weakest.

The tragedy of this moral defeat is that in attempting to suppress the opposition, the government suppressed the citizens on whose behalf it sought to govern. This kind of mindset and myopia disregards basic principles of democratic governance and accountability and separates citizens from the entire democratic equation, as the government – through its activists – even attacked ordinary passengers whose only crime was that they wished to enter Dhaka city. The argument that preventive action was taken as a matter of public security is at the very least questionable, if not deeply suspect. Such disregard for the fundamental rights of the people makes us ponder as to whether this is a sensible way for an elected government to handle dissent, including the voice of the opposition, and demonstrate a democratic ethos both to itself and to the world.

The issue is that the months leading to the January 2014 election, after the CTG abolition, showed a repressive face of the government, which demonstrated that it would not hesitate to take measures, however harsh, to use any coercive instrument of the State, impose any amount of suffering on ordinary people, tell concocted stories regardless of what the truth was, and impose needless restrictions on public movement to prevent the opposition from carrying out the protest activities permitted in any democracy. Much of this, but probably not all of this, could be justified on the grounds of public interest and the need to maintain public order and tranquillity. The need for some sort of a neutral body presiding over the election and allowing the EC to function freely is – and remains to a large extent – a legitimate demand of the people that the government should not wish away. Here, the opposition may be right and the ruling party wrong. The government perhaps needed to concede to this point if it wished for a participatory election in January 2014. Terming the opposition's actions as 'attempts to subvert the war crimes trials', although it may have had a substantive grain of truth, did not mean that the opposition's demand for a neutral administration to oversee elections was a misconceived strategy. Although BNP's position regarding the war crimes trials is highly questionable, its demands for an interim government for free and fair elections seem justified, given the historical and socio-legal realities of the nation (Anam 2012). Perhaps the government arguments about public safety, in particular, are not entirely baseless either, given the past history of violent conflicts in the name of rallies, strikes and protests, repeated again in January 2015 by BNP. But this highly explosive scenario clearly shows that none of the previous gravity of intense conflict and mistrust has been remedied by two decades of CTG involvement. Important lessons about the need for constructive democratic cooperation have apparently not been learnt. The palliative of the CTG was able to curtail the cancer of lawlessness and violence at critical election times, but it has not rendered the body of the nation of Bangladesh free from the continuing threat of remission. The wish-kite may still crash as a result of new violent turbulence over election-related issues in the near future because whatever progress the nation has made regarding election-time modality and fairness through the CTG structure over a period of 20 years now stands demolished.

Bangladesh's iccher ghuri and the CTG

The serious trust deficiency in the political and social mosaic of Bangladesh is so deeply entrenched that it has spread through each stratum of society. Bangladesh had found a way to break away from past undemocratic practices after having survived not only the British and Pakistan eras, but also the autocratic rule and military regimes of its own independent existence. In 1990, the political parties and the peoples' will attempted to begin afresh by putting behind the legacy of unconstitutional rule and election engineering through creating a CTG structure. This was indeed a promising beginning. While an unusual system internationally, the CTG had been relatively effective in delivering largely credible elections in the highly polarised political environment of the country. To that extent, the core finding of this book is that the CTG as an institutional legal tool restored faith and trust to the electoral governance of Bangladesh. Although it is difficult to measure trust, the fact that every election in Bangladesh's history conducted under a CTG administration had resulted in a change of government while every election conducted under a political government had returned that same government, points to two probable conclusions: firstly, that this is a cause of concern for whoever is in opposition, since it appears that an election conducted by the incumbent will never be fair and hence a threat of boycott and brinksmanship by the opposition looms large. Secondly, that all the elections conducted by the CTGs, including the controversial fourth military-backed CTG, ultimately restored trust as far as conducting 'electoral governance' is concerned. Although it seems rather odd that an unelected body could better carry the burden of upholding trust in electoral governance than an elected political government could, this poignantly depicts the unreliability of a political government in refraining from election engineering and illustrates the reality of Bangladesh's fragile state of democracy.

After the well-run elections of 1990, 1996, 2001 and 2008 – all carried out through the CTG mechanism – there was general optimism among the electorate that the perennial troubles associated with holding credible elections had been addressed, despite the drama of the political crisis of 2006 which led to the military-backed technocrat CTG taking over for almost two years. The CTG system was seen as a structure which honoured 'the will of the people' and the basic split of the popular votes between the two major political parties, the AL and the BNP, resonated that 'will' in every election, resulting in the opposition winning. However, two aspects were still left unaddressed: first, it did not address the problem that the 'winner-takes-all' system does not reflect the basic split of the popular votes, as 30–35 per cent of the popular vote remains with the opposition irrespective of the number of seats allocated to the opposition in parliament. Second, during the 20 years of the CTG's existence, there had been little progress towards democratic consolidation by any political government in power; the nation rather returned to a worse acrimonious political environment prior to the 2014 election which took the nation to a repeat crisis, as witnessed prior to the 2006 election. What is even more perturbing is that future elections are likely to be even more aggressive and traumatic unless steps are taken to hold free, fair and participatory elections.

One could of course argue that the CTG structure was only meant to deliver credible elections, and to that extent, each CTG has done so. This was reflected in the author's fieldwork results, as the stakeholders who were interviewed were clear about the issue that the CTG did not foster democracy as such, but greatly assisted in consolidating 'electoral democracy'. The people interviewed could clearly distinguish between fostering 'democracy' and nurturing 'electoral democracy'. The practice of law-making, first through 'executive ordinances of the CTGs' which were 'later validated by the parliament' – a legacy which the civilian governments adopted from the military regimes – continued even after the restoration of democracy in 1991. Between 1991 and 1996, 34 per cent of laws were passed by the parliament which were first promulgated as ordinances by the CTG and later placed before the parliament for approval; between 1996 and 2001, this trend of approving ordinances of the CTG as laws in parliament diminished; between 2001 and 2006, less than five per cent of laws originated as ordinances; between 2009 and 2013, however, legal cover was given to most of the ordinances of the fourth military-backed CTG (Jahan 2014). Another legacy of military regimes adopted by civilian governments is that of 'election engineering'. As democratically elected governments attempted to use State agencies to influence election results, the EC was purposely never empowered to act independently and hold the government accountable for violations of election guidelines. As far as this second legacy is concerned, the CTGs addressed this issue and therefore not only had they provided autonomy to the EC, but they could take credit, particularly the fourth CTG, in having completed an almost error-free voter roll, issuing national identity cards to almost all adult citizens and conducting a peaceful and fair election despite a delay of almost two years. Among other things, their efficiency also fostered a degree of trust as far as the credibility of elections was concerned.

While this was a useful outcome, much to the credit of the CTG regimes, it did not lead to a process of consolidated democratic development for the nation, and the *iccher ghuri* or the kite journey has been constantly exposed to turbulence in various forms. The nation's democratic journey had not been smooth as it had often lost its direction and walked on the wrong paths. Although the nation began as a parliamentary democracy, within four years it witnessed both a 'one-party' rule and fell under 'military regimes' which then continued from 1975 to 1990. It was the people's unwavering commitment and movement which brought the nation back to the path of democracy in 1990, resulting in the end of those long years of military rule and renewing the nation's democratic journey. From 1990 to 2006, gradual progress was made in fulfilling three minimum criteria of being classified as an electoral democracy and the CTG clearly played a vital role in that journey. Firstly, the regular CTG's organising of free, fair and contested elections in 1990, 1996 and 2001; secondly, each time the regular CTG organised elections, there was a peaceful transfer of governmental power as a result of these elections; and thirdly, the nation was able to establish civilian control over policy and institutions (Jahan 2014). However, the *iccher ghuri* stumbled again in 2006 when the two major political parties, the BNP government and AL opposition, failed to agree on the ground rules for organising the elections in 2007. In these circumstances of extreme violence and aggression, the nation witnessed a quasi-military takeover and was then ruled, as we know, by a military-backed CTG (irregular CTG) for the next two years. This irregular CTG period witnessed a suspension of fundamental rights and freedoms but their intervention put a halt to the mindless violence and anarchy in the political and social realm. However, it was clear this time that Bangladeshis would not let their *iccher ghuri* be pulled in different directions for too long by the military. The latter, being sensitive to its own image in the international arena, the revenues it was earning and the sensing of the people's pulse that politics, howsoever flawed, should remain the mandate of the politicians only and not any other class, understood that it had to succumb to the 'will of the people' and the 'international players'. We see that this may be a highly relevant new factor which goes well beyond the analysis of the CTG in the present work as a matter of internal domestic law. For this now strays into the potential impact of international law and global monitoring of standards of governance. This was beginning to become significantly relevant and may be a sign of the times that we are now living in. The clear evidence is that since the army was acutely aware that the UN peacekeeping remittances might be jeopardised and its reputation might be at stake if they crossed the line too far, they negotiated a safe exit. Despite their attempts to reform the political system and having failed to achieve those ambitious objectives, they eventually concentrated on organising a free and credible parliamentary election on 29 December 2008 and handed over power to the democratically elected AL government. Rare in South Asian history, the incident of a voluntary peaceful transfer of power from a *de facto* military government to an elected civilian government was witnessed and indeed welcomed nationally and internationally.

There were hopes that the political reforms that were initiated by the fourth military-backed CTG would provide sufficient impetus for the nation's political élite to at last work towards a transparent, accountable and participatory democratic system (Riaz 2013b). There was also the expectation that the nation's *iccher ghuri* would see long-term changes in the political culture. Since the fourth CTG remained in power longer than the others, there was also hope that their actions or efforts would succeed henceforth in bringing transparency to the electoral institutions in the long term, which is essential for the smooth functioning of any democracy.

But that was not to be. On the contrary, the nation's *iccher ghuri* not only did not fly in that direction but saw a regression in how matters unfolded over the next few years. Although many steps taken by the CTG were ratified by the parliament after the elections of 2008, there was an apprehension that the ruling party would take any opportunity to scrap the CTG system altogether as their existence as a political class felt threatened by the last CTG because of the extent the latter went to in arresting and questioning the polity. This fear of not wishing to continue with the CTG provision arose because despite the legal loopholes – procedural errors resulting in the fourth CTG regime's failure to convict top political figures – the entire episode loudly demonstrated to the people that politicians are not invincible and may indeed be challenged.

That opportunity to scrap the CTG system arrived when the Appellate Division of the Supreme Court declared the Thirteenth Amendment of the Constitution unconstitutional in a verdict in 2011. There is naturally no official evidence that this judicial decision was made under government pressure. However, the government wasted no time and hurriedly pushed through the Fifteenth Amendment of the Constitution abolishing the CTG, despite the full judgment not being written and despite the Court's short verdict declaring that the CTG system could be utilised for another two parliamentary elections so that during this time, effective electoral institutions would be allowed to be built. The *iccher ghuri* once again faced serious turbulence.

As a consequence, from mid-2011, Bangladesh was faced with a situation where the two political parties had taken opposing stands regarding the election time modality and had not come to any negotiated settlement despite repeated appeals by civil society and international stakeholders. This led to the flawed January 2014 election without a CTG and without opposition participation. At present, Bangladesh faces the risk of not even being classified as an electoral democracy with its *iccher ghuri* again at a crossroads and there is an urgent need to make another fresh start to sustain the fragile democratic process. Although there is a vital need to break away from the patterns and practices of antagonistic politics and governance, this does not seem to be forthcoming.

Despite the initial criticism of such a farcical and non-participatory 2014 election, the geostrategic role of Bangladesh as a Muslim-majority country meant that the world perhaps did not wish to see it slide into potential political Islamism if it fell into the perceived wrong hands (Harrison 2013: 107–110). If we were to see the trend of election results held under the CTG, there was a possibility that if the CTG had conducted the January 2014 election freely, fairly and inclusive of all parties (at the risk of sounding presumptuous), there might have been a change of government and consequently BNP with its alliance with JIB may have secured more seats (on the basis that each election by the CTG saw the opposition's return to power) than AL and taken the helm of power. That is certainly what the BNP had been arguing to justify its protest movement. However, this is perhaps not what the international community wished to see at this juncture of global politics (as BNP/JIB is perceived to be non-secular in its ideology), with the rise of what the West brands as 'Islamic terrorism'. And of course, nor would this please the AL, which seems to claim ownership of steering the direction of the *iccher ghuri* of Bangladesh for now, especially to see the end of the war crimes trials, which quite certainly would have been halted if power went into the hands of the BNP/JIB alliance.

The stark reality after the 5 January 2014 election is that the silent non-presence of the CTG seemed even more acute in terms of its role in delivering credible elections over the last 20 years. Even after the last election sans CTG, each of the opposing political forces attempted to portray the election as a 'victory' for its side. The AL-led forces argued that the mere organisation of the uncontested elections, no matter the flaws, was a genuine victory as they were able to overcome all the obstacles created by the opposition. On the other hand, the BNP claimed moral victory pointing to the lack of credibility of the elections, organised by the government, which cannot be trusted to organise a fair and credible election as they had predicted. While both sides pushed forward their respective claims and counterclaims of victory, the nation remained shell-shocked from the mindless death and destruction caused by the violence, *hartals* and *oborodhs* by the BNP/JIB and the incredulous elections engineered and orchestrated by the AL. There may be debates over which side has won, but it is clear as to which side has lost: the electorate (Jahan 2014). The stark price in terms of loss of life, property, earning, sense of security, peace and a regular life is immeasurable. Bangladesh has even fallen from the image that it can at least have outwardly free and competitive elections without creating any democratic and accountable governance.

It is therefore clear that the CTG had been a useful temporary tool in the learning process of Bangladesh about how to fly its electoral kite. It must be borne in mind that ultimately 'the will of the people' and their perception of fairness may be more important than theoretical debates about whether the CTG was a prerequisite for electoral democracy in Bangladesh or not. If people feel that the CTG is crucial to their sense of fairness in electoral democracy, and if knowing that their individual preference is counted at the moment of voting, that is the only true test of rudimentary electoral democracy. Bearing that in mind, it may be unsurprising that the CTG, even in its depleted state, is imagined as more precious than typical Western-style democratic (electoral) governance. Fair elections may be one element in the process towards democracy but where democracy has been marred by bias and mistrust, a fair election process may represent the only hope. After all, what is democratic governance without it?

Former CTG advisor Dr. Akbar Ali Khan, during an interview with the author, suggested bringing a shift in the 'winner takes all' political culture of Bangladesh. He proposed 'changing the Constitution and creating the scope for proportional representation, which might force the political parties to form a coalition and work together. That might gradually help decrease the mistrust between them'. Going beyond this, former CTG advisor Abdul Muyeed Chowdhury suggested in a similar interview that 'In addition to a percentage of the constituency seats given as proportional representation, there should be a bicameral legislature which would create a system of checks and balances. Bangladesh could have provincial governments, because it is not possible for the central government to deal with all relevant matters'. But for any of the suggestions above, there is a need for an effective dialogue between the AL and BNP MPs inside the parliament. For such dialogue to develop there is a need, first of all, for a participatory and credible election. And that election will be credible only if conducted by an 'acceptable mechanism' of some kind, renegotiated and agreed by the polity, with the support of its electorate.

Now that the CTG is gone, the challenges are not gone at all, but a new method of managing the existing tensions will need to be found, and it will need to be found soon. The stress on democracy is evident because the constitutional amendment to abolish the CTG has created significant roadblocks to participatory elections. It is only a matter of time before coercive measures and an unwillingness to go through discourse or to reach a compromise between the government and the opposition will not work anymore, and confrontations will only lead to the casualty of democracy and peoples' *iccher ghuri*. But meanwhile the steady international support that Bangladesh is receiving through nongovernmental organisations' advocacy and research on peoples' better understanding of electoral governance is commendable as that is clearly a foundation to work on.

Petulant preservation of privileges of power

Although Bangladesh is not perhaps strictly a multicultural society (in the sense that London as a city is, for example), it is deeply affected by multiple differences, leading to a culture of mistrust based on secular and religious identity, perceived pro-liberation and anti-liberation dichotomy, creating a deeply bipolar or rather multi-polar society due to the clashes between confrontational political and cultural identities. This at times makes Bangladeshi society a far more divided society than any multi-cultural one, which is exacerbated further by political intolerance of the other. The severity of this multi-polarity or 'super-diversity' (Vertovec, 1997), which is in reductionist fashion generally presented for Bangladesh as bipolarity (BNP/AL, Islamism/secularism, to name but two), remains a major predicament for people's understanding of their own problems and also for academic analysis. Even if the 'secularism versus Islam' dichotomy is hypothetically addressed, there may a perception that there will be progress. If the desired end result is an all-Muslim State set-up, as perhaps the far right would like to see, there would be huge problems for Muslim secularists as well as the non-Muslim Bangladeshis. It is also probable that the next argument may be about which Muslims are the right Muslims.

Conversely, one cannot disregard religion completely as that would not work either. This alone confirms that legal pluralism along the lines suggested by Menski's pluralist theorising and the practical application of such structures is unavoidable. Uniformising trends, in religion as well as more evidently in politics, are not the ideal prism through which to assess the potential for sustainable solutions in conditions of deep-seated plurality. In terms of electoral policy, specifically, no amount of manipulation, bar very significant changes in electoral laws, will result in the termination of the bipolar party politics that mar the country. The proof of this is in the aborted strategy of 'minus two', i.e. the removal of the two warring Begums, as it was realised that not only did they have a strong grass-roots support, even if they were forcibly exiled or removed, they may have been replaced by other warring protagonists of adversarial positions and the feud of AL/BNP would have gone on.

The argument that there is a need for wrestling the discourse on secularism out of the stale and misguided believer-nonbeliever dichotomy and for explaining that the trespass of religion into politics and vice versa is dangerous for both politics and religion is of course well-known. However, this is not the main strand of the argument in this book and its discussion would sidetrack from the key issues of failures in basic, much-needed, electoral governance. An-Na'im (2009: 260), to that effect, has argued that secularism should be defined as the neutrality of the State regarding all religions as a framework for regulating the political role of religion and not the means of excluding religion from the public domain. This is similar to Menski's advice: confront the problems which oppose pluralist management – do not seek to suppress them. Various amendments of the Bangladesh Constitution depict the tension of a constant tug of war between secularism and Islam. Indeed, handling the simmering religious conflicts needs to become the responsibility of the politically conscious and democratically oriented non-partisan individuals and groups of Bangladesh. But one has to bear in mind that this conflict is also portrayed as a strategy of distraction in moments of crises, to fall back on religious differences and worse still, to engage in religiously motivated violence of the kind seen in Bangladesh. Hence debates over the relationship between Islam, the State and society tend to create at times misleading dichotomies and raise unnecessary dilemmas. The key issue is still the focus on the processes of election management and their democratic credentials. Yet, observing the aftershocks of the controversial election of January 2014 raises questions as to whether a deliberate strategy to keep out Islamism is a semi-hidden aspect of the whole debate. The political class should seek to ensure that the religious sentiments of people and freedom of expression do not become mutually exclusive.

The problem is not merely the law or the institutions – it is also, as we know, the political sphere. There needs to be a fresh effort to seek a national renewal, based on the recognition of internal plurality and the need for interactive cooperation along democratic lines. What palpably stares at us from all of this is political expediency – political parties had made a demand for the CTG for the sake of democracy or rejected it as undemocratic according to their need. When AL demanded the CTG to be part of the Constitution in 1996, it nevertheless had the backing of popular support but its unilateral removal through the Fifteenth Amendment of the Constitution, in the absence of popular support, brings to question the AL government's motive. The BNP's resistance to the Fifteenth Amendment illustrates its own motives of expediency, as the BNP used similar arguments to resist the CTG in 1996 as the AL is using today (Khan 2015). In passing the Fourteenth and Fifteenth Amendments to the Constitution, constitutional institutions have been used as an instrument of executive power rather than serving as a check and balance between the executive, legislature and judiciary.

Hence, good governance is not possible through reliance merely on positivist law. Law is related to values, to people's ideas and ambitions, and good governance these days has to respect human rights and international legal principles, the 'new natural law' (Menski 2011: 13a). The public space that Habermas, as a political theorist, talked about in previous decades is neither free of values nor often very personal emotions; rather, in the case of Bangladesh, petulant preservation of privileges of power of the Begums still seems to prevail over everything else. At least it may seem so to many external observers. For example, Riaz (2016a: 143) illustrates an example about the deliberations and decision-making of the parliamentary committee on the constitutional amendment in 2011 in which 15 members were appointed, including members of BNP, in order to participate. BNP unhelpfully declined to participate in this important national debate. Riaz continues that the proceedings of the committee show that it had unanimously concluded that the CTG system should be maintained and that a strict limit of 90 days be imposed on its tenure. In one of the meetings, the committee gathered opinions from three former CJs; ten constitutional lawyers/experts; representatives from six political parties including the AL, which was represented by Prime Minister Sheikh Hasina; 18 intellectuals; editors of 18 newspapers and media; and the leaders of the sector commanders forum. Most participants urged the committee to keep the CTG provision but to look into the inadequacies of the mechanism and alter it accordingly and only a few suggested its complete abolition. The committee, as a result, formulated its recommendations on 29 May 2011, echoing the voice of those consulted and proposing only minor changes to the CTG provision. Despite this recommendation of retaining the CTG provision, after meeting the PM, the committee decided to make a complete about-turn, scrapping article 58, the basis for the CTG in the Constitution. This aberration of democratic practice, according to Riaz (2016a: 144), stems from party constitutional provisos and practices which establish 'patron–client relationships' between party members and the leadership and ensures

> A patrimonial political culture on the one hand, while establishing a highly personalized, authoritarian style of leadership on the other. The patron–client relationship legitimizes hierarchy and the right or obligation of the superior to be superior and protect the lesser.

Kochanek (2000: 548), cited in Riaz (2016a: 144), also identifies this aspect and reiterates that 'leaders are expected to be authoritarian and authority becomes highly personalized'. Riaz (2016a: 144) concludes that

> This kind of leadership exercises extra-constitutional power within the party and with state power when elected to public office. The primary

> sources of their authority remain outside the constitutional realm and therefore it is natural that they emerge as the 'tutelary power' and inhibit democratic transformation.

We see with the above example a glimpse of Austinian abuse of power. If the BNP leader Khaleda Zia now calls for an unlimited strike to bring about its desired agenda, we will again see a glimpse of Austinian abuse of power and of a prominent political leader's position. If Prime Minister Sheikh Hasina is unaccommodating vis à vis holding a participatory free and fair election in 2019, it will also be a sign of Austinian abuse of her power. That this is damaging to the nation as a whole, whether it comes from BNP or AL, has long been known. Thus, the urgent need to adhere to accountability, democratic norm and looking into public interest or rather 'higher public interest' is essential for all major actors if Bangladesh desires to fly its *iccher ghuri* peacefully in the sky.

At present, this journey remains treacherous for a number of reasons. The worrying thought occurs that even in this day and age, the individual discretion of a ruling figure remains a potent threat to even the most basic principles of good and responsible electoral governance. Clearly, the Begums are unhappy about being reminded of the need to balance different corners of the kite and rather prefer to see themselves as hegemonic centres of power. One may call this some typical kind of South Asian matriarchy, or 'petulance' in a more personal sense, but it is indeed remarkably akin to an Austinian way of thinking and self-justification, a positivist allergy against the competing claims of Chiba's 'legal postulates' and thus the ultimately dominant values of 'higher public necessity'. Seen from this wider perspective, the current struggles and turbulence in the electoral governance of Bangladesh would still appear to be nothing more than excesses of positivist legal discretion, albeit motivated by a toxic mix fed on a climate of mistrust at personal and broader levels. One could relate this back to the troublesome start of the nation in 1971. Regrettably, this nation is still not at ease with itself vis à vis its vision as a nation, and thus strategically adroit protagonists continue to fight over the use of law as a tool for good and responsible electoral governance.

The Bangladeshi electorate does not want to have the accolade of a failing State, though 'the right kind of thinking, the right kind of leadership which would take the nation forward, at a pace the nation wants, having the quality the nation wants', as voiced by the former CTG advisor Dr. Hossain Zillur Rahman in an interview with the author, is regrettably amiss (Research interview with the author). The minimal strand of a democratic element that existed in the polity, the system of holding elections through a neutral structure, the CTG, stands demolished. As the country is manifestly held to ransom by many types of petulant abuses of power, the top figures of leadership, as potential role models of good governance, are seen to fail the nation and the electorate, ruining the peaceful sailing of the *iccher ghuri* of the people of Bangladesh. That such behaviour and the resulting actions may have negative fallout for future elections and may be manifestly counterproductive is palpable. The relevant lesson becomes even clearer: basic bad electoral governance, for whatever reason, does not pay off in the long run – it only achieves short-term gains. More troubling though are the negative effects on the most vulnerable members of the electorate, those citizens of Bangladesh whose claims to have a voice in the future of the country are being violently denied in a variety of ways. CTG or no CTG, that specific problem for Bangladesh must also form the subject of another study.

What stands more manifestly proven than before, from a vantage point in 2017, is the need for a permanent, neutral and effective institution, which is not only able to conduct credible elections periodically but would also assist in healing the deeply embedded trust deficit which exists in the political sphere. The credibility of the institution has to be such that whichever political party is in power, it would be an irrelevant consideration to holding regular elections, because that institution would remain far away from the influence and clutches of the executive. The weather forecast for the *iccher ghuri* remains based on warnings about alertness to such sustainable democratic standards. Bangladesh had a functional electoral system through the CTG which would now need to be rediscovered and perhaps revitalised through a process of socio-political and legal mobilisation. The need therefore continues for as much constructive cooperation and renegotiation between different stakeholders as possible. This problem cannot be legislated away – the solution lies in the skilful operation of given structures, not their manipulative reconstitution, and maybe also a good deal more concern about the obligations of a leader as a public figure to the nation as a whole, rather than insisting on one's privately motivated right and claim to rule.

BIBLIOGRAPHY

Abel, C F and Sementelli, Arthur (2002) 'Power, emancipation and the administrative state'. *Administrative Theory & Praxis*, 24(2): 253–278.

Acemoglu, Daron and Robinson, James A (2009) *Economic origins of dictatorship and democracy*. Cambridge: Cambridge University Press.

Agar, Herbert (1938) 'Bases of democracy'. *The Public Opinion Quarterly, Special Supplement: Public Opinion in a Democracy*, 2(1): 86–88.

Ahmad, Khurshid (2000) 'Islam and Democracy: Some conceptual and contemporary dimensions'. *The Muslim World*, 90(1–2): 1–19.

Ahmar, Moonis (2005) *Violence and terrorism in South Asia 1971–2004*. Colombo: Regional Centre for Strategic Studies.

Ahmed, A F Salauddin (1965) *Social ideas and social change in Bengal 1818–1835*. Dhaka: RDDHI.

Ahmed, A F Salauddin (2007) *History and heritage: Reflections on society politics and culture of South Asia*. Dhaka: University Press Limited.

Ahmed, Emajuddin (1988) *Military rule and the myth of democracy*. Dhaka: University Press Limited.

Ahmed, Emajuddin (2005) 'Military rule, civilization and electoral corruption: Bangladesh and Pakistan in perspective'. *Asian Studies*, 25(I): 73–94.

Ahmed, Fakhruddin (1998) *The Caretakers: A first hand account of the interim government of Bangladesh (1990–1991)*. Dhaka: University Press Limited.

Ahmed, Moeen U (2007) 'The challenging interface of democracy and security'. *The Daily Star*, (4 April).

Ahmed, Moudud (1995) *Democracy and the challenge of development*. Dhaka: University Press Limited.

Ahmed, Moudud (2014) *Bangladesh, Emergency and the Aftermath*, Dhaka: University Press Limited.

Ahmed, Nizam (2004) *Non-party caretaker government in Bangladesh: Experience and prospect*. Dhaka: University Press Limited.

Ahmed, Rafiuddin (1981) *The Bengal Muslims 1871–1906: A quest for identity*. Delhi: Oxford University Press.

Ahmed, Sufia (2011) *Diaries of Justice Muhammad Ibrahim (1960–1966)*. Dhaka: Academic Press and Publishers Library.

Ahmed, Syed Refaat (ed.) (2008) *The Ishtiaq Papers*. Dhaka: University Press Limited.

Ahsan, Syed Badrul (2006) *Impressions: Bangladesh 1975 and other writings.* Oxford: Wessex Press (Wantage) Ltd.

Ahsan, Syed Badrul (2011a) 'Battling it out in Bangladesh'. *The Indian Express*, (20 August).

Ahsan, Syed Badrul (2011b) 'Forty years on.' *The Indian Express*, (11 April).

Ahsan, Syed Badrul (2011c) 'Ground realities'. *The Indian Express*, (18 June).

Ahsan, Syed Badrul (2012) 'The generation trap'. *The Daily Star*, (5 October).

Ahsan, Syed Badrul (2014) *From rebel to founding father Sheikh Mujibur Rahman.* New Delhi: Niyogi Books.

Aidt, Toke S and Dutta, Jayasri (2005) 'Policy compromises: Corruption and regulation in a democracy'. 25 pp.

Ain O Shalish Kendra (ASK) (2006) *Annual report.* Dhaka: Ain O Shalish Kendra.

Al-Jabri, Mohammed Abed (2009) *Democracy, human rights and law in Islamic thought.* New York: I. B. Tauris & Co Ltd. in association with Centre for Arab Unity Studies.

Alamgir, Jalal (July 2009) 'Bangladesh's Fresh Start', *Journal of Democracy*, 20(3), p. 51 cited in Riaz (2016a: 87).

Ali, Kazancigil (1997) 'Connecting political institutions to democracy'. In: Hepper, Metin, Ali, Kazancigil and Rockman Bert A. (eds.) *Institutions and democratic statecraft.* Boulder: Westview Press, pp. 299–308.

Ali, S M (1973) *After the dark night: Problems of Sheikh Mujibur Rahman.* Dhaka: University Press Limited.

Ali, Tariq (1970) *Pakistan: Military rule or people's power.* New York: William Morrow.

Alim, Syed Fattahul (2012) 'Confrontational or infantile politics?' *Forum (A monthly publication of the Daily Star)*, 6(4): (April).

Allen, Amy (2011) *Democracy in what state.* New York: Columbia University Press.

Allott, Anthony (1980) *The limits of law.* London: Butterworths.

Alvarado, Ruben (ed.) (2009) *The doctrine of state & the principles of state law: Friedrich Julius Stahl.* Aalten: Worldbridge Publishing.

Amnesty International (2011) 'Crimes unseen – Extrajudicial executions in Bangladesh', (August). *Amnesty International Report.* London: Amnesty International.

An-Na'im, Abdullahi Ahmed (1996) *Toward an Islamic reformation: Civil liberties, human rights, and international law.* New York: Syracuse University Press.

An-Na'im, Abdullahi Ahmed (2009) *Islam and the secular state: Negotiating the future of sharia'a.* Cambridge: Harvard University Press.

Anam, Mahfuz (2011) 'Abolition of the caretaker system: Now the proponent is the opponent and the opponent, and the opposer is the supporter'. *The Daily Star*, (30 June).

Anam, Mahfuz (2012) 'Awami League's moral defeat: Government holds Dhaka city hostage'. *The Daily Star*, (13 March).

Anam, Mahfuz (2015) 'Internment of BNP Chief: A dangerous precedent'. *The Daily Star*, (8 January).

Anam, Mahfuz (2016) 'Democracy is what the winner says it is'. *The Daily Star*, (6 December).

Anam, Tahmina (2014) 'Bangladesh does not have to go back to being a basket case'. *The Guardian*, (7 January).

Andaleeb, Syed Saad (2007) *Political culture in Bangladesh: Perspectives and analyses.* Dhaka: University Press Limited.

Anderson, James (ed.) (2002) *Transnational democracy: Political spaces and border crossings.* London: Routledge.

Anderson, Lisa (ed.) (1999) *Transitions to democracy.* New York: Columbia University Press.

Anderson, Robert S (1976) 'Impressions of Bangladesh: The rule of arms and the politics of exhortation'. *Pacific Affairs,* 49(3): 443–475.

Anisuzzaman, (1993) *Creativity, reality and identity.* Dhaka: International Centre for Bengal Studies.

Armstrong, Jerome and Zuniga, Markos Moulitsas (2006) *Crashing the gate: Netroots, grassroots and the rise of people-powered politics.* White River Junction, VT: Chelsea Green Publishing Company.

Aronowitz, Stanley and Bratsis, Peter (eds.) (2002) *Paradigm lost, state theory reconsidered.* Minneapolis: University of Minnesota Press.

Asafuddowlah (2010) *Of pains and panics.* Dhaka: Adorn Publications.

Asian Human Rights Commission (2014) 'Bangladesh: Authoritarian obstinacy wins, democracy loses', (08 January).

Askvik, Steinar and Ishtiaq, Jamil (2013) 'The Institutional Trust Paradox in Bangladesh'. *Public Organisation Review,* 13(4): 459–476.

Avari, Burjor (2007) *India: The ancient past: A history of the Indian sub-continent from c. 7000 BC to AD 1200.* Oxford: Routledge.

Axtmann, Roland (2004) 'The state of the state: The model of the modern state and its contemporary transformation'. *International Political Science Review,* 25(3): 259–279.

Bakht, Farid (2007) 'Caught on the back foot'. *Economic and Political Weekly,* 42(48): 8–9.

Bandyopadhyay, Sekhar (2004) *From Plassey to partition: A history of modern India.* Hyderabad: Orient BlackSwan.

'Bangladesh general elections: Bangladesh will hold its 10th general elections on 5 January amid serious questions over the credibility of the electoral process' (2014). *BBC News,* (03 January).

'Bangladesh's new friends' (1975) *New Statesman,* (22 August). p. 217.

Barman, Dalem Ch, Rahman M Golam and Siddiqui, Tasneem (2002) 'Democracy Report for Bangladesh'. *Country Reports for the IDEA State of Democracy Project.* Stockholm: Institute for Democracy and Electoral Assistance.

Barnes, Marian and Newman, Janet and Sullivan, Helen (2007) *Power, participation and political renewal: Case studies in public participation.* Bristol: The Policy Press.

Barrow, Clyde W (2005) 'The return of state: Globalization, state theory and the new imperialism'. *New Political Science,* 27(2): 123–145.

Bass, Gary J (2014) *The blood telegram: Nixon, Kissinger and a forgotten genocide.* London: Hurst & Company.

Baswedan, Anies Rasyid (2004) 'Political Islam in Indonesia: Present and future trajectory'. *Asian Survey,* 44(5): 669–690.

Baxter, Craig (1971) 'Pakistan votes – 1970'. *Asian Survey,* 11(3): 197–218.

BBC (2014) 'Bangladesh general elections: Bangladesh will hold its 10th general elections on 5 January amid serious questions over the credibility of the electoral process' *BBC News,* (03 January).

Belamy, Richard (2007) *Political constitutionalism.* Cambridge: Cambridge University Press.

Bell, Daniel A (2006) *Beyond liberal democracy: Political thinking for an East Asian context.* Princeton: Princeton University Press.

Bentham, Jeremy (1843) *The Works of Jeremy Bentham (11 Volumes)*, (ed.) John Bowring.

Bergman, David (2017) 'Recording of Bangladesh Paramilitary Officer lifts lid on extra-judicial killings and forced disappearances', *The Wire*, (06 April).

Bertocci, Peter J (1982) 'Bangladesh in the early 1980s: Praetorian politics in an intermediate regime'. *Asian Survey*, 22(10): 988–1008.

Bertocci, Peter J (1985) 'Bangladesh in 1984: A year of protracted turmoil'. *Asian Survey, A survey of Asia in 1984: Part II*, 25(2): 155–168.

Bhattacharjee, Arun (1973) *Dateline Mujibnagar.* Delhi: Vikas. p. 38.

Bhaumik, Subir (2017) 'Behind the 'RAW' tirade.' *The Daily Star*, (18 March).

Bhaumik, Subir (2014) 'Difficult Victory'. *The Telegraph*, Calcutta, India, (26 January).

Bhowmick, Nilanjana (2015) 'Political turmoil sparks fresh violence in Bangladesh'. *The Time*, (15 January).

Bhuian, Mohammad N (2012) *The fundamental right to freedom of the press in Bangladesh.* London: SOAS (Unpublished Ph.D. thesis).

Bingham, Tom (2011) *The Rule of Law.* London: Penguin.

Bjornlund, Eric C (2004) *Beyond free and fair: Monitoring elections and building democracy.* Washington, DC: Woodrow Wilson Center Press.

Blaug, Ricardo (2010) *How power corrupts: Cognition and democracy in organizations.* Basingstoke: Palgrave Macmillan.

Bose, Sarmila (2005) 'Anatomy of violence: An analysis of civil war in East Pakistan in 1971'. *Economic and Political Weekly*, 40(41) (October): 8–14.

Bose, Sugata and Jalal, Ayesha (2011) *Modern South Asia: History, culture, political economy.* London: Routledge.

Boucher, David and Kelly, Paul (eds.) (2003) *Political thinkers: From Socrates to the present.* Oxford: Oxford University Press.

Bowman, Kirk S (1996) 'Taming the tiger: Militarization and democracy in Latin America'. *Journal of Peace Research*, 33(3): 289–308.

Brandt, Michele and Kaplan, Jeffrey A (1996) 'The tension between women's rights and religious rights: reservations to CEDAW by Egypt, Bangladesh and Tunisia'. *Journal of Law and Religion*, 12(1): 105–142.

Brass, Paul R (ed.) (2013) *Routledge handbook of South Asian politics: India, Pakistan, Bangladesh, Sri Lanka, and Nepal.* Oxford: Routledge.

Bressman, Lisa Shultz(2007) 'Deference and democracy'. *Public Law and Legal Theory Working Paper*, 06–20. 45 pp. Nashville: Vanderbilt University Law School.

Brooks, Rosa Ehrenreich (2005) 'Failed states, or the state as failure?' *The University of Chicago Law Review*, 72(4): 1159–1196.

Broomfield, J H (1968) *Elite conflict in a plural society: Twentieth century Bengal.* Berkeley: University of California Press.

Brown, Judith M (2003) *Nehru: A political life.* New Haven: Yale University Press.

Buncombe, Andrew (2010) 'Battle of the Begums' brings Bangladesh to a standstill.' *The Independent*, (1 December).

Button, Mark E (2008) *Contract, culture and citizenship: Transformative liberalism from Hobbes to Rawls.* University Park Pennsylvania State University Press.

'CA announces 7 priority tasks for administration'. (2001) *The Bangladesh Observer*, (20 August).

Cane, Peter and Conaghan, Joanne (eds.) (2008) *The new Oxford companion to law*. Oxford: Oxford University Press.

Canfora, Luciano (2006) *Democracy in Europe: A history of an ideology*. Oxford: Blackwell Publishing.

'Caretaker government: "Partisan" persons included: Hasina' (2001) *The Bangladesh Observer*, (24 July).

'Caretaker govt has taken partisan steps: Kibria'. (2001) *The Bangladesh Observer*, (21 August).

'Caretaker govt's faulty steps' (2001) *The Bangladesh Observer*, (24 August).

'Caretaker system declared illegal' (2011) *The Daily Star*, (11 May).

'Caretaker system declared illegal: SC' (2011) *New Age*, (10 May).

Carothers, Thomas (ed.) (2006) *Promoting the rule of law abroad in search of knowledge*. Washington, DC: Carnegie Endowment for International Peace.

Cawthra, Gavin and Luckham, Robin (eds.) (2003) *Governing insecurity: Democratic control of military and security establishments in transitional democracies*. London: Zed Books Limited.

Chabal, Patrick (1998) 'A few considerations on democracy in Africa'. *International Affairs*, 74(2): 289–303.

Chadda, Maya (2000) *Building democracy in South Asia: India, Nepal and Pakistan*. Boulder: Lynne Rienner Publishers Inc.

Chambers, Robert (1997) *Whose reality counts? Putting the first last*. Rugby: Practical Action Publishing.

Chambers, Samuel A (2005) 'Working on the democratic imagination and the limits of deliberative democracy'. *Political Research Quarterly*, 58(4): 619–623.

Chambers, Simone and Kopstein, Jeffrey (2001) 'Bad civil society'. *Political Theory*, 29(6): 837–865.

Chandra, Anjana Motihar (2007) *India condensed: 5000 years of history & culture*. Singapore: Marshall Cavendish International (Asia) Private Limited.

Chandra, Bipan (1979) *Nationalism and colonialism in modern India*. Hyderabad: Orient BlackSwan.

Charles, Guy-Uriel E (2007) 'Democracy and distortion'. *Cornell Law Review*, 92(30): 101–173.

Chatterji, Brig. (ret.) S K (2014) 'Bangladesh's bumpy ride'. *The Diplomat*, (14 February).

Chattopadhyay, Saayam (2011) 'Bengali masculinity and the national masculine: Some conjectures for interpretation'. *South Asia Research*, 31(3): 265–279.

Cheema, G Shabbir (2005) *Building democratic institutions: Governance reforms in developing countries*. Bloomfield: Kumarian Press Inc.

Chiba, Masaji (ed.) (1986) *Asian indigenous law*. London: KPI Limited.

Chiba, Masaji (ed.) (1989) *Legal pluralism: Toward a general theory through Japanese legal culture*. Tokyo: Tokai University Press.

Chiba, Masaji (ed.) (1998) 'Other phases of legal pluralism in the contemporary world'. *Ratio Juris*, 11(3): 228–245.

Chiba, Masaji (ed.) (2002) *Legal cultures in human society. A collection of articles and essays*. Tokyo: Shinzansha International.

Chibundu, Maxwell O (2006) 'Political ideology as a religion: The idolatry of democracy'. *University of Maryland Law Journal of Race, Religion, Gender and Class*, 6(1): 117–157.

Chomsky, Noam (2006) *Failed states: The abuse of power and the assault on democracy.* New York: Henry Hold and Company, LLC.

Chu, Yun-Han, Diamond, Larry, Nathan, Andrew J. and Shin, Doh Chull (eds.) (2008) *How East Asians view democracy.* New York: Columbia University Press.

Chua, Amy (2002) *World on fire: Exporting free market democracy breeds ethnic hatred and global instability.* New York: Doubleday.

Chowdhury, Abdur Rahman (2012) 'Caretaker government – the best available option'. *New Age*, (7 June).

Chowdhury, Afsan (ed.) (2007) *Bangladesh 1971.* Dhaka: Mowla Brothers.

Choudhury, G W (1993) *The last days of united Pakistan.* Oxford: Oxford University Press.

Choudhury, G W (2011) *The last days of united Pakistan.* Dhaka: University Press Limited.

Choudhury, Shamila N (2013) 'Is Pakistan's military out of politics for good?' In: *Pakistan votes: A weekly look inside the historic 2013 elections.* Foreign Policy magazine, (7 March).

Citrin, Jack (1974) 'The political relevance of trust in government'. *The American Political Science Review*, 68(3): 973–975.

Coggan, Philip (2013) *The last vote: the threats to western democracy.* London: Penguin.

Cohen, Stephen Philip (2004) *The idea of Pakistan.* Washington, DC: Brookings Institution Press.

Cooke, Bill and Kothari, Uma (eds.) (2004) *Participation: The new tyranny?* London: Zed Books.

Corbridge, Stuart and Harriss, John (2000) *Reinventing India: Liberalization, Hindu nationalism and popular democracy.* Cambridge: Polity Press.

'Corruption, nepotism dog civil service recruitments: Insiders blame political intervention'. (2005) *New Age*, (27 November).

Cotterrell, Roger (1995) *Law's community: Legal theory in sociological perspective.* Oxford: Clarendon Press.

Cotterrell, Roger (2006) *Law, culture and society.* Hampshire: Ashgate.

Coulson, Noel J (1964) *A history of Islamic law.* Edinburgh: Edinburgh University Press.

Coulson, Noel J (1968) 'Islamic law'. In: Derrett, J D (ed.) *An introduction to legal systems.* London: Sweet & Maxwell.

Coulson, Noel J (1969) *Conflicts and tensions in Islamic jurisprudence.* Chicago: Chicago University Press.

Cownie, F C (2004) *Legal academics: Culture and identities.* Oxford: Hart Publishing.

Cox, Caroline and Marks, John (2003) *The 'West', Islam and Islamism: Is ideological Islam compatible with liberal democracy?* London: Institute of the Study of Civil Society.

Cox, Oliver C (1947) 'Modern democracy and the class struggle'. *The Journal of Negro Education*, 16(2): 155–164.

Croce, M (2014) 'What is legal pluralism all about?' *Jura Gentium*, Vol. XI: *Pluralismo Giuridico*, pp. 166–186. Annuale 2014.

'CTG should not be disturbed by any means' (2001) *The Bangladesh Observer*, (25 July).
Cunningham, Frank (2001) *Theories of democracy: A critical introduction*. London: Routledge.
'The curious case of caretaker government' (2013) *The Bangladesh Chronicle*, (30 July).
Curtis, Lisa A (2007) 'Protecting democracy in Bangladesh'. *Web Memo*, No. 1559 (17 July). Washington, DC: The Heritage Foundation.
Dahl, Robert A (1971) *Polyarchy: Participation and opposition*. New Haven: Yale University Press.
Dahl, Robert A (1989) *Democracy and its critics*. New Haven: Yale University Press.
Dahl, Robert A (1998) *On democracy*. New Haven: Yale University Press.
Dalrymple, William (2006) *The last Mughal: The fall of Delhi, 1857*. London: Bloomsbury Publishing.
Dalrymple, William (2015) 'The great divide'. *The New Yorker*.
DAM, Shubhankar (2004) 'Is Indian democracy dependent on a statute?' *Research Collection School of Law, Singapore Management University*, Paper 7.
Das, Gurcharan (2003) 'Democracy and capitalism in India'. *Globalist*, (11 May).
Datta, Sreeradha (2007) 'Islamic militancy in Bangladesh'. *South Asia: Journal of South Asian Studies*, 30(I): 167–168.
Datta, Sreeradha (2009) *Caretaking democracy: Political process in Bangladesh, 2006–2008*. New Delhi: Institute for Defence Studies and Analysis.
D'Costa, Bina (2012) 'Bangladesh in 2011: Weak state building and different foreign policy'. *Asian Survey*, 52(1): 147–156.
De, Amalendu (1977) 'Bengali Intelligentsia's attitudes to the Permanent Settlement'. *Social Scientist*, 5(8): 18–40.
De Burca, Grainne (2008) 'Developing democracy beyond the state'. *Columbia Journal of Transnational Law*, 46(2): 221–278.
Dearden, Lizzie, (2016) 'Bangladesh attacks: ISIS militants tortured hostages who could not recite Quran in 12-hour siege at Dhaka Cafe'. *The Independent*, (2 July).
D'Entreves, A P (1965) *Aquinas selected political writings*. Oxford: Basis Blackwell.
Derrett, J Duncan M (1968) *Religion, law and the state in India*. London: Faber & Faber.
DeSouza, Peter Ronald (2010) 'Bangladesh building an effective, capable and inclusive state – democracy, nationalism and the state in Bangladesh'. *Background paper for UNDP democratic governance group, community of practice meeting, Senegal* (February): pp. 12–18.
'Despicable offence committed' (2011) *The Daily Star*, (19 July).
Dharamsdani, M.D. (ed.) (2001) *Multi-party democracies in South Asia*. New Delhi: Anmol Publications (P) Ltd.
Diamond, Larry and Plattner, Marc, F. (eds.) (1996) *Civil – military relations and democracy (A Journal of Democracy Book)*. Baltimore: Johns Hopkins University Press.
Dias, R W M and Hughes, G B J (1957) *Jurisprudence*. London: Butterworths.
Di Palma, Giuseppe (1990) *To craft democracies: An essay on democratic transitions*. Berkeley: University of California Press.
Dil, Anwar S (2000) *Bengali language movement to Bangladesh*. Dhaka: Ferozsons.

Donlan, Seán Patrick and Urscheler, Lukas Heckendorn (2014) *Concepts of law*. London: Ashgate.

Doorenspleet, Renske (2006) *Democratic transitions: Exploring the structural sources of the fourth wave*. New Delhi: Viva Books Private Limited.

Dovi, Suzanne (2014) 'Political Representation'. In: Edward N. Zalta (ed.). *The Stanford Encyclopaedia of Philosophy*.

Dowding, Keith (1996) *Power: Concepts in the social sciences*. London: Open University Press.

Dryzek, John S (2003) 'Social choice theory and deliberative democracy: A reconciliation'. *British Journal of Political Science*, 33(1): 1–28.

Dunleavy, Patrick and O'Leary, Brendan (1987) *Theories of the state: The politics of liberal democracy*. New York: Palgrave Macmillan.

Dunn, Judy (1988) *The beginnings of social understanding*. Oxford: Blackwell Publishers Ltd.

Dyson, R W (2008) *Aquinas political writings*. Cambridge: Cambridge University Press.

Dyzenhaus, David (2006) *The constitution of law: Legality in a time of emergency*. Cambridge: Cambridge University Press.

Eaton, Richard M (1993) *The rise of Islam and the Bengal frontier, 1204–1760*. Berkeley: University of California Press.

Eaton, Richard M (2001) 'Who are the Bengal Muslims? Conversion and Islamisation in Bengal'. In: Rafiuddin Ahmed (ed.), *Understanding the Bengal Muslims: Interpretative Essays*. New Delhi: Oxford University Press.

The Economist (2012) 'The path through the fields: Bangladesh and development'. *The Economist*, (3 November).

The Economist (2013a) 'The campaign trail: The ruling party will win Bangladesh's election. The country will lose'. *The Economist*, (21 December).

The Economist (2013b) 'Zero sum politics: As an election looms, Bangladesh's feuding leaders live down to expectations'. *The Economist*, (02 November).

The Economist (2014a) 'Electoral farce in Bangladesh: The minus one solution'. *The Economist*, (03 January).

The Economist (2014b) 'One and only one'. *The Economist*, (20 September).

The Economist (2014c) 'Dialling down: Politics and the past in Bangladesh'. *The Economist*, (1 November).

Economist Intelligence Unit (2012) 'The frequency of street protests increases', (7 March). London: The Economist.

Economist Intelligence Unit (2010a) 'Country forecast: Bangladesh'. London: The Economist.

Economist Intelligence Unit (2010b) 'Country report: Bangladesh'. London: The Economist.

Edel, Abraham (1944) 'The relations of science and democracy'. *The Journal of Philosophy*, 41(26): 701–710.

Edgar, Andrew (2006) *Habermas: The key concepts*. Oxford: Routledge.

Edgeworth, Linda and Finn Daniel (2000) *Pre-election technical assessment: Republic of Bangladesh*. Washington, DC: International Foundation for Election Systems.

'EC to exercise more power' (2001) *The Bangladesh Observer*, (21 August).

Ehrlich, Eugen (1936) *Fundamental principles of the sociology of law*. Cambridge: Harvard University Press.

Ehrlich, Eugen (2009) *Fundamental principles of the sociology of law.* London: Transaction Publishers.

Eickelman, D F and Piscatori, J (1996) *Muslim politics.* Princeton: Princeton University Press.

Eisgruber, Christopher L (2002) 'Dimensions of democracy'. *Princeton Law and Public Affairs Working Paper Series*, 02–007. 50 pp. Princeton University: Program in law and Public Affairs.

El-Solh, Raghid (1993) 'Islamist attitudes towards democracy: A review of the ideas of al-Ghazali'. *British Journal of Middle Eastern Studies*, 20(1): 57–63.

Elkins, Zachary (2000) 'Gradations of democracy? Empirical tests of alternative conceptualizations'. *American Journal of Political Science*, 44(2): 293–300.

Elshtain, Jean Bethke (1993) *Democracy on trial.* Concord, Ont.: Anansi.

Ely, John Hart (1980) *Democracy and distrust: A theory of judicial review.* Cambridge: Harvard University Press.

Esposito, John L (ed.) (1995) *The Oxford encyclopedia of the modern Islamic world.* Oxford: Oxford University Press.

Esposito, John L, Voll, John O and Baker, Osman (eds.) (2008) *Asian Islam in the 21st century.* Oxford: Oxford University Press.

Euben, J Peter (1993) 'Democracy ancient and modern'. *Political Science and Politics*, 26(3): 478–481.

Evans, Geoffrey and Whitefield, Stephen (1995) 'The politics and economics of democratic commitment: Support for democracy in transition societies'. *British Journal of Political Science*, 25(4): 485–514.

Fair, Christine and Levitas, Kerem (2005) *Peace Brief* (May). Washington, DC: United States Institute of Peace.

Fairfield, Paul (2008) *Why democracy.* Albany: University of New York Press.

Farrell, David M (2001) *Electoral systems: A comparative introduction.* New York: Palgrave Macmillan.

Femia, Joseph V (1993) *Marxism and democracy.* Oxford: Clarendon Press.

Feng, Yi and Zak, Paul J (1999) 'The determinants of democratic transitions'. *The Journal of Conflict Resolution*, 43(2): 162–177.

Fidrmuc, Jan, (2001) 'Economic reform, democracy and growth during post-communist transition'. *William Davidson Institute Working Paper* 372 (March). Ann Arbor: William Davidson Institute.

Fiorino, Nadia and Ricciuti, Roberto (2007) 'Determinants of direct democracy'. Presented at *CESIFO Area Conference on Public Sector Economics*, (April). Munich: CESIFO.

Fisher, Rebecca (ed.) (2013) *Managing democracy, managing dissent: Capitalism, democracy and the organization of consent.* London: Corporate Watch.

Fisher, William F (1997) 'Doing good? The politics and antipolitics of NGO practices'. *Annual Review of Anthropology*, 26: 439–464.

Fishkin, James S (1997) *The voice of the people: Public opinion & democracy.* New Haven and London: Yale University Press.

Fishkin, James S (2009) *When the people speak: Deliberative democracy and public consultation.* Oxford: Oxford University Press.

Foblets, Marie-Claire (2012) 'Religion and rethinking the public-private divide: Introduction'. In: Ferrari, Silvio and Pastorelli, Sabrina (eds.) *Religion in public spaces: A European perspective.* Surrey: Ashgate.

Foucault, Michel (1988) *Power/knowledge: Selected interviews and other writings 1972–1977.* Gordon, Colin (ed.). New York: Pantheon Books.

Freeden, Michael (1998) 'Is nationalism a distinct ideology?' *Political Studies*, 46: 748–765.

Freeman, M D A (2001) *Lloyd's introduction to jurisprudence.* London: Sweet & Maxwell.

French, Patrick (2011), *Liberty or death: India's journey to independence and division.* London: Penguin Books.

Frey, Bruno S (2003) 'Direct democracy for transition countries'. *Institute for Empirical Research in Economics, Working Paper Series*, (July) 165. 36 pp. Zurich: University of Zurich.

Fukuyama, Francis (1995) *Trust: The social virtues and the creation of prosperity.* New York: Free Press Paperbacks.

Fukuyama, Francis (2004) *State building: Governance and world order in the twenty-first century.* London: Profile Books.

Fukuyama, Francis (2011) *The origins of political order.* London: Profile Books.

Gallo, Carmenza (1992) 'Review: Democracy by default?' *Sociological Forum*, 7(4): 711–718.

Gandhi, Mohandas Karamchand (2008) *Autobiography: The story of my experiments with truth.* BN Publishing.

Gani, Aisha (2014) 'Bangladesh has little to celebrate after the most violent election day in its history'. *The Guardian*, (15 January).

Gankovsky, Yuri V (1974) 'The social structure of society in the People's Republic of Bangladesh'. *Asian Survey*, 14(3): 220–230.

Gardner, James A (2005) 'Democracy without a net? Separation of powers and the idea of self-sustaining constitutional constraints on undemocratic behaviour'. *St. John's Law Review*, 79: 293–317.

Ghosal, U N (1957) *Studies in Indian history and culture.* Calcutta.

Ghosh, Partha S (1993) 'Bangladesh at crossroads: Religion and politics'. *Asian Survey, South Asia: Responses to the Ayodhya crisis*, 33(7): 697–710.

Ghosh, Partha S (2015) 'The other side of partition: Resonances on cultural expressions'. *South Asia Research*, 35(1): 42–60.

Ghosh, Subhasri (2014) 'Population movements in West Bengal: a study of Nadia district, 1947–51'. *South Asia Research*, 34(2): 1–20.

Gillin, J L (1919) 'The origin of democracy'. *The American Journal of Sociology*, 24(6): 704–714.

Gills, Barry, Rocamora, Joel and Wilson, Richard (eds.) (1993) *Low intensity democracy: Political power in the new world order.* London: Pluto.

Gleditsch, Kristian S and Ward, Michael D (1997) 'Double take: A re-examination of democracy and autocracy in modern polities'. *The Journal of Conflict Resolution*, 41(3): 361–383.

Goode, Luke (2005) *Jürgen Habermas: Democracy and the public sphere.* London: Pluto Press.

Goyal, Ashima and Jha, A K (2004) 'Dictatorship, democracy and institutions: Macropolicy in China and India'. *Economic and Political Weekly*, 39(42): 16–22.

Grifith-Jones, Robin (ed.) (2013) *Islam and English law: Rights, responsibilities and the place of shari'a.* Cambridge: Cambridge University Press.

Grofman, Bernard (1993) 'Lessons of Athenian democracy: Editor's introduction'. *Political Science and Politics*, 26(3): 471–474.
Gross, Oren and Aolain, Fionnuala Ni (2006) *Law in times of crisis: Emergency powers in theory and practice*. Cambridge: Cambridge University Press.
Grover, Virender (ed.) (1993) *Political-thinkers of modern India, volume 22*. New Delhi: Deed and Deed Publications.
Guha, Ramachandra (2008) *India after Gandhi: The history of the world's largest democracy*. London: Pan Books.
Habermas, Jürgen (1962) *The structural transformation of the public sphere: An inquiry into a category of bourgeois society* (German: *Strukturwandel der Öffentlichkeit. Untersuchungen zu einer Kategorie der bürgerlichen Gesellschaft*). Translated by Burger, Thomas and Lawrence, Frederick (1989). Cambridge: Polity Press.
Habermas, Jürgen (1979) *Communication and the evolution of society*. New York: Polity Press.
Habermas, Jürgen (1989/1962) *The structural transformation of the public sphere. An inquiry into a category of bourgeois society*, Burger, Thomas and Lawrence, Frederick (trans). Cambridge: Polity Press.
Habermas, Jürgen (1996/2012) *Between facts and norms: Contributions to a discourse theory of law and democracy*. Cambridge: Polity Press.
Habermas, Jürgen (1998) *Inclusion of the other: Studies in political theory*. In: Cronin, Ciaran and Degrieff, Pablo (eds). Cambridge: Polity Press.
Habermas, Jürgen (2001) 'Constitutional democracy: A paradoxical union of contradictory principles'. *Political Theory*, 29(6): 766–781.
Habermas, Jürgen (2003) *Truth and justification*. Cambridge: Polity Press.
Habermas, Jürgen (2006) 'Religion in the public sphere'. *European Journal of Philosophy*, 14(1): 1–25.
Habermas, Jürgen (2011a) *The structural transformation of the public sphere*. Cambridge: Polity Press.
Habermas, Jürgen (ed.) (2011b) *An awareness of what is missing: Faith and reason in a post-secular age*. Cambridge: Polity Press.
Habermas, Jürgen and Seidman, Steven (ed.) (1989) *Jürgen Habermas on society & Politics*. Boston: Beacon Press.
Hagerty, Devin T (2007) 'Bangladesh in 2006: Living in interesting times'. *Asian Survey*, 47(1): 105–112.
Hagerty, Devin T (2008) 'Bangladesh in 2007: Democracy interrupted, political and environmental challenges ahead'. *Asian Survey*, 48(1): 177–183.
Haider, Zaglul (1999) 'The role of military in the politics of Bangladesh: Mujib, Zia and Ershad regimes'. *Journal of South Asian and Middle Eastern Studies*, 23(3): 65–68.
Hailsham, Lord (1976) 'Elective dictatorship'. *Richard Dimbleby Lecture* (9 October).
Hajari, Nisid (2015) *Midnight's furies: The deadly legacy of India's partition*. Stroud: Amberley Publishing.
Hakim, Muhammad A (1993) *Bangladesh politics: The Shahabuddin interregnum*. Dhaka: University Press Limited.
Hakim, Muhammad A (1994) 'The Mirpur parliamentary by-election in Bangladesh'. *Asian Survey*, 34(8): 738–747.
Hall, Peter A (ed.) (1986) *Governing the economy: The politics of state intervention in Britain and France*. Oxford: Oxford University Press.

Hansen, Mogens Herman (1992) 'The traditions of the Athenian democracy A.D. 1750–1990'. *Greece & Rome*, 2nd Ser., 39(1): 14–30.

Haque, A K M Masudul (2008) 'Emergency powers and caretaker government in Bangladesh'. *Journal of the Australian Law Teachers Association*, 9(1): 81–94.

Hardin, Russel (2003) *Liberalism, constitutionalism and democracy*. Oxford: Oxford University Press.

Harris, J W (1980) *Legal philosophies*. London: Butterworths.

Harris, John (2003) *India: the bitter fruits of grandiose ambition*, (March). The Hague, the Netherlands: In: Clingendael Institute (Unpublished). (Mimeograph with the author).

Harrison, Frances (2013) *Political Islam & the elections in Bangladesh*. London: New Millennium.

Hart, H L A (1961) *The concept of law*. Oxford: Oxford University Press.

Hart, H L A (2012) *The concept of law*. Oxford: Oxford University Press.

Hartmann, Thom (2004) *What would Jefferson do? A return to democracy*. New York: Harmony Books.

Hasan, Ahmad (1984) *The doctrine of Ijma in Islam*. Islamabad: Islamic Research Institute.

Hasan, Manzoor and Zakaria, Sultan Mohammed (2016) 'Reflection on Bangladesh's democratic governance', *The Daily Star*, (30 July).

Hasan, Mubashar (2011) 'Democracy and political Islam in Bangladesh'. *South Asia Research*, 31(2): 97–117.

Hasan, Mubashar (2012) 'The geopolitics of political Islam in Bangladesh'. *Harvard Asia Quarterly*, Vol: 14(1–2): 60–69.

Hasanuzzaman, Al Masud (1998) *Role of opposition in Bangladesh politics*. Dhaka: University Press Limited.

Hashmi, Arshi Saleem (2009) 'Religious and militant groups in Bangladeshi politics: A case study'. *Institute of Regional Studies*, (December). Islamabad: Institute of Regional Studies.

Hashmi, Nader (2009) *Islam, secularism and liberal democracy*. Oxford: Oxford University Press.

Hawkins, Darren (2001) 'Democratization theory and nontransitions: Insights from Cuba'. *Comparative Politics*, 33(4): 441–461.

Hay, Collin, Michael, Lister and David Marsh (eds.) (2006) *The state – theories and issues*. Hampshire: Palgrave Macmillan.

Hayek, F A (2006) *The constitution of liberty*. London: Routledge.

Hepper, Metin (1997) 'Introduction'. In: Hepper, Metin, Ali, Kazancigil and Rockman Bert A (eds.) *Institutions and democratic statecraft*. Boulder: Westview Press, pp. 3–9.

Herzog, Siegfried (2013) 'Bangladesh 2013 – a year of political crossroads'. *Fur Die Freiheit*.

Hetherington, Marc J (1998) 'The political relevance of political trust'. *The American Political Science Review*, 92(4): 791–808.

Hewitt, Vernon (2008) *Political mobilisation and democracy in India: States of emergency*. Oxford: Routledge.

Hoppe, Hans-Hermann (2007) *Democracy: The God that failed*. London: Transaction Publishers.

Hoque, Ridwanul (2012) 'Constitutionalism and the Judiciary in Bangladesh'. In: Khilnani, Sunil, Raghavan, Vikram, and Thiruvengadam, Arun K. (eds.), *Comparative Constitutionalism in South Asia*. Oxford: Oxford University press.

Hossain, Akhtar (2000) 'Anatomy of hartal politics in Bangladesh'. *Asian Survey*, 40(3): 508–529.

Hossain, Golam (1995) 'Bangladesh in 1994: Democracy at risk'. *Asian Survey, A survey of Asia in 1994: Part II*, 35(2): 171–178.

Hossain, Golam (1996) 'Bangladesh in 1996: Politics of intransigence'. *Asian Survey, A Survey of Asia in 1995: Part II*, 36(2): 196–203.

Hossain, Kamal (2013) *Bangladesh: Quest for freedom and justice*. Dhaka: University Press Limited.

Hossain, Maneeza (2006) 'Countdown to elections: High stakes for Bangladesh'. *White Paper*, (July). Washington DC: Foundation for Defense of Democracies.

Hossain, Maneeza (2007) 'Bangladesh 2007: The new order and Islamism'. *White Paper*, (Spring). Washington, DC: Hudson Institute.

Hossain, Maneeza and Curtis, Lisa (2010) 'Bangladesh: Checking Islamist extremism in a pivotal democracy'. *Backgrounder*, Issue No. 2383 (15 March). Washington, DC: The Heritage Foundation.

Hossain, Sara and Alam, Tanjibul (2006) 'Separation of the judiciary from the executive in Bangladesh'. *UNDP Policy Paper, Bangladesh*. Dhaka: UNDP Policy Paper (26 November).

Hsin-chi, Kuan (1991) 'Power dependence and democratic transition: The case of Hong Kong'. *The China Quarterly*, 128: 774–793.

Huber, Evelyne, Rueschemeyer, Dietrich and Stephens, John D (1997) 'The paradoxes of contemporary democracy: Formal, participatory, and social dimensions'. *Comparative Politics*, 29(3): 323–342.

Huda, Nurul (2006) 'Caretaker government in an apprehensive polity'. *The Daily Star*, (4 November).

Huda, Nurul (2011) 'Behind the caretaker controversy' *The Daily Star*, (18 June).

Hughes, Kirsty (2007) 'Bangladesh: Moving towards or away from Democracy?' *Economic and Political Weekly*, 42(15): 1329–1331.

Human Rights Watch (2008) 'Human Rights in Bangladesh'.

Human Rights Watch (2009) 'Human Rights in Bangladesh'.

Human Rights Watch (2012) 'Human Rights in Bangladesh'.

Human Rights Watch (2014) 'Bangladesh: Elections scarred by violence. Government and opposition responsible for abuses before, during, after polls'.

Huntington, Samuel P (1991) *The third wave: Democratization in the late twentieth century*. Norman: University of Oklahoma Press.

Huq, Aziz Z (2006) 'Democratic norms, human rights and states of emergency: Lessons from the experience of four countries'. In: *Democracy, conflict and human society*. Stockholm: International Institute for Democracy and Electoral Assistance.

Huque, Ahmed Shafiqul and Hakim, Muhammad A (1993) 'Elections in Bangladesh: Tools of legitimacy'. *Asian Affairs*, 19(4): 248–261.

Hutchinson, Annan C and Colon-Rios, Joel (2007) 'What's democracy got to do with it? A critique of liberal constitutionalism'. *CPLE Research Paper*, 3(4): 1–49.

Hye, Hasnat Abdul (ed.) (2000) *Governance: South Asian perspectives*. Dhaka: University Press Limited.

Ibrahim, Syed Muhammad (2011) *Misrokothon*. Dhaka: Ananna.
Ikram, S M and Spear, Percival (1955) *The cultural heritage of Pakistan*. Oxford: Oxford University Press.
Imam, Husain (2008) 'Is the train on the right track?' *The Daily Star*, (25 August).
Inglehart, R (1997) *Modernization and postmodernization: Cultural, economic and political change in 43 societies*. Princeton: Princeton University Press.
Ingram, David (2010) *Habermas, introduction and analysis*. Ithaca: Cornell University Press.
Inoguchi, T, Newman, E and Keane, J (1998) 'Introduction: The changing nature of democracy'. In: Inoguchi, T, Newman, E and Keane, J (eds.) *The changing nature of democracy*. Tokyo, New York, Paris: United Nations University Press, pp. 1–19.
Institute of Governance Studies, BRAC University (2006) *State of governance in Bangladesh*.
Institute of Governance Studies, BRAC University (2008) *State of governance in Bangladesh*.
Institute of Governance Studies, BRAC University (2009) *State of governance in Bangladesh*.
Institute of Governance Studies, BRAC University (2010) *Governance Barometer Survey Bangladesh*.
International Crisis Group (2009) 'Bangladesh: Getting Police reform on track'. (Report no. 182 – 11 December) p.14.
International Crisis Group (2015) *Asia Report No. 264*, 'Mapping Bangladesh's Political Crisis', p. 9, (9 February).
'Invisible force working within CTG'. (2001) *The Bangladesh Observer*, (11 August).
Islam, Ashraful (2014) 'Rights groups demand disbanding of RAB'. *Deutsche Welle* (29 May).
Islam, Kazi Nazrul (2014 – originally published in 1364 Bengali year) *Sanchita*. Dhaka: Bangla Academy.
Islam, M Nazrul (2011) 'Two decades of democracy in Bangladesh (1991–2010): Disillusionment with practice'. *Berkeley Journal of Social Sciences*, 1(3): 1–26.
Islam, M Shirajul (2008) 'Bangladesh at crossroads'. *The Daily Star*, (13 September).
Islam, Mahmudul (2005) 'Rule of law in Bangladesh'. *Syed Ishtiaque Ahmed Memorial Foundation Lecture 2005*. Dhaka: Asiatic Society.
Islam, Md. Shafiqul (2009) *The effort of the non-party caretaker government to make the ninth parliamentary elections in 2008 in Bangladesh free, fair and credible*. Lunds: Lunds Universitet (Unpublished Master programme research paper).
Islam, Nurul (2003) *Making of a nation: Bangladesh: an economists tale*. Dhaka: University Press Limited.
Islam, Rafiqul (1992) *Bangladesh: shamorik shashon o gonotontrer shongkot*. Dhaka: University Press Limited.
Islam, Syed Serajul (1984) 'The State in Bangladesh under Zia (1975–1981).' *Asian Survey*, 24(5): 556–573.
Islam, Syed Serajul (1992) 'Bengal legislative assembly and constitutional development'. In: Sirajul Islam (ed.), *History of Bangladesh 1704–1971. Volume one: Political history*. Dhaka: Asiatic Society of Bangladesh.
Islam, Syed Manzoorul (1994) *Essays on Ekushey: The language movement 1952*. Dhaka: Bangla Academy.

Islam, Sirajul (1979) The permanent settlement in Bengal: A study of its operation. Dacca: Bangla Academy.

Issacharoff, Samuel (2004) 'Constitutionalizing democracy in fractured societies'. *Public Law & Legal Theory Working Paper Group*, 04–72. 32 pp.

Jacobs, Jane (1992) *Systems of survival: A dialogue on the moral foundations of commerce and politics.* New York: Random House.

Jacobson, Arthur J and McCormick John P (2005) 'The business of democracy is democracy'. *International Journal of Constitutional Law*, 3(4): 706–722.

Jahan, Rounaq (1972) *Pakistan: Failure in national integration.* New York: Columbia University Press.

Jahan, Rounaq (1973) 'Bangladesh in 1972: Nation-building in a new state'. *Asian Survey*, 13(2): 200.

Jahan, Rounaq (ed.) (2002) *Bangladesh: Promise and performance.* Dhaka: University Press Limited.

Jahan, Rounaq (2004) 'Bangladesh in 2003: Vibrant democracy or destructive politics?' *Asian Survey*, 44(1): 56–61.

Jahan, Rounaq (2005) *Bangladesh Politics: Problems and issues.* Dhaka: University Press Limited.

Jahan, Rounaq (2007) 'Bangladesh at crossroads'. Paper presented at *Experiments with democracy, a symposium on the Asian experience with democracy*, (August).

Jahan, Rounaq (2012) 'The parliament of Bangladesh: Challenges and way forward'. *The Daily Star* (3 June).

Jahan, Rounaq (2014) 'The state of democracy in Bangladesh'. *Dhaka Tribune*, (23–25 June).

Jahangir, B K (2002) *Nationalism, fundamentalism and democracy in Bangladesh.* Dhaka: International Centre for Bengal Studies.

Jalal, Ayesha (1995) *Democracy and authoritarianism in South Asia: A comparative and historical perspective.* Cambridge: Cambridge University Press.

Jamil, Ishtiaq, Askvik, Steinar, Dhakal, Tek Nath (Eds.) (2013) *In search of better governance in South Asia and beyond.* New York: Springer.

Joehnk, Tom Felix (2014) 'Sham election set dangerous standard for Bangladesh'. *East Asia Forum*, (09 February).

Kafaltiya, Anand Ballabh (2003) *Democracy and election laws.* New Delhi: Deep & Deep Publications Pvt. Limited.

Kahn-Freund, Otto (1974) 'On the uses and misuses of comparative law'. *The Modern Law Review*, 37(1): 1–20.

Kamal, Mahbub and Hossain, Mokammel (2011) 'Tin ghontay pash korechen, chchoi ghontay batil korun – Dr. Kamal Hossain'. *The Daily Jugantor* (9 July): 5.

Kang, Michael (2006) 'De-rigging elections: Direct democracy and the future of redistricting reform'. *Public Law and Legal Theory Research Paper Series*, 06–22: 46 pp. Atlanta: Emory University School of Law.

Kaplan, Robert D (1997) 'Was democracy just a moment?' *The Atlantic Monthly*, (December).

Karim, Abdul (1985) *A social history of the Muslims in Bengal (down to 1538 AD).* Chittagong: Baitush Sharaf Islamic Research Institute.

Karim, Fariha (2011) 'Bangladeshi force trained by UK police allowed to kill and torture'. *The Guardian*, (10 May).

Karim, Waresul (2004) *Election under a caretaker government*. Dhaka: University Press Limited.

Karsten, Frank and Beckman, Karel (2012) *Beyond democracy*. London: CreateSpace Independent Publishing Platform.

Kawsar, A B M Reazul Kabir (2012) *Bangladesh Nirbachon (1947–2012)*. Dhaka: Bangladesh Election Research Centre.

Keane, John (2009) *The life and death of democracy*. London: Pocket Books.

Keay, John (2010) *India, a history: From the earliest civilization to the boom of the twenty-first century*. London: Harper Press.

Kelly, Judith G (2012) *Monitoring democracy: When international election observation works, and why it often fails*. Princeton: Princeton University Press.

Kelly, Thomas (2014) 'Apples to oranges: Epistemological dissonance in the human rights case *Hadijatou Mani v Niger*'. *Quinnipiac Law Review*, 32: 311–333.

Khan, A A (2015) 'The politics of constitutional amendments in Bangladesh: The case of the non-political caretaker government'. *International Review of Law*, 9: 14.

Khan, Ali (1997) 'A theory of universal democracy'. *Wisconsin International Law Journal*, 16(1): 61–113.

Khan, Borhanuddin (2012) 'Necessity of a non-party caretaker government'. *The Daily Star*, (11 February).

Khan, Hamid (2009) *Constitutional and political history of Pakistan*. Oxford: Oxford University Press.

Khan, M Hafizuddin (2012) 'The Daily Star's wish list: A far cry'. *The Daily Star* (20 February).

Khan, Qamar-ud-Din (1982) *Political concepts in the Quran*. Lahore: Islamic Book Foundation.

Khan, Shamsul I, Islam, S Aminul and Haque, M Imdadul (eds.) (2008) *Political culture, political parties and the democratic transition in Bangladesh*. Dhaka: University Press Limited.

Khan, Sonia Zaman (2009) 'Let justice prevail: Law & war crimes in Bangladesh'. *BanglaCarta21 Seminar Report*. Seminar held in the House of Lords UK on 19 June 2009.

Khan, Sonia Zaman (2015) *Democratic transition and the Caretaker Government of Bangladesh in a culture of mistrust*. Unpublished doctoral thesis, London: SOAS.

Khan, Zillur R (1981) 'Politicization of Bangladesh military: A response to perceived shortcomings of civilian government'. *Asian Survey*, 21(5): 551–564.

Khan, Zillur R (1985) 'Islam and Bengali nationalism'. *Asian Survey*, 25(8): 834–851.

Khan, Zillur R (1993) 'Bangladesh in 1992: Dilemmas of democratization'. *Asian Survey, A Survey of Asia in 1992: Part II*, 33(2): 150–156.

Khan, Zillur R (1994) 'Bangladesh in 1993: Values, identity and development'. *Asian Survey, A Survey of Asia in 1993: Part II*, 34(2): 160–167.

Khan, Zillur R (1997) 'Bangladesh's experiments with parliamentary democracy'. *Asian Survey*, 37(6): 575–589.

Khan, Zillur R (2007) 'Aspirations and realities: Parliaments and the democratic culture'. In: Syed Saad Andaleeb (ed.) *Political culture in Bangladesh: Perspectives and analyses: Selections from the Journal of Bangladesh Studies*. Dhaka: University Press Limited. pp. 149–184.

Khan, Zillur R and Andaleeb, Syed Saad (eds.) (2011) *Democracy in Bangladesh: Political dimensions of national development*. Dhaka: University Press Limited.

Khandaker, A K (2014) *Bhetore Baire*. Dhaka: Prothoma Prokashon.

Khatib, A L (1981) *Who killed Mujib?* New Delhi: Vikas Publishing House (Pvt.) Ltd.

Khosru, Israfil (2012) 'The caretaker ordeal and a nation divided'. *New Age*, (7 October).

Kirschke, Linda (2000) 'Informal repression, zero-sum politics and late third wave transitions'. *The Journal of Modern African Studies*, 38(3): 383–405.

Klingemann, Hans-Dieter and Fuchs, Dieter (eds.) (1998) *Citizens and the state*. Oxford: Oxford University Press.

Klug, Francesca, Starmer, Keir and Weir Stuart (1996) *The three pillars of liberty: Political rights and freedoms in the United Kingdom (Democratic audit of the United Kingdom)*. London: Routledge.

Klug, Heinz (2007) 'Constitution-making, democracy and the civilizing of unreconcilable conflict: What might we learn from the South African Miracle?' *Legal Studies Research Paper Series*, 1046 (May). Madison: University of Wisconsin Law School.

Kochanek, Stanley (1996) 'The rise of interest politics in Bangladesh'. *Asian Survey*, 36(7): 704–722.

Kochanek, Stanley (1997) 'Bangladesh in 1996: The 25th year of independence'. *Asian Survey, A Survey of Asia in 1996: Part II*, 37(2): 136–142.

Kochanek, Stanley (1998) 'Bangladesh in 1997: The honeymoon is over'. *Asian Survey, A Survey of Asia in 1997: Part II*, 38(2): 135–141.

Kochanek, Stanley (2000) 'Governance, patronage politics, and democratic transition in Bangladesh'. *Asian Survey*, 40(3): 530–550.

Kochanek, Stanley (2010) 'Corruption and the criminalization of politics in South Asia'. In: Brass, Paul R (ed.) (2013) *Routledge handbook of South Asian politics: India, Pakistan, Bangladesh, Sri Lanka, and Nepal*. London: Routledge, 364–380.

Kohli, Atul (ed.) (2001) *The success of India's democracy (Contemporary South Asia)*. Cambridge: Cambridge University Press.

Kothari, Rajni (2007) *Rethinking democracy*. London: Zed Books.

Kramer, Gudrun (1993) 'Islamist notions of democracy'. *Middle East Report*, Political Islam, 183(Jul–Aug): 2–8.

Krisch, Nico (2010) *Beyond constitutionalism: The Pluralist Structure of Postnational Law*. Oxford: Oxford University Press.

Kugler, Jacek and Feng, Yi (1999) 'Explaining and modelling democratic transitions'. *The Journal of Conflict Resolution*, 43(2): 139–146.

Kukreja, Veena and Singh, Mahendra Prasad (2008) *Democracy, development and discontent in South Asia*. New Delhi: SAGE Publications Pvt. Ltd.

Kumar, Anand (2007) 'A blow to dynastic politics in Bangladesh'. *Institute for Defence Studies and Analysis, New Delhi, India*, (6 November).

Kumar, Sanjay (2014) 'For Bangladesh, elections bring little relief'. *The Diplomat*, (08 January).

Kumar, Venkatesh, B (2009) *Electoral reforms in India: Current discourses*. New Delhi: Rawat Publications.

Kumaraswamy PR and Datta, Sreeradha (2007) 'Democracy in Bangladesh: from fragility to collapse?' *Strategic Insight, E-journal published by the Department of national Security Affairs Center for Contemporary Conflict at the Naval Postgraduate School, Monterey, CA*, (No ISSN available), 6(4): 4 pp.

Kundu, Indrajit and Saha, Nirmal Kumar (2001) 'Democracy-development debate in Bangladesh: An analysis of some relevant issues'. *Chittagong University Journal of Law*, 6: 160–181.

Kuper, Andrew (2006) *Democracy beyond border: Justice and representation in global institutions.* Oxford: Oxford University Press.

Kurlantzick, Joshua (2013) *Democracy in retreat: The revolt of the middle class and the worldwide decline of representative government.* New Haven: Yale University Press.

Lai, Brian and Melkonian-Hoover, Ruth (2005) 'Democratic progress and regress: The effects of parties on the transitions of states to and away from democracy'. *Political Research Quarterly*, 58(4): 551–564.

Laslett, Peter (ed.) (1988) *Locke: Two treatises of government.* Cambridge: Cambridge University Press.

Lau, Martin (2006) *The role of Islam in the legal system of Pakistan.* Leiden/Boston: Martinus Nijhoff Publishers.

LeDuc, Lawrence, Niemi, Richard G and Norris, Pippa (eds.) (2010) *Comparing democracies: Elections and voting in the 21st century.* London: Sage Publications (Pvt.) Ltd.

Lee, Junhan (2002) 'Primary causes of Asian democratization: Dispelling conventional myths'. *Asian Survey*, 42(6): 821–837.

Legrand, Pierre (1997), 'The impossibility of legal transplants'. 4 *Maastricht Journal of European and Comparative Law*, 111–124.

Levey, Geoggrey Brahm and Modood, Tariq (eds.) (2009) *Secularism, religion and multicultural citizenship.* Cambridge: Cambridge University Press.

Levi, Margaret (1997) *Consent, dissent, and patriotism.* Cambridge: Cambridge University Press.

Levin, Michael (1992) *The spectre of democracy. The rise of modern democracy as seen by its critics.* New York: Washington Square Press.

Lienesch, Michael (1992) 'Response: Response to Mueller's "democracy and Ralph's pretty good grocery: Election, equality, and the minimal human being": Wo(e) begon(e) democracy'. *American Journal of Political Science*, 36(4): 1004–1014.

Lifschultz, Lawrence (1979) *Bangladesh: The unfinished revolution.* London: Zed Books.

Lijphart, Arend (1977) *Democracy in plural societies: A comparative exploration.* New Haven: Yale University Press.

Lijphart, Arend (1999) *Patterns of democracy: Government forms and performance in thirty-six countries.* New Haven: Yale University Press.

Lindberg, Staffan I (ed.) (2009) *Democratization by elections: A new mode of transition.* Baltimore: Johns Hopkins University Press.

Lindeman, Eduard C (1938) 'A summary statement of unifying influences in a democracy'. *The Public Opinion Quarterly, Special Supplement: Public Opinion in a Democracy*, 2(1): 94–96.

Linz, Juan J and Stepan, Alfred (1996) *Problems of democratic transition and consolidation.* Baltimore: Johns Hopkins University Press.

Lipset, Seymour Martin (1963) *Political man: The social bases of politics.* New York: Anchor Books.

Liton, Shakhawat (2012a) 'Full judgment vs short order'. *The Daily Star*, (19 September).

Liton, Shakhawat (2012b) 'Political culture key obstacle to fair polls'. *The Daily Star*, (29 September).

Liton, Shakhawat and Hasan, Rashidul (2011) 'Caretaker system abolished: Js passes constitution's 15th amendment bill amid BNP's absence'. *The Daily Star*, (01 July).

Liton, Shakhawat and Sarkar, Ashutosh (2012a) 'Caretaker system can still be legal' *The Daily Star*, (12 February).

Liton, Shakhawat and Sarkar, Ashutosh (2012b) 'Not all judges ruled it illegal'. *The Daily Star*, (17 September).

Locke, John (1740) *The works of John Locke*. 4th ed. London: E. Parker.

Lokken, Roy N (1959) 'The concept of democracy in colonial political thought'. *The William and Mary Quarterly*, 3rd Ser., 16(4): 568–580.

Lombardi, Clark B (2010) 'Can Islamizing a legal system ever help promote liberal democracy? A view from Pakistan'. *University of St. Thomas Law Journal*, 7(3): 649–691.

Lorch, Jasmin (2014) 'Elections in Bangladesh: Political conflict and the problem of credibility'. E-International Relations (2 February).

Ludden, David (ed.) (1996) *Contesting the nation: Religion, community and the politics of democracy in India (South Asia Seminar Series)*. University Park: University of Pennsylvania Press.

Ludden, David (ed.) (2011) 'The politics of independence in Bangladesh'. *Economic and Political Weekly*, 36(35): 79–85.

Luhmann, Niklas (1979) *Trust and power*. New York: John Wiley and Sons.

Lukes, Steven (2004) *Power: A radical view*. New York: Palgrave Macmillan.

McCann, Bryan (2008) *The throes of democracy. Brazil since 1989*. London: Zed Books.

McCarthy, Thomas (1998) 'Legitimacy and diversity: Dialectical reflections on analytical distinctions'. In: Rosenfeld, Michel and Arato, Andrew (eds.) (1998) *Habermas on Law and Democracy: Critical Exchanges (Philosophy, Social Theory & the Rule of Law)*. Berkley: University of California Press. pp. 115–153.

MacLean, James (2012) *Rethinking law as process: Creativity, novelty, change*. Oxford: Routledge.

Macpherson, C B (1965) *The real world of democracy*. Toronto: Canadian Broadcasting Corporation.

Machiavelli, N (1513) *The prince*. Translated by Skinner, Q and Price, R (1988). Cambridge: Cambridge University Press.

Madsen, Stig Toft, Nielsen, Kenneth Bo, and Skoda, Uwe (eds.) (2012) *Trysts with democracy: Political practice in South Asia*. Delhi: Anthem Press.

Magagna, Victor V (1991) *Communities of grain: Rural rebellion in comparative perspective*. Ithaca: Cornell University Press.

Mahmud, Tarek and Islam, Mohammed Serajul, (2017) 'Explosives in Sylhet attack were time bombs' *Dhaka Tribune* (27 March).

Mainwaring, Scott, O'Donnell, G and Valenzuela, J Samuel (eds.) (1992) *Issues in democratic consolidation: The new South American democracies in comparative perspective*. Notre Dame: University of Notre Dame Press.

Malik, Iftikhar H (1996) 'State and civil society in Pakistan: From crisis to crisis'. *Asian Survey*, 36(7): 673–690.

Maloy, J S (2009) 'The Aristotelianism of Locke's politics'. *Journal of the History of Ideas*, 70(2): 235–257.

Mandaville, Peter (2007) *Global political Islam*. Oxford: Routledge.

Mani, Rama (2006) 'Under-estimating the enemy and over-estimating ourselves? The quest for balance between democracy and security in the fight against terrorism'. Paper presented at the *Sixth International Conference for New or Restored Democracies*, Doha (30 October–1 November). 20 pp. Geneva: Geneva Center for Security Policy.

Maniruzzaman, Talukdar (1976) 'Bangladesh in 1975: The fall of the Mujib regime and its aftermath'. *Asian Survey, A survey of Asia in 1975: Part II*, 16(2): 119–129.

Maniruzzaman, Talukdar (1992) 'The fall of the military dictator: 1991 elections and the prospect of civilian rule in Bangladesh'. *Pacific Affairs*, 65(2)(Summer): 203–224.

Manisha, M and Mitra Deb, Sharmila (eds.) (2009) *Indian democracy: problems and prospects*. New Delhi: Anthem Press India.

Mann, Michael (1988) *States, war and capitalism*. New York: Basil Blackwell.

Manna, Mahmudur Rahman (2015) 'What a farce!' *The Daily Star*, (07 January).

Mansbridge, Jane J (1980) *Beyond adversary democracy*. New York: Basic Books.

March, J W and Olsen, J P (1989) *Rediscovering institutions*. New York: Free Press.

March, J W and Olsen, J P (1995) *Democratic governance*. New York: Free Press.

Markell, Parchen (2006) 'The rule of the people: Arendt, Arche, and democracy'. *The American Political Science Review*, 100(1): 1–14.

Markoff, John (1996) *Waves of democracy: Social movements and political change*. Thousand Oaks: Pine Forge Press.

Markovitz, Irving Leonard (1999) 'Constitutions, the federalist papers, and the transition to democracy'. In: Lisa Anderson (ed.) *Transitions to democracy*. New York: Columbia University Press, pp. 42–71.

Marmor, Andrei (2003) 'Authority, equality and democracy'. (January). *Public Policy Research Paper Series*, 03–15. 34 pp. Los Angeles: University of Southern California Law School.

Marshall, Charles B (1959) 'Reflections on a revolution in Pakistan'. *Foreign Affairs*, 37(2): 247–256.

Mascarenhas, Anthony (1971) *The rape of Bangladesh*. New Delhi: Vikas Publication.

Mascarenhas, Anthony (1986) *Bangladesh: A legacy of blood*. New York: Arnold Overseas.

Masud, Kazi Anwarul (2007) *Bangladesh crisis*. Dhaka: Salma Masud.

May, Christopher (2014) *The rule of law: The common sense of global politics*. Cheltenham: Edward Elgar Publishing Ltd.

Mayo, H B (1962) 'How can we justify democracy'. *The American Political Science Review*, 56(3): 555–566.

Mehdi, Rubya, Petersen, Hanne and Reenberg Erik (eds.) (2008) *Law and religion in multicultural societies*. Copenhagen: DJOF Publishing.

Meisburger, Tim (2012) 'Strengthening democracy in Bangladesh'. *The Asia Foundation*, (Occasional paper no. 13, June). Dhaka: Asia Foundation, Bangladesh.

Mejfa, Daniel and Posada, Carlos Esteban (2005) 'Populist policies in the transition to democracy'. (November). 40 pp.

Mendis, Dushyantha (ed.) (2008) *Electoral processes and governance in South Asia*. London: Sage Publications Ltd.

Menski, W and B. Chanda (eds.) (2005) 'Cancer of extremism in Bangladesh'. Proceedings of the *European Human Rights Conference on Bangladesh extremism*, *intolerance & violence*. London: Centre for Ethnic Minority Studies, SOAS and Bangladesh Conference Steering Committee.

Menski, Werner (2003) *Hindu law: Beyond tradition and modernity*. Oxford: Oxford University Press.

Menski, Werner (2006) *Comparative law in a global context: The legal systems of Asia and Africa*. Cambridge: Cambridge University Press.

Menski, Werner (2009–2010) 'Flying kites in Pakistan: Turbulences in theory and practice'. *Journal of Law and Social Research (Multan, Pakistan)*, 1(1): 41–57.

Menski, Werner (2010a) 'Fuzzy law and the boundaries of secularism.' *Potchefstroom Electronic Law Journal*, (ISSN 1727–3781), 13(3): 29–52.

Menski, Werner (2010b) 'Hindu law'. *Law & Justice. The Christian Law Review*, 164 (Hilary/Easter): 45–62.

Menski, Werner (2010c) 'Law, State and culture: How countries accommodate religious, cultural and ethnic diversity. The British and Indian experiences'. In: Marie-Claire Foblets, Jean-Francois Gaudreault-Desbiens and Alison Dundes Renteln (eds.) *Cultural diversity and the law. State responses from around the world*. Brussels: Bryylant and Editions Yvon Blais, 403–446.

Menski, Werner (2011a) 'Flying kites in a global sky: new models of jurisprudence'. *Socio-Legal Review*, 7: 1–22.

Menski, Werner (2011b) 'Flying kites: Managing family laws and gender issues in Bangladesh'. *Stamford Journal of Law*, 2 (March): 109–134.

Menski, Werner (2012a) 'Jürgen Habermas: Post-conflict reconstruction, non-hegemonic modernity, discourse about spaces and the role of religion'. In: Pradip Basu (ed.) *Modern social thinkers*. Kolkata: Setu Prokashani, 180–198.

Menski, Werner (2012b) 'Law, religion and democracy: The Indian experience'. In: Giovanni Filorama (ed.) *Religioni e modernita*. Torino: Giulio Einaudi Editore.

Menski, Werner (2012c) 'Plural worlds of law and the search for living law'. In: Werner Gephart (ed.) *Rechtsanalyse als kulturforschung*. Frankfurt and main: Vittorio Klostermann, 71–88.

Menski, Werner (2014) 'The liquidity of law as a challenge to global theorising'. *Jura Gentium*, Vol. XI: *Pluralismo Guiridico*. Annuale 2014, 19–42

Merriam, Charles E (1941) 'The meaning of democracy'. *The Journal of Negro Education*, 10(3): 309–317.

Metcalf, Barbara D and Metcalf, Thomas R (eds.) (2001) *A concise history of modern India*. Cambridge: Cambridge University Press.

Michelutti, Lucia (2008) *The vernacularisation of democracy: Politics, caste and religion in India*. Hyderabad: Routledge India.

Midlarsky, Manus I (1998) 'Democracy and Islam: Implications for civilizational conflict and the democratic peace'. *International Studies Quarterly*, 42(3): 485–511.

Miller, Arthur (1974) 'Political issues and trust in government: 1964–70'. *The American Political Science Review*, 68(3): 951–972.

Miller, Joseph Dana (1915) 'The difficulties of democracy'. *International Journal of Ethics*, 25(2): 213–225.

Mishra, Pankaj (2012) *From the ruins of empire: The revolt against the west and the remaking of Asia*. London: Penguin Books Ltd.

Mitchell, Kate L (1943) 'India today and tomorrow'. *Political Affairs*, 16(2): 185–188.

Moaddel, Mansoor (2002) 'The study of Islamic culture and politics'. *Annual Review of Sociology*, 28: 359–386.
Mohan, C Raja (2007) 'Balancing interests and values: India's struggle with democracy promotion'. *The Washington Quarterly*, 30(3): 99–115.
Mohiuddin, Yasmeen (2008) 'Sheikh Hasina and Khaleda Zia: Bangladesh's military is desperate to bring down these two former leaders: and it's dragging the whole country down with them'. *International Journal*, 63(2): 461–468.
Molla, Gyasuddin (2000) 'Democratic institution building process in Bangladesh: South Asian experience of a new model of a care taker government in a parliamentary framework'. *Heidelberg Papers in South Asian and comparative politics, Working Paper no. 3.* South Asia Institute, Department of Political Science, University of Heidelberg, (December).
Momen, Mehnaaz (2009) 'Bangladesh in 2008: Déjà vu again or a return to democracy?' *Asian Survey*, 49(1): 66–73.
Momen, Mehnaaz (2010) 'Bangladesh in 2009: The peril within'. *Asian Survey*, 50(1): 157–163.
Monibot, George (2004) 'A thousand dusty codicils filed under: law & order protest; Little by little, democracy is being banned', *The Guardian*, (3 August).
Mookherjee, Nayanika (2006) '"Remembering to forget": Public secrecy and memory of sexual violence in the Bangladesh war of 1971', *Journal of the Royal Anthropological Institute*, (N.S)12: 433–450.
Moore, Jr. Barrington, (1966) *Social origins of dictatorship and democracy. Lord and peasant in the making of the modern world.* Boston: Beacon Press.
Morison, John (2008) In: Cane, Peter and Conaghan, Joanne (eds.) *The Oxford companion to law.* Oxford: Oxford University Press.
Morlino, Leonardo (2002) 'What is a "good" democracy? Theory and empirical analysis'. Lecture delivered at the conference on 'The European Union Nations State, and the quality of democracy. Lessons from Southern Europe'. University of California, Berkeley, October 31–November 2. 44 pp.
Morrison, Wayne (2005) *Jurisprudence: from the Greeks to post-modernism.* London: Cavendish Publishing Limited.
Moskos Jr., Charles C and Bell, Wendell (1964) 'Attitudes towards democracy among leaders in four emergent nations'. *The British Journal of Sociology*, 15(4): 317–337.
'Most people satisfied with government' (2014). *The Bangladesh Chronicle*, (31 August).
Moten, A Rashid (1979) 'Varieties of instability: A theoretical and methodological critique'. *Journal of Modern African Studies*, 17(4): 703–709.
Mueller, Denis C (1996) *Perspectives on public choice: A handbook.* Cambridge: Cambridge University Press.
Muhith, A M A (1992) *Bangladesh: Emergence of a nation.* Dhaka: University Press Limited.
Mukerjee, Hiren (1958) *Gandhiji: A study.* Delhi: National Book Agency.
Mukherjee, Rudrangshu (2014) *Nehru & Bose: Parallel lives.* New Delhi: Viking (India).
Muller, Edward N and Seligson, Mitchell A (1994) 'Civic culture and democracy: the question of causal relationships'. *The American Political Science Review*, 88(3): 635–652.

Munck, Gerardo L (1994) 'Democratic transitions in comparative perspective'. *Comparative Politics*, 26(April): 355–375.

Munck, Gerardo L and Leff, Carol Kalnik (1999) 'Modes of transition and democratization: South America and Eastern Europe in comparative perspective'. In: Lisa Anderson (ed.) *Transitions to democracy*. New York: Columbia University Press, 193–216.

Muro, Diego, Alonso, Gregorio (eds.) (2011) *The politics and memory of democratic transition: The Spanish model*. New York: Routledge.

Mushrafi, Mokhdum-E-Mulk and Rahaman, Hasibur (2009) *Bangladesh politics and governance*. Dhaka: Mowla Brothers.

Nahar, Sultana (2005) *People, politics and religion: Communalism in Bangladesh and India*. Dhaka: Pathak Shomabesh.

Naik, Rineeta (2007) 'Bangladesh: The caretaker's burden'. *Economic and Political Weekly*, 42(35): 3540–3542.

Nasstrom, Sofia (2007) 'The legitimacy of the people'. *Political Theory*, 35(5): 624–658.

Nazrul, Asif (2012) 'Politicians.., if not the court'. *The Daily Star*, (30 September).

Nehru, J (1936) *Jawaharlal Nehru: An autobiography with musings on recent events in India*. Publisher: John Lane The Bodley Head.

Neocleous, Mark (1995) 'From civil society to social'. *British Journal of Sociology*, 46(3): 395–408.

Newman, Janet and Clarke, John (2010) *Publics, politics and power: Remaking the public in public services*. London: Sage Publications (Pvt.) Ltd.

Norris, Pippa (2005) 'Stable democracy and good governance in divided societies: Do power sharing institutions work?' *Faculty research working paper series*, RWP05–014 (February). Harvard University: John F. Kennedy School of Government, 41.

Nussbaum, Martha and Myers, Joanne J (2004) *Electoral engineering: Voting rules and political behaviour*. Cambridge: Cambridge University Press.

Nussbaum, Martha and Myers, Joanne J (2008) *The clash within: Democracy, religious violence, and India's future*. Cambridge: Harvard University Press.

Ober, Josiah (2008) *Democracy & knowledge: Innovation & learning in classical Athens*. Princeton and Oxford: Princeton University Press.

Odhikar (2014/2015) *Annual Human Rights Report on Bangladesh*. Dhaka, Bangladesh.

O'Donnell, G, Schmitter, Phillipe C and Whitehead, Lawrence (1986) *Transitions from authoritarian rule: Tentative conclusions about uncertain democracies: Prospects for democracy*. Baltimore: Johns Hopkins University Press.

O'Flynn, Ian (2006) *Deliberative democracy and divided societies*. Edinburgh: Edinburgh University Press.

Oliver, Dawn and Fusaro, Carlo (2011) *How constitutions change: A comparative study*. Oxford: Hart Publishing.

Olson, Kevin (2007) 'Paradoxes of constitutional democracy'. *American Journal of Political Science*, 51(2): 330–343.

Opello Jr., Walter C and Rosow, Stephen J (1999) *The nation state and global order: A historical introduction to contemporary politics*. Boulder: Lynne Rienner Publishers.

Oppenheimer, Daniel M and Edwards, Michael A (2012) *Democracy despite itself: Why a system that shouldn't work at all works so well*. Cambridge: MIT Press.

Osborne, Roger (2011) *Of the people, by the people: A new history of democracy*. London: The Bodley Head.

Pakistan Institute of Legislative Development and Transparency (2005) *Background paper, free, fair and credible elections in Pakistan*. Islamabad.

Pakistan Institute of Legislative Development and Transparency (2006) *Background paper, Caretaker government during election: A comparative study of Pakistan, Bangladesh and India*. Islamabad.

Pakistan Institute of Legislative Development and Transparency (2007) *Background paper, Required electoral reforms before general election 2007/2008*. Islamabad.

Paley, Julia (2002) 'Towards an anthropology of democracy'. *Annual Review of Anthropology*, 31: 469–496.

Palmer, Parker J. (2011) *Healing the heart of democracy: The courage to create a politics worthy of human spirit*. San Francisco: Jossey-Bass.

Park, Richard L (1975) 'Political crisis in India, 1975'. *Asian Survey*, 15(11): 996–1113.

Parens, Joshua (1994) 'Whose liberalism? Which Islam? Leonard Binder's "Islamic liberalism"'. *Political Science and Politics*, 27(3): 514–515.

Parnini, Sayeda (2014) 'Democracy's no-show at Bangladesh's elections'. *East Asia Forum*, (09 February).

Pattanaik, Smruti S (2006) 'The neutral caretaker government interregnum in Bangladesh'. *Institute for Defence Studies and Analysis, New Delhi*, (9 November).

Pattaro, Enrico (2005) 'An overview on practical reason in Aquinas'. *Scandinavian Studies in Law*, 48: 251–267.

Paxton, Pamela (2002) 'Social capital and democracy: An interdependent relationship'. *American Sociological Review*, 67(2): 254–277.

Pearl, David and Menski, Werner (1998) *Muslim family law*. London: Sweet & Maxwell.

Pellegrini, Lorenzo and Gerlagh, Reyer (2005) 'An empirical contribution to the debate on corruption, democracy and environmental policy'. *FEEM (Fondazione Eni Enrico Mattei) Working Paper No. 08.05*, (January): 27 pp.

Peters, Rudolph and Bearman, Peri (2014) *The Ashgate research companion to Islamic Law*. London: Ashgate.

Piliavsky, Anastasia (ed.) (2014) *Patronage as politics in South Asia*. Cambridge: Cambridge University Press.

Pitkin, Hanna Fenichel (1967) *The concept of representation*. Berkeley: University of California Press.

Pocock, J G A (1987) *The ancient constitution and the feudal law: A study of English historical thought in the seventeenth century*. Cambridge: Cambridge University Press.

Polanyi, Karl (1944) *The Great Transformation*. New York: Farrar and Rinehart.

Ponser, Richard A (2003) *Law, pragmatism and democracy*. Cambridge: Harvard University Press.

Potter, David, Goldblatt, David, Kiloh, Margaret and Lewis, Paul (eds.) (2010) *Democratization*. Cambridge: Polity Press.

Powell, Arvil (ed.) (2011) 'Special issue: Knowledge, pedagogy and Muslims in colonial north-west India'. *South Asia Research*, 31(1) (February).

Powell, G Bingham JR (2000) *Elections as instruments of democracy*. New Haven and London: Yale University Press.

Power and Participation Research Center, PPRC (2007) *Bangladesh governance report: Unbundling governance – indices, institutions, process, solutions*. Dhaka: PPRC.

Preece, Alun A (2000) 'Democracy and the military: The role of the military in the evolution and maintenance of democracy'. Paper delivered to the *International Conference on The Military and Governance in the Asia-Pacific Region*, (27 April). Brisbane: Griffith University.

'President signs ordinance reforming electoral laws' (2001) *The Bangladesh Observer*, (9 August).

Price, Gareth (2007) 'Bangladesh: Political paralysis'. *The World Today*, 63(1): 24–25.

Price, Pamela and Engelsen Ruud, Ariid (eds.) (2010) *Power and influence in India: Bosses, lords and captains.* Hyderabad: Routledge India.

Przeworski, Adam, Susan, C Stokes and Manin, Bernard (1999) 'Elections and representations'. In: Przeworski, Adam, Susan, C Stokes and Manin, Bernard (eds.) *Democracy, accountability and representation.* Cambridge: Cambridge University Press, pp. 1–54.

Putnam, Robert D (1995) 'Bowling alone: America's declining social capital'. *Journal of Democracy*, 6: 65–78.

Quigley, Kevin F (1997) 'Political scientists and assisting democracy: Too tenuous links'. *Political Science and Politics*, 30(3): 564–567.

Qvortrup, Mads (2002) *A comparative study of referendums: Government by the people.* Manchester: Manchester University Press.

Rabinow, Paul (ed.) (1991) *The Foucault reader: An introduction to Foucault's thought.* London: Penguin Books.

Raghavan, Srinath (2013) *1971 A global history of the creation of Bangladesh.* Cambridge: Harvard University Press.

Rahim, Abdur (1994) *The principles of Islamic jurisprudence.* New Delhi: Kitab Bhavan.

Rahman, A T R (1974) 'Administration and its political environment in Bangladesh'. *Pacific Affairs*, 47(2): 171–191.

Rahman, A T Rafiqur ((2006) *Bangladesh in the mirror: An outsider perspective on a struggling democracy.* Dhaka: University Press Limited.

Rahman, F (1958) 'Muslim modernism in the Indo-Pakistan sub-continent'. *Bulletin of the School of Oriental and African Studies, University of London*, 21(1/3): 82–99.

Rahman, Anisur (2011) 'Bangladesh plans to scrap caretaker government system'. *Gulf News*, (31 May).

Rahman, Fazlur (1970a) 'Islam and the constitutional problem of Pakistan'. *Studia Islamica*, 32: 275–287.

Rahman, Fazlur (1970b) 'Islam and social justice'. *Pakistan Forum*, 1(1): 4–5 and 9.

Rahman, Hossain Zillur (2009) 'Unbundling governance'. Lecture at the Institute for Global Leadership, Tufts University, Medford, USA. Dhaka: Power and Participation Research Center.

Rahman, Latifur (2002) *The caretaker days and my story.* Dhaka: Mullick Brothers.

Rahman, Masihur (2010) *Democracy in crisis.* Dhaka: University Press Limited.

Rahman, Md. Ataur (1983) 'Bangladesh in 1982: Beginnings of the second decade'. *Asian Survey, A survey of Asia in 1982: Part II*, 23(2): 149–157.

Rahman, Muhammad Habibur (2010) *Tattabodhayak shorkarer daibhar.* Dhaka: Prothoma Prokashan.

Rahman, Syedur (1990) 'Bangladesh in 1989: Internationalisation of political and economic issues'. *Asian Survey, A survey of Asia in 1989: Part II*, 30(2): 150–157.

Rahman, Wali-ur (2009) 'An analysis of the Supreme Court judgment of the fifth amendment of the constitution of Bangladesh'. *Journal of International Affairs*, 13(2) (July–December).

Rahman, Wali-ur (2011) *Transition to democracy: Kaleidoscope of a changing world.* Dhaka: University Press Limited.

Rai, Anil Kumar (1996) *Concept of state and fundamental rights.* New Delhi: Deep and Deep.

Rainer, Helmut and Siedler, Thomas (2006) 'Does democracy foster trust?' *IZA Discussion Paper*, (May) 2154. 29 pp. Bonn: Institute for the Study of Labor.

Rajan, Sudhit Chella (2005) 'Is democracy possible, Part II: Cosmopolitan ideas and the problem of global political community'. Presented at the annual meeting of the *Western Political Science Association*, (16–19 March). 21 pp. Oakland: California, USA.

Rajpal, Shilpi (2015) 'Colonial psychiatry in mid-nineteenth century India: The James Clark Enquiry'. *South Asia Research*. 35(1).

Ramachandran, Sudha (2014) 'Bangladesh: Democracy in peril: The Hasina–Zia feud threatens to return the country to military rule'. *The Diplomat*, (07 January).

Ramnath, Kalyani (2012) 'We the people: Seamless webs and social revolution in India's constituent assembly debates'. *South Asia Research*, 32(1): 57–70.

Ramney, Austin and Kendall, Willmoore (1951) 'Democracy: Confusion and agreement'. *The Western Political Quarterly*, 4(3): 430–439.

Randeria, Shalini (2006) 'Entangled histories: Civil societies, caste solidarities and legal pluralism in post-colonial India'. In Keane, John (ed.) *Civil Society: Berlin perspectives.* New York: Berghahn Books, 213–242.

Rashid, Harunur (2001) 'Can a CTG make a policy decision.' *Dhaka Courier*, 18(4) (17 August): 27.

Rashiduzzaman, M (1994) 'The liberals and the religious right in Bangladesh'. *Asian Survey*, 34(11): 974–990.

Rashiduzzaman, M (1997) 'Political unrest and democracy in Bangladesh'. *Asian Survey*, 37(3): 254–268.

Rawls, John (2005) *A theory of justice.* Cambridge: Harvard University Press.

Ray, James Lee (1995) 'Global trends, state specific factors and regime transitions, 1825–1993'. *Journal of Peace Research*, 32(1): 49–63.

Rehg, William (1998) 'Against subordination: Morality, discourse, and decision in the legal theory of Jürgen Habermas'. In: Rosenfield, Michel and Arato, Andrew (eds.) *Habermas on law and democracy: Critical exchanges.* Berkeley: University of California Press, 257–271.

Rejai, Mostafa (1967a) *Democracy. The contemporary theories.* New York: Atherton Press.

Rejai, Mostafa (1967b) 'The metamorphosis of democratic theory'. *Ethics*, 77(3): 202–208.

'Restore caretaker govt system' (2011) *The Daily Star*, (24 August).

Reydams, Luc, Wouters, Jan and Ryngaert, Cedric (eds.) (2012) *International Prosecutors.* Oxford University Press, 169.

Rhodes, R A W, Binder, Sarah A and Rockman, Bert A. (eds.) (2006) *The Oxford handbook of political institutions.* New York: Oxford University Press, USA.

Riaz, Ali (2004) 'Bangladesh in 2004: The politics of vengeance and the erosion of democracy'. *Asian Survey*, 45(1): 112–118.

Riaz, Ali (2006) 'Bangladesh in 2005: Standing at a crossroads'. *Asian Survey*, 46(1): 107–113.
Riaz, Ali (2010a) *Islamic militancy in Bangladesh: A complex web.* Oxford and New York: Routledge.
Riaz, Ali (ed.) (2010b) *Religion and politics in South Asia.* London and New York: Routledge.
Riaz, Ali (2012) 'Inconvenient truths about Bangladeshi politics'. *The Daily Star* (1 January)
Riaz, Ali (2013a) 'Bangladesh in turmoil: A nation on the brink?' *Congressional Testimony before the Subcommittee on Asia and the Pacific Committee on Foreign Affairs, United States House of Representatives*, p. 3.
Riaz, Ali (2013b) 'Democracy in Bangladesh: A report card'. *South Asia Journal*, (Issue 7 – January).
Riaz, Ali (2014a) 'A crisis of democracy in Bangladesh'. *Current History*, 113(762): 152–153.
Riaz, Ali (2014b) 'Shifting tides in South Asia: Bangladesh's failed election'. *Journal of Democracy*, 25(2): 119–130.
Riaz, Ali (2015) 'The troubled democracy of Bangladesh: 'Muddling through' or 'a political settlement'? *Institute of South Asian Studies (ISAS) Special Report* No. 25, 8, (14 July).
Riaz, Ali (2016a) *Bangladesh: A political history since independence.* London and New York: I.B. Tauris.
Riaz, Ali (2016b) 'What does democracy mean to Bangladeshis?' *The Daily Star* (6 December).
Riaz, Ali and Fair, Christine C (eds.) (2011) *Political Islam and governance in Bangladesh.* London and New York: Routledge.
Riker, William H (1965) *Democracy in the United States.* New York: Colier Macmillan.
Rizvi, Gowher (1991) 'Bangladesh: Towards civil society'. *The World Today*, 47(8/9): 155–160.
Robinson, Nick and Sattar, Nawreen (2012) 'When corruption is an emergency: "Good governance" coups and Bangladesh'. *Fordham International Law Journal*, 35: 737–779.
Rosanvallon, Pierre (2007) *Democracy: Past and future.* New York: Columbia University Press.
Rosenfeld, Michel (2001) 'The rule of law and the legitimacy of constitutional democracy'. *Public Law Research Paper*, 36 (March). 70 pp. New York: Jacob Burns Institute for Advances Legal Studies, Cardozo Law School.
Rosenfeld, Michel and Arato, Andrew (eds.) (1998) *Habermas on law and democracy: Critical exchanges (philosophy, social theory & the rule of law).* Berkley: University of California Press.
Rousseau, Jean-Jacques (1980) *The social contract.* London: Wordsworth.
Roy, Asim (1987) 'The Bengal "cultural mediators" and the Bengal Muslim identity in the nineteenth and early twentieth centuries'. *South Asia*, 10(1): 11–34.
Rubin, Edward L (2001) 'Getting past democracy'. *Public Law and Legal Theory Research Paper Series*, 1–4. 64 pp. Philadelphia: University of Pennsylvania Law School.
Rushdie, Salman (1992) *The Satanic Verses.* Delaware: The Consortium Inc.

Russel, Ralph (1972) 'Strands of Muslim identity in South Asia'. *South Asia Review*, 6(1): 25.

Rustow, Dankwart A (1970) 'Transitions to democracy: Toward a dynamic model'. *Journal of Comparative Politics*, (April 1997).

Ruud, Arild Engelsen (2012) in Madsen, Stig Toft, Nielsen, Kenneth Bo and Skoda, Uwe (eds.) *Trysts with democracy: Political practice in South Asia (Anthem South Asian Studies)*. London: Anthem Press, 53–54, 67–68.

Ruud, Arild Engelsen (2014) 'The political bully in Bangladesh'. In: Piliavsky, Anastasia (ed.) *Patronage as politics in South Asia*. Cambridge: Cambridge University Press, 304.

Sadiki, Larbi, Wimmen Heiko, Zubaidi Al, Layla (eds.) (2012) *Democratic transition in the Middle East: Unmaking power*. New York: Routledge.

Sadurski, Wojciech (ed.) (2005) *Constitutional theory*. Aldershot: Ashgate.

Safi, Michael (2016) 'Indian Court orders cinemas to play national anthem before films'. *The Guardian*, (30 November).

Sahlins, Marshall (1974) *Stone Age economics*. London: Tavistock.

Salik, Siddiq (1997) *Witness to surrender*. New Delhi: Lancer Publishers & Distributers.

Saramago, Jose (2004) 'The least bad system is in need of change: Reinventing democracy'. *Le Monde Diplomatique*, (August).

Sarker, Jadunath (1977) *History of Bengal, Muslim period, 1200–1757*. Kolkata: J Prokashan.

Sartori, Giovanni (1987) *Theory of democracy revisited*. Chatham: Chatham House.

Sattar, Maher (2012) 'Dhaka's death squad shoots for a makeover'. *Global Post* (29 January).

Saxonhouse, Arlene W (1993) 'Athenian democracy: Modern mythmakers and ancient theorists'. *Political Science and Politics*, 26(3): 486–490.

Sayeed, Sinha MA (2012) 'Lessons from past non-party caretaker governments and the way forward'. *The Financial Express*, (7 May).

Schacht, Joseph (1979) *The origins of Mohammedan jurisprudence*. Oxford: Clarendon Press.

Schacht, Joseph (1984) *An introduction to Islamic law*. Reprint. Oxford: Oxford University Press.

Schaffer, Teresita and Saigal-Arora, Hemani (1999) 'India: A fragmented democracy'. *The Washington Quarterly*, 22(4): 143–150.

Schendel, Willem van (2009) *A history of Bangladesh*. Cambridge: Cambridge University Press.

Schmitter, Philippe C and Karl, Terry Lynn (1991) 'What democracy is … and is not'. *Journal of Democracy*, 2(3): 76.

Schoenbrod, David (2003) 'Democracy by decree: What happens when courts run government'. *Public law and legal theory Research Paper Series*, 2: 3–19.

Scholte, Marianne (2014) 'No "Basketcase"'. *Development and Cooperation*, 41(12): 463–465.

Schopflin, George (2000) *Nations, identity, power: The new politics of Europe*. London: Hurst & Company.

Schwartz, Paul M (2002) 'Voting technology and democracy'. *New York University Law Review*, 77: 625–698.

Schwartzberg, Melissa (2004) 'Athenian democracy and legal change'. *American Political Science Review*, 98(2): 311–325.

Schwartzberg, Melissa (2009) *Democracy and legal change*. Cambridge: Cambridge University Press.

Sen, Swadhin (2002) 'Community boundary, secularized religion and imagined past in Bangladesh: Archaeology and historiography of unequal encounter'. *World Archaeology*, 34(2): 346–362.

Sengupta, Nitish (2001) *History of the Bengali-speaking people*. New Delhi: UBS Publishers' Distributors Pvt. Ltd.

Serajuddin, Alamgir Muhammad (2011) *Muslim family law, secular courts and Muslim women in South Asia*. Karachi: Oxford University Press.

Serra, Narcis (2010) *The military transition: Democratic reform of the armed forces*. Cambridge: Cambridge University Press.

Shah, Prakash (2005) 'Globalisation and the challenge of Asian Legal Transplants in Europe'. *Singapore Journal of Legal Studies*, 348–361.

Shah, Prakash (2005) *Legal pluralism in conflict: Coping with cultural diversity in law*. London: Glass House Press.

Shah, Prakash (2014) 'Critiquing the western account of India studies within a comparative science of cultures'. *International Journal of Hindu Studies*, 18(1): 67–72.

Shain, Yossi, Linz, Juan J. (eds.) (1995a) *Between states: Interim governments and democratic transitions*. Cambridge: Cambridge University Press.

Shain, Yossi, Linz, Juan J. (eds.) (1995b) 'Introduction: Interim government and their legitimating myths'. In: Shain, Yossi, Linz, Juan J. (eds.) *Between states: Interim governments and democratic transitions*. Cambridge: Cambridge University Press, 6–7.

Sharansky, Natan and Dermer, Ron (2006) *The case for democracy: The power of freedom to overcome tyranny and terror*. New York: Public Affairs.

Sharma, Mohan Lal, Peacock, Olivia and Gopal, Krishnan (2002) *Globalisation, democracy and governance in South Asia*. New Delhi: Kalinga Publications.

Sharma, Mukul (2007) 'Bangladesh's repressive regime'. *Economic and Political Weekly*, 42(32): 3294–3295.

Sharma, Shalendra (1999) *Development and democracy in India*. Boulder: Lynne Rienner Publishers.

Shashtri, Amita, and Wilson, Jeyaratnam A (eds.) (2001) *The post- colonial states of South Asia: Democracy, development and identity*. New York: Palgrave Macmillan.

Shehabuddin, Elora (2011) 'Bangladeshi civil society and Islamist politics'. In: Riaz, Ali and Fair, Christine C (eds.) (2011) *Political Islam and governance in Bangladesh*. Oxford: Routledge, 91–114.

Shennan, J H (1974) *The origins of the modern European state, 1450–1725*. London: Hutchinson.

Siaroff, Alan (2000) 'The fate of centrifugal democracies: Lessons from consociational theory and system performance'. *Comparative Politics*, 32(3): 317–332.

Siddiqui, Kamal (2006) *Towards good governance in Bangladesh: Fifty unpleasant essays*. Dhaka: University Press Limited.

Sihag, Balbir S. (2007). 'Kautilya on administration of justice during the fourth century B.C.'. *Journal of the History of Economic Thought*, 29(3): 359–377.

Singh, Baljit (1964) 'The sources of contemporary political thought in India – A reappraisal'. *Ethics*, 75(1): 57–62.

Sisson, Richard, and Rose, Leo E (1990) *War and secession: Pakistan, India, and the creation of Bangladesh*. Berkeley: University of California Press.

Skinner, Q (1978) *The foundations of modern political thought, Vol 1: The renaissance*. Cambridge: Cambridge University Press.

Skinner, Q (1989) 'State'. In T Ball et al. *Political innovation and conceptual change*. Cambridge: Cambridge University Press.

Sloss, David (2006) 'Using international law to enhance democracy'. 47 Va. J. Int'l L. 1 2006–2007. Santa Clara Law Digital Commons. Santa Clara University.

Sobhan, Rehman (2012) 'Bangladesh at 40: Looking back and moving forward'. *The Daily Star* (2 January).

Sobhan, Zafar (2006) 'Conspiracy theories in Bangladesh'. *Economic and Political Weekly*, 41(30): 3275–3276.

Sobhan, Zafar (2007) 'New game in Bangladesh'. *Economic and Political Weekly*, 42(10): 806–807.

Sobhan, Zafar (2008a) 'Back to square one in Bangladesh'. *Economic and Political Weekly*, 43(39): 8–9.

Sobhan, Zafar (2008b) 'Finishing line in sight in Bangladesh?' *Economic and Political Weekly*, 43(47): 8–9.

Sobhan, Zafar (2009) 'State of shock'. *Economic and Political Weekly*, 44(11): 8–9.

Soguk, Nevzat (2010) *Globalization and Islamism: Beyond fundamentalism*. Lanham: Rowman and Littlefield Publishers.

Somek, Alexander (2005) 'Democratic minimalism: Turning the clock back from democracy to democratization'. *University of Iowa Legal Studies Research Paper*, 05–10: 36 pp.

Spencer, Jonathan (2007) *Anthropology, politics and the state: Democracy and violence in South Asia (New Departures in Anthropology)*. Cambridge: Cambridge University Press.

Starr, Harvey (1991) 'Democratic dominoes: Diffusion approaches to the spread of democracy in the international system'. *The Journal of Conflict Resolution*, 35(2): 356–381.

Starr, Harvey and Lindborg, Christina (2003) 'Democratic dominoes revisited: The hazards of governmental transitions'. *Journal of Conflict Resolutions*, 47(4): 490–519.

'Statement of the National Democratic Institute (NDI)/The Carter Center pre-election delegation to Bangladesh's 2001 Parliamentary elections' (2001). *National Democratic Institute/The Carter Center*, (4 August). Atlanta: The Carter Center.

Stern, Robert W (2001) *Democracy and dictatorship in South – Asia: Dominant classes and political outcomes in India, Pakistan, and Bangladesh*. Westport: Praeger Publishers.

Stoker, Gerry (2006) *Why politics matters: Making democracy work*. New York: Palgrave, Macmillan.

Strindberg, Anders and Warn, Mats (2011) *Islamism*. Cambridge: Polity Press.

Sulkenen, Pekka (2007) 'Re-inventing the social contract'. *Acta. Sociologica*, 50(3): 325–333.

Suvin, Darko (2006) 'Terms of power, today: An essay in political epistemology'. *Critical Quarterly*, 48(3): 38–62.

Sztompa, Piotr (1999) *Trust: A sociological theory*. Cambridge: Cambridge University Press.

Talisse, Robert B (2007) 'Folk epistemology and the justification of democracy'. *Vanderbilt University Working Paper Series*, (August).

Tamanaha, Brian Z (2005) *On the rule of law: History, politics, theory.* New York: Cambridge University Press.

Tamanaha, Brian Z (2006) *A general jurisprudence of law and society.* Oxford: Oxford University Press.

Tamanaha, Brian Z (2009) 'Law'. In: Katz, Stanley N (ed.) *The Oxford international encyclopedia of legal history.* Oxford: Oxford University Press. Volume 4. pp. 17–23.

Tamanaha, Brian Z (2010a) *Beyond the formalist–realist divide: the role of politics in judging.* Princeton: Princeton University Press.

Tamanaha, Brian Z (2010b) 'A vision of social-legal change: Rescuing Ehrlich from Living Law'. *Legal Studies Research Paper Series*, Paper no. 10-10-05: (8 October). St. Louis: School of Law, Washington University in St. Louis.

Tamanaha, Brian Z., Sage, Caroline, and Woolcock, Michael (eds.) (2012) *Legal pluralism and development: Scholars and practitioners in dialogue.* Cambridge: Cambridge University Press.

Tannock, Charles (2014) 'Between secularism and shariah, Bangladesh's division widen'. *The Daily Star (Lebanon)*, (11 February).

Tessler, Mark (2002) 'Islam and democracy in the Middle East: The impact of religious orientations on attitudes towards democracy in four Arab countries'. *Comparative Politics*, 34(3): 337–354.

Teubner, Gunther (1998) 'Legal irritants: Good faith in British law or how unifying law ends up in new divergences'. *The Modern Law Review*, 61(1): 11–32.

Thomas, P. (1997) 'Socio-legal studies: The case of disappearing fleas and bustards'. In: Phil Thomas (ed.) *Socio-Legal Studies*, 1–22. Dartmouth: Aldershot.

Tibi, Bassam (2012) *Islamism and Islam.* New Haven and London: Yale University Press.

Tocqueville, Alexis de (1969) *Democracy in America.* J.P. Mayer (ed.). Translated by George Lawrence. Garden City: Doubleday.

Torres, Jose Arsenio (1962) *Asian Survey*, 72(2): 79–105.

Transparency International Bangladesh (2006) *Corruption perception index (CPI) 2006: Results, questions and answers*, (6 November). Dhaka: Transparency International Bangladesh.

Transparency International Bangladesh Report (2014). *The Independent (Bangladesh).* Dhaka: Transparency International Bangladesh.

Tripathi, Salil (2014) *The colonel who would not repent: The Bangladesh war and its unquiet legacy.* New Delhi: Aleph Book Company.

Turner, John C (2005) 'Explaining the nature of power: A three-process theory'. *European Journal of Social Psychology*, 35: 1–22.

Twining, William (1973) *Karl Llewellyn and the realist movement.* Cambridge: Cambridge University Press.

Twining, William (1974) 'Law and social science: the method of detail'. *New Society*, 27 June, pp. 758–61.

Twining, William (2000) *Globalisation and legal theory.* London: Butterworths.

Twining, William (2009) *General jurisprudence: Understanding law from a global perspective.* Cambridge: Cambridge University Press.

Uddin, Sufia M (2006) *Constructing Bangladesh: Religion, ethnicity and language in an Islamic Nation.* Chapel Hill: University of North Carolina Press.

'UN threatens Bangladesh's peacekeeping role'. (2007) *The Daily Star*, (12 January).

Upretti, B C and Gopal, K (eds.) (2012) *Democracy in South Asia*. New Delhi: Kalinga.

Uslaner, Eric M (2000) 'Trust, democracy and governance'. Prepared for the *European Consortium for Political Research (ECPR) Workshop 13 on 'Voluntary associations, social capital and interest mediation: Forging the link'*. Copenhagen: Denmark, p. 41.

Van Creveld, Martin (1999) *The rise and decline of the state*. Cambridge: Cambridge University Press.

Van de Watering, Richard (2008) *A. V. Dicey, Lectures on the relation between law and public opinion in England during the nineteenth century*. Indianapolis: Liberty Fund.

Vanhanen, Tatu (2000) 'A new dataset for measuring democracy, 1810–1998'. *Journal of Peace Research*, 37(2): 251–265.

Vanhanen, Tatu (2004) 'Problems of democracy in ethnically divided South Asian countries'. Paper presented at *The 18th European Conference on Modern South Asian Studies, Panel 32: Problems of Democracy in South Asia*, (6–9 July). Lund: Sweden.

Vertovec, Steve and Peach, Ceri (1997) *Islam in Europe: The politics of religion and community*. Basingstoke: Macmillan.

Vigoda-Gadot, Eran and Mizrahi, Shlomo (2014) *Managing democracies in turbulent times: Trust, performance, and governance in modern states*. Heidelberg: Springer.

Vincent, Andrew (1987) *Theories of the state*. Oxford: Wiley-Blackwell.

Viroli, M (1992) *From politics to reason of states: The acquisition and transformation of the language of politics, 1250–1600*. Cambridge: Cambridge University Press.

Vohra, N N (ed.) (2001) *Culture, democracy and development in South Asia*. New Delhi: Shipra Publications.

Von Tunzelmann, Alex (2007), *Indian summer: The secret history of the end of an empire*. New York: Henry Holt & Company.

Waldegrave, William and Selborne, Palmer (1913) *The state and the citizen*. London: Frederick Warne and Co.

Warren, Mark E (1993) 'Can participatory democracy produce better selves? Psychological dimension of Habermas's discursive model of democracy'. *Political Psychology, Special Issue: Political Theory and Political Psychology*, 14(2): 209–234.

Warren, Mark E (1999) *Democracy & trust*. Cambridge: Cambridge University Press.

Watson, Alan (1993) *Legal transplants: An approach to comparative law*. Athens: University of Georgia Press.

Weinbaum, Marvin G (1996) 'Civic culture and democracy in Pakistan'. *Asian Survey*, 36(7): 639–654.

Weiner, Myron (1987) 'Empirical democratic theory'. In: Weiner, Myron and Ozbudun, Ergun (eds.) *Competitive elections in developing countries*. pp. 3–34. Durham: Duke University Press.

Wejnert, Barbara (2005) 'Diffusion, development, and democracy, 1800–1999'. *American Sociological Review*, 70(1): 53–81.

Welchman, Lynn (2002) 'Islamic law: Stuck with the state?' In: Huxley, Andrew (ed.) *Religions, law and tradition*. London: Routledge Curzon, 61–83.

West, Cornel (2004) *Democracy matters*. London: Penguin Books.

'Why pressurise Caretaker Govt?' (2001) *The Bangladesh Observer*, (26 July).
Wignaraja, Ponna and Hussain, Akmal (eds.) (1989) *The challenge in South Asia: Development, democracy and regional corporation.* New Delhi: SAGE Publications Pvt. Ltd.
Wilde, Alexander (1999) 'Irruptions of memory: Expressive politics in Chile's transition to democracy'. *Journal of Latin American Studies*, 31(2): 473–500.
Wollack, Kenneth (2005) 'Political competition as an anti-corruption tool'. Washington DC: Center for International Private Enterprise (21 June): 5 pp.
Wollheim, Richard (1958) 'Democracy'. *Journal of the History of Ideas*, 19(2): 225–242.
Wolpert, Stanley (1984) *Jinnah of Pakistan.* Oxford: Oxford University Press.
Wynbrandt, James (2009) *A brief history of Pakistan.* New York: Checkmark books.
Yeates, Nicola (2001) *Globalization and social policy.* London: Sage.
Yilmaz, Ihsan (2005) *Muslim laws politics and society in modern nation states: Dynamic legal pluralisms in England, Turkey and Pakistan.* London: Ashgate.
Yturbe, Corina (1997) 'On Norberto Bobbio's theory of democracy'. *Political Theory*, 25(3): 377–400.
Zafarullah, Habib Mohammad (1987) 'Public administration in the first decade of Bangladesh: Some observations on developments and trends'. *Asian Survey*, 27(4): 459–476.
Zahed, Iqthyer Uddin Md (May–June 2013) 'An analysis of US policy in the Liberation war of Bangladesh, 1971'. *IIOSR Journal of Humanities and Social Science (IOSR JHSS)* Volume 12, Issue 2, p. 124 where the author refers to the work of Iqbal, M Z (2009), *History of the Liberation War*, Dhaka.
Zahur, A B M S (2008) 'End of line?' *The Daily Star*, (8 September).
Zakaria, Fareed (2004) *The future of freedom: Liberal democracy at home and abroad.* New York: W.W. Norton.
Zaman, Farhana (2012) 'Bangladeshi women's political empowerment in urban local governance'. *South Asia Research*, 32(2): 81–102.
Zamindar, Vazira Fazila-Yacoobali (2010) *The long partition and the making of South Asia. Refugees, boundaries, histories.* New York: Columbia University Press.
Ziring, Lawrence (1984) 'From Islamic Republic to Islamic state in Pakistan'. *Asian Survey*, 24(9): 931–946.
Ziring, Lawrence and LaPorte Jr., Robert (1974) 'The Pakistan bureaucracy: Two views'. *Asian Survey*, 14(12): 1086–1103.

TABLE OF CASES

Abdul Bari Sarker v Bangladesh 46 DLR (1994) AD 37.
Abdul Mannan Khan v Bangladesh ADC Vol. IX (A), 10 (2012).
(The Constitution of Bangladesh [Thirteenth Amendment Act Case]).
Anwar Hossain Chowdhury v State BLD (1989) (Spl) 1.
Asma Jilani Case PLD (1972) SC 139 (*Asma Jilani v Government of Punjab*).
Bangladesh Italian Marble Ltd. and Others v Bangladesh BLT (2006) (HCD) 1, Special Issue. (The Constitution of Bangladesh [Fifth Amendment Act Case]).
BLAST (Bangladesh Legal Aid and Services Trust) v Bangladesh and Others (Fatwa Case), 63 DLR (HCD) 1.
Dosso's Case PLD (1968) SC 533.
Idrisur Rahman v Bangladesh (2008) 60 DLR 714.
Kesavanda Bharati v State of Kerala AIR (1973) SC 1461.
Mohinder Singh v Chief Election Commissioner AIR 1978 SC 85.
Rameshwar Prashad and Others (VI) v Union of India (2006) 2 SCC 1.
Secretary, Ministry of Finance v Masdar Hossain 20 BLD (2000) AD 141. (Separation of judiciary case).
Special Reference No. 1 of 2002 AIR 2003 Sc 87 or (2002) 8 SCC 237.

INDEX

For Product Safety Concerns and Information please contact our EU representative GPSR@taylorandfrancis.com Taylor & Francis Verlag GmbH, Kaufingerstraße 24, 80331 München, Germany